Monash Asia Institute

To be free

Chee Soon Juan

About the author

Chee Soon Juan is a neuropsychologist by training and was formerly a lecturer at the National University of Singapore. Schooled in Singapore, he received his tertiary education in the United States, where he obtained his PhD from the University of Georgia in 1990.

In 1992, he joined the opposition Singapore Democratic Party. Three months later, he was sacked from the National University of Singapore, allegedly for misusing research funds for postage. He was subsequently sued for almost US$350,000 by his department head, a ruling party member of parliament, for disputing his dismissal.

He is now the Secretary-General of the Singapore Democratic Party and a Research Associate at the Monash Asia Institute.

Titles by the same author

Dare To Change: An Alternative Vision for Singapore.

Singapore, My Home Too.

Effective Parenting for the Asian Family
(with Huang Chih-mei).

Cover design by Cecilia Lim
Maps © Monash Asia Institute

To be free: stories from Asia's struggle against oppression

Chee Soon Juan

Published by
Monash Asia Institute
Monash University
Clayton 3168
Australia

reprinted 1999

National Library of Australia Cataloguing-in-Publication Data:

Chee, Soon Juan, 1962–
To be free: stories from Asia's struggle against oppression.

Bibliography
Index
ISBN 0 7326 1173 3.

1. Human rights - Asia. 2. Human rights workers - Asia. 3. Political rights - Asia. 4. Asia - Politics and government - 20th century. I. Monash University. Monash Asia Institute. II. Title : Asia's struggle against oppression.

323.095

Preface

Years ago when I was studying in the United States, I received a transcript that had my particulars printed on it. Under 'City' someone typed in 'Singapore', in the space for country 'CHINA'.

To many Westerners, Asia can be just a blur on the atlas, far removed from their lives. Nonetheless, recent events have shown that the world is tied together more intricately than we sometimes realise. Political developments in Asia, like it or not, do affect circumstances in the rest of the world.

Then there is my fellow Singaporean who once asked an academic who told her that he was teaching politics at the university, 'Is that legal?'

This is a book about political developments in Asia, in particular, the fight for democracy. It is not written for the academic specialising in Asia, but the lay reader interested in learning, however rudimentary, more about the goings-on of the region's politics. It is meant to inform, to warn and to encourage. As such, there are no historical minutiae to bore the reader nor footnotes to clutter the text. Reference notes are provided at the end of the book.

The difficulty in writing such a book is to decide what to leave out rather than include. For every dissident who is mentioned in this book, hundreds more have been left out. The dissidents in China, for instance, have not been included because they are so numerous, and their stories are enough to make up a separate book. The stories of the people mentioned in the following chapters must, therefore, for the time being, stand as representatives for those who have sacrificed themselves, and as inspiration for those who continue to yearn for democracy.

Chee Soon Juan
8 September 1998

Acknowledgements

For every author's name that appears on the cover of a book, several others have contributed towards the finished script. This one is no exception. I am especially grateful to Ann Ng and Glyn Howells for their involvement in every stage of the writing, and more.

This book could not have been written if not for the support of the Monash Asia Institute, in particular Professor John MacKay, Director. I would also like to thank Dr Damien Kingsbury for his insightful review of the manuscript and Leon Comber for his invaluable suggestions. Special thanks to Emma Hegarty for so patiently and meticulously editing the text, and all the effort involved in its production. I am also indebted to Juliet Yee for her kind assistance in helping me settle in at the Institute.

Thanks to David Hudson at Swinburne University, who spent much time in refining the manuscript and making precious suggestions, for which I owe much gratitude. I would also like to thank Kevin Magee for his input and for challenging me to think deeper and higher in my arguments.

In addition, I am thankful to the Council of Asian Liberals and Democrats Secretariat, Alternative Asean for Burma, the Asian Forum for Human Rights and Development, Focus on the Global South, Forum of Democratic Leaders in the Asia-Pacific, the New Taiwan Foundation, Chilin Foundation, Cheng Nan-rong Foundation, Benigno Aquino Foundation and the Special Broadcasting Service (Australia).

To those who have contributed to making this book a reality, I am eternally grateful: Joy Balazo, Alex Bardsley, Bonar Tigor Naipospos, Ceasar Chang Mou-hsiung, Chen Mei-chih, Damai, Michael Davies, Raul Daza, Herb Feith, Andrew Gunawan, Susan Hong, Huang Ming-tah, Margaret John, Leslie Kean, Ker Tzy-chao, Kim Sei-ung, Kit Magisco, Binky Mendoza, Miel Moreleda, Park Jun-hee, Gary Swinton, Amanda Tibbey, Noel Williams, Garry Woodard and Dick Wootton.

I must express my utmost thanks to Martin Lee for writing the Introduction, as well as to his former assistant Minky Worden for facilitating the process.

To those who have helped in one way or another but whom I have inadvertently failed to mention, my deepest appreciation. To all my friends, especially those in Burma and Singapore, who have assisted in making this project such an experience and education, but who must for now, remain anonymous for security reasons, my sincere gratitude.

Finally, to my wife, who is also my best friend—thank you.

Contents

Introduction

by Martin Lee

Chairman of Hong Kong's Democratic Party

The life of an Asian democrat over the past decades has not been an easy one. In the post-colonial era, Asia has made great strides economically as much of the region has been lifted out of poverty by the efforts of its people. However, political reform has lagged far behind economic developments. In some cases, economic success has given Asian tyrants the excuse for crushing political dissent.

Indeed, the struggle for democracy in Asia has known many dark moments and has often depended upon the leadership of extraordinary individuals. Though the stories told here span six countries, numerous decades, and very different national circumstances, they are linked together: the courageous Asians profiled in this book all speak eloquently of the imperative of freedom. These are leaders of such remarkable moral stature that despite imprisonment and exile, they—and the causes for which they stand—have remained in their peoples' hearts and in the world view. The profiles in the book are also connected by the fact that each provides a strong rebuttal to the so-called 'Asian values' argument, which Asian leaders have so often used to justify repressive rule.

The author of this important new book, Dr. Chee Soon Juan, has experienced first-hand the perils of pushing for political reform in Singapore—a nation which has perfected the art of quashing dissent and punishing dissenters. His story is not included here, but should be. A prominent opposition politician and neuropsychologist in Singapore, Dr. Chee was forced out of his teaching position and subsequently faced with trumped-up charges of defamation when he attempted to dispute his dismissal. Although he is now in exile from the country he loves and still considers home, Dr. Chee continues to labour to find ways to express his aspiration that democracy, human rights and the rule of law will one day define Singapore. I consider him to be one of the best hopes for effecting change in Singapore—and indeed, as this book shows—across Asia.

The Myth of Asian Values

The oppression and persecution of political dissidents in Asia is all too-often explained and excused in terms of what has become known as 'Asian values'. Regional autocrats often appeal to Asia's unique historical and social values and argue that these 'Asian values' render criticism of a government inappropriate and undesirable. Inappropriate because Asians allegedly do not want a greater voice in the government. Undesirable because the centralized power of authoritarian states is said to be conducive to high rates of economic growth. Yet, not even Confucius, whose teachings are alleged to have instilled devotion to authority among the Chinese, advocated blind allegiance to the state. When asked how one should serve a prince, Confucius replied, 'Tell him the truth even if it offends him.' And yet, those who dare speak the truth to authoritarian governments in Asia are all too often threatened, beaten, jailed, exiled and even executed by offended leaders.

It is time to put to rest, once and for all, the myth that human rights and democracy are not appropriate for Asians. The 1998 financial crisis in Asia exposed as fallacious the assertion that authoritarian governments can deliver better rates of economic growth than representative forms of government. Moreover, recent political developments in Indonesia and Hong Kong have proven to the world what the courageous democracy advocates profiled in this book have known all along: the stereotype that Asians do not care about democracy and only care about wealth is not true. Rather, the assertion by Asia's leaders that democracy and Asian values are mutually exclusive is more a matter of self-serving convenience than a matter of fact.

The 'Asian values' argument relies, in part, on the assumption that there exist distinctly Asian characteristics which lend themselves to a preference for authoritarian rule. This claim is simply preposterous. For one thing, given the rich diversity of beliefs and traditions in Asia, it is not at all clear that one can even speak about such a thing as 'Asian values.' Even if we assume that it is possible to find common values which cut across the many languages and religions of Asia, it is still far from clear how democracy and these Asian values are mutually exclusive.

The chief proponents of 'Asian values'—notably Singapore's Senior Minister Lee Kuan Yew and Malaysia's Prime Minister Mohammed Mahathir—make their case by imputing the concept with anti-colonialist sentiment. Defending 'Asian values,' they argue, is tantamount to defying unwarranted western interference and struggling to retain what is distinctly Asian. However, there is no conflict between recognizing that Asia may have different values from the West and still believing Asians have the right to choose their own leaders through democratic elections. Certainly, to the extent to which we Asians can, in fact, lay claim to the positive traits of strong family ties, reverence for education and a strong work ethic, we should struggle to maintain these values. We should celebrate those things which make us unique. However, we must also celebrate those things which bind us together with the rest of the world.

Political developments in Asia in 1998 prove that political freedom is not inimical to Asian sensibilities, but rather a right all people wish to exercise. South Koreans have elected Kim Dae Jung—resilient defender of democracy and former political prisoner—as President. Indonesian students have taken to the streets to demand from their government a greater voice for the people. In Hong Kong's May 1998 elections, a record-breaking voter turnout dramatically illustrated public dissatisfaction with the Beijing-appointed government. The popular vote in these elections—Hong Kong's first polls as a part of China—overwhelmingly supported the pro-democracy candidates who had been thrown out of office at the time of Hong Kong's handover to China.

Indeed, when Asian values are articulated by the people rather than by their leaders, these values include a strong desire for democracy and responsible, accountable governance. Asia's governments who otherwise have no basis of legitimacy, exploit regional pride and anti-colonialist feelings. Stripped of its nationalistic pretensions, the 'Asian values' argument is a naked attempt to justify the personal power of the autocratic elite.

I am confident that history will ultimately recognise that the supposed conflict between democracy and Asian values is a false distinction. There is no friction between Asians retaining their own unique characteristics and Asians believing that there are indeed some aspirations which are universal among all people. If you take a European, an African and an Asian and twist their arms, all will feel pain. If you arbitrarily jail them, they will all desire to be free. If you put a bullet in their heads, they will all die. Thus the claim that fighting for democracy in Asia amounts to disrespect towards Asian values is a false assertion. Rather, it is the suggestion that Asians are somehow culturally incapable of exercising basic rights which really smacks of racism.

Democracy: Enhancing Economic Stability

The Asian and international business community, along with proponents of the 'Asian values' argument, have often praised authoritarian governments such as Indonesia and China for their supposed ability to promote rapid economic development. Often, they go further, mocking the 'inefficiency' of democracies like India and the Philippines and asserting that democracy in Asia is bad for economic growth. Asia's 'economic miracle,' as the argument goes, is not tied to market factors but rather to a distinct Asian cultural and political identity which emphasizes order, discipline and authoritarian power structure. The assumption that strong, centralized government is necessary for high growth rates and economic prosperity, however, is deeply flawed. If anything, a suitable environment for foreign investment and economic prosperity relies on the rule of law, transparency and accountable government. In fact, the correlation between a stable democracy and long-term high rates of sustainable growth has been well-documented.

This is not to say that high economic growth and authoritarian regimes cannot ever simultaneously exist. Certainly, we have seen this happen on occasion. But this situation is intrinsically unstable—witness the spectacular collapse of President Suharto's 32-year rule in Indonesia. Formal institutions which serve to check centralized power—elected legislatures and independent judiciaries, for example—are necessary in the long run for economic stability. Without institutional controls on state power, there is little to prevent the growth of corruption and 'crony' capitalism as we have seen in Indonesia, Thailand and South Korea. In systems where the government's power goes unchallenged, the ruling elite abuse the trust placed in them to run the economy, handing out cheap credit and bad loans to friends and family. It should then, come as no surprise that rulers in Indonesia, Thailand and China have taken advantage of the wealth created by foreign investment and their own people and used it to line their own pockets.

Authoritarian governments are also poorly situated to deal with economic troubles. The countries that have weathered the Asian financial storm the best are democracies—Taiwan, the Philippines and Japan. Again, this is not surprising; Government which is not answerable to its people will not be likely to have open markets or the institutions required to impose the discipline necessary to overcome financial crises. In Indonesia, lack of transparency in the markets allowed President Suharto and his powerful business allies to cover up the information which might have forewarned investors and curtailed speculation. Countries with non-representative governments are also inherently more vulnerable to social unrest during times of economic trouble. Where a government's mandate is not derived from the people, its legitimacy is likely to be tied to its ability to provide financial stability. Again, the example of Indonesia is instructive. The currency crisis there caused political chaos, in part, because the government breached the only social contract which existed between itself and the people: the promise of prosperity.

For those who care about freedom and prosperity in Asia, the battle ahead is about creating institutions which will guarantee political and financial stability in the region. The importance of having formal institutions which check the accumulation of state power cannot be overemphasized. In order to accomplish this goal, the democracies of the world must seek not only economic restructuring from Asia's teetering autocratic regimes, but substantial political reform as well.

A Vision for Asia

As we approach the end of the 20th century, the world community can take pride that more people in more countries are more free than ever before. However, while Asians can look across our vast continent and see significant political reforms have taken place in Taiwan, South Korea and Japan, many Asians still live in countries where basic political liberties are not respected. Much of the government-sponsored repression detailed in this book continues today.

The future of political reform in Asia depends on recognizing that true Asian values are in no way incompatible with democracy and accountable government. Toward this goal, this book is an invaluable contribution. Each of the compelling stories told in this collection of profiles represents a repudiation of the 'Asian values' argument. Aung San Suu Kyi's tremendous popularity among her fellow Burmese speaks to the democratic aspirations of the Burmese people. But for the brutal military force which annulled the results of the 1990 election and the military which placed Aung San Kuu Kyi under house arrest, Burma would be a democracy today.

Similarly, the phoenix-like rise of Kim Dae Jung—from jailed dissident to President of the Republic of Korea—proved that the Korean people want to choose their own leaders and want leaders that will protect their political freedoms. Pramoedya Ananta's willingness to criticize the government in spite of the grave personal costs is a testament to the strength of conviction of all opposition figures in Asia, including the author himself. In the Philippines, the public outrage which followed the assassination of Benigno Aquino showed the world that the Filipino people had been underestimated when it was believed that they were apathetic to Marcos' iron rule. For Shih Meng-teh, disheartened after a decade of imprisonment, he had himself come to believe that the Taiwanese were indifferent to politics. Subsequent developments, however, convinced him that the Taiwanese people did want and were willing to fight for political reform. Chia Thye Poh's story—twenty two years in jail without having been charged or tried for any crime—is a telling example of the might a government can bring to bear on an individual in regimes such as Singapore.

The extraordinary individuals profiled here do not have identical beliefs or identical prescriptions, but they share a collective vision: an Asia where the human rights of every individual are respected and protected by law. Only when this vision is realized will Asia cease to be merely a large continent and become a truly great one.

Martin Lee is the Chairman of the Democratic Party, Hong Kong's first, largest and most popular political party. Despite being thrown out of the legislature following Hong Kong's July 1 handover to China, the democrats triumphed in the May 1998 elections, with Martin Lee emerging as the top vote-getter in the elections. If Hong Kong were a democracy, Mr. Lee would have been forming the government.

RUSSIA
RUSSIA
OUTER MONGOLIA
NORTH KOREA
SOUTH KOREA
CHINA
JAPAN
TIBET
INDIA
TAIWAN
BURMA
HONG KONG
LAOS
THAILAND
VIETNAM
CAMBODIA
PHILIPPINES
Pacific Ocean
South China Sea
BRUNEI
MALAYSIA
SINGAPORE
INDONESIA
Indian Ocean
AUSTRALIA

Prologue

The Struggle Begins

To Benjamin Franklin's two certainties in life, death and taxes, let me add a third—oppression. For as long as there has been more than one in a group, man has sought to subjugate man. Consider the following allegory:

'Friday,' said Robinson Crusoe, 'I'm sorry, I fear I must lay you off.'

'What do you mean, Master?'

'Why, you know there's a big surplus of last year's crop. I don't need you to plant another this year. I've got enough goatskin coats to last me a lifetime. My house needs no repairs. I can gather turtle eggs myself. There's an overproduction. When I need you I'll send for you. You needn't wait around here.'

'That's all right, Master, I'll plant my own crop, build my own hut and gather all the eggs and nuts I want myself. I'll get along fine.'

'Where will you do all this, Friday?'

'Here on this island.'

'This island belongs to me you know. I can't allow you to do that. When you can't pay me anything I need I might as well not own it.'

'Then I'll build a canoe and fish in the ocean. You don't own that.'

'That's all right, provided you don't use any of my trees for your canoe, or build it on my land, or use my beach for a landing place, and do your fishing far enough away so you don't interfere with my riparian rights.'

'I never thought of that, Master. I can do without a boat, though. I can swim over to that rock and fish there and gather sea-gull eggs.'

'No you won't, Friday. The rock is mine and I own riparian rights.'

'What shall I do, Master?'

'That's your problem, Friday. You're a free man, and you know about the rugged individualism being maintained here.'

I guess I'll starve, Master. May I stay here until I do? Or shall I swim beyond your riparian rights and drown or starve there?'

'I've thought of something, Friday. I don't like to carry my garbage down to the shore each day. You may stay and do that. Then whatever is left of it, after my dog and cat have fed, you may eat. You're in luck.'

'Thank you, Master. That is true charity.'

'One more thing, Friday. This island is overpopulated. Fifty percent of the people are unemployed. We are undergoing a severe depression, and there is no way that I can see an end to it. No one but a charlatan would say that he could. So keep a lookout and let no one land here to settle. And if any ship comes don't let them land any goods of any kind. You must be protected against foreign labour. Conditions are fundamentally sound, though. And prosperity is just round the corner.'

Sometimes Friday sees through the ruse and sometimes he doesn't. When he does, all hell breaks loose. It did in Asia after World War II when the peoples decided that their European conquistadors were no longer worthy of worship, especially after being so thoroughly drubbed by the Japanese Imperial Army.

And so the war-cry of nationalism was sounded and the locals went to war against the colonial Crusoes. The Fridays wanted equality and liberty, and nothing was going to stop them from driving out their overlords.

God-like to many Indonesians, Sukarno staged a frenzied campaign against the 'Dutch dogs' and ran them out of every one of the islands in the Indonesian archipelago.

A shrill voice railed against the British in Singapore in 1956: 'If you believe in democracy, then you must believe in it unconditionally.' Lee Kuan Yew, then a young opposition member of parliament, went head-to-head with the colonialists and badgered the British until they packed and left.

Further north in Kuala Lumpur, wild-eyed screams of '*Merdeka*!' (Independence) rattled the bullies in London so much so that by 1957, Malaysia graduated from colony to congress.

The French in Indochina were feeling the strain of battling their hitherto servile subjects and left after the Dien Bien Phu defeat in the 1970s.

In the Philippines, the 'little brown brothers' were frugal in their fraternity to the 'Yankee Monkee' they wanted out of the country.

In Burma, the 'Thirty Comrades', needled and wheedled the British until they got their own Union of Burma.

The Chinese were finally able to rid themselves of those 'foreign devils' after a prolonged and humiliating subjugation of their motherland.

It was a time of fervent nationalism. Man Friday had finally wised up and he wanted what was his. The story didn't end there, however. Hardly had the cheers of independence died when the leaders of the liberated began their oppression and brutality on their own peoples which, in many ways, were far more horrendous than the atrocities the colonialists ever inflicted on their subjects.

Under the New Order regime of Suharto masses were slaughtered in the name of communist-cleansing; five times more people were killed in a matter of months than in the whole of the Vietnam War. One who survived to tell his story, and many other tales, was Pramoedya Ananta Toer. Beaten until deaf and banished to an island where life takes on a moribund quality, the author climbed out of the pit of doom and wrote his way to international recognition. His mammoth four-book epic, the *Buru Quartet*, has since been translated into twenty languages and undergone countless reprints.

But even Pramoedya could not have written a tale as tragic as that of Shih Ming-teh, a long time political prisoner in Taiwan. The island's remarkable openness today belies the grimness of Shih's fate when he struggled for freedom in his lonely cell. Sentenced to life imprisonment, then pardoned, then re-arrested and sentenced to life again, Shih waged a relentless war on authoritarianism with nothing more than an unshakeable belief in freedom and democracy.

If Taiwan has grown from dictatorship to democracy, then Singapore has seen its political status go in the reverse direction, and together with it Chia Thye Poh's struggle. Locked up for 22 years by the father of 'Asian values', Lee

Kuan Yew, Chia has never stopped believing in the 'worldwide democratic movement', which for many years abandoned him to the cruelty of the Singapore regime. Since his release from prison, the Government continues to decide where he can go, who he can see, and what he can write.

Kim Dae Jung also paid for his belief in democracy with years of exile, imprisonment and near assassinations. His political battles with Park Chung Hee and Chun Doo Hwan are nothing short of legendary. He survived the political strife and today enjoys success as President of South Korea.

Benigno S. Aquino Jr's assassins made sure that they hit their target on September 21, 1983, when the Philippine opposition leader stepped out of the aeroplane after three years in exile and was executed on the tarmac. The killing ignited a revolution that saw dictator Ferdinand Marcos fall from years of plunder. He left the Philippines one of the poorest countries in Asia, with the people still picking up the pieces left behind from the years of misrule.

Poverty in Asia is perhaps most evident in Burma. Raped in every manner possible by its military dictatorship, the Golden Land is now anything but. One woman has stood up to confront the brutish regime and, more importantly, scares them. Not with guns and grenades but reason and reconciliation. Aung San Suu Kyi continues to work towards democracy for a people who found the wherewithal to face the brutality of its rulers and whose dreams for freedom at one time seemed desolately distant. At the time of writing this book, Aung San Suu Kyi defies the military regime by travelling out of Rangoon to meet the people. Few doubt that the will of the Burmese will prevail.

Asian values, under the guise of Confucianism, have been used by Asia's autocrats to repeatedly subjugate their peoples and to ward off Western criticisms about their undemocratic ways. This is discussed in greater detail in the Conclusion. There will always be those who will argue that democracy is not important for economic progress. The current Asian crisis has opened up a new can of worms, and it is becoming clearer that openness and accountability, in other words democracy, is essential for economic progress.

But that's not the point.

Others argue that democracy is a Western concept not suited to Eastern cultures and races. The irony is that it was the West which subjugated and oppressed Asia for much of the 19th and 20th centuries. Freedom from colonialism was not given but won; the rebellion was instinctual. In short, the longing for equality, justice and freedom is not Asian or Western—it is primordial.

But that's not the point either.

Human beings must learn to live together in a world where Friday does not have to collect Crusoe's garbage and eat his leftovers, where after winning his freedom, Friday does not, in turn, oppress his own people, and where humankind works out a way to live in peace and on the premise that human equals human.

That's the point.

All too often we talk about the movements, forces and paradigms that shape political change. We become desensitised by such impersonal descriptions and fail to see the pain, the tears, the terror, the broken bones and minds, the dark years in even darker cells that Asian dissidents have had to go through to achieve democracy. We become so callused that when they called out to the world, few heard. Yet, they kept on with their beliefs and stayed true to their faiths, not because there was money in it, for riches could be made if one supported—not opposed—the autocratic regimes, and not because there was power to be gained, for they could not predict when their lives were going to end in the hands of their oppressors. But because freedom was there.

They fought no less fearlessly than Nelson Mandela; in fact, some of these battles have been even more bitter. But because theirs was an Asian to Asian struggle, their stories have not triggered the raw emotion, and together with it the publicity, that comes in a White-oppress-Black struggle.

Some have succeeded, others are still in the midst of their struggles. Whatever fate has dealt them, they have left an indelible mark in the history of Asia and their courage must stand as testimony to the region's continuing struggle for freedom and democracy. For those who will listen and those who care, these are their stories...

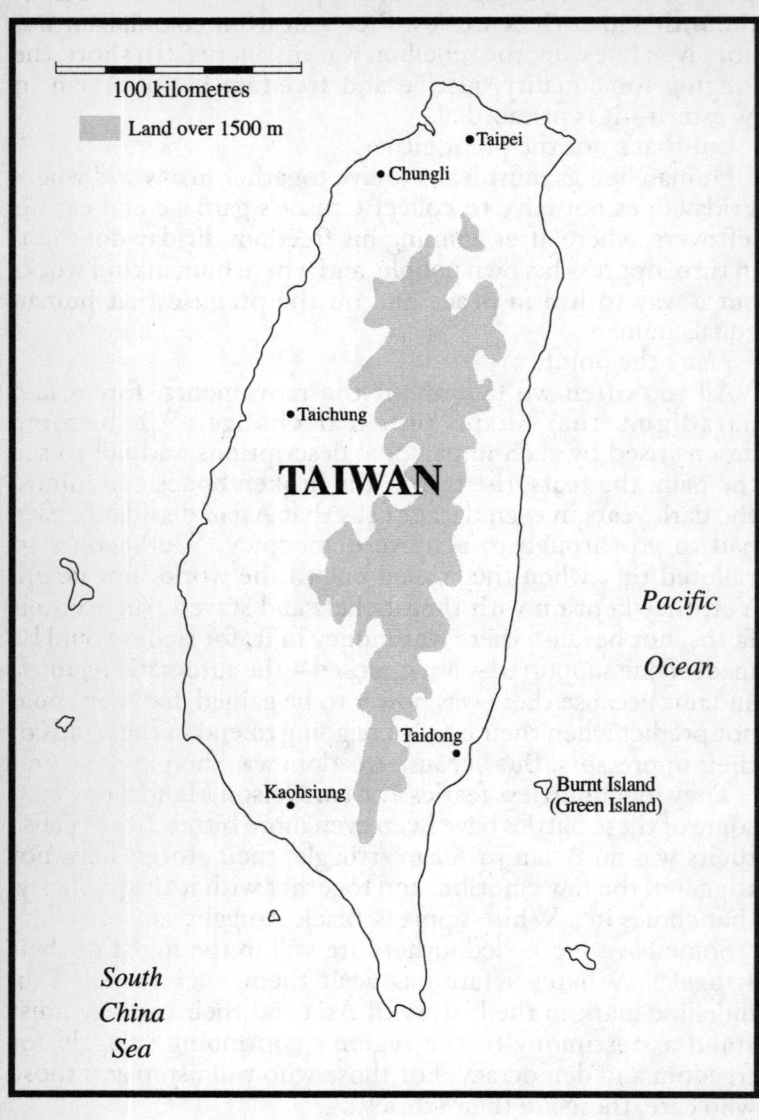
100 kilometres
Land over 1500 m
Taipei
Chungli
Taichung
TAIWAN
Taidong
Kaohsiung
Burnt Island
(Green Island)
Pacific
Ocean
South
China
Sea

I
Taiwan
Shih Ming-teh

The escape

'Nori! They're here to arrest you!' Linda screamed.

It was just a few hours since he first dozed off at about midnight, after returning home from a meeting with his compatriots. He was in a daze, having woken to the choleric ring of the doorbell and the fretful screams of his wife.

He instinctively reached for the telephone to warn the others. The line was dead. He put on his clothes and ran to the living room where Linda was frantically barricading the door with sofas, shelves and just about anything else she could find.

'Quick! Run!' she shouted.

Nori was desperately trying to figure out what to do but his thoughts were aggravatingly uncooperative.

The doorbell continued. Linda ran to the back door to see if their neighbours could help. Suddenly, the front door shook with an angry pounding.

'Mr Shih, open the door.'

The pounding continued.

'Who are you?' Linda cried out

'We're from the local police.'

'I know the local police officer. Don't lie to me,' Nori replied.

'I've just been posted here yesterday.' Without waiting for a response, the officer started kicking the door down.

Nori returned to the bedroom and switched off all the lights. He fumbled his way to the kitchen and went out through the back door. His apartment was on the second storey with a fire escape that led to the flat below, but experience told him that intelligence agents would have already surrounded the ground floor. He found the wall that formed the outer fencing of the block of apartments and half-slipped, half-groped his way along the narrow strip of moss-covered concrete which led to the roof of the neighbouring flats. Overhanging branches of a tree reached out to lend a chivalrous hand and Nori grabbed them appreciatively.

At 39 years of age, he surprised himself with his nimbleness and strength, despite the less than graceful trek across the concrete ledge. The military training in his younger days was coming in handy. After a couple of feet, he heard Linda scream. The officers must have broken the door down, he thought. Nori looked back but saw only darkness. He was confident that she would not be harmed as she was an American citizen.

Nori continued crawling until he reached a four storey building. The whole area was dark and he couldn't see how high he was. He looked up the wall for a second appraisal.

His legs hit the ground hard. The pain spread through his body and for minutes he lay unable to move or to yell out. Slowly he picked himself up and took refuge in the shadows. He saw that his left thumb was cut and bleeding profusely. Strangely—and thankfully—he felt no pain.

As he emerged from the alley, he saw intelligence agents milling around in the distance. He knew that he had to get out of the area before daylight. It was one of those times when morning wasn't welcome. Just as he was about to make a dash for it, a policeman suddenly appeared around the corner of the block. Too late, the officer had spotted him.

He sensed that this policeman didn't recognise him. 'Good morning, officer,' Nori gambled. He risked a radiant smile as he pretended to perform callisthenics, while doing his darnedest to hide his bleeding hand. His heart was pounding, but it assuredly wasn't from the morning exercise.

'Good morning,' the officer paid Nori his winnings and walked on.

Nori closed his eyes and let out a huge sigh of relief. He started walking towards the main thoroughfare and flagged down a taxi. That was the easy part, now he had to decide where to go. As Taipei yawned with the breaking of a new day, Nori looked out the window and smiled wistfully at his fellow citizens going about their day's activities. His mind raced back to the time when he had first been arrested 18 years ago.

Masters of our own fate

Shih Ming-teh was born on 15 January 1941 into a wealthy family in Kaohsiung, a city in southern Taiwan. His father, Shih Kuo-tsuei, a practitioner of traditional Chinese medicine as well as a believer in the Roman Catholic faith, was rather successful in his medical practice which very quickly translated into several pieces of real estate. His wife had given birth to three sons and five daughters, with the sons all dying when they were still infants. Notwithstanding his Christian beliefs and in full observance of that most contentious of traditions where boys are preferred, Shih Kuo-tsuei took a young second wife, who bore him another six children, this time all but one of them boys. Shih Ming-teh squeezed in at number four.

The Portuguese had named Taiwan 'Formosa', or Beautiful Island, when they first set foot there in the eighteenth century. Long considered an inconsequential island compared to the vastness of the Asian continent, Taiwan lies like loose change falling out of the hip-pocket of motherland China. With a mountain range for a spine, the island is muscularised with fertile pockets of loam on the coasts. As early as the Ming Dynasty, peasants from the Fujian province on the mainland came across in search of arable land. Since then, generations have settled on the western half of the island, with few traversing the mountain range to the eastern coast. Taiwan was already inhabited by natives of Polynesian stock, who possessed a darker complexion and an altogether distinct culture. For centuries these *shandiren*, or mountain people as the Taiwanese call them, coexisted peaceably with the early settlers.

Young Shih grew up under the heat of the Rising Sun where everything—lock, stock and *barreru*—was melted down and remoulded in the image of the Japanese masters. His name 'teh' (which means 'virtue') is pronounced 'Nori' in Japanese, and he has been stuck with it ever since.

When he was four, Shih experienced the terrifying storm of American bombers on the imperialists in Taiwan. As World

War II drew to a close with the Japanese surrender, Shih witnessed the islanders' elation when they were finally rid of their conquerors.

But the joy was shortlived. The departure of those wretched Japanese soldiers only heralded the arrival of those wretched Chinese soldiers. Led by General Chen Yi, who was later appointed governor, the ragtag team who came to liberate Taiwan in order to oppress it were an appallingly undisciplined bunch. They forced the locals into harsh labour, harvesting crops and extracting minerals which were shipped to the Chinese mainland to support the Kuomintang (Nationalist Party) army in its ongoing fight with the communists. Little was left for the locals.

Trying to make sense of the violence that he had seen, Shih asked his father why the Taiwanese had been ruled by Japan.

'Son,' his father sighed wearily, 'even with the war over and the Japanese gone from our land, we Taiwanese will never be masters of our own fate.'

Shih very quickly learned what his father meant.

The problem with the Chinese army was more than just militaristic bellicosity. The Taiwanese had lived on the island for generations. Rather than assimilate into their new surroundings, the uniformed bumpkins set out to impose their supremacy which strained ties even more. Besides, the locals contended, it was mainland China which had so readily ceded Taiwan to Japan in 1895 as part of a humiliating peace settlement following the Sino-Japanese War.

The schism that subsequently developed between the locals and the mainlanders (who were, even with later arrivals, outnumbered ten to one) grumbled portentously on the island. The two communities sat like the components of a bomb: inert by themselves but, when mixed, would explode with a vengeance.

Someone in Taipei hit the plunger and the bomb went off on 28 February 1947 with such fury that its effects are still felt half a century later. An elderly woman was hawking contraband cigarettes when police officers accosted her and tried to confiscate her goods, whereupon she put up a fight. The officers, unaccustomed to such effrontery, charged her with resisting arrest, convicted her of the offence and sentenced her to a beating (though not necessarily in that order) which they proceeded to administer on the spot. Bystanders came to the woman's aid, and a scuffle developed. Suddenly a shot rang out and before anyone could make sense of the situation, a civilian lay dead.

This event, which came to be known as the 2-2-8 Incident (named after the date on which it occurred), triggered widespread protests among the Taiwanese. The disquiet between the locals and their mainland rulers now turned into hatred, and rapidly engulfed the major cities.

Governor Chen Yi cabled the mainland Government for reinforcements for his diminutive garrison. When they arrived, the full force of the military was unleashed on the people. The bloodletting spread mercilessly across the country; by the time the situation was brought under control, it was estimated that between 10,000 and 15,000 civilians had been killed.

Martial law was imposed and the army, like a hateful headmaster, set out to teach the locals a lesson that they would remember forever. Those convicted of taking part in the uprising, often in dubious legal proceedings, were publicly executed. The grisly show-and-tell became a routine event across the whole country. Before each execution, a gong would be sounded to signal that class was about to begin.

When he was six years old, Shih Ming-teh slipped out of his house to witness one such session. The executioner stepped up to the condemned man, who was kneeling with hands bound behind his back, pointed the rifle to the back of his head and pulled the trigger. Bones and brain littered the pavement. One eyeball flew off and impaled itself on the branch of a tree close to where Shih was standing, staring bitterly at him and permanently scarring his psyche.

His own father was not spared the Government's wrath. Suspected of taking part in the uprising, Shih Kuo-tsuei was imprisoned and subjected to interrogation which maimed him physically and psychologically. He was released a few months later when no evidence was found against him, but never recovered from the trauma and died two years later.

With martial law, political parties were banned as they had been under the Japanese, even more books were deemed 'undesirable' and declared illegal, and Mandarin became the official language which, like the Japanese language, was not the mother tongue of the Taiwanese who spoke Taiyu, a provincial dialect. 'When we were in school, we had to wear a big label which read: "Please speak Mandarin." Those who used Taiyu were fined,' my Taiwanese mother-in-law recalled.

Meanwhile on the mainland, Mao Zedong, driven by the rubric and revolution of Marx, came out of his historical Long March and led a ruthless onslaught on Chiang's troops, taking city after village. Humiliated and emaciated, the Kuomintang army fled to Taiwan in 1949. Chiang Kai-shek declared that the island would be used as a base from which to launch the recovery of China from the communists. What was left unsaid was that Taiwan was not home to the Kuomintang. As far as Chiang and his army were concerned, it was nothing more than a military base, a political outpost. This callousness was to have far-reaching consequences for the later development of the Beautiful Island.

When the Communist Party took over China, Chiang Kai-shek knew that the war was well and truly lost. To save himself from complete loss of face, the leader of the Kuomintang relinquished his post of President of the Republic of China as proclaimed by Dr Sun Yat-sen when he overthrew the Qing Dynasty in 1911.

Ever the impresario of modern Chinese politics, Chiang left the lame duck presidency to his deputy Li Chung-ren while he quietly staged a massive haul of national treasures from the motherland. A total of 151 crates of gold, silver and cash from the central bank were shipped off to Taiwan. Chiang was also prescient enough to take priceless relics and museum treasures along with him. President Li Chung-ren, assailed by thoughts of being dragged from pillar to post by the communists, had in the meantime resigned the presidency and escaped to the United States.

Once in Taiwan, Chiang's appointed National Assembly, according to script, pleaded with the Generalissimo to resume the presidency of China. The stage was set for the former President to take control again. In 1949 he declared Taipei to be the temporary capital of all China and vowed that the Kuomintang would one day 'make a glorious return to the mainland'.

The 2-2-8 Incident had lit the flame of independence in the hearts of a group of young Taiwanese whom Shih was to later lead—a flame that burned unstoppably in the decades that followed. More than anything else, Shih wanted the Taiwanese people to be able to defend themselves against foreign powers. Resisting the mainland rulers would be an arduous task. But for every journey of a thousand miles, someone had to nurse the anxious hope that someone else would take that first fearless step.

Shih was a thin, timid man who never looked like a leader of his people. With a stick of a body, he was not disposed to grandiloquent displays of wit and oratory. His preferred method of leadership was to work in the background and influence his contemporaries with quiet diligence. He quickly developed a zest for philosophy, politics and law, and participated in discussion groups organised by students. Wherever these groups gathered together, there would also be talk about social issues, with poverty and discrimination against the locals being the leitmotif. The meetings were conducted in different places, including the Shihs' family run hotel.

Shih was determined to lead inspite of himself. Firstly, he had to overcome his aversions to everything from public speaking to darkness, which triggered phobic reactions. With a single-mindedness that proved to be his greatest source of strength in his struggle for freedom, Shih doggedly challenged his timorous nature. He would often go out into the cemetery after sundown to confront his intense dread of the dark. This exercise was extremely helpful during the years he spent in solitary confinement.

A self-confessed romantic, Shih told his friends that he would be willing to die for two things: love or his beliefs. Love was not forbidden in Taiwan and Shih took to it like duck to water. At 18 he fell in love with Chen Li-chu who later became his wife and bore him two daughters. It was his obdurate belief in Taiwanese self-determination that very nearly cost him his life.

In his high school days, Shih Ming-teh showed keen interest in military matters. He was fascinated by the strategies of warriors such as Napoleon, Hannibal and Alexander the Great. It was as a logical extension of his interest that he enrolled in a military school. Ironically, this only compounded his misgivings that the Kuomintang Government never really saw (much less treated) the Taiwanese people as their equals. Unofficial language, up until recently, still referred to the local Taiwanese people as *benshengren* which means 'local province people'. The *benshengren* have a term of their own for the mainlanders: *waishengren* or 'foreign province people'. These terms are not used disparagingly but are a reflection of the political situation Taiwan has had to deal with since the end of World War II.

After graduating from military school, Shih was assigned to combat duty on an island off the coast of China called Hsiao Jin Men or the 'Little Golden Gate'. By then, the fighting between the communists and the Kuomintang had petered out to the occasional and often ritualistic strafing of artillery on the Chinese coastline. With little to keep them occupied, the soldiers turned to the less hazardous activities of tending gardens and raising pigs.

In 1962 at the age of 21, while he was still performing his tour of duty, Shih Ming-teh was suddenly placed under arrest and taken to the sister island of Da Jin Men ('Big Golden Gate'). For six days and nights during which he was not allowed to sleep, the young soldier was repeatedly asked about his involvement with political groups. Well briefed thugs were able to reveal the discussion groups that Shih had participated in as far back as his high school days. They even cited the books he had read, the company he had kept and the words he had spoken.

After 18 days of detention, Shih was charged with being involved in a conspiracy to form the Taiwan Independence League, advocating the overthrow of the Kuomintang Government. More bemused than angry, he retorted that the League was just a group of students who discussed political and social issues. The discussions were political kindergartens and there was no intention to take them any further, let alone to take up arms. Besides, Shih maintained, he had lost contact with his friends in Taiwan after being posted to Hsiao Jin Men.

Shih was flown back to Taiwan where he thought he would be released. Instead, he found himself being dragged from one prison to another, and it dawned on him that the authorities weren't about to set him free.

The dark years

In prison Shih met two other detainees whom he recognised from his military training, and lost what little cheer he had left when they told him that the minimum sentence that such prisoners received was two years. 'Two years!' the thought seared his mind. For a young man experiencing the most delicious period of his life, it might as well have been two hundred.

When the other two inmates hatched a plan to escape to the nearby mountains where one of them had a relative, Shih was right there in the front row. But the map showing the way to the rendezvous house fell into the hands of the guards.

Escape attempts breed wrath. Shih was sent with his fellow collaborators and 17 other prisoners to the Taiwan Garrison Command's Security Centre—the army's favourite torture house—in the heart of Taipei. Their heads shaved, the prisoners were shackled together at the ankles and squeezed into a small cell. Given the opportunity to bathe only twice a week, the odour that reeked from the cell became positively dreadful.

The new interrogators said little, preferring to deal out slugs and kicks. Shih was led to the interrogation room with his hands cuffed behind him. The same questions were put to him again. 'What was the Taiwan Independence League all about?' growled a scruffy looking questioner.

'There was no such organisation when I was in Taiwan,' Shih explained for the umpteenth time.

'What were the League's activities?'

'I was posted to Hsiao Jin Men. I don't know what happened after that...'

Crack! came the sound of rifle butt meeting bone.

Shih literally didn't know what had hit him. He just felt the impact of a blow on his back. His body lurched forward and fell to the ground. Because he was handcuffed, he couldn't break his fall and landed face first on the unyielding floor.

'Aauuhh...' Shih let out a drawn-out groan after he recovered his senses.

His face, by now a bloody mess, contorted in pain. All he could feel were the spasms down his back and the cuts in his mouth. Blood was flowing from his nostrils. His eyes rolled back and, for a moment, he nearly passed out from the pain. Unable to breathe through his nose, Shih tried to gulp in air. That was when he felt pieces of broken teeth in his mouth. He spat out the fragments, gasping desperately. Everything was spinning around him. He couldn't see clearly because his eyes were watering.

From where he was lying, Shih could only see the boots of his interrogators shuffling about. They were all shouting at him. Then he caught sight of the toe-cap of a menacing boot coming towards him. All he could do was close his eyes. With sadistic accuracy, the boot smashed into his already broken mouth, dislodging more teeth. As more blows rained down, Shih remained motionless. Involuntary grunts came from his throat as each fist and boot made contact.

Shih was dragged back to his cell barely conscious. For the next few days he was left alone to recover. He couldn't eat as his mouth was swollen and bruised. Even swallowing his own saliva was an ordeal. The sharp ache in his back made lying down more agonising than sitting up. Six months later, the rest of his teeth dropped out due to the lack of dental treatment and hygiene. Medical assistance came only in the form of painkillers. All this time he slept in a sitting position.

Throughout his stay at the security centre, Shih heard screams and saw prisoners being dragged to and from the interrogation rooms. Methodology varied little as the interrogators played out the good-cop-bad-cop game, intimidating and enticing their hapless victims to reveal their conspiracy, real or imagined.

Humiliation was upgraded to a sport. Female prisoners had their nipples pinched and their vaginas scraped with hair brushes. Many couldn't walk after the painful sessions. Male detainees were made to strip and ordered to masturbate, often for hours. Their penises were tied to a string and they were led around the room while the interrogators laughed. One prisoner was forced to drink his own urine every morning.

Following his ordeal at the centre, Shih was taken to the Police Headquarters Martial Law Department and arraigned. There he was finally permitted to write to his family. In May

1963 they visited him—the first time since he was arrested. His mother, wife and daughter, whom he had never seen, were allowed into the visitors' room. When Shih saw them he broke into a toothless smile and held them tight. Then his wife, Li-chu, turned to their daughter, 'Call Papa.' Frightened by the unfamiliar surroundings and the strange man, the little girl began to cry.

Shih learned that his brothers Ming-cheng and Ming-hsiung had also been imprisoned. Ming-cheng's involvement with the group was largely incidental as he had attended the meetings only occasionally, more out of curiosity than concern. Shih's second elder brother, Ming-hsiung, had been away at medical school and didn't even know about the meetings. As the Government's imagination grew, so did its tentacles which ultimately rounded up 30 people whom it accused of subversion.

Trials that cared little about evidence and even less about justice delivered foul sentences of death, life imprisonment, twelve years and five years. Each of Shih's brothers received five.

Shih's own trial did not come until about a year later. In the meantime, political prisoners from all over the island were given the death sentence as a matter of course. Those facing the executioner were given their last meals before being dragged off to be shot. On the day of the execution, the guards would knock open the rusted chains around their ankles. The clanging of the shackles and sobbing protests of the condemned caused weak knees and nausea in the other prisoners. On those days, none of them could eat. While awaiting his fate before the military court, Shih passed his time by reading whatever his jailers allowed him, which was usually not much more than propaganda extolling the virtues of Chiang Kai-shek and his Government. But, as the Chinese say, in the absence of fish, prawns are just as good.

Shih held on to his belief that the Taiwanese people would one day be able to determine their own destiny. He knew that Taiwan's prospects for autonomy were dependent upon American foreign policy. And as long as Chiang Kai-shek continued to harbour his delusion about returning to the mainland, Taiwan would forever be pinned under the authoritarian rule of the Kuomintang.

When the Republican Party had nominated Richard Nixon as its presidential candidate in 1960, the Kuomintang assiduously courted him and openly supported his campaign. Shih believed that John F. Kennedy, the Democratic candidate, was more amenable to the idea of Taiwan becoming an independent nation. When Nixon lost the elections, Chiang scrambled to send his ambassador to cosset Kennedy, who reportedly said, 'I may forgive but I will not forget.' It seemed then that history would move in Shih's favour. But history, ever so fickle, also saw Kennedy assassinated midway through his presidency.

Missed opportunities occur in places both great and grim. Prisoners were allowed to receive small sums of money from their families to purchase snacks and toiletries. A favourite was the delectable Taiwanese beef noodle soup. Shih was savouring his meaty stew one day when he noticed a fellow inmate who looked pitifully hungry but was unable to afford food as he had no family to give him pocket money. Shih told himself that he would buy this man a bowl of beef noodles the next time the vendor came around. As chance would have it, Shih was caught in the toilet when the noodleman came to take orders, and he felt it a trifle indelicate to yell for food whilst in the process of discarding its remnants. Maybe next time, he thought. But there was to be no next time. The prisoner was executed days later.

Shih's morale grew weaker as the days wore on. Talk was going around that he would be given the death sentence, as his accusers felt he had played a major role in the group's activities. In 1964 he was finally brought before the tribunal for judgement: guilty as charged and sentenced to life imprisonment. Shih shivered with relief. At that point, anything was better than dying, and he ecstatically announced the glad tidings to his prison-mates when he returned to his cell.

The coin finally dropped, and Shih realised the full impact of his sentence:

> To many people, they see the torturing and beatings of political prisoners as most cruel. Yes, the tortures were painful. But those times were very short compared to the long jail terms. For people like me who have been jailed

for a quarter of a century, the pain during the torture and question sessions was just like a comet that came and went in a few seconds.

Taiyuan prison is a concrete monolith rising up from a plateau on the remote fringe of the Chongyang mountain range. Situated on the southeastern coast of the island, access to the maximum security facility from Taipei is an arduous 24 hour trip by road, rail and sea. Inside its walls are narrow dungeon-like cells from which escape is but a fantasy. Small windows that provide limited ventilation peek through the top end of the otherwise bare cells and tease their victims with the open space that lies beyond. The prison's water supply came from a creek that coursed through farms situated further uphill. Pesticides contaminated the water and led to the deaths of several prisoners. During the rainy season the water was constantly muddy, turning the rice cooked in it to inedible mirk.

With a daily routine of 30 minutes of outdoor exercise, one hour of leisure after lunch and two hours of visits to other cells, Shih's life became one enormous ennui. The highlight of the week was the thought that another one had passed and that, soon, he could get to see his loved ones who came to visit him at the end of each month. In Taiyuan, there was no fear of beatings and torture. Despair had replaced terror. A life in perpetual captivity drains the body of spirit and the mind of reason, and a desperate battle is waged just to keep both afloat. The thought of never seeing open skies again, of never walking down the street and smiling and talking to friends and, most of all, of never going home again is only one remove from that of suicide.

When he first arrived in Taiyuan, Shih felt that there was little difference between those serving a 15 year sentence and his life imprisonment. But when the 15 years were up and his cellmates started to leave after completing their sentences, it dawned on him that his was really a life bereft of hope.

But Shih refused to go under. To stay alive, he had to manufacture hope. Apart from reading whatever books the security officers allowed his family to bring him, he started to learn Japanese from an old inmate. Over the years, he acquired enough proficiency to translate Japanese books into Chinese. He also found succour for his mind by writing letters to his family. To facilitate his writing—which for a prisoner becomes one's coach, companion and counsellor—he constructed a makeshift table from his books and piles of scrap paper.

Tales of infinite sadness were told about political prisoners in Taiyuan. Families broke up because they could not endure the strain of the prolonged separation. Fathers and mothers passed away heartbroken that they never saw their sons again. One inmate, Chen Shui-chuan, regularly wrote to his mother during his years of incarceration. No one dared tell him when she passed away for fear of snapping the flimsy string that held his mental being together. He continued to pen his filial missives and was not told the truth until his release years later.

Another incident had all the elements of a tragi-comedy. Lai Chen-fu, had just a few weeks to go before completing his 10 year term. One morning he innocently asked a fellow prisoner for the day of the week, which in the Taiwanese dialect includes the words 'pai gui'. The phrase takes a semantic skid into another expression meaning 'to worship the devil', which a dimwit of a guard overheard and interpreted as an imprecation on Generalissimo Chiang who was celebrating his birthday that very day. Lai's term was extended by another three years.

Shih had his share of sorrow in prison. His mother passed away in 1968, four years into his incarceration at Taiyuan. On her death-bed, too weak to talk, she kept gesturing with her two fingers. Everyone was trying to figure out what she was trying to say. Some thought that she was referring to her second son who was away in Hong Kong. In the end Shih's wife, Li-chu, realised that she was reminding the family not to forget to send the monthly 200 Taiwan dollars (about US$3) to Shih Ming-teh in prison. When she got their assurance, she took her last breath.

The grieving of his mother's death and the analgesics Shih took for his back injury precipitated gastric pains. As the intensity grew, he was sent for medical observation where the preliminary diagnosis was stomach cancer. With continual entreaties from Li-chu, the authorities finally sent him for treatment at the nearby Taidong County Hospital. His wife rented a room next to the hospital and persuaded the sentinel to allow her to stay with her husband on several occasions.

The six months he was hospitalised turned out to be his happiest days. Li-chu prepared home cooked meals which, for someone used to the repulsively insipid prison fare, were a gastronomic goldmine. He spent much time with his daughter, who was by then nine years old, frolicking in the backyard chasing butterflies and frogs, and helping her with her homework. 'This is the only real family life that I have known my whole life,' he later reminisced. 'It gave me beautiful memories to last a lifetime.'

All too soon, he had recovered and had to return to Taiyuan. The blissful respite ended on a bittersweet note: sweet because Li-chu was pregnant with their second child, bitter because the baby girl would also grow up fatherless.

On 8 February 1970, six political prisoners in Taiyuan decided to escape. It was either that or die an obscure death in jail. They had two objectives. One, of course, was to break out of prison. More than that, they wanted to jolt the Taiwanese people out of their apathy by capturing a nearby radio station and broadcasting a call for a glorious revolt against the Kuomintang. The trouble with grand schemes is that they have to be executed, which almost always leads to chaos.

With his military background, Shih's views were much sought after and he was urged to join. He declined. The prisoners stormed the watch command officer's post and demanded the unlocking of all the cell blocks. A struggle broke out between a guard and a prisoner; and the commotion drew the attention of other guards. Despite the hitch, the six prisoners still managed to escape and find sanctuary in the surrounding mountains. After a massive search, they were back in prison within two weeks. All but one were executed. Guards found guilty of negligence were also given the death sentence.

Not content with the executions, the authorities embarked on a witch hunt to find out the extent of the conspiracy. For not reporting the plot, Shih was sentenced to solitary confinement. Shih Ming-teh found himself in a tiny cell. Actually, it was more like a coffin, measuring a little over three feet in width: with a shoulder pressed against one wall, the other palm could be squarely placed on the opposite wall. When he lay down, his head scraped the inner wall as his feet touched the door. Food was unceremoniously passed in via a serving hole. A sealed window sat near the high ceiling.

At first Shih was asked to reveal the names of all the prisoners involved in the conspiracy. He was alternately threatened with the death penalty for not talking and enticed with early release if he cooperated. For someone facing the prospect of never being free again, such a promise was seduction by the devil himself. Having witnessed what the authorities did to those who were implicated, Shih remained abidingly stalwart.

That was not always the case with some other prisoners. The infirm of spirit would inform on their fellow inmates for much less, sometimes for nothing more than easier daily chores.

A small bulb provided light at night because the officials did not want their charge to commit suicide. Shih was allowed reading materials which he devoured. In a life where all that glitters is the hope of feeling sunshine on one's face again, the written word is gold. Night traded places with day as he turned to reading after dusk, because it was brighter then than during the day when the light was turned off. As the books accumulated, he spread them on the hard floor and used them as bedding.

His first human contact came after three months when his wife was allowed to visit him. When he emerged from the decrepit cell, he looked sub-human. Not having spoken for such a long period, his tongue had difficulty shaping the words he wanted to say.

After the tryst with daylight and fresh air, Shih was led back to dark solitude. It became a struggle just to pass each minute, let alone the hours and days. He had no idea when his captors would show some mercy and let him out of the miserable hole. He started to make conversation with an imaginary friend and recited passages from books he read, in an interesting mixture of Chinese, Japanese and English.

Shih was repeatedly offered a reduction in his jail term if only he would name names. The officials were determined to break his will. Shih was just as resolute. It was a stand off. Stand offs usually come about when the antagonists are equally matched in might; in this case, power was overwhelmingly stacked on one side. And so, admitting defeat, the authorities let their prisoner out of the cell after an incredible 11 months.

Adjusting to Change

Outside Taiyuan was altogether another world. Taiwan's economy was expanding rapidly, with the GDP showing annual increases of eight to ten per cent. The GNP per capita had bounded from US$50 in a once soporific, agrarian society to US$2,500 in an economy that had become a redoubtable trading juggernaut. With much fanfare, the Republic of China gloated over its economic accomplishment at the expense of those less sophisticated political infidels across the Taiwan Straits.

But all was not sunshine and *Shaoxing* wine for Taiwan, still labouring under martial law. With intellectual and economic attainment, the middle class became more assertive. The *benshengren* had no special affiliation with China, and that 'glorious return to the mainland' had all but become a fatuous fantasy of a dislocated band of old Kuomintang soldiers. To the Taiwanese, the island was home and no nationalistic exhortation was going to alter that fact. Meanwhile many of them were becoming restive at being shut out of the governing process.

Half a world away, embarrassed by its ally's authoritarian streak, the United States mounted pressure on Chiang Kai-shek to introduce political reforms. In order not to ruffle feathers in Washington—which Taiwan depended on for its defence weaponry—Chiang grudgingly allowed elections at the provincial level, which had little effect on his control of the national government. As political parties were still illegal under martial law, opposition politicians ran as independent candidates and were referred to as the *dangwai* or 'outside of the [Nationalist] Party.'

The mood among the people was remoulding, imperceptibly at first but with increasing momentum. Political undercurrents came to a head when Chiang Ching-kuo, son of the President and Prime Minister of Taiwan, visited the United States in 1970. During the visit, two Taiwanese students attempted to assassinate him. Chiang Ching-kuo escaped unharmed but the message was clear: some Taiwanese were no longer content to sit idly by while the Chiangs prepared themselves for a dynastic reign. If there were any doubts in his mind about the people's discontent, the attempt on his life quickly dispelled them. Fate, as Chiang realised, plays fast and loose with politicians—even entrenched autocrats.

In the years that followed, Chiang Ching-kuo cultivated the local Taiwanese population by co-opting some of its more prominent members into the higher echelons of the Kuomintang. One of them was Lee Teng-hui who was appointed mayor of Taipei. Prime Minister Chiang also began to pay more attention to improving the island's infrastructure that had hitherto been neglected by his father who had always considered Taiwan a transitory point unworthy of investment. In 1974 the Prime Minister, who was by then assuming more responsibilities in the daily administration of the island, embarked on major infrastructure projects: the island-long North-South Highway, the Chiang Kai-shek International Airport, an international port in the city of Taichung, and several nuclear power plants.

Unlike Chiang Kai-shek who carried himself with courtly austerity, the heir-apparent knew that political circumstances had altered and that he would have to display a more well-disposed mien. In contrast to his father's slim and chiselled physique, the teddy-bearish and bespectacled Chiang Ching-kuo had a less forbidding appearance, which may have helped him when he tried to convince the people that he was earnest about change.

It was not as if Chiang Ching-kuo had undergone political conversion and was now willing to play pat-a-cake with the *dangwai*. He kept a stranglehold on the national government and, if properly enraged, could inflict pain with as much egalitarianism as his father. Elections were restricted to the provincial level. Members of the two legislative bodies, the National Assembly (the body that also elected the president) and the Legislative Yuan had their terms extended indefinitely from the time they set foot in Taiwan. Political parties were still banned. Chiang abided by his father's immutable attitude towards political prisoners: 'We do not have political prisoners here. Those who are alleged to be political prisoners actually have committed crimes.'

Following his release from solitary confinement, Shih and the rest of the political prisoners in Taiyuan were transferred to an even more remote and inhospitable facility on a small island 33 kilometres off the eastern coast where escape was even more unthinkable. The uninhabited atoll was so dismal, with its blackened and windswept features, that it was unlovingly christened Burnt Island. The fact that the Government changed its name to the more welcoming Green Island did nothing to ease the prisoners' desperation.

Shih's physical problems continued to plague him. A few months after being transferred to Burnt Island, he developed acute appendicitis that left him barely able to walk. Again, the prison warden refused to send him to hospital for treatment. It was only after the doctor threatened that he would not be responsible if Shih died that the warden relented. Even then, the prison administration flew him to Taidong only 50 hours later where he underwent surgery immediately.

Shih continued his program of self-study to keep his mind from turning to mulch. He started developing a written system for the Taiwanese language which eventually led to a compilation entitled *Design Principles and Rules of Usage for a New Taiwanese Script*. Unfortunately, the manuscript was lost years later when he fled before his second arrest.

It was now even more difficult for the families to visit the prisoners. Shih's wife stepped up her efforts to get her husband released. With each passing month she grew increasingly despondent. Desperate, she knelt down in front of the Presidential Palace and tearfully begged Chiang Kai-shek to release her husband. A former fellow prisoner who was released after serving a 12 year sentence joined up with Li-chu to campaign for Shih's release. Li-chu found solace in this man, and solace tripped into romance. The thought of never being able to be with Shih for the rest of her life proved to be more than she could bear. She finally gave up and decided to go with her new companion.

Li-chu broke the news of her affair to her husband on one of her visits and, not surprisingly, he became intensely bitter. Bitterness turned into hatred for everything that had happened to him, and hatred into revenge. He wanted to punish those who had brought him so much misery and injustice. The emotional torment translated into physical aching in his heart which he desperately tried to ease by all means possible, even lying prone on the floor in the hope that the pressure would somehow suppress the pain. His whole existence seemed like a recurring nightmare with each episode more sanity-sapping than the one before. Every night in his darkened cell a maniacal fusion of pain, loneliness, confusion and disillusionment dragged him this way and that, and every night he quietly cried to himself—except when pain became so vile that he only managed to cling on to his mind by letting out a long, lonely wail.

As a Christian, Shih always looked forward to Christmas. But Christmas on Burnt Island was like Christmas on the moon—one experienced a lightness of being but with no one to share the happiness. Months had passed since his marriage ended but he was still reeling from its aftermath. Why, he asked, was peace not coming to him? He began to realise that his feelings of recrimination and bitterness were driving him to desolation. To retaliate, if he was ever freed, was to cause misfortune to others as well as to destroy his belief in non-violent resistance. All the years he spent behind bars could not be allowed to degenerate into gratuitous retribution. There must be a higher purpose to his suffering. Jesus, he remembered, not only forgave his enemies but loved them as well.

Loving the Kuomintang was a distant if not altogether unimaginable proposition, especially as he sat rotting in jail. The least he could do, he thought, was not to hate his persecutors and, more manageably, to forgive them. And thus began the healing process. Shih said a long prayer that Christmas night and found forgiveness in his heart. Soon, for the first time in many months, he fell into a restful sleep. He had finally woken up from his nightmare.

Before their separation, his wife had continued to bring him small amounts of money. When she left him, so did the cash, and without it he was unable to buy toiletries. Exigency inspires innovation. Strips of cloth from old prison wear made for decent toilet paper that could be washed and reused when supplies ran out. Broth from the morning's ration of porridge, when carefully decanted into little containers, served admirably as a substitute for shampoo and soap.

Later, when his siblings found out that Li-chu had left him, they brought him the money that he so badly needed all the same.

In America, Richard Nixon was elected President. Acrimony towards China in the past now melted into accommodation with Secretary of State Henry Kissinger pushing for normalisation of ties with the Middle Kingdom. Nixon's visit to China in February 1972 signalled a shift in the United States' policy on Taiwan, which was no longer recognised as the Republic of China but a lonely province of the People's Republic of China.

Following rapprochement between the two countries, Japan, with the tacit acquiescence of the United States, broke off diplomatic ties with Taipei and recognised Beijing instead. Other countries soon followed suit, and by the 1980s Taiwan's international diplomatic relations whittled down to just a handful of countries in Latin America, Africa, the West Indies and the Pacific Islands.

Just the year before on 25 October 1971, Taiwan had left the United Nations to avoid the indignity of expulsion. At about the same time, Beijing was pushing for representation.

When the international community recognised the Beijing Government, Shih's hopes for the Taiwanese people to be free from Chinese domination were now burning as bright as a wet matchstick. All the years of imprisonment he endured became even more incomprehsible. The Chinese Communist Party now claimed Taiwan as one of its provinces, and countries had to accept this if they wanted to enjoy full diplomatic relations with China. To the Taiwanese people, the only difference was that the regime in Beijing was even more brutal than the one in Taipei.

In the high stakes game of Taiwanese politics, it sometimes takes the demise of men to bring about respite for others. In April 1975, Chiang Kai-shek passed away and the Government announced an amnesty for political prisoners, reducing Shih's life sentence to 15 years. Prisoners were usually sent to a halfway house two years prior to their release to prepare them for the world of the living. Since he had already served 13 years, Shih was due for such a transfer. But freedom was not to be had quite so easily, as the authorities refused to release him.

Jimmy Carter was elected United States President the following year and pressed for Shih's release, which eventually happened 11 months before his 15 years was up. He was transferred to the Tu-cheng Rehabilitation Centre in Taipei.

In the meantime, Vice-President Yen Chia-kan took over from Chiang Kai-shek to finish the presidential term and then, like a dutiful uncle, stepped aside for Chiang Ching-kuo.

Chiang Ching-kuo was acutely aware that he was presiding over a Government whose octogenarian leaders, when they showed signs of life in between bouts of political narcolepsy, were insufferably out of sync with society. He knew that he would have to co-opt more locally born Taiwanese into his Government. One such inductee was Hsu Hsin-liang, who would play a crucial role in Taiwan's quest for freedom. Hsu had been awarded a scholarship to study in the United Kingdom. Before completing his studies, he fell victim to politics and returned to Taiwan to stand for elections under the Kuomintang which he duly won.

As a member of parliament in the provincial legislature, Hsu was a fearsome exponent in the Way of the Political Hand. When let loose in the ring, and to the mortification of his managers, Hsu started punching and poking the Kuomintang trainers in his own corner. Openly criticising Government policies and personalities, the maverick became more of a bane to his Party than anyone had expected—or could tolerate.

Hsu wanted to go places with his political career. In 1977 he had his mind fixed on becoming the magistrate of his county. But after his death defying performance at the provincial level, the Kuomintang was in no mood to nominate him as its candidate. Confident of his own political appeal, Hsu bolted the Party and stood as a *dangwai* candidate. 'I won't be campaigning for a magistrate's post but instead for a democratic movement,' he warned. 'If we can't have democracy, then it's revolution.' He knew exactly where to hit the Kuomintang, and his ferocious campaign deepened the open cut between the *waishengren* and the *benshengren*.

On polling day, an election official was caught entering a ballot booth with a voter. When you toss a match into an ammunition dump, you don't just get a pop. The indiscretion sparked off a heated quarrel which grew into imputations that the Government was trying to rig the process. This triggered an angry protest and, before the day was over, the nearby

Chung-li city police station was burned down wall to wall, ashes to ashes.

The army was on standby in the area, but Chiang could not afford a bloody incident on his hands, especially as he was about to take his seat as President and one which the United States could make very warm. He ordered the military to show restraint, which to many who had lived through the years of his father's rule, had become a most unfamiliar sight but which was nonetheless interpreted as a victory, albeit a tad nervously.

That night when the results were announced, Hsu had trounced his opponent. Buoyed by triumph on two fronts, the irrepressible *dangwai* leader sensed that the time had come for the groundswell to be organised into a more structured movement. The people of Chung-li had served notice on Chiang that they were serious about political reform. Chiang grudgingly acknowledged it, and within months, appointed more Kuomintang *benshengren* into key cabinet posts.

On 16 June 1977 Shih was free to leave the Tu-cheng Rehabilitation Centre. Ironically, he woke up that morning not feeling terribly excited about joining the outside population. And little wonder. He was 36 years old, had no family to return to as his estranged wife wanted a divorce, no house to call his own, and only a couple of hundred dollars that his relatives had saved up for him. He had no idea what to do for a living.

Before he left, the inmates warned him not to look back: 'Just walk away. Don't even say goodbye. If you do, you'll end up coming back.' In Chinese, the only equivalent of goodbye was 'zai-jian' or 'see you'. But Shih was not given to superstition. He resolved that if he had to come back to prison because of his political beliefs, then so be it. As he was about to leave, Shih turned around, smiled and waved goodbye to everyone.

'The streets have changed,' Shih thought with trepidation. In place of tall fields of corn and sugar stood taller buildings of concrete and steel. Knobless, transparent doors provided an impeccable telepathic service, stairs moved so that feet didn't, and toilets extended an uplifted welcome unlike those surly holes that one had to straddle in prison. One could even talk to relatives and friends in distant lands from a telephone right in one's living room.

It wasn't the new technology that bothered Shih. It was how much the people had changed that gave him much cause for vexation. Talk was all about assets and accounts, profits and portfolios. Political discussions were nervously eschewed; societal aspirations took the form of stockmarket appreciations. Even friends he had known before his imprisonment distanced themselves, wanting little to do with an ex-political prisoner. Decades of control by the Nationalists where the word of one man had virtually become law, coupled with a scissor-happy media, had battered political life into a critical condition.

Even his relatives pragmatically averred: 'You say you suffered for your ideals, but who cares? Nowadays, people measure each other's worth in terms of a car or a house.' Others would counsel: 'You'd best forget about fighting the Government, you're banging your head against the wall. Better get yourself a wife and earn some money.'

At the same time as Hsu Hsin-liang was running for Magistrate of Taoyuan, another important election was taking place at the provincial level, where the wife of former political prisoner Su Tung-chi was a candidate. Su, like Shih Ming-teh, was released upon completing his discounted life sentence. As ex-political prisoners were banned from running for office, Su's wife stood in his place on a platform of human rights issues.

Shih was approached to manage the campaign. Getting directly involved in political activities so soon after being released could mean a quick trip back to Burnt Island. But he wanted, more than anything else, to find out how much people cared about freedom and democracy. A compromise of sorts was reached and Shih, taking on a pseudonym, plunged into the campaign, boots and all. The proof of the daring was, it seemed, in the polling as the team pulled off a stunning upset. It was more than an election victory, Shih thought: 'I won back my confidence.'

Following the win, Shih was pleasantly surprised by an offer of a reporter's job with the *Taiwan Times* which he readily accepted. The newspapers were beginning to show some backbone and trying to steal away, ever so cautiously, from the control of the Government. Shih began publishing booklets calling for, among other Kuomintang provoking ideas, another legislative body to be set up to counter the puppet National Assembly and the Legislative Yuan. The Government banned them.

The booklets also caught the eye of a young human rights campaigner by the name of Chen Chu who had herself become a permanent feature article in the journals of the Kuomintang intelligence unit for her stand on human rights. Over the years she had painstakingly cultivated an impressive network of *dangwai* activists in and around Taiwan. Chen Chu was assisted by a PhD candidate from Stanford University, Linda Gail Arrigo, who was doing research on women factory workers in Taiwan and who had also taken an active part in discrediting the Kuomintang over the Chung-li affair, an endeavour which earned her the undying dislike of the regime.

Chen Chu recognised the complementary nature of Shih Ming-teh's and Linda Arrigo's circumstances. It would, she calculated, be a killing of the two proverbial birds with one marriage. Shih, whose latest publication had made him a prime candidate for re-arrest, would be accorded some form of protection if he was married to an American citizen. That was at least the theory. Married to a Taiwanese, Linda would similarly have a little more leverage if the authorities decided to deport her.

On 15 June 1978, Shih got wind that the secret police were on his trail. He and Linda hurried to the United States embassy and, with Chen Chu as the witness, obtained a marriage contract notarisation. They immediately went into hiding in the house of an acquaintance who happened to be an American GI. That day, Chen Chu's house was raided and she too had to go into hiding. A week later, she was apprehended. Linda immediately activated her contacts in Taiwan and abroad; within a month, after pressure from the Carter administration, Chen was released.

Under further pressure from the United States, Chiang Ching-kuo was forced to open up the Legislative Yuan for elections and 23 December 1978 was to be the polling day—the first time that the national legislative body had called for elections in its almost 30 year reign. The announcement made for an exciting curtain raiser which did not necessarily raise the curtain on anything. Political parties were still banned and, without a base, *dangwai* candidates had little chance of beating the omnipotent Kuomintang machine.

Again, Chen Chu was instrumental in pulling the amorphous opposition together. With political meetings still illegal, she suggested that Shih and Linda Arrigo host a wedding dinner and invite opposition leaders and supporters. The invitation list quickly grew to 400 and the angelic couple soon found themselves entertaining a heretical bunch of *dangwai* politicians, newspaper editors, writers and ex-political prisoners at the wedding-cum-opposition summit.

As champagne flowed and dumplings disappeared, Shih got together with Hsu Hsin-liang to discuss strategies for the upcoming elections. They were joined by other prominent freedom fighters such as Huang Hsin-chieh, Chang Chun-hung, Lin Yi-hsiung and Yao Chia-wen. That meeting proved to be the linchpin of Taiwan's historic lurch towards a fully fledged democracy. The Dangwai Campaign Coalition would be formed to assist opposition candidates, with Shih Ming-teh as its executive secretary.

Financed by Yu Deng-fa, Kaohsiung county's Magistrate, the coalition ran a respectable campaign focusing on human rights and democracy issues. Chiang had the old benefactor and his son arrested, charging them with conspiring with the communists. The *dangwai* took to the streets to protest the arrests in their first ever public demonstration. With Yu in prison, the financial baton was passed onto Huang Hsin-chieh, who sold several pieces of farmland to raise funds for the opposition candidates who were brimming with hope.

But destiny sneezed and democracy was blown away. At two in the morning, one of Chiang's aides woke him with the news that the United States had finally decided to sever official ties with Taipei and acknowledge the Beijing Government as the authority of all China. The announcement would be made in a few hours. Chiang had known that the decision would come sooner or later but he was hoping that it could have been later, much later. Overnight, literally, Taipei had ceased to exist in the official mind of Uncle Sam who had abandoned it to the detested stepmother Mao. The Kuomintang Government would not go quietly, however. Carter sent Assistant Secretary of State Warren Christopher to pacify the Taiwanese who welcomed his delegation with eggs and tomatoes.

Orchestrated and stoked by the Government, anti-American sentiment was at fever pitch. Chiang lambasted Carter's decision for affecting the interests of not only the Republic of China but, a trifle disingenuously, of 'the entire free world'. By branding the *dangwai* politicians as bedfellows with Americans who were 'supporting communist bandits' in selling out the country, the Government pulverised the opposition movement. With the local media in brilliant castigating form, the popularity of the *dangwai* leaders plunged to an all time low. Chiang capitalised on the situation and cancelled the 23 December elections, citing that most elastic of reasons—national security.

But this was not a time to defer to dread. Shih and the other *dangwai* leaders doggedly pushed ahead with their calls for political reform. They grew bolder with each meeting, and soon public forums and demonstrations were organised all over the island. The Kuomintang responded by arresting opposition workers and closing their offices. Thugs were sent in to rough up its supporters whenever public meetings were organised, and the local media dutifully played up scenes of 'unruly' and 'violent' *dangwai* gatherings.

Meanwhile, Shih had come under intense surveillance by the Taiwan Garrison Command. This became so obvious that one evening while he and Linda were heading for a Christmas dinner, they noticed two intelligence agents waiting in a car. Unable to hail a taxi, the two casually walked up to their minders and requested a ride. The red faced officers sheepishly obliged.

'We used to conduct our meetings in the car,' Yao Chia-wen told me as we walked down a street lined with flags reminiscent of imperial China whenever a triumphant warlord was ushered into a newly conquered territory. But these flags were not beckoning any emperor; they carried the crisp smile of an opposition candidate in a crisp suit vying for a city council post in Taipei. 'Opposition parties were illegal then under martial law. In order not to get caught, we would pile into a car and conduct our meeting in it as we drove along. Someone would take the minutes and the driver always ended up being the chairman as he had to concentrate on driving instead of arguing.' Yao argued all the way to the Legislative Yuan where he was a prominent member of the opposition.

By the late 1970s, the *dangwai* had become an opposition party in all but name. The leaders now decided to publish the *Mei Li Dao Magazine*. *Mei Li* means 'beautiful' and *Dao* indicates 'island', an apparent reference to Formosa. Shih Ming-teh was asked to take charge of the publication. On 10 December 1979, in conjunction with International Human Rights Day, the Mei Li Dao group organised a mass rally in Kaohsiung, despite warnings that the event was illegal. When the police pulled out their batons, the *dangwai* brandished their banners, determined to proceed with their protest at the Kuomintang's continued abuse of human rights.

That night, as the crowd swelled to 30,000, the organising committee braced itself for trouble from toughs dispatched by the Kuomintang. The mood was one of taut anger; only the night before, the Taiwan Garrison Command had arrested two *dangwai* activists and severely beaten them. Before the assembled protesters could begin to march, the police stopped Shih Ming-teh and Yao Chia-wen, the designated leaders of the demonstration. As the two were summoned into the police station, riot troops encircled the demonstrators. Suddenly screams and cries were heard as the police fired canisters of tear gas into the crowd. As people tried to escape the fumes, the riot police tightened the cordon. In desperation, the marchers punched and kicked their way out.

The organisers appealed for calm, which for a moment seemed to work. The crowd reassembled outside the magazine's office where speeches were scheduled. Just when the audience began to settle down, the troops charged again, clubbing with one hand and gassing with the other. The crowd returned ruthlessness with ruthlessness. Soon the peaceful rally had degenerated into a full-scale riot that ended with heavy casualties on both sides.

As the stinking fumes of tear gas swirled and the injured were carried away, leaders of the Mei Li Dao group wondered what lay ahead for the organisation. 'If I have to sit in jail for the rest of my life for beginning this movement so that the people can stand up to the dictator,' Shih grimly said to Linda, 'I am willing.'

The following days saw more *ad hominem* attacks by the press. The Mei Li Dao leaders visited those who were hospitalised in the clash and held a press conference the following day to tell their side of the story. Lin Yi-hsiung, in a fit of uncontrollable pique, yelled at the Taiwanese reporters, 'I look down upon all of you!' Not that it did anything to change their hostile attitude towards the *dangwai*, but it was chicken soup for his soul. Following the press conference, they left for Yao Chia-wen's house for a meeting that ended a little after midnight. Government security agents were by then out on a sweep.

Trying times

'Where to, mister?' the cab driver asked. 'I can't be driving around the whole day.'

His cut thumb began to throb although the bleeding had ceased. The jump from the ledge had also aggravated his back injury, sending shots of pain through his spine and down his legs.

'New Taipei Park, please,' he said, for want of a better place.

Shih wondered how many of his colleagues had been arrested. He could not know that he was the only Mei Li Dao leader to have escaped the dragnet.

He got out of the taxi and thought about going to the United States embassy. No, he caught himself, it was no longer an embassy and he could not be sure of getting refuge there. Relatives and friends were also out of the question, as the intelligence agents were bound to be watching them.

Shih ended up in a restaurant owned by a friend's parents. He knew he couldn't remain at any one place for too long, and over the next couple of days stayed at different locations. His fugitive status received an unwelcome boost when he heard on the radio that the Government had launched a nationwide search for him. Posters with his photograph were all over the island:

Wanted and Reward

Name	Shih Ming-teh
Sex	Male
Age	39
Birthplace	Kaohsiung City
Height	172 cm
Charge	Treason
Reward	NT$500,000

Identity of informant will be kept strictly confidential.

Hiding or covering up for a fugitive is punishable by death penalty, life imprisonment or jail for 10 years or more.

The nightly news splashed his face across television screens and repeated the bounty of US$15,000.

'Belief and faith is more valuable than reward,' the Reverend Wu Wen, a pastor of the Presbyterian Church of Taiwan, assured Shih. 'Don't worry, you're safe with us. Now get some rest, you'll need it.'

Later that evening, the pastor and his wife came into their guest's room and shared with him a chapter from the book of Psalms, assuring Taiwan's most wanted man that God never abandons his children. That night Shih rested well. When morning came, he got ready to move again. He took out his dentures, put on a hat, and—with escorts, pretending to be his children, clasping his arm as he hobbled—instantly aged several years.

Over the next 12 days he stayed with Lin Wen-chen, a church elder, as the Government stepped up the hunt and doubled the reward for his capture. Television and radio pumped out broadcasts about his past activities and announced that the reward had increased yet again. The reward was now US$70,000.

Dr Chang Wen-ying, a dental surgeon and Mei Li Dao colleague, then ignited a debate when she suggested that she perform plastic surgery to modify Shih's features. Chang was a surgeon of the mouth, not the face, a friend pointed out the obvious; yes, but Shih's situation was one that called for desperate measures, argued another. As in most controversies, each side had a point. But whatever their differences, there was agreement on one fact—Shih was the only one who could decide.

Chang began the surgery on Shih's eyelids but was forced to abort the operation because she found the procedure too risky. When she administered the anaesthetic Shih, in his weakened condition, lost consciousness, and was quickly brought around and put on a drip. When he was ready again, Chang started a five hour operation to broaden his jawline, constantly praying that he wouldn't die during the surgery (Chang later went on to become the mayor of Taichung city).

Following the operation Shih moved again, this time to an apartment in downtown Taipei which was the home of Hsu Ching-fu, a movie distributor and friend of Shih's brother. By now it had become too dangerous for Shih to move about during the day, even with his bandaged and toothless jowl as additional disguise. The Kuomintang had, in the meantime, redoubled efforts to hunt down its quarry.

Two former inmates of Taiyuan prison volunteered to help Shih. 'We'll put him in a wooden crate and smuggle him out by ship,' said one, a Thai Chinese who went by the name of Shui.

'Where will he go?' the Reverend Wu enquired.

'That can be decided later,' Gao, his partner, interjected.

'Why don't you meet Shih Ming-teh and discuss this with him?' asked the pastor.

'We don't need to see Shih, just tell us where he is and we'll make the necessary arrangements,' replied Gao.

That night Pastor Wu told Shih of the plan to smuggle him out of Taiwan by ship. Shih, tired after being on the run for more than three weeks, agreed.

On 8 January 1980, the doorbell rang in a pre-arranged pattern. It was 1 p.m., the appointed time when the two would pick Shih up. When the door opened, intelligence agents rushed in and placed him under arrest. They handcuffed him, secured his ankles in chains, put a helmet on his head and led him out. He had been on the run for 26 days.

By the time he was arrested, Shih Ming-teh had become something of a mythical figure, a daring hero to some and the devil incarnate to others. The public had followed his escape and subsequent arrest with morbid fascination. To his detractors, Shih had already lived one day too many, and news of his capture was greeted by a triumphant spectacle of exploding firecrackers. To this day, no one can be sure whether Shui and Gao were the ones who had betrayed Shih. They had left Taiwan and have never been heard from again.

Shih's ordeal also focused the attention of the international media on the political situation in Taiwan. This was crucial when the Mei Li Dao leaders were later tried for treason and sedition.

The few who had helped Shih were also arrested. The Presbyterians were mainly *benshengren* and, not coincidentally, were most involved in assisting him. The Reverend Kao Jun-ming, General-Secretary of the Presbyterian Church of Taiwan, whose involvement had been peripheral and who had met Shih only once years before, had extended his hand out of 'Christian love and sympathy'. That was enough to earn him a seven year term. Hsu Ching-fu received a similar sentence; elder Lin Wen-chen ended up with five years imprisonment; Reverend Wu Wen, dentist Dr Chang Wen-ying and five other church members each received two.

The sentences were relatively light, only because the matter had attracted the attention of religious bodies all over the world. With added political pressure from the United States, the Kuomintang had to maintain a semblance of a fair trial.

But a bigger trial was yet to come. Over 150 people had been arrested for the riot in Kaohsiung. Eight were charged with treason. They were Huang Hsin-chieh, Chang Chun-hung, Lin Hung-shuen, Lin Yi-hsiung (who were provincial members of parliament), Yao Chia-wen (the group's lawyer), Annette Lu Shiu-lien (a women's rights activist), Chen Chu, Hsu Hsin-liang and Shih Ming-teh. Hsu was overseas at the time of the arrests.

Before the trial could get under way, tragedy struck one of the defendants. Lin Yi-hsiung's wife was attending a court hearing on the Mei Li Dao case. She had left their three daughters, a 9-year-old and 7-year-old twins, with Lin's widowed mother. She always made it a point to call home whenever she was out. That day, no one answered the telephone. Concerned, she rang and asked the secretary in her husband's law firm to check on the family.

Returning from school, 9-year-old Lin Huan-jun was let in by a man who suddenly pulled out a knife and plunged it repeatedly in her back. As blood splattered everywhere, Huan-jun managed to struggle free and run out of the house, hiding behind a bush in the garden. The man followed but ran off without finding her.

When the secretary arrived, she didn't notice anything unusual. She found Huan-jun lying in bed.

'Please don't shake me, *Ah Ee* (auntie), it hurts,' Huan-jun said.

'Where does it hurt? What's the matter?' the secretary asked.

'A thief took a knife and stabbed me in the back. *Ah Ee*, I'm very thirsty...'

The secretary quickly reached out and saw that the back of her school uniform was in shreds and her back was covered in blood.

'Where's granny and *mei-mei*?' she asked frantically.

'I don't know,' came the soft reply. '*Ah Ee*, I'm afraid, please don't leave.'

'I won't leave. Good girl. I'll get some water for you.'

On seeing Huan-jun on the hospital bed, Mrs Lin cried out and fainted.

The authorities allowed Lin Yi-hsiung out on bail. His friends took him to the hospital, telling him that it was for a physical examination, unable to bring themselves to relate the truth to him.

Lin was happy to see his comrades again and was sitting on his hospital bed chatting away excitedly.

'Come, let's go for a beer,' he said.

His friends did not reply.

'Why? What's wrong?' Lin asked.

'Your mother is dead. She had 13 stab wounds on her body.'

'Was it suicide?' he asked after a few moments.

'No. Your eldest daughter is injured. She's in the hospital.'

Lin sat motionless. He stared blankly into space and didn't say anything. After a long while, a friend hugged him: 'If you feel like crying, go ahead.' Only then did Lin breakdown.

Seventeen years after the murders, I sat next to Lin in his office. After his release from prison he left for the United States, Japan, and the United Kingdom to study political systems. He now runs a non-government organisation, the Chilin Foundation, to investigate social issues and to encourage young Taiwanese to take interest in social movements. He was elected Chairman of the opposition Democratic Progressive Party in June 1998.

Now in his fifties, Lin surprised me with his retiring demeanour. His white hair became even more striking when he blushed after a compliment. There was not the slightest hint of loathing or retribution. Instead, here was a man who understood what peace was about and possessed a quietude that inspired courage born of kindness and grace.

I asked him what he thought had triggered the killing. He recalled the time when he found out that his twin daughters had been stabbed to death with his mother in the basement of the house. Over the next few weeks, as police tried to piece the evidence together, Taiwan was in shock. The case was as complex as it was macabre.

The local media accused a fellow opposition member of the murders claiming they were to punish Lin for revealing too much when he was under interrogation after the Kaohsiung riots. The public remained largely unconvinced. Another suspect was found, this time a bearded occidental who had visited the Lin's residence prior to the murder. The police placed him under 'protection' and for three months refused him permission to leave the island.

That bearded suspect turned out to be Professor Bruce Jacobs, now head of the Department of Asian Languages and Studies at Monash University in Australia. 'It was a very dark period in Taiwan,' the professor said to me as we sat in his office amidst stacks of books and papers. 'America had just ceased its official recognition of Taipei and the mood of the people was one of intense bitterness and xenophobia.'

But how did he get involved? 'They were looking for a scapegoat and I was a convenient target,' Jacobs continued. 'In the end they had to release me because international pressure, especially from the United States and Australia, was intense. It took the personal intervention of Chiang Ching-kuo before I was allowed to leave. No one else dared to make that decision.'

Other scenarios were also ruled out. A random act by common criminals was dismissed because nothing had been stolen. It was widely believed that all the defendants' homes were under 24 hour police surveillance. Everything pointed to something more sinister.

The night that he was arrested, Lin had been asleep in his apartment. Shih Ming-teh had just escaped from his flat immediately above the Lins'. Suddenly, someone smashed the window and a group of men climbed through, one brandishing a knife. Lin was taken to a detention centre where he spent the next 40 days. He was repeatedly denied sleep for days at a time and beaten. One of the interrogators was specially assigned to inflict pain.

Lin was repeatedly punched on the upper body and kicked in the calves.

'I'll break all your teeth if you don't talk,' the torturer said. 'You know I'm not afraid to kill you if I have to. We'll just say that you committed suicide.'

With that, he dragged Lin down a flight of stairs to what looked like the basement. After punching his chest several times, always aiming for the left side, the man threatened to inject Lin with drugs. When the bruises choked dark red, the beatings stopped, only to resume a few days later. It went on like this until they extracted a confession. Lin's family was then allowed to visit him, but not before he was advised to caution them 'not to act recklessly outside or there will be unfavourable consequences.'

Foremost on their minds was whether Lin had been tortured and whether he was all right. Lin evaded their questions but finally said, 'You figure it out yourselves.'

'If you've been wronged, speak out,' Lin's mother urged. As the visit drew to a close, he heard her crying as she left the centre. It was the last time he saw her. Just before her death, it was reported that she had told some Japanese sympathisers that her son had been tortured.

No suspects were ever arrested for the Lin murders, and the case remains unsolved. Perhaps, the most ominous message that the perpetrators sent out was the date of the killing itself, 28 February, the date when the Kuomintang had unleashed its murderous troops on the Taiwanese people 33 years earlier.

When Lin recovered, he was brought before the military tribunal to answer the charges brought against him. All the defendants protested that they had been tortured into making signed confessions. At the opening of the trial, Huang Hsin-chieh denounced his own confession, saying that he had been put under 24 hour interrogation for two straight days. 'At that point,' he said, 'living is more painful than dying.'

Annette Lu Shiu-lien did the same thing. Her interrogators had been a little more sophisticated. They showed her gruesome photographs of a former female political prisoner who had just been executed, as well as a copy of the receipt that was issued when her family came to claim the body. Had they known then that their victim would later become the

Magistrate of Taoyuan county, they would have been a touch more tactful.

Yao Chia-wen repeated the charge that he signed the confession under duress. Besides, he did not write his confession but copied it from a model version. He said he was then warned by the prosecutor not to reveal the way the confession was obtained.

What did all this have to do with the judgement? It was one of those uncomplicated moments when veracity had to conform to the verdict, and justice, however left handed, had to take its course. Huang Hsin-chieh was given 14 years and the rest 12. Shih Ming-teh was sentenced to another life term. Again the sentences were light because the international community had been keeping an eye on the Kuomintang's brand of justice. Public sentiment had also turned against the Government following the Lins' murders, which helped to prick the blinkered minds of the tribunals. Otherwise, it would have been life imprisonment for all except Shih; he would surely have been executed.

Throughout the trial Shih had kept up a defiantly jaunty pose to show that he had not capitulated. But on the day he learned about the murder of the Lin family, he broke down and, in tears, told the court that he never knew that the opposition's cause could arouse so much viciousness. If it would help heal the sick wounds of Taiwan society, he pleaded to the judges, 'give me the death sentence, I beg you.'

The showdown

Less than three years after his reprieve, Shih Ming-teh found himself back in a cell on Burnt Island. He did not appeal his sentence because he refused to recognise the authority of the courts. He was just glad that he had the opportunity in those few short years to have been able to be part of Taiwan's awakening. The prison authorities went out of their way to inflict all kinds of indignities on him, from shaven head to solitary confinement. Outdoor activity was denied and he was allowed his first family visit only after five months.

When his family complained about his prolonged solitary confinement, the warden thought it a wonderful joke to put him in a cell with a demented detainee. For the first few nights, sleep seemed a terrible idea, as he had witnessed one particularly nightmarish incident when an insane inmate grabbed a sickle and slashed another in the torso with such force that he all but disembowelled the luckless prisoner. To have his struggle end so senselessly at the hands of a schizophrenic would without doubt bring immeasurable joy to the Kuomintang.

Shih spent one year in the same cell with his mentally maladjusted mate. With such a companion it was a daily battle just to stay mentally intact. Luckily his books and pen helped him through those dark years. But his physical condition had deteriorated. Apart from his back pain, Shih had high blood pressure. The prison officials gave him his medication irregularly which made his existence even less bearable.

In 1980, with all of the opposition leaders put away, Chiang Ching-kuo called for elections which he had cancelled two years before.

Up until then the *dangwai* camp had experienced growth by surge and lull. With the Mei Li Dao leaders behind bars, the opposition was almost comatose. Undaunted, the wives of the imprisoned politicians stood as candidates and, remarkably, won their contests with ease. It was the first time the Taiwanese were able to express their views on the Government's handling of the Mei Li Dao affair and they could not have done it in a more emphatic manner.

In the early 1980s, two events put in motion a chain of developments that would set the stage for a showdown between Shih and the President. It began with the visit of Dr Chen Wen-cheng, a 31-year-old assistant professor of mathematics at the Carnegie-Mellon University in Pittsburgh, Pennsylvania, who had returned to Taiwan to attend a conference. He was found dead one morning on a lawn in the National Taiwan University with 13 broken ribs, a fractured pelvis, three cracked vertebrae and ruptured internal organs.

The police said that he 'could have committed suicide or died in an accidental fall.' Only the day before, Chen had left his home in the morning to go to the Taiwan Garrison Command centre where he remained for 12 hours. The command officials explained that they just had a 'friendly' chat with him. Before he left, Chen had intimated to a friend that they had asked to see him and that he was afraid of being arrested. The officials accounted for the 12 hours by claiming that they met with him for a couple of hours, after which the professor stayed for lunch and dinner. The autopsy, however, revealed that Chen's stomach was empty.

Chen's death sparked a furore both in Taiwan and the United States. Shih Ming-teh immediately staged a month-long hunger strike to protest against the Kuomintang's brutality. He revealed that Chen had written to him when he was managing the *Mei Li Dao Magazine* and had pledged funds to help run the publication. This, Shih claimed, was what led to Chen's murder.

On 15 October 1984, three years after the Chen Wen-cheng murder, a Taiwanese writer by the name of Henry Liu was gunned down gangland-style in the garage of his Californian home. A few weeks earlier, Liu had announced that he was publishing a no-holds-barred exposé of Chiang Ching-kuo whose trigger happy, over zealous defenders believed that there can be no yin without yang, no exposé without murder.

FBI investigations had traced the killing to three Taiwanese men who had since returned home. Unable to get the Kuomintang to extradite the suspects, the FBI let out that they had evidence to show that the Taiwanese Intelligence Bureau was involved. Chiang then had his top three numbers in the bureau arrested, and ordered an investigation to placate the Americans. The bureau head, his deputy and two of the three assailants received life sentences. The third killer escaped to Brazil but was subsequently arrested and extradited to the United States.

The matter would take an even more unseemly turn. Before the assassination took place, one of the killers had a tape which eventually, but not accidentally, ended up in the hands of the FBI. The contents implicated Chiang Shiau-woo, Chiang Ching-kuo's son, in the murder. It seemed that one of the murderers had prepared the tape for use as a bargaining chip if he was arrested. When news of this broke, Chiang quickly dispatched his son to the Taiwan Trade Office in friendly Singapore.

Following the assassination, Shih announced that he would go on another fast until the Chiang dictatorship protected civil and human rights, including the right to form an opposition party. Foremost, he wanted the release of the Mei

Li Dao prisoners and he wanted it done by 28 February. Other political prisoners joined Shih in his hunger strike. Outside of prison, Shih's eldest brother and sister began their hunger strike, calling for public support to pressure the Kuomintang to stop terrorising its own people. His brother Shih Ming-cheng fasted to death.

By now Shih had grown in political stature both at home and abroad, and unlike before he was able to call the attention of the international community to the situation in Taiwan. Chiang Ching-kuo had a real fight on his hands.

Shih was taken to the General Military Hospital in Taipei twelve days into his hunger strike. An entire floor was cleared and the process of forced feeding began. Under pressure, especially from the United States Congress, the Kuomintang agreed to Shih's demand to release the Mei Li Dao prisoners. With this agreement, Shih resumed eating. But when 28 February came, only Chen Chu was freed. The Government said that it required more time to decide on the rest of the prisoners. Shih took this as a breach of faith, but agreed to give the Kuomintang one more month.

March came and went with no indication of any release. Shih embarked on his hunger strike again and announced that he wanted all his conditions met by July. Up until then, Shih had subsisted on milk and juice. If his wishes were not granted by then, he would go off the liquids as well. *Dangwai* activists were staging protests in Washington against Chiang Ching-kuo and pressing Congress to address the issue of human rights abuses by the Kuomintang Government. Like a shrewd poker player, Shih knew that he had a full hand, and he upped the ante by openly calling for the formation of the Taiwan Democratic Party.

Meanwhile, the Kuomintang attempted to show the world that it was not ill-treating its prickly captive. Government officials visited Shih, who was not made to wear prison garb, with photographers in tow. Family and friends were allowed frequent visits which Shih used to direct the affairs of the *dangwai* movement.

Behind the scenes, the Kuomintang resorted to psychological pressure to try to break Shih. Intelligence agents told him that the world didn't care whether he lived or died. They also lied that his American wife had fallen for another man. But it was becoming increasingly unclear just who was pressurising whom.

Meanwhile, Hsu Hsin-liang, who had been in self-imposed exile in the United States, felt that it was time to make a concerted push for democratic reforms. With Shih as the symbol of resistance at home, Hsu put together a committed, if somewhat limp, coterie of intellectuals to establish a political party in the United States that he would later take back with him to Taiwan *ą la* Benigno S. Aquino Jr of the Philippines and Kim Dae Jung of South Korea. He was whisked straight to jail when he stepped off the plane in Taipei.

In September 1986, despite repeated threats that the ban on opposition parties would be strictly enforced, the *dangwai* officially launched the Democratic Progressive Party in Taipei's Grand Hotel. The world's attention was focused on what the Kuomintang would do to the fledgling opposition party. In the following weeks, the political thermometer was registering levels of uneasy tension. Chiang, feeling more of the heat, backed down from a confrontation that he knew he could not win.

With the Democratic Progressive Party entrance into Taiwanese politics, martial law lost its purpose. After the tumultuous uprising against Marcos in the neighbouring Philippines, Chiang lifted martial law in July 1987. A heart attack had reminded him of his own mortality; eager to avoid historical damnation, the President announced that he was granting amnesty to all the Mei Li Dao prisoners.

Freedom was again not to be handed over on a platter, for Shih saw an invidious dagger beneath the silver that would fatally stab his political ideals. Amnesty, he insisted, was a pardon for criminals. To leave prison under such a circumstance would be tantamount to admitting that he was guilty of a crime and thereby undermine his legitimacy as a leader. Not leaving would mean sacrificing even more of his freedom. It was a most agonising time but in the end he made up his mind: thanks, but no thanks. He wanted an unconditional release.

Chiang Ching-kuo died six months later on 13 January 1988. He was succeeded by his deputy Lee Teng-hui who, himself a locally born Taiwanese, was more acceptable to the *dangwai*. More importantly, he did not carry with him the China political baggage with which his two predecessors were encumbered. Lee Teng-hui had the unenviable task of restoring the confidence of the people who had become, at best, wary and, at worst, downright scornful of the instruments of the state. His initial efforts were carried out with the aplomb of a knuckle dustered, beercan crushing bruiser (some say they were a result of pressure from the hardline Kuomintang factions).

Former journalist Cheng Nan-rong started the pro-opposition weekly *Freedom Times*, and was continually harassed by the security police. When the magazine carried an article calling for the republic's constitution to be amended to reflect the independence of Taiwan as a nation, the Government charged him with treason and issued a summons for his arrest. The Kuomintang was spoiling for a fight and duly got one. Cheng responded by barricading himself in the magazine's office in downtown Taipei, where he vowed that the Kuomintang could never arrest him but only his corpse. It was a warning that the ruling party dearly underestimated.

The Government sent the police to Cheng's office and repeatedly warned him to surrender. A tense stand off followed which lasted for more than two months. On day 71, the security officers stormed the premises. Before they could break through, smoke started billowing from the vents of the office and flames could be seen burning inside the room. By the time they gained entry, all they found was a burnt-out office. On the floor lay the charred body of Cheng, who left behind a wife and a 9-year-old daughter. Cheng's wife would later carry on his struggle and is today a Democratic Progressive Party member of the Legislative Yuan.

Shih Ming-teh sent a letter of protest to the President and warned him of the dire need to open up the political process. The death rocked Taiwanese society, jolting people out of their political apathy. One of Cheng's close associates, deeply distressed by his death, also died of self-immolation during the funeral procession. As more and more Taiwanese joined the demonstrations, confrontation with the Government looked certain. Sensing that the emotions of the people had reached a critical level, the Kuomintang prudently backed off.

All this time, Shih continued his hunger strike. Under strict orders not to let him die, the hospital staff continued its twice daily force feeding program. Plastic tubes were shoved into his oesophagus via the nasal passage, and a liquid mixture was then pumped into his stomach. Every day, twice a day, for four years, Shih was fed in this manner.

The fast was taking its toll on Shih's body. His weight had dropped to 40 kilograms. Weak as he was, Shih went about his daily activity of reading and writing. Chores such as washing his underwear gradually became more difficult as he weakened. Psychologically, Shih was also becoming vulnerable. Prison officials never stopped their psychological warfare against him. Shih started to experience bouts of depression, and his mood swings became more frequent.

In the meantime, international pressure intensified. Lee Teng-hui knew that he could not sustain authoritarian control the way that the Chiangs had done. In 1990 he repeated the offer of amnesty to Shih. On 20 May 1990, seeing that his conditions had been finally met—all other political prisoners had been freed, martial law had been repealed, the Democratic Progressive Party was at its rambunctious best, and the killing and intimidation of the Kuomintang's opponents had come to a halt—Shih ended his hunger strike which had lasted four years and two months.

As far as the Kuomintang was concerned, he was free to go. Shih said that if he was going to leave the prison hospital, it would have to be on his own terms. When he left, he told the Government, he did not want the sentinels to be around. They disappeared.

But one more hitch remained. Prisoners pardoned by amnesty had to sign a release form before they were allowed to leave. Shih insisted that he had been wrongfully incarcerated; if anyone should sign any forms, it was the Government. The prison administration insisted that Shih had to acknowledge the discharge papers. Once again, there was a stand off. But the authorities also knew that the odds of them besting their prisoner in such a contest was somewhere between 'negligible' and 'delusional'.

Shih walked through the gates of the hospital which had served as his prison for the previous four years and tore up his release form in a final gesture of defiance. And as he savoured the warmth of the sun on his face on a beautiful spring morning on 21 May, the last political prisoner had become a free man again. Taiwan had finally begun to heal its wounds. Shih had taken that first step and thereafter many more along that arduous journey of a thousand miles. After spending a quarter of a century in prison, Shih Ming-teh took that final, proud step out of prison and forever into history books.

Don't worry, I forgive you

'The most difficult part during my imprisonment was not the harsh conditions that I had to endure,' Shih recalled as we chatted. 'Those were very bitter and lonely days. But overcoming the suffering was easy; it's resisting the temptation that is hard.'

Shih was referring to his decision about rejecting Chiang Ching-kuo's pardon just before the President's death.

'At that time, I wanted more than anything else in the world to be free again,' he continued. 'I was 46 when I was given amnesty in 1987. I had been in captivity for more years than I had been free. But I had to resist that temptation to leave prison because the system still did not guarantee the Taiwan people their freedom. It was the most difficult decision I ever had to make.'

If prison did him any good, it was to freeze his aging process. At 57, he looked youthful for a man who had been through hell on earth. He wore a thin moustache and, below it, a kindly smile which suddenly disappeared as his tongue reached in to pull out a set of dentures.

'You received quite a bashing, didn't you?' I asked.

'Yes, that's the temptation authoritarians cannot resist—the use of power to be cruel to those who disagree with them. I was very bitter and full of hatred in the beginning, but a person who carries bitterness in his heart cannot do anything good for society.'

He described how he managed to survive in prison all those years. Firstly, he said, it was important to see that in exchange for losing one's freedom, one gained time for study and learning. Secondly, as deplorable as prison conditions are, it is crucial that one adapts to the environment. Finally, never despair: refuse to accept that the situation is hopeless.

'I knew what I was in prison for,' he continued, 'and I knew that that was the price that I had to pay.'

During those lonely years in prison, Shih had written:

> In every era, there are always those who will struggle for freedom. These people play a difficult role, their paths are paved with pain and loneliness. Their own generation will not accept them. In fact, they will be rejected, bullied, humiliated, imprisoned and even killed. These freedom fighters crawl along a narrow path. But in the end, those who follow will widen the path into a broad avenue. Freedom fighters may rot physically but their courage and commitment will enhance human civilisation and last forever. Freedom fighters don't belong to today, but they will live on tomorrow.

'I still remember that period,' said my wife, a Taiwanese. 'As a student, I, too, thought you were a criminal. The television stations and newspapers kept painting such a fiendish picture of you, it was difficult to believe otherwise. At that time, it was hard for the people to understand the extent the controlled media shaped our perception.'

Shih said nothing and just smiled.

But not everybody shunned him, he reminded, referring to the church members who had risked everything to help him when he was on the run. Our conversation conveniently took a Biblical turn. Shih said that his Christian faith had much to do with his prison survival. 'I like the New Testament,' he added. 'Jesus always showed the way with love and kindness, unlike in the Old Testament when God was so authoritarian.'

Although born and raised a Catholic, Shih was dismayed at the stand of Taiwan's Catholic church. 'It didn't allow its priests and nuns to participate in any of the public demonstrations. Yet Jesus was also conducting public forums and rallies during those days,' Shih mused, harking back to the years when the *dangwai* were organising their illegal rallies. 'People would gather around him and he would preach to them in public places, often against regulations. When the soldiers came, the crowd would disperse and Jesus would go on his way.

'Remember the story about the fish and the loaves of bread which He fed to the masses at one of the public gatherings?

We were giving out refreshments too,' he chuckled.

The more we talked, the more I realised that it was not just a political objective that Shih Ming-teh was chasing. It was a way of life that kept him struggling against his oppressors, a way that signalled tolerance and forgiveness. In forgiving, he found confidence and pride in himself and his people.

After his release in 1990, Shih was invited to testify before the United States Congress on the situation in Taiwan. When he accepted the invitation, Taiwanese at home and in America wanted him to complain about the human rights abuses that the Kuomintang had perpetrated. Others wanted him to use the opportunity to press for Taiwan's independence from China. Some even thought it a good opportunity for Shih to rebuke the United States Government for its part in helping to sustain the Kuomintang dictatorship for its own interests. Shih did none of them:

> I have not come here to plead or to make accusations. Neither am I here to ask America to save Taiwan or to protect the rights of the Taiwanese people. I have also not come to attack my own Government nor to plead with the People's Republic of China to let Taiwan become independent.
>
> I have brought with me only one message which is that the present generation of Taiwanese has absolute confidence in ourselves. We will not bow to any superpower or oppressor. We deeply believe that we will overcome difficulties and challenges that we face with our own strength, wisdom and ability. We will fight injustice and human rights abuses and build an equal society in Taiwan. We will protect the independence of our country from any intruder. This is my faith, and this is what I relied on to overcome all the suffering and temptation during my 25 years in prison. And this generation of Taiwanese people has this faith as well.

In 1992 Shih was elected as a member of the Legislative Yuan, representing the Tainan County.

When he rose to make his maiden speech, a hush came upon the House. In one defining moment before starting his speech, Shih turned to the Kuomintang ministers and legislators: 'Don't worry, I forgive you.'

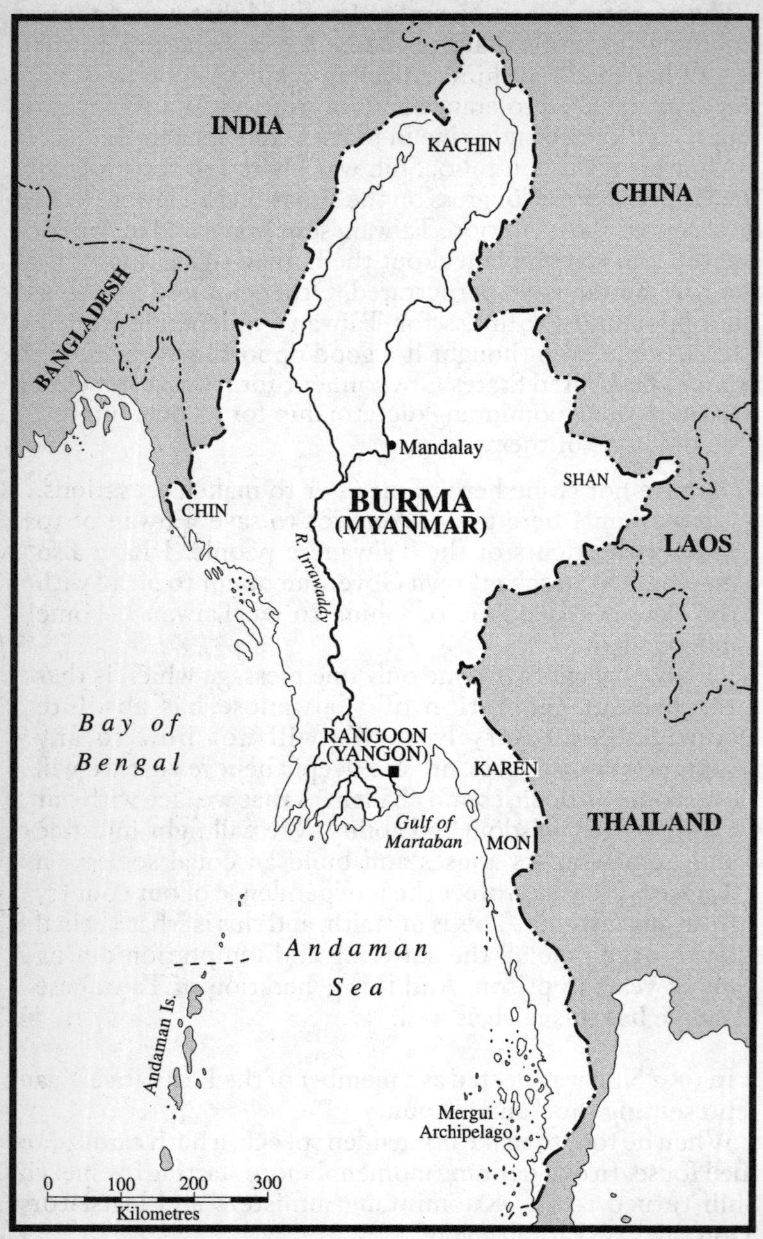
INDIA
KACHIN
CHINA
BANGLADESH
Mandalay
SHAN
BURMA
(MYANMAR)
CHIN
LAOS
R. Irrawaddy
Bay of
Bengal
RANGOON
(YANGON)
KAREN
Gulf of
Martaban
MON
THAILAND
Andaman
Sea
Andaman Is.
Mergui
Archipelago
0
100
200
300
Kilometres

2

Burma

Aung San Suu Kyi

As my father's daughter

Engines roared and seats shook as the captain brought the aircraft to ground speed. Most passengers get a tad jittery at such times, but nerves are quickly soothed when a pleasant chime introduces the reassuring voice of the chief flight attendant.

'Welcome to Myanmar,' a soft voice greeted us. After telling us about the local weather and time, she customarily signed off: 'We hope you've enjoyed your flight and we thank you for flying Thai Airways.'

A few moments later, like an afterthought, the voice came on again: 'The baggage claim will take a very long time.' The words hung in the cabin air, challenging their listeners to interpret them. Smirks broke out on the faces of some passengers. Others just attributed the 'very long time' to an underdeveloped baggage handling system.

Inside the terminal, immigration officials sullenly checked visas. A separate counter, the 'ASEAN line', was reserved for those with 'most favoured nation' travelling status. As the queues lengthened, burly security agents wearing their Indian tunic tops and *longyis*—the traditional Burmese dress of ankle-length cloth expertly swaddled around the waist and tied into a neat ball around the navel—paced deliberately between the lines. They were joined by two dour looking Caucasians in their more mundane jeans and T-shirt. All were looking and searching, for what it was unclear. It reminded me of those adorable narcotic-sniffing beagles at the Los Angeles airport.

But adorable isn't exactly how one would describe these men. Neither were they searching for drugs. Anyone trying to smuggle narcotics into the country obviously hadn't been paying attention during their drug trafficking lectures. Burma, or Myanmar, is the biggest producer and exporter of heroin and opium, the trade being a significant source of funds for the cash strapped military government.

Another way of raising money is to hit visitors for cold hard cash. Before getting past the security agents, I was herded to another counter where a minimum of 300 American dollars—only the greenback was accepted—had to be bartered for the Foreign Exchange Currency (FEC).

'Three hundred dollars, sir,' the lady politely demanded. 'One FEC is equivalent to one dollar.'

'I haven't got 300 dollars,' I said.

'But you must change 300 dollars, sir,' she said with impeccable politeness.

'I'm sorry, but all I have is 100,' I replied.

A man with a full head of curly black hair and a thick moustache who had been looking over the shoulders of the tellers inched across and whispered something in Burmese. The lady then turned back to me and apologised: 'I'm sorry, sir, but you need to change 300 FECs.'

'So what do I do? I don't have 300.'

After a brief pause, the hirsute supervisor gave an almost imperceptible nod and moved on. My polite teller then lowered her voice to a conspiratorial level: 'Do you have a present?'

'No,' I whispered back, trying to look as perplexed as I could.

She stared at me in exasperation. Then she straightened up and resumed a more officious tone: 'Next time you must bring 300 US dollars.'

'Thank you, I will.'

She scribbled something on a chit and handed it to me. It was a receipt for 100 FECs. On the counterfoil, she penned '300'. My puzzlement was now genuine: how was she going to balance the accounts at the end of the day? Some questions are better left unasked.

And as I picked up my bag to leave, I could hear the teller beside me murmuring to her Japanese looking customer, 'Do you have a present?'

'Taxi to hotel? Cheap, very good taxi, new taxi!' claimed a middle-aged man. He produced the best smile that his weary face could summon. I gave him the name of the hotel. 'Yes, very good hotel, new hotel! Wait here.' With that, he disappeared.

Minutes later, a light blue taxi rolled up and the exuberant driver came bounding. 'See, new taxi, right?' he said, obviously pleased that his asseveration had been vindicated. My eyes widened when I noticed the logo on the bonnet. It was a navy blue ring with the word 'Comfort' across it. This was the unmistakable trademark of a state-run taxi company in Singapore, a country whose efficiency could not be in more stark contrast with its indigent neighbour, but whose Government rarely passes up the chance to make a quick buck.

As we headed towards downtown Rangoon, I noticed that there was almost no traffic; having just left Bangkok, the feeling bordered on sensory deprivation. Rangoon looked, smelled and even tasted like a city which time had carelessly misplaced. There was no indication that life here had anything remotely tied to a schedule, save for the digital timer below the traffic lights which gave motorists a countdown to the next change of red to green. Ten, nine, eight...the seconds ushered, clearly setting the pace: Ready, set, go!

Yes, go. But where? This is one of the poorest and most isolated countries in the world, and commerce is under anaesthesia. Few countries would trade with the military regime in power and, of those who do, little goes into laying the foundation for sustained economic growth.

Unable to extricate itself from destitution, Burma, once known as the Golden Land, has become a haven for the profane and the slothful. The large majority of the Burmese people, however, continue to yearn for relief from their military rulers.

I took a closer look at the FEC bills. They resembled the hellbank notes that the Chinese offer to the deceased for the afterlife. Even Monopoly currency looked less apocryphal. The catch was that the FEC was not reconvertible to dollars; anywhere else in the world, Kleenex tissue would have been more valuable. The Burmese themselves did not accept the nondescript bills, preferring the reassuring smile of George Washington. It was the most expensive—perhaps the only—airport entry tax in the world.

The hotel lobby, modest as it was, seemed altogether another world compared to the decrepitude in the streets. A man came up and identified himself as my contact. With the barest of salutations, he briefed me about the program for my stay. Just when we got to discussing my visit with Aung San Suu Kyi—the Burmese leader who, in the words of a pro-democracy activist, had become 'the country's most celebrated but censored tourist attraction'—the hotel's resident crooner suddenly belched forth into song: 'Every breath you take, every step you take...I'll be watching you.' If any song should be banned in Burma, this was it.

Burma is ruled by a dictator named Ne Win, who ironically started as a young revolutionary in the independence movement when the country was a British colony. In his twenties, he joined with 29 other nationalists to drive out their British overseers. They called themselves 'The 30 Comrades', sounding like a gang straight from a Hong Kong kung-fu movie.

Among them was another young activist, Aung San. Both were determined to rid the country of foreign rule. There the similarities ended. While Ne Win was an incorrigible gambler and womaniser, Aung San gained the respect of his comrades as an upright leader. Given the polarity of their dispositions and the narrow political bed they shared, friction between the two soon followed.

Aung San went to Japan in the 1930s to train in guerilla warfare with the 30 Comrades. He returned with the Japanese troops during World War II. When he saw what the Japanese were really up to (some say when he realised that the Japanese were about to be defeated), Aung San revolted and escaped to the hills. There he formed the bluntly named Anti-Fascist People's Freedom League (AFPFL) to fight the Japanese.

At the end of the war, Aung San, together with another well respected Burmese, Nu, wasted no time in demanding independence. The British had looked favourably upon the leadership of Aung San during the war, even though he initially fought on the 'wrong side'. The British Prime Minister, Clement Attlee, eventually promised that Burma would gain full independence within one year.

General elections were held in April 1947 and the AFPFL under Aung San, whose mass appeal was by then indubitable, swept to victory with 248 of the 255 seats in the National Assembly. Aung San was called upon to form a government. At the age of 32, his popularity was at an all time high, and he was affectionately referred to as the people's *bogyoke* or leader.

But, like many youthful leaders, Aung San was dealt the fateful card of premature success. On the morning of 19 July 1947, while a cabinet meeting was in progress, gunmen in army uniform swept into the room and sprayed it with rifle fire. It took only seconds for them to accomplish the assassination, after which they fled in military jeeps. Nine people lay dead, including Aung San.

The British asked Nu to continue in Aung San's place. He became Prime Minister when Burma gained its independence on 4 January 1948, and remained in office until Ne Win staged a coup in 1962.

Aung San died at the age of 32 and left behind a wife, Khin Kyi, two sons and a two-year-old daughter named Suu Kyi. 'Do you know how she got her name? It's so cute,' an activist friend volunteered. 'You see, their first two children were boys and Aung San wanted their third child to be a girl. *Suu* in Burmese means "gift," so Aung San Suu Kyi means Aung San's gift to his wife, Khin Kyi,' she beamed.

And a gift Aung San Suu Kyi was. Following the assassination of her father, she stayed close to Khin Kyi. The widow reluctantly took over her husband's post as a member of the National Assembly, even though politics was not her predilection. Having been a teacher and a nurse, she was more inclined to social work. She resigned in 1948 to become a manager of social welfare organisations.

Aung San Suu Kyi travelled with her mother to China, Europe, the United States and Southeast Asia before settling down in New Delhi at the age of 15, when her mother was appointed ambassador to India. After graduating from high school there, she went to England to pursue a degree in philosophy, economics and politics at St. Hugh's College in Oxford, where she met Dr Michael Aris, a British scholar who specialised in Tibetan studies. They married and she joined her husband in Bhutan, where he worked in a government translation department.

The couple returned to London in 1975. In the meantime, Suu Kyi had given birth to two sons, Myint San Aung

(Alexander) and Htein Lin (Kim). In 1988 she was in the midst of her doctoral studies at London University's School of Oriental and African Studies when her mother suffered a stroke. She returned to Burma in April to tend to her mother, whose condition was rapidly deteriorating. By then, trouble was already brewing. But her mind was more on her mother's wellbeing than on the portentous political developments. 'During my visits to Rangoon I would sometimes spend three or four months with my mother,' she said, 'and always when friends came over, at some time or the other, the conversation would inevitably turn towards the situation of the country.'

She never involved herself in Burmese politics, much less participate in the demonstrations that were rocking the country. 'I'm just the sort of person who generally does not like to take part in demonstrations...I admired those who did what they did. I was totally behind what they were doing...I was just one of the large silent majority who were supporting them.'

Even then, the sense of duty was already ingrained in her. Months before her wedding on 1 January 1972, she had written to Michael Aris: 'I only ask one thing, that should my people need me, you would help me to do my duty by them. How probable it is I do not know, but the possibility exists.'

The possibility turned out to be one of those instances when kismets collide and people are left with little choice but to follow their destiny. Just months before she had returned to Burma to tend to her ailing mother, students were staging protests against Ne Win's rule which had made Burma's already unhappy situation absolutely critical. Many of them paraded Aung San's portraits when they marched, and hung on to them even as they were shot by the soldiers. Some Burmese had looked to Aung San's first born, Aung San Oo, to lead the democratic fight. But Aung San Oo did not have the inclination for politics and had emigrated to the United States. The second son, Aung San Lin, died when he was still a child, drowning in a nearby pond.

Seeing that her father had become symbol of resistance to Ne Win, Suu Kyi relented to pressure and decided to take up her father's role to lead the nation against the dictator. Intelligent and articulate, she stepped naturally into the role of *bogyoke* in her own right.

On 26 August 1988 close to half a million people waited expectantly at the Shwedagon Pagoda, an ornate temple in the heart of Rangoon, for the arrival of their new leader. Her father's portrait formed the backdrop of the modest looking stage. Monks had been taking turns since the day before, acting as security to prevent the army from disrupting the rally. Students combed the stage for explosives.

Then she arrived. People stood up and strained to see what she looked like, this daughter of their national hero. Aung San Suu Kyi did not disappoint them. She looked self-assured and spoke with conviction, and was every bit the leader that the people had been longing for. In *The Voice of Hope*, Alan Clements described her as 'fine porcelain, a beauty whose features are as classical as a Japanese haiku; nothing is out of place, neither the flowers in her hair, nor the perfectly pressed traditional Burmese dress she wears with such elegance.' It is difficult to fault this portrait.

Here was a diminutive lady—Gandhi-like in her tenacity with moral fibre to match, intellectual hostage to none, an archetype of Asian comeliness—fighting a hideous monster of a military regime.

With each charge she made against the regime, the applause intensified. Hers was not the expansive hyperbole that politicians dish out. She spoke plainly about the situation that confronted the country and challenged the State Law and Order Restoration Council (SLORC) to cease its oppressive rule. It was a down-to-earth address that connected with the very soul of the resistance movement that the people had so perilously created. The audience cheered wildly.

'The present crisis,' Suu Kyi concluded, 'is the concern of the entire nation. I could not, as my father's daughter, remain indifferent to all that was going on. This national crisis could, in fact, be called the second struggle for independence.' The invocation of the image of Aung San and the memory of the fight for Burma's independence more than 50 years ago was a potent mix, and the crowd went berserk.

'Daw Suu instilled confidence in the people and we were ready to lay down our lives for the revolution,' a young student told me (*Daw* is the honorific title the Burmese use for women, *U* is the male equivalent). 'Up until then, only the braver students and monks were ready to resist till the end. Now her speech touched a chord among the ordinary people.'

By the end of the rally, there was little doubt that Aung San Suu Kyi had emerged as perhaps the only leader who stood any chance of delivering the Burmese people from the clutches of Ne Win.

It all began in the teashop

I made my way down to the 'city' to see what life was like in downtown Rangoon. You know a country is in trouble when its capital is devoid of the familiar Golden Arches and the ubiquitous Real Thing. Instead the streets were littered with 'tea shops', small and often rundown shacks sparsely furnished with wooden tables and stumpy stools that raise your knees to about your neck, serving Burmese cuisine from meagre victuals. I had to see for myself what a teashop was like because it was in one of these unpretentious stalls that a revolution was ignited and the world's attention focused on Burma.

That day was Saturday, 12 March 1988. Three students at the Rangoon Institute of Technology (RIT), one of Burma's most prestigious universities, sauntered into a tea shop. A tape recorder was serenading the customers with songs by a local entertainer. The students asked the proprietor to put on another tape. A group of drinkers, who looked like they had had one too many beers, objected. One unmannerly remark led to another, and soon a heated argument broke out. One of the drinkers picked up a chair and brought it down on the head of Win Myint, a second year student, who was rushed to hospital. The incident was reported to the police who subsequently apprehended the culprits. That was that.

Or so it seemed. Next day, the accused were released without so much as an investigation. When word reached the RIT campus, the indignant students set out to confront the police. The more they found out, the angrier they became. The youth who had struck Win Myint with the chair was the son of the chairman of the local people's council, an administrative arm of the one party state. The students made their way to the council's office and demanded an explanation for the abrupt release of the drunken assailants. When their effort came to nought, they pelted the office with stones. Some entered the premises and trashed the furniture.

Still seething, they went downtown that evening to challenge the authorities. By now their number had swollen to a couple of hundred. En route they ran into a phalanx of riot police armed with clubs and automatic rifles. The sight of the detested and dreaded *Lon Htein* troops provoked an almost knee-jerk reaction in the students. Rocks and debris started flying in the direction of the riot squad, which countered with an unexpected round of gunfire, killing 23-year-old Maung Phone Maw. Maung was a highly regarded student leader whose death enraged his fellow students.

Several other injured demonstrators were rushed to the Rangoon General Hospital, where more soldiers were waiting. Instead of going to the operating theatres, the injured were chained to their beds, and doctors and nurses were prevented from administering medical attention. After a few days, two of the students died, one with a bullet in his liver and the other in his colon and bladder.

That night the students huddled in their dormitories, trying to come to grips with the death of Maung Phone Maw. Many of them stole back to the spot where the fatal confrontation had taken place, offering prayers, placing flowers, and all vowing justice for their slain leader.

When Monday came, classes at the RIT resumed, but the atmosphere was not one of learning. The students exploded into nervous activity when they spotted the *Lon Htein* policemen quietly surrounding the campus. There was nowhere to run, and soon predator and prey were staring at each other, one in hungry anticipation and the other in nervous perspiration. The students organised themselves, distributing pamphlets calling for support for their friends slain over the weekend. The campus grounds were soon full of demonstrators. All the while, the troops remained stoic outside the university walls.

Next afternoon, military trucks rammed through the gates. Blindly clubbing at anything that moved, the soldiers grabbed as many students as they could. Those who were defiant enough to put up a struggle were pounded mercilessly with truncheons and boots. The state controlled Burma Broadcasting Service announced that the rioting on the RIT campus had to be put down after negotiations with the student leaders ended in a stalemate. The official state newspaper, the

Working People's Daily, ran a similar story and reported that Maung Phone Maw had died in a clash with local civilians.

On Wednesday, Rangoon University students at the main campus staged a demonstration in support of their counterparts at the RIT. A march to the affiliated Hlaing campus was organised the same afternoon. The procession had acquired a carnival-like atmosphere with young rollicking students chanting anti-government slogans. They were later joined by high school students. When they neared their destination, they suddenly found themselves accosted by the military (*tatmadaw*). Concertina wire had been uncoiled across the road and soldiers were lined up behind it with rifles at the ready. Behind them was an armoured vehicle with a machine gun sitting on its hood.

The students instinctively turned to look back and panicked when they saw files of helmeted *Lon Htein* troops massed behind them. To the left was a row of shophouses and to the right a flight of steps leading to the edge of the Inya Lake. It was a classic snare, and the prey was cornered. Before they could react the *Lon Htein* troopers charged from one end and the *tatmadaw* soldiers from the other. Unable to escape, the students were sitting ducks for troopers, who took particular aim at their heads. As they fell, the soldiers snatched their watches and jewellery. Some of the students ran towards the lake and were drowned. The luckier ones managed to scale the walls of the shophouses and escape. Others ran into nearby houses where residents provided temporary shelter.

Trucks then rumbled onto the scene to cart away the broken bodies. Following close behind were fire engines which hosed away the bloody evidence; within minutes there was no trace of the carnage.

The next day, in a half-gesture to appease the students, the Government announced that it would conduct an inquiry into the death of Maung Phone Maw. There was no mention of the killings at the Inya Lake. If the statement had any effect, it was to stoke the embers of the student movement. Meanwhile, the army went on a frenzied attack, raiding hostels and carting students off to the eerily named Insein prison. Many died of suffocation inside the enclosed trucks, which were deliberately driven around in the sun for hours. An eyewitness told of how security agents dragged three teenage girls to the banks of the Inya Lake and gang-raped them, leaving them barely conscious and bleeding from their vaginas. One died from a ruptured uterus. Hospital staff confirmed that this was just one of many cases.

The students responded by staging more demonstrations and riots of their own. Government buildings, traffic lights, public vehicles, telephone wires and anything that was state owned came under attack. The rioting had now spread to include the population at large, and the *Lon Htein*, in the time honoured tradition of restoring order after mocking morality, responded with more brutality.

The Government activated army units in an attempt to contain the crisis which was quickly spiralling beyond control. Military guards were positioned outside government offices and the Presidential Palace, and armoured cars went around the streets ordering residents to stay indoors. By the week's end, Rangoon was in chaos. As barricades lay strewn across roads and buildings smouldered, the people and their rulers were taking stock of the situation. What precipitated the unrest lay deep in the country's repressive past, but other horrors were yet to come.

Number One and Number Nine

Burma stretches from southern China down to the Isthmus of Kra where it jostles with its eastern neighbour Thailand. It also shares an extensive border with India in the northwest. The Irrawaddy River begins its life at the northern tip of the country, wanders south and dies in the Andaman Sea, giving birth in the process to vast forests and bountiful fertile land replete with precious minerals. As a result of this rich stock of natural resources, Burma emerged from World War II with the highest standard of living in Asia.

With their distinctly Buddhist culture—the population of 40 million includes one and a half million monks and nuns—Burmese people exude a most congenial air of genteel pride. Well known for their creative intellect and love of the cultural arts, they form an extraordinarily diverse culture of 64 ethnic groups and 200 languages and dialects, one of the most kaleidoscopic countries in Southeast Asia.

But with the diversity came fractiousness. The ethnic minorities such as the Arakans, Was, Chins, Shans, Karens, Karennis, Mons and Kachins living along the borders have long sought their independence. Together, they make up about a third of the Burmese population. When the nation proclaimed its independence in 1948 as the Socialist Republic of the Union of Burma, these minorities seized the opportunity to begin agitating for their own independence. What followed was an unreadable and bewildering tale of endless violence, of feuding territories controlled by armies whose chiefs maintained their own law and seemed in no hurry to bring respite to their peoples. In particular, the Shans and Karens battled the central Government in Rangoon, which was itself embroiled in a political and economic quagmire.

In 1962 Prime Minister Nu was forced to enter into negotiations with the minority leaders to grant them autonomy. The army baulked. With their abundant resources, the ethnic territories were a goldmine. Led by General Ne Win, the armed forces rumbled into Rangoon and placed Nu under arrest. The General installed himself as President, and wasted little time in announcing that the army was assuming the responsibilities of government due to the 'greatly deteriorating conditions of the Union'. And thus began Ne Win's rape of Burma.

To describe Ne Win is to labour in psychology. He is a despot, undoubtedly, and an eccentric one at that. But unlike other autocrats in his league he is also a recluse, not given to megalomaniacal aspirations to be worshipped and idolised by the masses. There are no statues and busts of him in Rangoon, nor are there portraits of him in government offices. He shuns public appearances and rarely addresses the people.

Now in his eighties, Ne Win lives in a resplendent mansion on the banks of the Inya Lake. With servants and helpers to cater to his emperor-like whims, the President models his reign on traditional Burmese monarchies, sometimes even appearing at public functions dressed in ancient royal costumes. The mansion is protected by soldiers—and landmines.

A licentious man with a libido matched only by his ruthlessness, the General, at last count, took on seven wives and a colossal concubinage. 'Number One', as he is sometimes called, is an apt description of his strength, both political and amorous. And as far as double standards go, Ne Win is not to be outdone. Debauched as his life is, it has not prevented him from imposing strict moral codes on his countrymen, even to the extent of forbidding the display of pictures of kissing couples.

Although manifestly xenophobic, Ne Win's penchant for private excursions to the West is boundless. Spending months at a stretch trekking across Europe, mostly visiting health centres seeking anything from rejuvenation in the spas of Lake Geneva to Jungian psychoanalysis in Vienna, Number One would always be escorted by his number twos and threes, taking breaks to buy property and precious stones.

Astrology and numerology are held close and dear. His inexplicable fascination for the digit nine and everything arithmetically related to it brings political *feng-shui* to extreme, and often comical, heights. He believes that events, especially the less amusing ones, can be anticipated and their outcomes altered to one's advantage. When revolts flared in the 1970s among the right-wing groups, driving in Burma was suddenly switched from the left-hand side of the road to the right, with the subsequent suppression of the uprising cited as justification for the change. Armed Forces Day is auspiciously set on 27 March (the third month and 27th day), the arrest of opposition leaders in 1989 took place on 20 July (month and day add to 27), the 1990 elections were called on 27 May, and so the extraordinary list involving the number nine goes on.

While travelling from the airport to Paris on a state visit to France, an outrider accompanying Ne Win's motorcade had the misfortune to fall off his motorcycle. He apparently did not feel the pain as much as his honoured guest who, remembering his father's warning to leave a place immediately if he 'witnessed a bad omen', abruptly cancelled the visit, U-turned and left behind a trail of fumes and flabbergasted diplomats. Ne Win's wacky world grew even weirder. When soothsayers warned him of an imminent violent uprising, the dictator stood in front of the mirror, stomped on a piece of meat and shot his reflection, presumably to defeat the flesh and blood of his enemies.

His whims brought unspeakable hardship to the people. By the mid-1980s Burma, once among the richest countries in Asia, had become an economic basket case. It was forced to apply to the United Nations for 'Least Developed Country' status when the economic situation threatened to spin out of control. In 1987, the President suddenly announced that the 75, 35 and 25 denominations of the kyat would no longer be legal tender. No reasons were given. They were replaced with new 45 and 90 kyat banknotes.

Overnight, the old notes—about three-quarters of the country's money in circulation—became worthless scraps of paper, wiping out savings and turning businesses topsy-turvy. People were understandably apprehensive about accepting the new notes for fear of another capricious demonetisation. Financial transactions, from the buying of cups of coffee in tea shops to formal business deals, were carried out in small kyat notes, the equivalent of a few cents.

Observers at that time regarded the matter as something of a cruel joke, but no one was laughing, least of all the university students. And if Ne Win was looking for a fight with them, he was rewarded. When they were told that the old currency could no longer be used to pay their fees, the students, predictably, rioted in the streets. Public property bore the brunt of their anger and the junta responded by closing down the universities. Caught out themselves, the military officers frantically searched for a plausible explanation. They finally pontificated that the change in currency was to counter inflation, neutralise the ethnic insurgents and check black marketeers.

Practice has the infuriating habit of confounding theories, especially obtuse ones. People rushed to exchange goods for the new notes for fear that they would be rendered worthless as well. Demand for goods increased, prices escalated and the inane explanation of curbing inflation never got off the ground. As for countering the insurgents, soldiers of the ethnic armies who lived near the borders of Thailand and China used mainly the currencies of these countries and were hardly affected by the decision. Finally, the hocus-pocus that the demonetisation was an attempt to stymie black marketeers also proved to be a non-starter. With the price of goods rising, people turned to the black market for better bargains.

The real reason behind the change was nothing more than Ne Win's obsession with the number nine, the 45 and 90 kyat notes being multiples of the digit. Enough was enough. Unable to stomach Number One's stunts any longer, the people joined the students to stage protests that increased in regularity as the year wore on. It was not until the following year, after the incident in the tea shop involving the RIT students, that the situation deteriorated into open confrontation.

On 23 July 1988, Ne Win surprised everybody by announcing during a special conference of the Burma Socialist Program Party (BSPP) that he was taking responsibility for the incidents in March and June and was resigning as Chairman of the Party which he had founded after the 1962 coup. He almost floored the public when he added that he would call for a referendum to see if the people wanted a multiparty system and, if they did, he would hold general elections. To top off the heady news, the General, apparently losing his political marbles, announced that he would 'completely retire' from politics 'whatever the results of the referendum and whatever the new government'.

The news was, of course, too good to be believed. It bordered on the fantastic. Why would Ne Win, with no one to challenge his authority, suddenly show compunction for atrocities that he never had qualms committing during the more than 25 years of his reign? Hardly anyone believed that he was genuinely remorseful about the brutal killings. Besides, international opinion had little effect on the dictator who had cut off Burma from the rest of the world.

The melodrama, like good soda water, was all fizz. It was another of Ne Win's schemes, this time to stage some sort of political opera, a Burmeseque drama that would create a scene which would allow him to make a graceful exit and give him room to operate without further staining his unsanitary repute. The script continued with the BSPP conference promptly voting down Number One's proposal. Flattered and feted as the indispensable national leader, the General was pleaded with to stay on as President. Ne Win declined, saying he would step down immediately.

The people were not duped, however. Tin Oo, the Deputy Chairman of the National League for Democracy, the political party that would later thump the junta in the 1990 general elections but be denied the reins of power, shook his head as he told me: 'He is very clever. He is a man who is always calculating for himself. He realised that the economy was in trouble and, in order to save face, he stepped down.' There was also never any doubt that Ne Win would continue to pull the levers from backstage. 'He had put all his henchmen in place to continue his one party rule,' Tin Oo continued.

Never too squeamish to rub salt into his opponents' wounds, Ne Win appointed General Sein Lwin as his successor. If there was anyone the Burmese people reviled more than the brutal despot, it was the brutal despot's hatchet man. Sein Lwin, nicknamed the 'Butcher', had been the architect behind most of the massacres. Through the decades that Ne Win was ruler, whenever sporadic unrest erupted, the Butcher had been despatched to conduct his slaughter; the *Lon Htein* his cleaver and the streets his abattoir.

Immediately after Ne Win grabbed power in 1962, Rangoon University students occupied the students union building in protest. Following a tense stand-off with the police which lasted two days, Sein Lwin ordered his men to open fire. Students fell by the dozen. When the demonstrators ran for cover, the *Lon Htein* continued to gun them down, spraying bullets at the building. Sein Lwin then ordered the building dynamited. The Butcher claimed his first scalps as hundreds of students lay dead on the university grounds.

In 1974 Thant, the Secretary General of the United Nations and one of Burma's most respected citizens, died in New York. Ne Win's xenophobia had placed Burma in such a hermetic position that participants in the Cold War came to see its isolation as neutrality. So, ironically, a nation that wanted little to do with the rest of the world had one of its nationals elected as Secretary General of the United Nations. As Thant's restrained and sober political disposition had not endeared him to Ne Win, his coffin was not officially received when it was flown back to Rangoon. The body was to be buried unceremoniously in a desolate spot outside the capital.

To the students, this was an unpardonable sacrilege. A group snatched the casket and hijacked it to the campus for burial. Their audacity gained the support of Buddhist monks as well as the public, and demonstrations broke out all over Rangoon. If the people's reaction was foreseeable, the Government's response proved no less predictable: martial law was imposed. When the students defied the ban, Sein Lwin moved in again and his troops mowed down no less than 300 students with machine guns.

Now, in 1988, Ne Win was trying to produce and direct his own play with Sein Lwin in a starring role. If Sein Lwin was the lead character, then the ordinary people were the disposable extras. Within weeks of his assuming command, people took to the streets of Rangoon in mass protests which spread to other cities. By early August, students were gathering in the streets every day, chanting anti-Government and, more precisely, anti-Sein Lwin slogans: 'Crack Sein Lwin's head! Off with Sein Lwin's head!'

The students knew they had made progress when monks began to join them. At the Shwedagon Pagoda, the monks conducted their own rally and joined in the chorus calling on workers to stage a nationwide strike on 8 August, the fiftieth anniversary of the departure of the British. A General Strike Committee passed messages throughout trades and professions, urging people to cease work on that day.

The combination of the 8.8.88 date and the infectiousness of the monks' courage proved irresistible. Clad in their *longyis*, tens of thousands converged on the streets, creating a sea of bobbing heads and fists in a tumultuous show of people power. Even the elderly and children joined in. Demonstrators from other cities arrived in cars, buses, trains and lorries to reinforce the protest. They camped out in the city centre, occupied the main thoroughfares and congregated outside government buildings, schools and hospitals. There were impromptu speeches condemning the Government. Comedians entertained the crowd with uproarious satirical performances about the generals. Residents clapped and cheered from their balconies. Sections of the crowd spontaneously broke into song, the national anthem the favourite refrain. The revelry did not reflect the gravity of the situation. But nobody cared. After 26 years of repressed anger, they had finally found the courage to tell Ne Win that the emperor had no clothes.

A few days before the planned general strike, Sein Lwin declared martial law and ordered everyone back to their homes. The people remained defiant. They were determined to confront their greatest fear—the Butcher himself. When the soldiers took up their positions, crowds converged upon them and urged them to defect. Calling them brothers and showering them with praise, the people were confident that the *tatmadaw* would not open fire. For a moment, as the soldiers smiled and chatted, a military implosion appeared a distinct possibility.

The marchers headed towards City Hall where hurriedly erected stages became the centre of public denunciations of the Government. The BBC reported these events in Burmese. Teashops were doing a brisk business with people crammed into the stalls, with ears straining to catch the latest reports and eyes watching for security agents.

On 8 August 1988, workers in the various towns of Moulmein, Tavoy, Mergui, Toungoo and several others walked out of their jobs and joined the nationwide protest. That afternoon, a general arrived at City Hall and warned the protesters to disperse. Otherwise, they would be fired upon. The announcement was greeted with catcalls of such magnitude that the General retreated. Speakers urged the crowd to remain disciplined and not to attack the General and his men: 'We want a peaceful demonstration! We want democracy!'

Just before midnight, troops stormed the demonstration. Machine gun fire rattled amidst screams and cries. People scurried for the nearest shelter as truckloads of soldiers arrived and poured lead into the thickest parts of the crowd. Protesters dropped by the hundreds. Some got up and ran. Others died on the spot. Within hours, the area in front of City Hall was cleared of all but the dead.

Remarkably, the people came out again the next day, and so did the soldiers, who were now firing at anything that looked alive. The demonstrators responded by tearing through the city and storming police stations. Any soldier or *Lon Htein* trooper foolish enough to be caught alone met with a gruesome death. It was a war, but only one side was armed.

As the days passed, the *tatmadaw* continued their bullet and bayonet orgy. Even monks meditating by the pavements were arrested, disrobed and shot. High school students were lined up, made to kneel with hands on their heads and shot point-blank. The unfortunate ones who survived the first shot were bayoneted in the throat. Thousands were taken to the Rangoon General Hospital, some dead, some seriously wounded. When the hospital staff could not cope with the casualties and protested in frustration, the *tatmadaw* opened fire on them too.

It was an insane scenario, with both sides refusing to yield. It boiled down to whether the soldiers would run out of bullets first or the people would run out of rioters.

All They Have Are Guns

As suddenly as it had erupted, the fighting ceased. On 12 August the Government announced that Sein Lwin was stepping down as President. Stunned by the announcement, the people celebrated what was to be a pyrrhic victory. On 19 August (19 plus 8 equals 27) General Maung Maung—another of Ne Win's close associates—was named as Sein Lwin's replacement.

Unlike his predecessor, the new President had the political resilience of warm butter. He immediately moved to appease the masses and promised elections within three months. The opposition rejected this offer of seemingly sweet reasonableness and called for the new President's immediate resignation. They wanted an interim government that included opposition leaders to oversee the running of the elections. A stalemate emerged over the next few weeks with the people demanding and the generals fencing.

What happened during Maung Maung's presidency, which lasted less than a month, stunned even the most optimistic of political pundits. As the demonstrators continued their push, the army suddenly beat a hasty retreat. The troops pulled back from the streets and returned to their camps where they remained for the next few weeks. The atmosphere was one of a bizarre and somewhat unnerving truce.

Finding themselves in the unfamiliar situation of protesting without staring down barrels and bayonets, the people hailed their victory in the name of democracy. As Burmese from every walk of life—civil servants and army personnel included—joined in the celebrations, jubilation turned into euphoria. Everyone thought that they were witnessing the unfolding of history and envisaged a Philippine-style people's revolution where Ne Win, like Marcos, would be forced to flee the country.

The press, straightjacketed by years of censorship, suddenly exploded with exposés about Ne Win and his cronies. Headlines denouncing the dictatorship became daily fare. Even the *Working People's Daily* began to be more even-handed in its reporting. It seemed like the start of a national renaissance.

In the run-up to the elections, political parties were allowed to form. No fewer than 233 sprouted, most of which were no more than discussion groups that offered precious little to the situation at hand. One party did emerge to bring Burmese politics some semblance of pride and direction. The National League for Democracy (NLD) was formed on 24 September by Aung Gyi, Tin Oo and Aung San Suu Kyi, who became its Chairman, Deputy Chairman and Secretary General respectively.

Aung Gyi was as puzzling as political enigmas came. He had served under Ne Win as an army officer but in the 1960s became increasingly critical of the regime. In 1988 he openly defied the junta by participating in the uprising. During his drift towards democracy, the former General was imprisoned several times for his criticisms of the Government's human rights abuses and its economic non-policies.

Yet he continued to speak warmly of the President even after the 1988 massacres. Suspicions of his motives were a constant source of friction between him and the other NLD leaders. But his opposition credentials were never closely scrutinised until he accused Tin Oo and Aung San Suu Kyi of being communists. When he failed to dislodge them from the party leadership, he resigned and blundered from the political scene.

Tin Oo had also been one of Ne Win's officers, serving as chief of staff and defence minister from 1974 to 1976. Midway through his career, he was accused of participating in a coup attempt and locked up for four years. Unlike Aung Gyi, Tin Oo has remained a steadfast critic of Ne Win. 'Come, come, please help yourselves,' he urged in an avuncular tone as he poured me a generous serving of coffee. Laid out on the coffee table were Burmese finger-foods wrapped, fried and baked in every sumptuous way imaginable. 'They must have wondered why I'm eating so much,' he laughed. He was referring to the security agents living down the road who seemed to have degraded the fine art of political voyeurism into a not-so-subtle practice. They had commandeered a neighbour's house fronting the lane that led to Tin Oo's residence to photograph every coming and going there, making no effort to conceal their surveillance.

After the initial flurry of courtesies, we settled down and Tin Oo, now in his seventies, traced the events that led to the electoral showdown between the NLD and the military regime, which had formed the National Unity Party to replace the BSPP. The frenzy of political activity did not seem to lead anywhere. The junta would not say when the elections were going to be held apart from dropping unhelpful hints that it would be before the middle of 1990. Meanwhile, they continued to hammer down any political nail that protruded, arresting anyone who contravened an order forbidding public gatherings of more than four people.

Not one to yield to intimidation—'All they have are guns' she steels the faint-hearted—Aung San Suu Kyi took her campaign into the countryside and implored the people to unite under that most dangerous of worthy banners—democracy. Scrambling to counter her infuriating habit of ignoring their script, the generals responded by going around the townships warning residents not to come out onto the street to greet her.

With no scheme too contemptible, the regime distributed crudely drawn caricatures depicting her and her husband engaged in various sexual positions; their captions called her, among other expletives, a prostitute and demanded that she and her 'foreign bastard' leave Burma.

Torn between the desire to just shoot her and bring an end to their misery, and the fear of triggering a revolt that would engulf the entire country if they did that, the Government was exhibiting signs of operational schizophrenia. On 5 April 1989, when she had finished a day of campaigning in the town of Danubyu, Aung San Suu Kyi was returning home with a group of NLD officials. A flag bearer was walking in front when suddenly a small troop of soldiers knelt across the road, ready to gun them down.

'Get off the road!' the captain ordered.

Aung San Suu Kyi told the flag bearer to step aside as he was the first in the line of fire. The captain warned that his men would open fire if the group continued to walk in the middle of the road.

'Fine, all right,' Suu Kyi replied. 'We'll walk on the side of the road.'

The captain hadn't seen that coming. Regaining his wits, he yelled that he would shoot even if the group walked on the side of the road.

If he's going to shoot us even if we walk on the side of the road, well, perhaps it is me they want to shoot, Suu Kyi calculated. She decided not to budge which set tensions rising. One order from the captain and the group could have lived their last day.

Just then a major who had been accompanying the campaigners came running up and started arguing with the captain. Without another word, Aung San Suu Kyi led her supporters down the middle of the road and right past the bewildered soldiers. As they muttered nervously among themselves, the captain threw a tantrum, tearing the insignia from his shoulder and cursing that he was not allowed to shoot.

'The point is that demonstrations are not allowed,' foreign minister Ohn Gyaw explained to Stan Sesser, author of *Lands of Charm and Cruelty*. 'This is a land of law and order. Be it Aung San Suu Kyi or a passer by, if people didn't listen to the authorities, what would happen? This is not the West. Here they can express themselves inside some hall.'

The incident was not the first that brought Suu Kyi in direct confrontation with the *tatmadaw*. On another occasion, she was travelling with some of her colleagues to a village when her convoy was stopped by soldiers. Her secretary got out of the car to find out what was wrong. Suddenly a burst of gunfire sounded. Aung San Suu Kyi immediately got out of her car. 'Why are you shooting?' she asked calmly. When the officer in charge saw that it was her, he quickly apologised, explaining that the gunshots were an accident and allowed the convoy to proceed.

Aung San Suu Kyi also had the sense to avoid a showdown with the military when circumstances dictated it. The opposition planned to commemorate Martyrs' Day on 19 July 1989, the anniversary of Aung San's assassination. Suu Kyi was to address the rally. The generals quickly announced that anyone attending the event would be arrested. The soldiers, regardless of rank, were given the authority to sentence their captives to three years' hard labour, life imprisonment or execution. Troops converged on the streets of Rangoon. Not wanting to precipitate a bloodbath, Aung San Suu Kyi called off the rally.

The SLORC versus the NLD

While he was promising elections, Ne Win moved to tighten his hold on power. Through his trusted head of the Directorate of Defence Services Intelligence (DDSI), Colonel Khin Nyunt, Number One was stalking the protesters and planning his future strikes.

His first move was to secure himself financially. He ordered soldiers to remove hundreds of millions of kyats in cash reserves from the Foreign Trade Bank. Next, some 9,000 common criminals were suddenly released from prison. The official version was that simultaneous 'uprisings' in prisons all over the country had taken place, leading to fires and mass breakouts. Criminals suddenly found themselves in situations where law enforcement was almost non-existent. Lootings and robberies plunged the cities into anarchy, with Rangoon being worst hit. In attempts to protect their property, residents set up vigilante teams and armed themselves with home-made spears and clubs.

There were even reports that DDSI agents were poisoning water supplies. Earthen containers that provided drinking water for demonstrators and marchers were feared to be laced with chemicals. When monks noticed a couple of suspicious looking loiterers, they chased and caught one who was carrying a bottle. The suspect denied that the solution was poison, whereupon the crowd made him drink it. He did, and died.

On another occasion, three men and one woman were caught snooping around the Rangoon Children's Hospital. Several demonstrators pounced on them; upon interrogation, two confessed that they had instructions to poison the water tank. The incensed mob decapitated them on the spot.

Arsonists went on a burning spree, targeting government offices and warehouses. Before the buildings were set on fire, looters would cart everything away in a free-for-all, with the soldiers joining in. Eyewitnesses said that the *tatmadaw* were the first to remove the stocks and food supplies from the warehouses, leaving the doors open for other looters. The accounts were corroborated by vigilantes who arrested the looters and found them intoxicated. The looters revealed that they had been given pills by DDSI agents before being sent out on their assignments.

The scenario in Rangoon was one of confusion. On the one hand, Maung Maung had promised elections and the junta seemed to be softening its hardline stance. On the other hand were these reports about poisonings and lootings that the DDSI appeared to be instigating. What was going on?

The question was answered on 18 September (the eighteenth day of the ninth month) when Ne Win resurfaced. The Burma Broadcasting Service ominously cut short its usual program and started playing militaristic tunes. These were soon followed by an announcement that 'in order to bring a timely halt to the deteriorating conditions on all sides all over the country,' the armed forces were taking direct control of the Government through the State Law and Order Restoration Council (SLORC). General Saw Maung, yet another of Ne Win's close associates, was appointed Chairman.

The BSPP had been disbanded. Nonetheless, there was a promise that the multiparty elections would proceed. A curfew was imposed and demonstrations were banned, even though the SLORC knew that warnings had by now become largely platitudinous. Next day, machine guns were positioned on top of buildings overlooking the American embassy, where the demonstrators had been mostly gathering. Not knowing that they were set up for the kill, the people continued to stream in. When the crowd was sizeable enough, the *tatmadaw* opened fire.

As the first volley ceased and the people were running every way, the soldiers moved in. They gave chase and continued to unload their ammunition into the backs of the fleeing demonstrators. Where bullets missed, bayonets cleaned up. The bodies were picked up by trucks and driven off to the crematorium. Amnesty International reported an account by a soldier who was on duty there but who had since deserted the army:

> [The furnace] was supposed to burn only one body at a time but up to six were burned until the machinery could cope no longer and broke down. Operations then moved to a crocodile farm where dead bodies were chopped up and fed to these reptiles. [This soldier] has stated that he was an eyewitness to the [killings] and to seeing hundreds of bodies crammed into three disused oil storage tanks, towed behind a patrol boat, presumably to be sunk at sea. He claims to have seen a secret register in which the names of 40,000 people in the Rangoon area were killed by SLORC troops. According to this eyewitness this number does not include the dead or wounded who subsequently died and were taken away by friends or family. The burnings and the feeding of the decomposed bodies went on for nearly a month.

Those who had the misfortune to be captured were taken to interrogation centres and forced to reveal the names of the leaders and monks involved in the movement. Doctors, teachers and civil servants were also arrested. The month when Maung Maung was President and the Government seemed to be in an inexplicable recession was actually a time when the people were lulled into thinking that they had triumphed and could remove the bandannas and handkerchiefs covering their faces. The cunning variant of Mao Zedong's 'let one hundred flowers bloom' stratagem allowed the DDSI to identify the main activists, which they did with uncharacteristic efficiency.

At the torture houses, the 'softening' of each prisoner would begin with an intense round of slaps, punches, and kicks. The prisoners were given the morbid 'privilege' of choosing their own punishment. I met one who lived to tell the tale. Myint (not his real name) was a graduate student in engineering, now in his late twenties. He is a lanky man who told his story softly but deliberately.

'What do you want? Choose!' yelled an officer.

With snot coming out of his nose and a mixture of blood and saliva running down the corner of his mouth, Myint looked shell-shocked. His right eye was swollen from a punch. He was kneeling.

'Which one? Do you want to walk on the seashore or ride a motorcycle?' the soldier asked.

Myint didn't answer. In one unbroken motion, the officer swept his boots across Myint's jaw. The pain reverberated through his head. All he could hear was 'Choose! Choose!'

Myint struggled to ask, 'Choose what?'

The other soldiers standing around started laughing.

'The seashore or motorcycle?'

Desperately trying to avoid another blow, Myint chose the seashore, without a clue as to what it meant.

'Oh! Brave man!' the soldiers laughed. They hauled him to an area strewn with gravel and bottle caps. One soldier kicked the back of Myint's knee, forcing him to buckle into a kneeling position. Another tied his hands behind him.

'You want to walk on the seashore? Now walk!' the officer shouted.

There was a ghastly smorgasbord of torture techniques. 'Riding a motorcycle' meant that one had to hunch over as if riding a motorbike while standing on tiptoe. When 'flying a helicopter', the prisoner would be tied upside down to a ceiling fan and whirled around. One's head would be dunked in water during a ride in a 'wet submarine', while the 'iron road' meant pressing an iron bar up and down on one's shin until bone showed.

When Myint hesitated, the officer stung him with a slap on the ear: 'I said walk!'

Myint placed one knee on the sharp stones and rusted metal caps. When he took another step, his whole weight bore down on the first knee and the gravel cut in. Myint's body shook in pain. 'I screamed,' he said blandly. 'The soldiers just laughed.'

'Walk some more!' the officer demanded.

When Myint hesitated, a soldier kicked him in the face again. Myint took another step when he recovered from the kick.

'Who is the leader and who organised the demonstrations?'

'There are no leaders. Everyone acted spontaneously,' Myint replied.

The officer cursed: 'Don't lie to me. Who is your leader?'

The questioning continued for about an hour, with Myint still kneeling on the 'seashore'. When the soldiers realised they could not get anything useful from him, they untied him and threw him in the cell with other prisoners. All of them looked lifeless. After a few minutes, Myint passed out.

On 20 July 1989, at 6:30 a.m., the *tatmadaw* surrounded Aung San Suu Kyi's home and placed her and several other NLD leaders under house arrest. Suu Kyi reacted calmly; she had anticipated the detention, although she wasn't sure if she would be taken to Insein Prison. That afternoon, some colleagues came over to her house for a meeting, lunching and joking their way through a most depressing day.

More than 2,000 leading members of the NLD were arrested and taken to Insein. To make room for these political prisoners and for the thousands more whose arrests were pending, the SLORC released more than 18,000 criminals. The NLD was now in a forlorn state. Under years of crippling censorship, oppositional forces were inexperienced and divided. Former Prime Minister Nu, now an elderly man, saw the opportunity and unilaterally announced that he was the rightful leader because Ne Win had unlawfully wrested power from him in 1962. Without consulting the other opposition leaders, Nu formed his own 'government' with himself as Prime Minister. Without the support of the NLD leaders, however, his initiative went nowhere. Without a political party, opposition supporters coalesced around Aung Gyi, Tin Oo and Suu Kyi. Kyi Maung, another notable NLD leader who had been arrested and imprisoned several times, took over as Chairman of the Party.

For the generals, there had never been a better time to pull out the ballot box. With everyone who needed to be jailed behind bars and every law to ensure victory in place, the regime confidently called for elections on 27 May 1990 (the date is again divisible by nine). So confident was the SLORC that its chief, General Saw Maung (who was later replaced by Than Shwe) pledged that the army would abide by the results of the elections whatever the outcome, and political matters would be left to the elected government. It was a pompous cloak that the SLORC had donned, and its subsequent defrocking would prove to be an excruciating discomfiture. When the results were announced, the generals' jaws dropped like a mishandled bowling ball. The NLD won 392 of the 485 seats.

The SLORC's National Unity Party captured only ten seats, with the remainder going to parties allied with the NLD.

'The NLD even won in the military constituencies,' chuckled the former Australian ambassador Garry Woodard as we sat talking in his garden. 'Aung San Suu Kyi was directly criticising Ne Win and calling on the army to switch their allegiance. The army at that time had an element of fragility. In fact, Ne Win and his leaders were earlier looking to get out. There were helicopters in his garden and even rumours that the Americans were on hand to assist the democrats.'

Khin Nyunt, head of the DDSI, quickly claimed that the elections had only been for a 'constituent assembly' that was to draw up a new constitution. The elected MPs did not constitute a parliament because 'only the SLORC has the right to legislative power'. The newly promoted Brigadier-General added that the junta would not accept a constitution drawn up by the NLD to claim power. It was a make-up-the-rules-as-you-go-along state of affairs.

Why did the SLORC generals conduct the elections if they had no intentions of handing over power in the first place? Stan Sesser surmised that:

> The most likely explanation is that the dictatorship had originally envisioned a Guatemalan-type solution for Burma—with the military pulling the strings behind the scenes and a powerless civilian government creating a facade that would allow a resumption of foreign aid and investment.

But the 'Guatemalan-type' order could only come about if the people were convinced that the generals were best placed to run the country. 'The SLORC held elections because it wanted to discredit democracy by showing how divided the parties were and how easy it is to buy off unprincipled politicians,' Woodard commented. On both counts, the junta was way off target.

Following the election debacle, it was the monks' turn to show their displeasure at the SLORC's flagrant disregard for common decency. On 8 August, the first anniversary of the 1988 uprising, the *sangha* order of monks took to the streets. Instead of staging a demonstration, they gathered in huge numbers and went on their usual morning alms round. Crowds offered them food. A few students, sensing the significance of the event, hoisted the NLD flag.

Without warning, the soldiers opened fire on the monks. A bullet ripped through the chest of a young novice, killing him instantly. Nine other monks and two bystanders were also hit. In response, more than 7,000 monks decided to refuse alms from military officers and their families; in the context of Burmese society, this was a grave act of excommunication. The SLORC warned the *sangha* order to rescind its boycott. When the monks ignored the threat, the army retaliated by raiding all the 133 monasteries in Mandalay and arresting several abbots. This scandalous act in a deeply Buddhist country revealed the army's desperation: not taking action against the monks, who were revered by the people, would have seemed that the military acknowledged that there were limits to its abuse of power.

The SLORC seized the opportunity to arrest Kyi Maung, the NLD Chairman, and 65 NLD MPs-elect, further decimating the ranks of the Party. Those who escaped made their way out of the country and organised themselves into the National Coalition Government of the Union of Burma. Its leader and prime minister in exile was Dr Sein Win, Aung San Suu Kyi's cousin, whose father (Aung San's brother) had also been killed in the attack in 1947.

'It's difficult to reason with the SLORC,' Sein Win said to me during a conference. 'But we can't give up hope. All these years we've been trying to show them the only ones to suffer are the Burmese people themselves. All they seem to care about is to hang on to absolute power.'

And with absolute power comes turpitude. The soldiers' behaviour, by comparison, made the baseness of the common criminals look decidedly pedestrian. Rape and torture became routine. Amnesty International reported:

> Naw Mya Thaung, a 36-year-old mother of two, arrived in Mannerplaw in 1992, telling of the week long orgy of destruction and murder that took place when the units of the *tatmadaw* came to her village. Villagers were not allowed to leave and were accused of being related to the rebels. Every woman in the village was systematically gang raped, young and old, married or unmarried. Not one

woman was spared. When her turn came she had to hand her 18-month-old son to another woman before going into the trench full of soldiers, or she would have been killed. Through that week, monks were beaten, villagers repeatedly raped and murdered, crops and houses burned, all livestock shot. Even pots and pans were broken. By the time the soldiers left, the village had ceased to exist. The villagers had no choice but to leave.

Private Maung Po Pain recounted the following story to Amnesty International:

> With my company were ten women porters—eight Karen and two Burmese. We were free to rape them at any time and they were raped very badly, especially the Karen women. But I didn't rape them because I felt they could easily have been my sisters or my motherl'The soldiers in my company always slapped, kicked and punched the porters and sometimes used rifle butts on them.

Political prisoners were commonly used as porters for soldiers. Many become slave labourers in the construction of railway lines. Others have been deployed as human minesweepers to clear paths mined by the ethnic minority troops in their fight against the SLORC. Children are forced to labour in fields and construction sites. This treatment continues till today.

Friends of SLORC

The political sump that SLORC had created provoked widespread condemnation by the international community and cuts in economic aid. Without funds, how was the SLORC going to purchase arms? Enter Singapore. It has been reported that the island republic supplied recoilless gun ammunition, mortars, automatic rifles, small arms ammunition, surface to air missiles and radars. Bertil Lintner wrote in *Outrage: Burma's Struggle for Democracy*:

> In order to maintain the new 'law and order,' the supply of arms and ammunition for the army was a main consideration, and foreigners began to speculate how long

the present supplies would last, especially since the state coffers had been almost depleted of foreign exchange. But late in the evening of 6th October [1988], there was a curious black out along Prome Road in Rangoon, which only affected the three closest rows of house on either side of the thoroughfare. Meanwhile, heavily laden army trucks rumbled past from the city's port up to the Mingaladon military area north of the airport. Prome Road residents counted 75 trucks making three trips each; in the port, workers had seen boxes marked 'Allied Ordnance, Singapore' being unloaded from a ship. (Allied Ordnance is a joint venture between Nobel Industries and Shengli Holdings, an investment group of the Singapore Government).

Lintner explained that some of the weapons manufactured by the Chartered Industries of Singapore (CIS), a Government run arms manufacturing company, were under licence from the parent Swedish company Forenade Fabriksverken (FFV). Apparently an agreement had been entered into by the two companies stating that CIS had to obtain approval from FFV before any of the material and products could be re-exported to a third country. The CIS 'never even applied for such a permit'.

China, Israel, Pakistan and South Korea were also reported to be supplying the SLORC with military equipment. But Andrew Selth of the Strategic Defence Studies Centre at the Australian National University observed that:

> The first country to come to the regime's rescue was Singapore. In August 1989 Singapore was again accused of providing arms to the SLORC when weapons and ammunition originating in Belgium and Israel were transshipped to Burma, apparently with the assistance of SKS Marketing, a newly formed Singapore-based joint venture with the Burmese military regime.

As recently as 1997, the *Asian Defence Journal* reported that Singapore was supplying high-tech equipment to the SLORC for its Cyber Warfare Centre in Rangoon, a military set-up which taps 'domestic phone, fax and e-mail lines on a countrywide basis'. Singapore is also 'thought to be training large numbers of Burmese secret police'.

Singapore has been on the friendliest of terms with the Burmese dictatorship. In 1986 Prime Minister Lee Kuan Yew visited Burma and during a banquet gushed: 'My first visit to Rangoon was in April 1962, when I got to know General Ne Win. Our friendship has grown these last two and a half decades. Burma-Singapore relations have been close and friendly. No problems have disrupted the even tenor of our relations.'

These 'close and friendly' relations were taken a step further at the international level. On 19 November 1990, Sweden spearheaded a move at the United Nations to draft a resolution which censured the SLORC for it rapacious conduct and for not honouring the election results. Singapore was particularly vocal in supporting a counter-resolution of 'non-interference in the internal affairs of member States in their electoral process'.

Years later Lee Kuan Yew would add that Aung San Suu Kyi should remain as a symbol of democracy and leave the running of Burma to the SLORC which, in his view, is the only organisation capable of doing the job despite the overwhelming millions of Burmese who thought differently, many having given their lives for their convictions, and his policy of international 'non-interference'.

Desperate for foreign exchange, the SLORC was forced to end the country's hermetic existence and establish relations with other countries, with the prime intention of attracting funds needed to maintain the resources of its army. Investment laws were amended to encourage outsiders to do business in the ravaged country. When the expected capital infusion failed to materialise, the generals turned to selling Burma's natural resources. Petroleum companies from America, Australia, Britain, Canada, Japan and the Netherlands came to explore for oil.

With logging banned in Thailand, the avaricious Thai logging companies, many of which were owned by some Thai army generals as well as Sein Lwin's son and relatives, lustily eyed the vast teak forests across the border. By early 1989 several concession areas had been awarded; within a year, more than half a million tonnes of timber was exported from Burma. Ne

Win's son-in-law, Aye Zaw Win, was put in charge of the lucrative industry which regulates the fishing rights of domestic and foreign fisheries. The young entrepreneur wasted no time in expanding his business links, and now 'has direct business interests and connections in Singapore through the office of the State Pearl and Fishing Rights Enterprise.'

Unscrupulous governments continued to do business with the junta, providing it with cash. Steve Erlanger of the *New York Times* wrote: 'So it is no surprise that the Thais, South Koreans and Singaporeans are keeping the regime supplied with hard currency through the purchase of fishing, timber and oil drilling rights.' The gluttony of the SLORC at one end and the political constipation of the body politic at the other will in due course end in a grotesque national explosion.

House Arrest

The intelligence agents next door bustled with activity when she arrived at our meeting place. Earlier on, my contact and I had been stopped at the checkpoint when we went to her house on University Avenue. A sentinel sulking under the sun in his thick cotton tunic pointed to the 'no entry' sign in the middle of the road and impatiently waved my taxi away. 'No one, no one,' was how he kept visitors from calling on Aung San Suu Kyi.

But if, like unsociable parents, the SLORC didn't allow us to come to the house to see the country's favourite daughter, she could always come out to see us.

As we settled down for the interview, the lights suddenly went out. There was a power failure, or so it seemed. Without batting an eyelid, Aung San Suu Kyi laughed: 'It may seem strange in your country but it's quite normal here.' For some odd reason, the blackout had been triggered by the security agents down the road. It was, perhaps, their way of signalling their unhappiness about the meeting. It could also have been, as my contact theorised, that without the electromagnetic field generated by the electricity, electronic eavesdropping was much more effective. As it was a beautiful, sunny morning, we got on perfectly well without the electricity.

Just then a military intelligence agent popped up outside the gate at the end of the driveway to steal a peek into the house. 'Don't worry, they're just curious,' one of the NLD officials assured.

Our conversation eventually turned to Singapore. When the subject of arms sales cropped up, she smiled a sad smile: 'Singapore is so rich, does it need money from the arms? Are you going to have less to eat because you do not engage in that? I think Singapore is economically strong enough not to depend on such business even in spite of its present problems.'

I mentioned my country's investment in hers, and how some circles had come to see Singapore as the model for other Asian countries. 'The difference between Burma and Singapore is so great I don't know where to begin,' she sighed. 'Let's start with the size of the country. Don't forget that we are an agriculturally based country. Eighty per cent of our people still live in the countryside. Singapore is in quite a different situation altogether.'

There he was again, the man from military intelligence (MI) stealing another peek.

She was right. Administering Singapore is unlike governing any other country in Asia, except perhaps Brunei.

All through our conversation, Aung San Suu Kyi remained supremely composed and showed nothing of the strain that she had been under in the last decade. Her mother Khin Kyi died in December 1988 after a series of strokes. Suu Kyi had stayed in the hospital with her and brought her home only towards the end. When she died, crowds started gathering outside the compound.

The regime's top generals—Saw Maung, Khin Nyunt, and Phone Myint—nervous about the emotions that the death of Aung San's wife might generate, promptly made their way to University Avenue to sign the condolence book. Aung San Suu Kyi amiably invited them in. She seized the opportunity to remind her guests of their promise to return Burma to democracy. Resorting to evasive doublespeak, the generals committed themselves to nothing and quickly departed.

'You know, I've never felt vindictive towards the SLORC,' Suu Kyi told Alan Clements. 'Of course I've been angry at some of the things they've done. But at the same time I can sense their uneasiness—their lack of confidence in good, as it were.' This is quintessential Aung San Suu Kyi. Steeped in her

Buddhist faith, she has always confronted the SLORC with boldness, accompanied by her message of nonviolence and conciliation: 'I liked most of them as human beings—I could never help seeing the human side of them.' Her refusal to resort to armed struggle won her the Nobel Peace Prize in 1991. This benevolent attitude has drawn criticism from the more militant opposition quarters who feel that the SLORC must pay, and pay dearly, for their atrocities.

Her conciliatory approach does not masquerade nor dilute her resolve to confront the authoritarian regime. At every opportunity she makes plain her views about the need, especially in Buddhism, to confront autocrats. She said to Clements:

> In Buddhism, as you know, we believe that you will pay for all the bad things that you've done. And I think because of that, a lot of Buddhists think that because the authorities are cruel and unjust, you don't have to do anything at all, they will get their own desserts. I don't accept that. I don't think that one should just sit back and expect *karma* to catch up with everybody else. I remind people that *karma* is actually doing. It's not just sitting back. Some people think of *karma* as destiny or fate and that there's nothing they can do about. But *karma* is not that at all. It's doing, it's action. So you are creating your own *karma* all the time. Buddhism is a very dynamic philosophy and it's a great pity that some people forget that aspect of our religion.

So what is her preferred method of resistance? 'People must ask questions and not just accept everything,' she insists. At the weekly addresses to her supporters at her house (which had since been banned by the junta) she remained abiding in her creed that violence must be eschewed but the will to challenge the authorities must remain unbending:

> I've always said that they really must learn to question people who order them to do things which are against justice and existing laws. Ask, according to which law are you forcing me to do this? What right do you have to make me do this? They've also got to ask themselves should we do this?

But more than just maintaining a questioning stance, she believes that action is just as essential: 'Complacency is very dangerous. Actually with a lot of people, it's not a sense of complacency either. I think that many people accept things out of either fear or inertia. This readiness to accept without question must be removed.'

Intellectual integrity takes centre stage in her struggle. In this regard, Vaclav Havel, the President of Czechoslovakia, has influenced her:

> But what impressed me most about Czechoslovakia was the intellectual honesty that some of the best people maintained. They would rather be plumbers, roadworkers, street-cleaners and bricklayers than compromise their intellectual integrity by joining a university or the government. They accepted the superiority of the mind over the body and they placed the importance of intellectual integrity far above that of material comfort.

Her propensity to not 'just accept everything' strikes consternation in the generals. Time and again when there were calls for her release from house arrest, the SLORC said that they would do so on condition that she leave Burma and promise never to return. Even after they set her free in 1995, they have kept a nervous eye glued on her movements.

On the morning of her arrest in 1989, a relative had arrived to tell Suu Kyi that soldiers were all over the place and that something was wrong. Then Tin Oo's son came over and said that soldiers had prevented his father from going for his morning walk. All of them thought that the Insein prison was their next destination.

Suu Kyi packed her things for prison. Her two young sons, Kim and Alexander, were with her. She explained to them that they would have to go back to England. The decision did not come easily but she knew what needed to be done:

> As a mother, the greater sacrifice was giving up my sons, but I was always aware of the fact that others had sacrificed more than me. Obviously, it is not a choice that I made happily, but one that I made without any reservations or hesitation. But I would rather not have missed all those

years of my children's lives. I would much rather have lived together with them.

But this was out of the question, for the SLORC wanted the Aris family on another planet if it was possible. A visa for husband Michael sometimes seems harder to come by than peace in the Middle East. On the rare occasion that her sons are with her, they try to enjoy each other as other families would. 'When my younger son visited me the last time he had his birthday, I took him out to shop,' she said, trying to sound like the average mother. 'It was a little difficult with the people gathering around.'

During the years of her house arrest, Aung San Suu Kyi kept to a strict timetable. Getting up at 4:30, she would meditate for an hour, after which she would try to catch up on international affairs over the radio, which often included learning what the SLORC was up to. After exercise she bathed and ate her breakfast, then did household chores:

> I had a lot of things to do. It was not like sitting in a prison cell. I had a house to look after that had to be kept tidy and clean. I could listen to the radio and read. I could sew. I could do all the normal things that I would have imagined that many people do every day, with the exception of going out and having friends come in.

Things were not always that simple. At first she had refused to accept anything from the authorities, even food. She sold her furniture in order to purchase her own provisions through a helper who came round once a week. She went on an 11 day hunger strike to protest her detention. It was a time when defiance had to make do for money. She ran dangerously low on funds and could not even afford groceries. Undernourished, her hair began to fall out and at one point she could hardly get out of bed. But she was still philosophical about her situation, as she told me:

> One should be grateful for suffering in a sense, because it helps us to think more of other people and I think it teaches us greater humility, understanding and compassion. I think the fact that we have suffered so much, the more we suffer, the more sympathetic we will be to those who have suffered.

Aung San Suu Kyi takes pains to avoid building a personality cult. Her secretary said that she even disliked waving to the crowd from inside her car as she felt that it looked too much like royalty. She only relented after her assistants told her that not doing so would appear arrogant, something which was far removed from her personality. Besides, they added, the people would treasure an acknowledgment from her.

She has repeatedly called for dialogue with the generals to negotiate a peaceful resolution to the political impasse. Each time, the SLORC would react as if it was aggrieved by her, not she by it. Aung San Suu Kyi is not surprised, as she explained to Clements:

> I read somewhere that it is always more difficult for the perpetrator of a cruel deed to forgive the victim, than for the victim to forgive his tormentor. I found that very strange when I first read it, but I think it's true. The victim can forgive because he has the moral high ground as it were. He has nothing to be ashamed of...But the tormentor finds it difficult to forgive the victim because he knows that he has committed an act of shame. And every time he sees his victim he is reminded of his shame. That makes it harder for him to forgive...But the victim who has behaved well finds it quite easy to forgive the tormentor. Because every time he sees the tormentor, I'm sure he is empowered by the reminder of his own noble behaviour—his courage. He might say: 'I stood up against that man's tortures with dignity.'

On 10 July 1995, a SLORC soldier walked up to Kyi Maung's house. The NLD Chairman had been released earlier by the military and was reading in his study when the officer arrived.

'There's an intelligence officer at the door,' his wife informed him.

Kyi Maung went to see what the soldier wanted: 'What is it?'

'Daw Aung San Suu Kyi wants to see you,' he intoned.

'Is she seriously ill?' asked Kyi Maung.

'No, she's not ill.'

'Are you here to give me a lift?'

'No,' the officer replied dryly, 'come in your own car. Daw Aung San Suu Kyi would like to see your wife too.'

After the brief encounter, the soldier left. Kyi Maung and his wife quickly drove to their Party leader's house. When they got there, they were greeted by a smiling Suu Kyi: 'Uncle, what took you so long, six years to drive a mile?'

The SLORC had finally decided to release their captive from house arrest.

Drugs and money laundering

Ne Win was now determined to put a stop to the unrest once and for all. His patient orchestration of the events—his resignation as President, the release of criminals, the looting and descent into anarchy—had given him the pretext that he needed to 'restore' law and order through the SLORC. Like the Orwellian pigs who did not hesitate to subjugate their comrade-creatures that they were supposed to liberate, the generals showed little hesitation in breaking any law and wreaking whatever mayhem to restore 'law and order'. The barbarous but meticulously planned crushing of the demonstrations left no doubt that the generals would stop at nothing to wipe out the opposition movement.

Before the massacre in 1988, there had already been a steady trickle of people leaving the cities for safer havens along the borders. Since then, students and other activists have fled by the thousands to these areas. The SLORC embarked on a campaign to track down the student leaders, who had found a natural ally in the ethnic armies, particularly the Karens, who had been at war with Rangoon since 1948. These armies financed themselves by cultivating poppy plants. When Chiang Kai-shek was defeated by the communists in China in 1949, his Kuomintang troops retreated to Taiwan, but some who were fighting in southern China found themselves cut off from the main force. The only route available to them was the hills of Burma. There they set up their base to relaunch their attack on Mao Zedong's forces.

The Kuomintang soldiers had brought with them modern military equipment which the Burmese ethnic groups needed for their struggle. In return, the Chinese army stumbled upon the opium growing farms. With worldwide demand for the drug, the Kuomintang soldiers soon succumbed to the lure of cash and all but forgot their fight with their sworn communist enemies. In no time, an opium empire sprang up in the ethnic bases, especially in the northeastern regions of the Shan, Wa and Kachin states.

With the new supply of arms, the war between the central Government and the ethnic groups, who were joined by the Communist Party of Burma (CPB), intensified. The *tatmadaw* launched fierce raids into the ethnic states, who responded with equal ferocity. Finally, in 1989 the SLORC scored a decisive victory over the CPB. With their key ally destroyed, many of the ethnic armies entered into a ceasefire agreement with Rangoon.

The SLORC saw its chance. A ceasefire with the ethnic insurgents proved doubly propitious. Firstly, the pro-democratic forces who had escaped into the ethnic regions would be deprived of allies. Secondly, some of the insurgents had become international drug barons by setting up massive refineries to process heroin from opium; among the most notorious were Khun Sa, Lo Hsing-han and Lin Ming-xian. By agreeing to stop the fighting and allowing the drug barons to operate unmolested, even providing protection for the trafficking routes, the SLORC could launder the drug money into businesses in Rangoon. This *quid pro quo* was most satisfactory to the dictators and druglords.

The generals abandoned their policy of disallowing bank deposits that were considered to be of dubious origin. Instead, they simply levied a tax on funds entering the country. As a result, money from the drug sales that had been deposited in safe havens outside Burma came flooding back. One of the main players in the game was Lo Hsing-han, who had upgraded his position from insurgent warlord to that of adviser to the SLORC's chief, General Khin Nyunt. In the boardrooms of downtown Rangoon, Lo directed his corporate empire through his flagship company, Asia World.

Companies threw caution to the wind and started investing in the country's ramshackle economy. Again, one of the first in line was the Singapore Government, which has since poured in more than one billion dollars. Some of the cash found its way into the Myanmar Fund, an investment fund set up to finance business projects. A couple of these businesses involved Lo Hsing-han's Asia World. In 1996 the Australia television network, the Special Broadcasting Service, exposed this relationship. The Singapore Government, feigning hurt, howled in protest. Invited by the station to tell their side of the story, both Singapore's High Commissioner to Australia and the Prime Minister himself declined. In the United States, the State Department then said that 'over half [of the investments in Burma] from Singapore have been tied to the family of narco-trafficker Lo Hsing-han.' In Singapore, there was silence.

Lo Hsing-han's son, Steven Law, banned from entering the United States for suspected drug activities, freely conducts his father's business in Singapore through Asia World. He is married to a Singaporean. The extravagant wedding in Rangoon was attended by eight Burmese cabinet ministers and Singapore's ambassador to Burma. Steven Law and the Singapore Government were publicly toasted by a Burmese minister as partners 'without whose support and encouragement, there would be very few Singaporean businessmen in our country.'

Singapore's premier Goh Chok Tong has repeatedly stonewalled questions about his Government's involvement with the 'King of the Golden Triangle'. Obviously stung by the barrage of criticism, the Government quietly announced in August 1997 that 'a majority of the shareholders voted in favour of winding up the Myanmar Fund.' Singapore's ruling People's Action Party, however, continues its 'even tenor' in relations with the SLORC, blithely ignoring its connections with the drug trade.

Principles, it is said, are easy to fight for but a real pain to live with. The Singaporean regime executes dope-runners found with no more than 15 grams of heroin. In recent years an average of one trafficker per week has been hanged. 'It's ridiculous that the small fry are executed while the [Singapore] Government goes about its business with the big fish,' said the exiled Burmese Prime Minister Sein Win.

Remember Us

The engine of her white Toyota started as three good sized men (smartly clad in their *longyis* with the NLD's badge of a fighting peacock proudly pinned on the left side of their orange tunics) stood up to escort their Secretary General home.

She pulled a small case out of her bag. After quickly powdering her face, she straightened up to say goodbye. 'One day when all this is over, we must get together and have a party to just have fun and not talk about politics at all,' she laughed.

'Yes, we must,' I replied. 'And when Burma democratises, don't forget about us in Singapore.'

She laughed heartily: 'No, we won't forget our friends. But for now, please remember us.'

We will, I thought to myself, as she got into the car flanked by her bodyguards. As it drove off, I couldn't help but feel that dark as the days are now, Burma's future was pregnant with hope.

Months later on 24 July 1998, Aung San Suu Kyi decided to take a trip to the countryside to meet with her NLD colleagues and supporters. Along the way, her car was stopped by the military. A stand-off ensued when she refused to turn back and the soldiers refused to let her proceed. The soldiers then carried her car to a disused bridge, away from the cool shelter of the trees. Twice, her driver drove the car back under the shade. Twice, the soldiers carried it back onto the bridge.

A woman from a nearby village brought a plate of food to the car and was beaten up by the soldiers for her effort. The army refused to allow any food and water to be brought to Suu Kyi and her colleagues, and after a few days, their supplies ran out.

When an officer approached her car, she wound up the window and refused to talk to him. The officer returned the greeting by kicking the vehicle. After four days without food and water, she became increasingly weak and had to lie on the back seat, covering herself with damp cloth to cool down. She was running a fever of 104.

One night, a burly officer opened the car door and forced her to sit up. Two policewomen got into the car and sandwiched her in middle. Another soldier got into the driver's seat and drove her back to her house. Along the way, 200 security agents lined the route, which was cleared of all traffic and in darkness with the streetlights switched off.

A couple of weeks later when she recovered, Aung San Suu Kyi got into her car to make a similar trip. A little distance from her house, she alighted and switched to a van. The Toyota TownAce was better equipped with food and supplies, including bedding, insect repellent and travel Scrabble. Again, the military stopped her vehicle half-way. Again an impasse followed. By this time, international concern was mounting, which the junta tried to placate by describing the situation as a 'camping holiday to the picturesque village on Anyarsu'. To make their description more believable, the authorities ordered a plastic picnic table to be placed near the van and a fresh flower to be put on it every day. Behind the props, however, Michael Jackson's 'Beat It' and Madonna's 'Material Girl' were blasted over speakers by day and Buddhist sermons by night. 'They have no idea of my taste [for music]' the NLD leader said later.

Days into the stalemate, her doctors told her that she was suffering from jaundice, kidney problems and low blood pressure, and persuaded her to return home. After almost two weeks, she agreed to end the stand-off.

The plane cleared the runway and the captain turned off the seatbelt sign. I loosened my tie and slipped the negatives out from under my collar. My neighbour looked at me and smiled politely. He had been standing in front of me when the agent on the ground kept taking photographs of me. I smiled back, too tired to explain the day's events.

After Aung San Suu Kyi left the meeting place, the lights flickered back on and things returned to as normal as the security agents allowed them to be. Seeing us emerge, the intelligence agents scurried into their hideout. One reappeared with a camera. Ignoring him, we made our way to the main road to catch a cab. The agent sputtered past us on his little scooter, pulled out his camera and started shooting again. I hauled out my lilliputian Olympus autofocus and returned the compliment. It was an unusual scene—both us standing on opposite sides of the road with him taking photographs of me taking photographs of him. Satisfied that he got his shots and I mine, I waved goodbye and we parted company.

My contact and I took separate taxis, just in case the agents decided to follow us. I told the driver to take me to the Bogyoke Aung San market in the heart of Rangoon. There I darted in and out of clusters of stalls hawking all manner of goods, looking for something to eat.

'No FEC,' said the shop woman.

'But that's all I have,' I replied, trying to pay for my lunch of noodles in piquant coconut curry.

'Kyat or dollar, no FEC,' the proprietor insisted.

Looking at the currency, my mind went back to the airport exchange counter and I muttered something about being ripped off by the regime.

'What?' the lady asked.

'Nothing. I'll come back, I need to change the FECs.'

I saw a shingle: 'Money Changer, Government Approved.' I asked if she accepted FECs.

'One dollar, one FEC,' she answered.

'Okay, what about kyats?'

'Hmmm...190,' she offered.

I attempted to negotiate but was swiftly crushed.

'Today, not possible. Best is 190 kyats, okay?' She was a fortress.

At least it was better than the junta's makebelieve official rate of six kyats to a dollar. (Months later, the rate had fallen to 320 kyats to the dollar).

As I wandered down the street, hawkers were everywhere, peddling anything from trinkets to half-used plastic cigarette lighters. Some older men were walking amidst the traffic selling newspapers, all in Burmese except one: it was *Newsweek*, with a sullen looking Bill Clinton illustrating a story about Monica Lewinsky.

Further down the road, a red billboard in English caught my eye:

People's Desire:

1. Oppose those relying on external elements acting as stooges holding negative views.

2. Oppose those trying to jeopardise stability of the State and progress of the nation.

3. Oppose foreign nations interfering in internal affairs of the State.

4. Crush all internal and external destructive elements as the common enemy.

When Ne Win first introduced his 'Burmese Way To Socialism', he obviously felt that the most effective method of introducing the concept to his countrymen was by sticking 'People' in front of everything. The city landscape is peppered with signs ranging from the patriotic 'People's Police Force' to the less stately 'People's Pride Hairdressing Saloon (sic)' to the unfortunate 'People's Toilet Industries'. In this socialistic ambience, the 'People's Desire' seemed to fit in nicely.

As I turned the corner, suddenly, from out of the squalor, there appeared a huge marble building. It was the Traders' Hotel, one of the very few luxury hotels in Burma. Sharply dressed doorboys snapped to attention, opened the heavy-set glass door and ushered me into the air-conditioned coolness. Thick, lush carpets, winsome lighting, mellifluous music, immoderate archways—everything was designed to caress.

But this hotel was different; it had a strange feel to it, unlike other hotels of its kind. Something was missing—people. The lobby was deserted and except for two men who were polishing the gold plated doorknobs of the toilet door and the lone waiter in the lounge tending to his lone customer sipping a colourful concoction, the place seemed like an elegantly furbished museum, an unaffordable ornament.

I approached the reception counter and was pleasantly greeted by a demure woman. When I enquired about the room rates she pulled out a pamphlet even before I could finish my question. 'We're giving a 30% discount on our rooms,' she enthused. Aung San Suu Kyi had mentioned to me that this was the tourist season in Burma. Yes, the season was here, all it needed now was the tourists.

My experience in the hotel where I stayed was just as instructive. Youthful employees were assigned to every floor, but their tasks were unclear—especially for the one who sat facing the elevator, agonisingly propping up his head whenever guests arrived, only to let gravity pull it back to the comics on his lap as soon as they filed past.

Checking into my room, one bellboy carried my bag, another poured a glass of water, one more turned on the bathroom light, a fourth adjusted the bedspread, a fifth held open the door for the first four, and all waited for a tip.

On the final day of my stay, I enquired about the late checkout as my flight was in the evening. 'What time do you want to check out, sir?'

'My flight isn't till eight tonight,' I said.

'You can checkout any time.'

The words were like pearls to a tired traveller. Still, one wonders about the viability of such munificence.

That evening I learned that my contact was also in the hotel. His itinerary had been a little less settled than mine. After we left our meeting with Aung San Suu Kyi, a man on a scooter had tailed him and he had weaved around the streets of Rangoon trying to elude his over-mindful attendant who was equal to the legerdemain. Exhausted, he finally made his way to the hotel and parked himself in the lounge. His minder duly followed and waited in the lobby. After a couple of hours, the agent suddenly got up and decided to leave. It was dinner time.

Next day I made my way to the airport, where officials had the habit of patting down Aung San Suu Kyi's guests before they were allowed to board the plane. I didn't want to lose the roll of film that I had taken during my visit, so before leaving the hotel I had it processed, then discarded the prints and hid the negatives. The strip of film fitted almost perfectly under my collar; the tie kept it in place.

'Do I look all right?' I asked the taxi driver.

'Yes, you look very nice,' he replied graciously.

Satisfied that I didn't appear too odd, I eased back into the seat.

Suddenly an outrider stopped the traffic. For a few moments, nothing seemed to be happening and I became increasingly tense. A convoy of cars zipped past, trailed by an ostentatious limousine.

'General Than Shwe, he's going home. Do you know who he is?' the cabbie asked.

'Yes, I do,' I answered. 'He's a very powerful man, is he not?'

He turned to me and smiled, then turned away and left my question hanging limply.

A little later, he gestured with his hand. 'That's the university.'

'Rangoon University?'

'Yes.'

The campus looked dilapidated and the weeds seemed the only sign of life there. The whole place was deserted.

'I studied botany before,' he said, brightening up a little. 'But now all the universities are closed.'

'Did you graduate?'

'No,' he said. 'But no difference.'

I cleared immigration uneventfully although a sprightly lady came bounding up as I was making my way to the terminal and asked me which hotel I had stayed in. It was the first time in all my travelling that I have been asked that question by immigration officials. The other place that shows such healthy curiosity about my movement is, of course, my home town of Singapore, where the PAP Government prefers to know which flights I take.

While I was waiting to board the aircraft, another *longyi*-clad, camera toting man appeared. He mingled amongst the passengers as nonchalantly as his dead giveaway subterfuge could muster. Whenever he thought I wasn't looking, he would shyly snap a shot, then disappear and a few minutes later pop up somewhere else.

Just as I was about to step into the bus which would take us to the plane, my rabbit-like photographer popped up again and took a few more shots; by now he had lost his coyness. When I started climbing up the ramp, there he was again, frenetically capturing my profile for intelligence posterity. Other passengers were looked bewildered and somewhat irritated.

As the plane made its way back to Bangkok, my mind returned to my botany trained taxi driver. In that short space of a cab ride, I learned a lot about Burma. It wasn't exactly a rambling conversation, but it wasn't what he said that struck me, it was the words that were left unspoken—a spirit left dangling in half-sentence, waiting for another era, another society. In the meantime Burma, savaged to its knees, continues to drag itself through agony and exploitation.

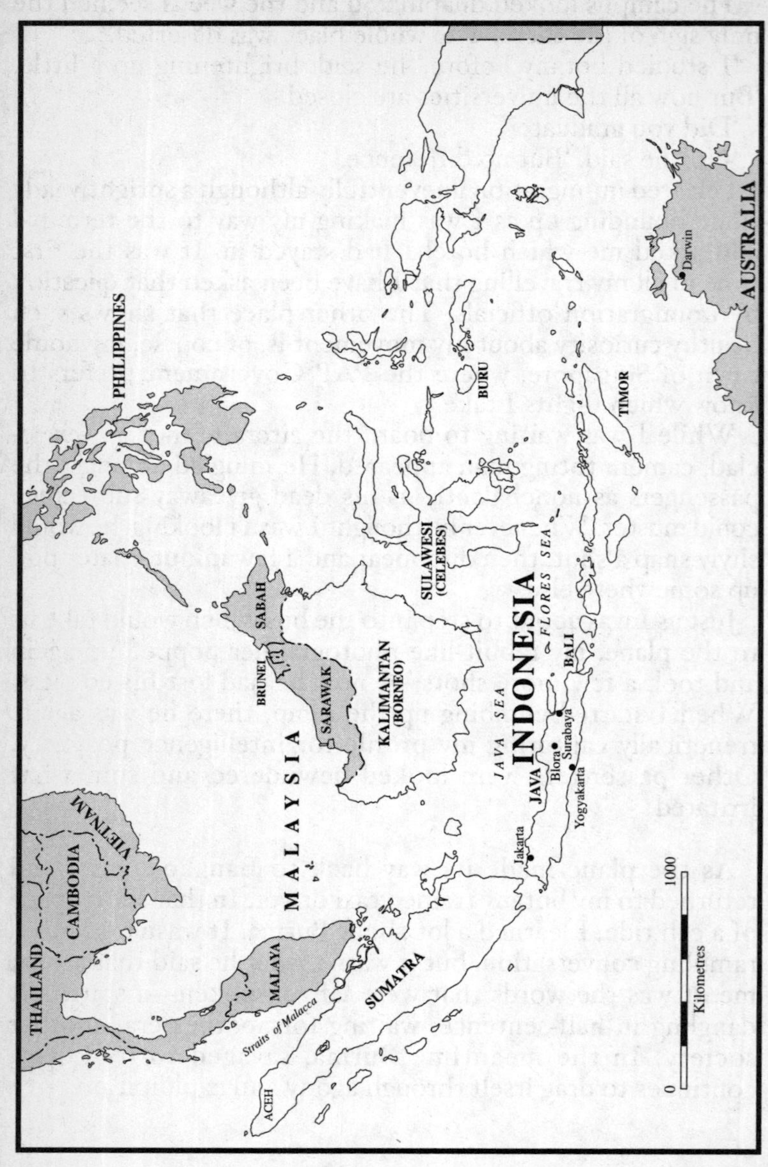
THAILAND
CAMBODIA
VIETNAM
MALAYA
M A L A Y S I A
Straits of Malacca
SUMATRA
ACEH
SARAWAK
BRUNEI
SABAH
KALIMANTAN
(BORNEO)
PHILIPPINES
SULAWESI
(CELEBES)
J A V A   S E A
INDONESIA
F L O R E S   S E A
Jakarta
JAVA
Blora
Surabaya
Yogyakarta
BALI
BURU
TIMOR
Darwin
AUSTRALIA
0
1000
Kilometres

3
Indonesia

Pramoedya Ananta Toer

Crocodile Hole

In the mid-1960s, Indonesia's political landscape was given such a tremendous jolt that powerful institutions were sent sprawling in its aftermath. The upheaval came in the form of a military putsch, an event so laden with conflicting circumstances and evidence that there is still no consensus as to its purpose and its primary movers.

It all started on 1 October 1965. Lieutenant-General Achmad Yani was asleep in his house when a band of soldiers entered through the front gate, overpowering his bodyguards. Yani heard the commotion and went to the living room where a sergeant confronted him with the news that President Sukarno wanted to see him urgently. Yani replied that he needed to put on his uniform first. The sergeant curtly said that this was not necessary, whereupon the Lieutenant-General shouted at his subordinate for being so insolent. That set up just the right mood for an ugly brawl. Yani not only out-ranked his opponent but out-slugged him as well, knocking the sergeant unconscious.

The General then turned to go back to his room when another soldier opened fire with his automatic rifle. Yani was cut down by the bullets but managed to stay alive. His children quickly ran to his side but were prevented from helping their father. The soldiers dragged his limp body and dumped it on the back of a lorry.

Meanwhile, soldiers also forced their way past the guards at another general's house, encircling it to prevent anyone from escaping. General Nasution was in bed with his wife when he heard the noises outside. When his wife got up to investigate, she saw a rifle barrel staring unsympathetically at her, and slammed the door shut. When Nasution did the same, the soldier ripped the door with a barrage of ballistic invective. The couple dropped to the floor, scurrying out of the room via another exit. Mrs Nasution told her husband to make a run for it as it was he whom the soldiers were after. In pitch darkness, he ran across the garden under a storm of gunfire and managed to scramble over the neighbouring Iraqi ambassador's fence to meet death another time. His five-year-old daughter was not as lucky, dying from three shots in her back.

Five other military generals were similarly targeted in the daring raids staged that night. All except Nasution, were taken to an air base at Halim on the outskirts of Jakarta. Those still alive were killed; the bodies were dumped into a well called *Lubang Buaya*, or Crocodile Hole, followed by a lot of cement. While some rebel units were carrying out these attacks, others had taken up positions surrounding the national radio station and the communications centre in Jakarta. Soldiers also stationed themselves close to the Presidential Palace. Led by Lieutenant-Colonel Untung, the operation was joined by 3,000 men from regiments in Central and East Java.

At dawn, Radio Indonesia announced that soldiers loyal to President Sukarno had smashed a conspiracy by several generals who had been plotting to stage a coup d'état with the aid of the United States Central Intelligence Agency. The broadcast also declared that the operation, code-named *Gerakan 30 September* (30 September Movement) or the G30S, had succeeded in saving the life of the President. The generals, it was claimed, had become corrupt and lived a lascivious life which the Indonesian people could not condone, and had thus been arrested. That they were lying lifeless in a well beneath hardened concrete seemed like one of those niggly little details that were better left unmentioned.

But reality and rhetoric make for unholy matrimony. That same day, the station, now completely in the hands of the 'counter-rebellion' forces, announced that the leaders of the G30S had appointed the Revolutionary Council of Indonesia to take over 'all the authority of the state'. Untung was named the Council's Chairman, and the President's cabinet was summarily dismissed. The only trouble was that Sukarno, whom the rebels claimed to be protecting, was not mentioned at all in the rambling proclamation. More niggly little details.

The rebellion was startling not only for its sheer audacity but also for the men who led the assault. Untung, an officer celebrated neither for his intellect nor influence, coordinated the operation so unlieutenant-colonelly that it was a wonder the coup lasted for as long as it did—a whole 24 hours. It ended in the hands of another general who would later rise to become President himself. Major-General Suharto was not on the hit list of the rebel forces, which itself seemed odd. Suharto was a powerful figure in the military and, by virtue of the cardinal role of the army in Indonesian politics, in the Government's hierarchy as well. He was seen by some to be more consequential than the other generals who had been murdered. Yet, the G30S had not targeted him.

Suharto was in charge of the *Komando Strategis Angatan Darat* (Kostrad), the Strategic Reserve Command, which was set-up to engage in confrontation with Malaysia. When he learned of the coup, he and Kostrad officers directly under his command, managed to round up troops loyal to him. By late afternoon Suharto, with Nasution, had commando, tank and armoured divisions ready to strike at the troops involved in the coup attempt. When he was ready, the Major-General sent an unambiguous message to the rebel camp: surrender or face annihilation. The G30S leaders promptly surrendered. By 7 p.m. Suharto had recaptured the radio station and the communications building. Jakarta was now under his command.

Following the surrender of the rebel troops, attention was suddenly turned to the *Partai Kommunis Indonesia* (Indonesian Communist Party, or PKI), which was accused by the army of masterminding Untung's plot to capture power. Untung was later tried and executed for his role. With victory in its hands, the military even ventured to suggest that President Sukarno himself may have been linked with the rebel movement, which to observers seemed a distinct possibility.

Meanwhile, Suharto and the conservative right were bent on wiping out the PKI and the socialist wrong which included Sukarno. The only problem was that Sukarno, or Bung

(Brother) Karno as he is often addressed, still enjoyed immense popularity; to move against him would in all likelihood plunge the country into civil war. The military resorted to a murderous campaign against Sukarno and the PKI. In the process, the political environment was destabilised and hundreds of thousands of people became targets of rampaging mobs, requiring the police to intervene and make massive arrests of, strangely, the victims, including Pramoedya Ananta Toer.

Romance with the typewriter

The fourth most populous country on earth, Indonesia, like a dismembered crib, cradles Southeast Asia with its archipelago of almost 1,400 islands. The influence of a mixture of Asian religions on the already spiritually oriented people, especially in Java, has created a culture steeped in mysticism. With the advent of Hinduism in Java and Sumatra, early tribal leaders claimed divinity to legitimise their rule. Often seen as descendants of Vishnu, the Hindu god-warrior, these leaders pursued the occult to give their reign an air of mythical grandeur. Such was the influence of the Asian subcontinent that even the name Indonesia is a derivation of 'Islands of India'.

Buddhism later made its way to Java where, like its predecessor, it was absorbed into the culture of the ethnic groups. Borobudur, a breathtaking 150-feet monument containing 400 statues and countless sculptures depicting the life of Buddha, stands just outside Jogjakarta in Central Java as testimony to the scale of Buddhist influence.

Islam was later added to this complex merging of religions, gaining wide acceptance among the indigenous people. Instead of replacing the mixture of Hinduism and the more animistic Javanese religions and traditions, the Shariah laws governing Muslim behaviour could only be superimposed on the existing religious practices.

It is from this amalgam of religious faiths that present-day Javanese culture has evolved. And it is from this culture that Pramoedya Ananta Toer emerged. Pramoedya's personality defies categorisation. He exudes expansiveness and yet is painfully timid; he is fiercely loyal to his culture but is determined to transform it; his liberal view of things political

Shih Ming-teh's wanted poster.
Courtesy New Taiwan Foundation

Shih Ming-teh with his daughter at Taidong Hospital, 1968.

Courtesy New Taiwan Foundation

Shih Ming-teh (second from right) with government officials during his hunger strike at the General Military Hospital.

Courtesy New Taiwan Foundation

Lin Yi-hsiung with his mother, wife and daughters.

Courtesy Chilin Foundation

The first public demonstration by dangwai, 1979.

Courtesy New Taiwan Foundation

Shih Ming-teh, Lin Yi-hsiung and Hsu Hsin-liang at a demonstration for direct presidential election.

Courtesy Chilin Foundation

Cheng Nan-rong, editor of the Freedom Times (inset), and the charred remains of his body, 1989.

Courtesy Cheng Nan-rong Foundation

Aung San with daugther Aung San Suu Kyi and sons Aung San Oo and Aung San Lin.

Courtesy Leslie Kean

Student protestor shot by the army, Burma 1988.

Student protestor kissing the boot of a soldier, Burma 1988.
Courtesy Ryo Takeda

Aung San Suu Kyi addressing supporters outside her house. Beside her are Tin Oo (left) and Kyi Maung (right).

Courtesy Leslie Kean

Aung San Suu Kyi with the author, 1998.

DDSI agent taking a photograph of the author after his meeting with Aung San Suu Kyi, 1998.

Burmese girls working as builders labourers, 1998.

blends effortlessly into his traditional outlook. Because (some would say in spite) of his idiosyncrasies, Pramoedya has earned himself the distinction of being Indonesia's finest writer.

Born in Blora, East Java, 6 February 1925, Pramoedya was the oldest of nine children. He was enrolled in a private school called *Budi Utomo*, or Noble Endeavour, which was set up by a group of reform-minded nationalists who wanted to wrest control of Indonesia from their Dutch overlords. As a student, Pramoedya was not academically or physically gifted. He grew up taking a rather cynical view of himself and the world around him, and his impoverished environment helped little.

His father, principal of the Budi Utomo School, helped even less. After completing his seven years of elementary school in ten, Pramoedya told his father he wanted to continue his education. 'Dumb kid, go back to elementary school!' his father scolded.

'I took my books and ran into the cemetery which lay between the school and home,' Pramoedya recounted. 'There was a castor bean tree there, and I grabbed hold of it and screamed. Even now when I am reminded of that, my eyes still get teary.'

Pramoedya eventually made it to a secondary school in the nearby city of Surabaya. As his family was not able to afford the expenses, Pramoedya would get up at 5 a.m. and go down to the padi fields to buy grain that had just been harvested so that he could sell it again when planting time came. The small profit enabled him to pay for his books and clothing; just before he left for Surabaya, he bought himself his first pair of shoes.

In 1942, before he could complete his schooling, the Japanese invaded Java in 1942. The Dutch started drafting young males to fight in their army. Refusing to die for the whites fighting the yellows in his country where neither was welcomed, Pramoedya left Surabaya and headed for home in Blora.

Out of school, Pramoedya had to fend for his family again. His father had lost his job when the school was disbanded. His mother died a few months later after giving birth to her ninth child, and Pramoedya left for Jakarta where he stayed with his uncle. There, Pramoedya was introduced to a typewriter. The acquaintance quickly developed into a love affair which survived the cataclysms of almost 50 years of political turbulence. It allowed the world to peer into the power and elegance of his universe of words. It also brought 14 years of imprisonment.

'The Japanese Are Your Elder Brothers,' an anthropologically incorrect banner taught, fluttering behind the triumphant Japanese flags fixed atop an endless column of invading trucks. At first, the locals greeted their new lords as liberators coming to save them from Western enslavement. But they quickly found out that welcomes, like milk, don't last very long under the Rising Sun.

The Dutch called the country the 'Netherlands East Indies' but it reverted to 'Indonesia' during Japanese rule. The Japanese, as in all the other conquered territories, treated their subjects with unsurpassed depravity.

Pramoedya sought the shelter of the printed page and got a job as a typist in the Domei News Java Service, which afforded him the luxury of being able to sit behind books rather than bars. In the museum library where he spent most of his spare time, he heard the clanking of chains and the groans of people being tortured by the *Kempetei* police headquarters next door. Every now and then an exhausted moan would waft through: 'Have mercy, sir!'

With the paltry salary he earned, Pramoedya was able to feed himself. He even saved enough to buy himself a set of dictionaries, something he had looked forward to all his life. 'I had to add to the sum some of the money I had received from selling my late mother's ring,' he later wrote. 'But walking home that day with those beautiful dictionaries in my arms, I felt like the smartest, most important fellow in the world.'

Just days following the Japanese surrender in August 1945, Sukarno declared Indonesia an independent state. This was followed by four years of bitter conflict between the nationalists and the colonialists. Pramoedya seized the opportunity and joined the newly formed revolutionary army. Within a year he attained the rank of a lieutenant. On 21 July 1947 he was arrested by the Dutch military for taking part in the resistance movement and put in Bukit Duri Prison.

While in prison, Pramoedya composed his first novel, *The Fugitive*. A fiery moral tale about a young patriot who returns to his birthplace after a long struggle with the Japanese occupiers, the story deals with the indignation of a subjugated man and his vengeful response to foreign powers who would humiliate him in his own homeland. Tragically, it ends with the betrayal of the protagonist by his girlfriend's father. The novel, which he wrote in one week using his bed as a desk, reflected much of Pramoedya's own angst during that period. At night, when lights were out, he crawled underneath his bunk and did his writing on the floor with a little lantern for company. Pramoedya also wrote several short stories; the manuscripts were smuggled out of prison by, ironically, a Dutch academic who saw to their translation and publication in Dutch journals and magazines. He remained in prison until the Dutch conceded power in 1949.

Prison had failed to arrest Pramoedya's spirit. 'I had confidence,' he would later remark, 'I was a young nationalist, twenty-four years of age, whose works were beginning to circulate in the free world...I saw myself as having boundless energy to write. I could release, through writing, the pressure of my soul's upheavals, the personal suppression, the unspoken pain, and the uncharted dreams my lack of self-worth had not permitted me to follow.'

Pramoedya witnessed the full glory of the birth of the new nation when the Dutch left. Tens of thousands of people had gathered outside the Gambir Palace (later renamed Istana Merdeka or Freedom Palace) to watch the Dutch national flag lowered for the final time and the hoisting of the Red and White over the sovereign soil of Indonesia.

After the euphoria of the hand-over subsided, Indonesia found that its problems did not leave with the Dutch. The hastily constructed Government was in shambles, unable to provide service and leadership to a nation of over 150 million people. Political splinter groups popped up all over the archipelago and threatened to pull the nation asunder. The economy was rudderless and its currency in a nosedive. Worst of all, the people themselves remained indifferent to the problems. Pramoedya lamented that the 'native' character, so often ridiculed by their former masters, now appeared at its worst.

At a personal level Pramoedya's marriage—he had married soon after he was released from Bukit Duri Prison—also took a turn for the worse. He was unable to find a job that paid enough to make a decent living. Besides, writing had become so critical in his life that he couldn't do anything else. The articles he sold were no longer making enough money. His solution was to increase the output of his work, which did nothing for its quality. 'Pram, you're not writing anymore; you're shitting!' lamented a friend. The financial situation did not improve and his writing got from bad to dysenteric.

Pramoedya's second daughter was born in 1953, the year that he received an invitation by a Dutch cultural foundation to spend 12 months' sabbatical in the Netherlands. He decided to leave with his family for Europe. The respite helped to relieve the nerves jangled raw between him and his wife through the months of poverty.

When they returned to Indonesia the following year, the old problems resurfaced. Income from his writing proved to be more elusive than ever. It seemed like a two-way race to the bottom between his financial and physical health, with his weight down to a miserable 49 kilograms. And he was not even 30 years old. Matters deteriorated to a point where his wife, pregnant with their third child, insisted on a divorce. Beggars can't be choosers and Pramoedya, feeling very inexpensive, went to his father-in-law to officially call off the marriage.

Distraught and in tears, he said, 'Today, I return to you your daughter. Forgive me for being unable to be your daughter's husband.'

'What about the children?'

'Your daughter will not allow me to take them.'

Just before he left, his ex-wife called out, 'You're never going to find another woman who can take care of you for five years!'

But he did. In 1955 Pramoedya married Maimunah Thamrin who remained with him through the years of debilitating poverty and political imprisonment. She bore him another six children and has remained with him.

Killing the left

Through the 1950s, President Sukarno was largely recognised as the only person skilful enough to keep Indonesia together as it fumbled its way into the post-colonial era. Bung Karno was variously described as an a demagogue, despot, father of the nation, Japanese collaborator, great revolutionary and a dirty, rotten hero, depending on where the beholder sat on the political spectrum.

His gift of oratory was unexcelled among his peers. Whenever he got up on stage in front of hundreds of thousands of people, he spoke with such élan that he could evoke tears of patriotism and screams of fervour from his listeners at will. He seduced the uneducated masses and waxed rhapsodic by invoking images of the epic battles of the *Mahabharata* and the *Ramayana* that the people knew through the *wayang kulit* (shadow-puppet theatre).

The play, accompanied by *gamelan* music from a small ensemble of gongs and cymbals, is narrated by a *dalang*, or puppeteer, who also lends voice to the characters. Likening himself to the great warrior in the stories who heroically overcomes his enemies, the Bung, like a starry eyed military general infatuated with the mirror, often cast himself as the Great Leader of the Revolution, part-god, part-man. His penchant for the parallels would later prove uncannily real when he was made to mouth the words of his *dalang*-general.

Behind the scenes Sukarno had to perform more like a tightrope walker than a battlefield general. Two major political forces had emerged: the *Partai Nasional Indonesia* (PNI) and the PKI whose socialist principles the President increasingly showed affinity to. As the economy continued its downward spiral and poverty entrenched itself, communism gradually gained greater favour with the masses. The PKI grew in strength, claiming at least three million members at its peak which made it the third largest communist party in the world. It won three seats in parliament in the 1955 elections.

The increasing popularity of the PKI was watched closely not only by the PNI and the right-wing military, but also by the Americans and British. Sukarno's bitter experience with the Netherlands had led him to see the world locked in a bipolar struggle: the industrialised Western powers on the one side and Third World nations on the other.

It was at this time that Sukarno found a natural ally in China. Exchanges between the two governments increased, with Sukarno visiting China in April 1965. But with the Americans in full battle cry against communism, it was only a matter of time before this alliance was smashed. In addition, the British were trying to contain the tense political situation in Malaysia and Singapore. With the Great Leader of the Revolution stoking the fires of nationalism from across the narrow Straits of Malacca, it would not have been a moment too soon for London if Sukarno just upped and disappeared.

Hostility begets suspicion begets a manic Bung. Suspecting that the British were involved in plotting for his political demise and planning to use military bases in Malaysia to launch strikes against Indonesia, Sukarno connived in 1963 to launch his own offensive against his neighbours in the form of *konfrontasi*, or confrontation, where youths were recruited for training at the Halim air base for combat in Malaysia. The British maintained that the confrontation was nothing more than political histrionics designed by an increasingly irrational dictator to distract attention. Both sides were, as usual, probably right.

The British embassy in Jakarta had come under siege, with protesters harassing its diplomats and raiding their homes. Weeks later Sukarno broke off diplomatic relations with London. The rage spread to include the Americans, who were also seen as part of Western imperialism. When the United Nations admitted Malaysia into its Security Council in 1965, Indonesia stormed out, with China's encouragement.

With Jakarta's opinion of the West growing increasingly dim (and vice versa), capitalism also came to be seen by the Indonesian people as a scourge. Army generals who had all along maintained a 'bourgeois' lifestyle came under attack. Sukarno was busily painting a portrait of his own regional power play and didn't stop until he painted himself into a corner. All the manoeuvring came to a head on 1 October 1965, when Untung launched his clumsy coup.

Immediately after the Crocodile Hole killings and the subsequent suppression of Untung's military adventure, Suharto blamed the communists for the insurrection. Right-wing army generals sounded the clarion call and the national bloodbath began. General Nasution, who had lost his daughter during raid on his house, led the way: 'They must be smashed immediately...they must be destroyed.'

The PKI headquarters in Jakarta was an early target for raging mobs. Armed with pistols, machetes and wooden staves, angry hordes of students destroyed everything in sight while police officers and firemen looked on. PKI members were singled out and taken to detention centres set up all over the country. Thousands died at the hands of their interrogators. As membership of the PKI cut across all segments of society, professors and peasants were persecuted alike.

Kampongs believed to be PKI strongholds were wiped out when soldiers indiscriminately opened fire on villagers, killing unarmed men, women and children. There was so much murdering to do that some troops rounded up anti-communist youths and organisations, trained them over a couple of days, and sent them out with one objective: to locate and kill communists. In Central Java alone, volunteers of the Civil Defence Corps killed over 800 suspected communists by cracking their heads with iron bars at the detention centres. In the armed forces, regiments which had responded to Untung's call to rebel were swiftly crushed. Within a few months, the rabid campaign claimed thousands of lives; with estimates varying between 300,000 and 700,000.

Many observers at that time were convinced that the communists were staging an uprising to overthrow Sukarno and establish a communist state. But the President had all along been drifting towards the left and making headway with his northern counterparts in China. It was the PKI that had everything to lose by removing Sukarno as head of state. Besides, the communists were gradually gaining momentum without having to resort to an armed confrontation which they knew they would lose.

This, however, did not rule out the fact that the PKI could have initiated the coup. It is entirely conceivable that the communists were so solicitous about the military taking over the Government after the demise of Sukarno, who was at that time not in the best of health, that they sought to eliminate the generals before the President passed away.

Sukarno himself was not cleared of complicity in the 30 September Movement. Even after the radio announcement was made about the 'arrest' of the six generals on 1 October, the Bung did not condemn it. In fact, it was a full two days after the putsch began that the President addressed the nation. Even then, he hemmed and hawed his way through and characteristically said much about nothing.

Some analysts believe, however, that the incident was not communist-inspired. The CIA, they claimed, had participated, or at least encouraged, the coup. With Sukarno making overtures to Beijing and spewing anti-Western propaganda, it would have indeed been remarkable if the United States was not involved in the political sleight to remove Sukarno and the PKI. The questions that remain unanswered seemed to be at what stage did the CIA become involved and how deep was this involvement?

One more piece of the puzzle was the role played by Suharto. The fact that the General was not targeted by Untung and his men led many to suspect that Suharto was involved in the conspiracy. Speculation has it that the General knew about the G30S plan but did not intervene, gently prodding Untung to kidnap the generals and later double-crossing him.

Subsequent hearings and investigations threw up evidence which was often contradictory and unreliable. In the illusory sphere of Indonesian politics where things are often not quite what they seem or seem not quite what they are, any one of the theories described above could have been the real reason behind the coup. No one could say who was the *dalang* and who the *kulit*, no one, that is, except the players themselves who are not talking because they had become either very powerful or very dead.

Whatever the reasons, Sukarno was, for all intents and purposes, rendered ineffectual following the military takeover. With the military now in his firm grasp, Suharto's control of the country had become axiomatic.

Following the 30 September failed coup, Sukarno appointed Major-General Pranoto Reksosamudro as chief of the military. Suharto did not like the dilution of his control of the capital. The up-and-crushing General quickly 'persuaded' the fence-sitters to declare their support for him.

On 23 February 1966, anti-communist students tried to storm the President's office. Sukarno retaliated by banning the student movement and closing down the universities. This only incited the protesters who were now openly calling for his resignation and indictment.

Sukarno was not completely without support, however. Sections of the navy and air force were still loyal to him, as were several community and political leaders. On 10 March the President issued a declaration that the student demonstrations and riots were backed by the CIA, and appealed to his countrymen to stand up to the foreign inspired insurgence. The next day, he called for a meeting of his cabinet to plan retaliatory action. Before the meeting could get under way, Suharto ordered his troops to surround the palace. When news of the siege reached him, Bung Karno made a quick getaway by helicopter to his residence in Bogor. The unseemly exit further signalled his incapacity to match his usurper and, more importantly, disillusioned his already irresolute supporters.

When Sukarno arrived in Bogor, Suharto's men were on hand to greet him, and pressed him to issue a decree transferring control of the Government to Suharto. Without Sukarno's cooperation, Suharto was in danger of a revolt from the sections of the military that were loyal to the President.

The following day, Bung Karno announced that he was directing Suharto to 'take all necessary steps to guarantee security and calm and the stability of the running of the Government and the course of the Revolution...'

After the massacre of anyone and everyone remotely connected with the PKI, there wasn't much left to deal with, but Suharto wanted to make doubly certain that the Party would never again seek power through left-leaning politicians. He turned his attention to the 108 member cabinet. Ministers who were still supportive of Sukarno were all placed under 'protective' custody. Suharto forced the President to reduce the cabinet to 24 members, all of them Suharto minions. Suharto moved to distance Indonesia's relations with China. At the United Nations he negotiated to bring Indonesia back into the international fold.

Even at the very last stages, Sukarno tried to bargain as much as he could for his foundering presidency. He continued to make public statements reproaching his subordinates, especially Suharto. Each time, the General moved decisively to cut off whatever headway his President tried to make.

The demonstrations were by now calling for Sukarno's death. Before an enormous crowd at Merdeka Square on Independence Day in 1966, the President, like the *kulit* in the *wayang*, mouthed almost everything his ventriloquist wanted him to say, including an end to *konfrontasi* with Malaysia and Singapore. To add to the humiliation, Sukarno was compelled to publicly take the blame, though not entirely without basis, for the economic mess that the country was in.

With the conquest, ministers in the Suharto camp boldly announced that President Sukarno no longer spoke for the Indonesian Government. Sensing that his time had come, Suharto insisted that Sukarno step down as President without further delay or conditions. With the Bung nowhere to be seen, the remnants of resistance to Suharto had crumbled.

In March 1967, Suharto was appointed Acting President (and then President one year later) until further elections. He proclaimed his New Order for the Republic, and called for support from his citizens, guaranteeing 'justice, progress and democracy'. He forbade Sukarno from ever engaging in politics again, consigning the broken ex-President to house arrest, where he remained a cipher until his death in 1970.

Please take care of my library

With Bung Karno out of the way, the army closed in on the PKI. One of the targeted groups was Lekra, a left-leaning cultural organisation. Like Sukarno, Pramoedya was not entirely comfortable with the communist ideology, but could see the benefits of the socialist movement. Lekra seemed an appropriate vehicle through which he could add to the already complex political process, and he had been quickly appointed to its higher echelons.

Pramoedya also supported Sukarno. He thought the President was giving fresh impetus to a nation struggling to free itself from the stranglehold of the Western world, but this support was not unqualified. In 1960, he wrote *Hoakiau di Indonesia* (The Chinese in Indonesia), a scathing criticism of the shoddy treatment the Chinese received from the Government when anti-Chinese sentiments ran high during the Cold War. When the words hit print, Pramoedya was arrested and imprisoned from 1960 to 1961. To his mind, however, Sukarno was the only one at that time able to rally the diverse and disparate ethnic groups. Pramoedya later wrote, '[Sukarno] was capable of creating a nation without shedding blood.'

That is a polite reference to Suharto's barbarous rule. Between 1983 and 1984, nearly ten thousand suspected criminals were summarily executed. Usually, a group of four to ten men would barge into the suspects' houses and pump a fusillade of bullets into their target, preferably the head—all in full view of wives, children and neighbours. And if the audience was not big enough, the victims were dragged off and dumped dead in the middle of bus terminals, schools, busy roads, cinemas, and markets. Anyone bold enough to write letters of protest were quickly persuaded to desist when parcels of heads and body parts were delivered to their homes. And when passers-by removed the corpse of a victim dangling outside a shop, the indignant military had them arrested and interrogated.

Having been closely linked with Sukarno and the PKI, Pramoedya knew that it was just a matter of time before the army came for him. In 1965, friends were urging him to run, but Pramoedya was determined to stand his ground: 'Why flee? What should I run away from? Myself? Why? If the attacking mob wants to come here, I will face them alone. My place is here.' Maimunah and the children had in the meantime gone to her parents' house.

Several days passed and there was no sign of the police or thugs. One evening his neighbour, an army lieutenant, started talking very loudly even though his audience was nowhere to be found. He was pacing outside Pramoedya's front gate and shouting that Sukarno was finished and the military had the upper hand. This happened again the following night. Pramoedya had no doubt that he was the target of the remarks. He took the *kretek* cigarette that he was smoking and threw it at his unneighbourly neighbour. It worked, for the broadcast stopped.

The writer then went about his writing; he was working on an encyclopaedia of Indonesian literature and was also studying the teachings of Prophet Muhammad. As he was alone in his house with his younger brother, he would turn off all the lights at night and sit out on the verandah to enjoy the quiet. But he was also waiting.

Then they came. It was 11 p.m., 13 October 1965. A group of men surrounded his house. Pramoedya heard the commotion outside. When he turned on the light in the yard, he spotted a masked man running away. Probably some thief who had just broken into another house, he thought. Seeing that there wasn't anybody around, he turned off the lights. Several men immediately appeared at the front gate. When he turned on the lights again, they ran for cover. Pramoedya went back into the house.

Suddenly, a huge rock crashed through the window and sent glass and furniture flying. More stones and rocks were tossed through the roof, ripping the tiles and ceiling. 'These people are trying to kill me,' his mind screeched. Instinctively, he reached for something to protect himself and grabbed a mop handle. That wasn't going to do the trick. Then he remembered that a friend of his had given him a small samurai knife from a visit to Japan. He grabbed that as well. His brother had slipped out the back and into a neighbour's house. But Pramoedya was not going to back down to these hoodlums. If this was going to be his last day, it was going to be in his own front yard.

'Is this what you call a struggle?' Pramoedya yelled out to his attackers. 'If it's a struggle, I've been struggling since I was young. But this is not the way to do it.'

The stones stopped flying and everything fell quiet. The mobsters were momentarily stunned into silence.

'Get your leader in here! What kind of a struggle is this?' Pramoedya called out.

Then a huge stone smashed through the front door. Pramoedya didn't have time to get out of its way. A sharp pain seared through his leg. His thigh had been hit and blood started to ooze from the gash. He couldn't do anything to the wound because the rocks started raining in again. By now, the besieged writer was hobbling on one leg, still clinging to his stick and knife.

'Where is the gasoline?' came a voice.

'Here, just burn it!' another said.

'Oh, no, please don't burn it,' pleaded a neighbour. 'If you do, my house would also get burned!'

A group of army and police officers came to Pramoedya's rescue. His younger brother also reappeared. During those riotous months, 'rescue' was not rescue. Instead of arresting the thugs who almost killed him, the soldiers came into the house and started admonishing him.

'It is useless to fight the people!' berated the commander.

'They're a mob, not the people!' Pramoedya shot back.

Not interested in starting a debate, the commander said, 'Get ready, *Pak*. Let's get you out of here safely.' (*Pak*, or father, is the honorific term for older men).

Under the circumstances, Pramoedya didn't think it was a bad proposition, but he also knew that he didn't have much of a choice. The rescue was actually a polite arrest. He quickly packed his typewriter and his manuscript, *Gadis Pantai* (Girl of the Coast). Even then he sought to extract some concessions, not for himself but for his manuscripts.

'Do you know who I am?' he asked, more out of concern than vanity.

'Yes, Pak.'

'Please make sure all these papers and my library are safe,' Pramoedya said.

'Yes, yes, I promise,' the commander hurried.

Out in the street, the politeness evaporated. Pramoedya and his brother were led to an empty plot behind his house. As he trudged along, the mob turned out to be larger than it had seemed. They continued to hurl insults at him, and he was a lot more terrified than his facade let on. The thugs wielded spears, krises, machetes and knives. His pole and knife would have been no match for this array of deadly weapons. The police tied Pramoedya's hands behind him, fastened the rope in a noose around his neck, and put him on the back of a truck. He knew that this was what happened to prisoners when they were taken away to be executed. Just as the mob started to close in, the truck moved off. As the vehicle bounced up and down the uneven road, the rope tugged painfully at his neck.

After a short distance, an army corporal came up to him; without a word, he raised his sten gun and brought it down on Pramoedya's face. With his hands tied, there was no way he could avoid the blow. He turned his head and braced himself for the smash. The metallic butt of the rifle met the side of his face, narrowly missing his eye. The force cracked his cheekbone and drew blood. Pramoedya fell on his side. His mouth and eyes could not move from the pain that reverberated through his head. His hands strained on the rope, which was strangling him. He gasped for air. Beside the bloodied figure bound like an animal were his typewriter and his unfinished manuscript. The picture was surreal.

Pramoedya was taken to Kostrad. When they were getting him off the truck, with his whole body covered in blood from the raw wounds on his face and leg, Pramoedya turned to the guard on duty and asked him to safeguard his documents and library. 'The Government can seize them so long as it does not damage them,' he pleaded. Again, the officer assured him that his request would be met. The typewriter and *Gadis Pantai* were taken away and Pramoedya was led into a holding cell. Several other men were lying on the floor and the writer joined them, curling up into ball. The cold hard floor was no comfort but he was too weak to stand.

A corporal then entered the room. He was young and, unlike his colleagues, had an amiable look about him. He started questioning Pramoedya, who thought that the soldier could carry on a civilised conversation, and asked him what his rank was. But one man's interest was another man's insult. The soldier landed a few more blows on the writer and then left as quickly as he had appeared. The brief encounter made absolutely no sense, just a lot more pain.

About two hours later, a truck pulled up. Soldiers carted its contents into the room where Pramoedya was. He recognised to his horror that the objects were from his library—card files, documentary photographs and negatives, 5,000 books and several tons of collected newspapers, the product of 15 years of painstaking work. A newly arrived prisoner told Pramoedya that he had witnessed the soldiers taking all his books and papers away. When they left, a mob started looting his house: 'They even shook the mango tree to get at the fruits. Nothing was left untouched. Your house is now one big empty hole!'

Pramoedya had built the house with his own hands. His father-in-law had given him 20,000 rupiah to buy bricks. It turned out to be a lot of bricks. And so Pramoedya ended up with a beautiful house along a humble street strewn with small huts. After the attack that night, the house was taken over by an army captain, who claimed it as his own and lived there for the next 20 years.

His library was torched. The manuscripts and books, which took years of research and writing, were destroyed. Until then, the police had broken only his bones. Now they were trying to break his spirit as well. A friend later saw typewritten sheets of paper used as fish wrap. They were marked 'Documentation Collection of Pramoedya Ananta Toer'.

Years later, recalling his arrest and the destruction of his house, Pramoedya wrote, 'Now don't think I have vengeful feelings about this. No... The level of the culture and civilisation of our armed forces is rather low and disheartening. We need to elevate them. When uncivilised things are done to you, don't respond in kind by being uncivilised. If you're able, respond with justice...'

That night, the room slowly filled up with *tahanan politik* (political detainees or *tapols*), all suffering one form of injury or another. When day came, more truckloads of prisoners arrived. Men and women were herded into the tiny holding centre. Many of them were roughed up so badly that they lay motionless on the truck deck. The military officers carelessly picked them up and threw them on the ground, breaking more bones. Then a group of reporters was brought in. Their faces were etched in pain, their knees a mangle of gnarled flesh and blood. They had been made to crawl on the gravel road all the way to the detention camp. The number of detainees soon outgrew the room, with many left lying along the hallway which worsened the stench of open wounds and nervous sweat. Groans and moans added to the putrescence.

The soldiers then came for Pramoedya—it was interrogation time. He was led into a dimly lit room and made to sit beside a younger man who was in agony. Looking down, Pramoedya saw that his interrogator, a slim, tall Arab-looking officer, was standing on the *tapol's* feet, grinding his army boots into the prisoner's instep. The man let out a sharp but tired grunt. The whole night, Pramoedya had heard howls coming from this interrogation room. Now he was about to experience it.

Not through with his victim, the soldier then took out a pencil from his trouser pocket and carefully placed it under the man's fingernail. He started pushing the pencil in, separating the nail from the soft flesh beneath. The scream was long and loud. The soldier smiled sadistically and asked, 'What's the matter? Why are you screaming?'

Pramoedya turned away and caught sight of an electric-shock machine standing in the corner. He was already in pain and was made to wait for more. His body tensed up, anticipating the onslaught. Surprisingly, however, the interrogator turned out to be a saint compared to his colleague.

'Why are you so bloody?' he started.

'I fell,' Pramoedya replied, not wanting to antagonise his captors.

'What is your opinion of the Untung movement?' the officer asked.

'I know nothing about it,' said Pramoedya. That was the truth. He had only learned about the Crocodile Hole massacre through the media.

'Do you approve of such a movement?' his questioner continued.

'If I got the chance to study the authentic facts about it, maybe in about five years from now I would be able to answer your question,' Pramoedya parried.

'Are you a member of the PKI?'

Pramoedya hesitated. He remembered a friend who had advised him that if he was asked whether he was a communist or not, the answer had better be 'yes' regardless of fact. Otherwise, the army had its way of extracting a confession. After seeing what had happened to the young man beside him, Pramoedya decided that survival was the better part of valour.

'Yes.'

'Do you believe this country would become communist?' the officer asked, growing increasingly tense.

Pramoedya knew he had to handle the question very carefully. One wrong answer and he could suffer immeasurable pain at the hands of his tormentors.

'Not within forty years,' Pramoedya cautiously answered.

'Why?'

Feeling safer, he replied, 'The geographic factor and Indonesian conservatism.'

He passed the examination; his interrogator moved on to more mundane issues and after some time allowed him to return to the holding room.

After a few weeks the prisoners were transferred to the Guntur Military Police Headquarters where they were registered and stripped of everything they possessed. In the meantime, his brother was released. For the next four years,

Pramoedya and the other *tapols* were taken from one prison to another. Undernourished and suffering from injuries, many died. At one stage, conditions were so abysmal that six people died in a single day.

Welcome to Buru Island

Adri XV, a 300,000 tonne ship, departed on Independence Day, 17 August 1969, bound for the Moluccas. The tired steel creaked as the vessel made its way across the Flores Sea. Deep in her bowels was human cargo—800 *tapols*—all bound for Buru Island. A large cell held the prisoners who had come from different jails throughout the country.

Before they boarded the ship, the *tapols* were made to squat at the wharf. Their hunger was intense. Some of the luckier ones who happened to be placed next to *bluntas* shrubs tore at the leaves and ate them. It didn't matter that the bushes were coated in dust; no one bothered to wash them because getting caught would result in a beating. Another prisoner caught a *cicak* as it was trying to scamper away. He expertly broke off the lizard's toe-pads, squeezed its nape with his thumb and forefinger to remove the contents in its head, and then put the still wriggling reptile into his mouth and swallowed it. Desperate bodies called for desperate eating habits, and the prisoners, craving for protein, ate rats and leeches whenever and wherever they could find them.

On the ship, Pramoedya squatted in one corner of the cell looking gaunt and feeling hungry. He didn't care what lay ahead. Just moving from one island to another was progress. He had to believe that. It was his only hope of keeping his wits about him, of surviving.

Like many of the other *tapols*, he had not eaten for days. His hunger reminded him of the miserable jails in Jakarta where life was one of constant darkness interspersed with moments of hysterical beatings. The guards would often take away the food left for the prisoners by their families. The daily rations amounted to nothing more than rice and watered vegetables that you could hold in your hand. After a year in detention, many of the prisoners weighed no more than 30 kilograms. Their eyes bulged and their skin was cracked and dry, and because their joints were tender, their movements were painfully slow. Dysentery was common, but medical treatment was scarcely available. Many of the *tapols* needed assistance just to get up or lie down and had to lie on the floor covered in their own vomit and excrement. The *ulama*, or Islamic religious leader, would come at the beginning of the fasting month of *Ramadan* and preach the virtues of fasting and controlling one's hunger and other bodily desires. It seemed like a cruel joke. Whenever the chief warrant officer came around, he would remind them: 'The only right you have is to breathe!' He wasn't exaggerating.

Pramoedya was jolted back to the present when he felt something crawl up his leg. It was a cockroach. There were heaps of them flitting all over the cell competing with the *tapols* for space. Meals were reduced to two tiny portions of rice sauteed with water and red chilli. Diarrhoea was a daily occurrence.

One day the small toilet in front of the cell choked causing faecal matter to collect into a huge dungheap. The frantic prisoners tried to clear the cesspool with brooms, pouring bucket after bucket of water into the hole, hoping to wash the horror down the drain which, as abomination would have it, remained hopelessly clogged. As the sea water rushed down from the deck whenever waves hit the side of the vessel, the toilet quickly filled up with a mixture of water and excrement. The prisoners could only look on helplessly as the level of water in the hull rose. Eventually, the contents in the toilet overflowed, flooding the entire cell with the brown liquid.

Along the way, the engine of the ship often ground to a halt. When it did the only sound left was the creaking of the hull and the lapping of water on its side as the crew tried to restart the motor. Some of the detainees prayed that it would sink and let the watery grave bring a welcome end to their tortured bodies. But each time the vessel would choke and gasp feebly back to life and continue the excruciating journey.

A journey by sea would not be complete without music, and this Buru-bound boat was to be no exception. Worn-out *kroncong* songs were played over and over on a worn-out recorder; the melody was morose and the lyrics filled with political and cultural propaganda chastising the listeners for their wrongdoings. Whenever the cycle of songs paused the voice of a religious minister would come on and a prayer for a safe journey to a new life would pervade the stinking cells: 'Good luck in your new life.'

From time to time, the *tapols* would be lectured on the importance of the *Pancasila*, a national moral code originally expounded by Sukarno. The prisoners were repeatedly reviled for their failure to abide by the code's five basic pillars: belief in one God, a just and civilised humanity, Indonesian unity, democracy and social justice.

After ten days at sea, the shoreline of Buru Island appeared in the distance. The iron door swung open and a guard yelled to the prisoners to get out. The stronger *tapols* came out from the cells carrying the weaker ones who had succumbed to disease and malnutrition. As the prisoners stepped out onto the deck, two landing craft came to take them to shore. When all the prisoners were on the quay in the little port of Namlea, a roll call was conducted. Then without warning, the soldiers started to thrust their rifle butts at the prisoners, while others used their fists. 'If you disobey orders, more of this will happen,' warned the head soldier. Welcome to Buru Island.

Meanwhile, the doors of Indonesia's economy had opened to the world's multinational giants. Corrupt Indonesian businessmen with the right connections set up mega-deals with Western corporate bigwigs and were soon rolling in money which seemed to multiply in miraculous fashion. Hotels and holiday resorts of unimaginable splendour, enormous buildings and banks radiating power, and playground-clubs for the rich and powerful sprouted all over Jakarta.

It had been four years since Pramoedya was arrested in 1965, but the end of his ordeal was still nowhere in sight. The Government had still not charged him with any offence. Pramoedya protested, 'How am I supposed to know how long we will be in exile? Until death? Or maybe only until we've reached semi-consciousness? Ask it to those who control the world's capital. Ask it to those who have experienced everything there is to experience, collected all there is to collect and regulated all that there is to regulate.'

'I have nothing against capitalism,' Pramoedya explained to me as we sat in his handsome but modestly furnished living room. 'But capital must be used for the good of all men and not at keeping others under a state of torment.'

Buru Island lies three degrees south of the equator in the South China Sea. To the west is Java, and to the south Darwin, Australia. About the size of Bali, Buru is only sparsely inhabited in small pockets by early Bugis settlers and indigenous tribes people. The island is full of treacherous and mosquito infested swamps. Large unwelcoming forests, and grass rising up above the heads of the prisoners, dominate the landscape.

Male detainees considered 'dangerous' were shipped to Buru. Every prisoner was issued one set of khaki coloured pants and shirt that he would wear for the rest of his existence on the island. No one wore shoes, for none were given. As a result, many of the prisoners had feet swollen from infection from leeches and insects.

The prisoners ranged from the very young, some only in their early teens, to the old. Brian May who visited Buru in 1969 described in his book, *The Indonesian Tragedy*, the concept that lay behind the island prison:

> Experienced farmers and young men were needed to get the settlement under way and to feed those who became too weak or too old to work. When those who were now middle-aged could no longer grow their own food there would be others, at present in their thirties, to look after them. These in their turn could be fed by those now in their twenties. Eventually, the settlement would dwindle to a few old people, rendered harmless and perhaps imbecilic by being cut off from normal human relationships for the greater part of their lives. In the end there would only be the dead.

The penal complex housed a total of 10,000 prisoners who were divided into 33 units, each with its own commander and guards. The units, usually a few kilometres apart, were connected to each other via tracks laid out by the prisoners.

The *tapols* were classified into three categories. Class A prisoners were 'confirmed' communists who would be tried in due course. Class B consisted of intellectuals, artists, academics and scholars suspected of leading the communist movement who, because of insufficient evidence for prosecution, were banished to Buru Island. Class C detainees were believed to be uncommitted ideologues who got caught up in the movement; they were released after relatively short periods of detention.

There was no way out of Buru Island. Even if a prisoner were to break out from the prison compound, the surrounding jungle and the open sea would see to it that he did not live to tell of his escape. In total isolation from the world, the prisoners were condemned to an existence devoid of humanity. When a prisoner was brought to Buru, he had to leave everything behind, including hope.

The small boats moved carefully up the river, hemmed in on both sides by thick undergrowth. Ancient trees with vines for beards stood like guardians along the river bank. Before long the small vessels docked at a rickety wooden platform. 'Get out! From here you walk,' the commander shouted.

The trek into the jungle was arduous. Many of the *tapols* were weak from hunger but still had to carry heavy loads of supplies. Huge tree trunks lay fallen across their paths and the only way round was to crawl underneath them. Razor-sharp thorns tore at bare knees and feet, and the humidity made conditions even more unendurable. Several prisoners fell in exhaustion which only added to the burden of the more able-bodied prisoners who had to carry their fellow travellers as well as their supplies. Those who could not continue were left behind. After a debilitating six hour trek, the prisoners reached a clearing where barracks stood, fenced in by barbed wire. At points on the perimeter, guard posts sprang up in an unsophisticated Orwellian spectre.

Everyone was given an identification number and assigned to a unit. The *tapols* were herded into barracks that were bare except the damp, pounded earth floor and a few trunks propping up a roof pleated from sago palm leaves. The walls consisted of bamboo staves loosely bound by rattan. Straw mats for beds lined the length of the huts with a narrow corridor running down the middle doubling as the dining area. The shacks were hardly able to house all the prisoners but that night nothing mattered to the prisoners. They piled on top of one another, just glad to be able to rest their sore bodies. Mosquito nets made slumber possible.

A few hours later a gong sounded and the guards yelled for everyone to get up before the sun did. As part of the routine, all prisoners had to perform morning exercises. 'Watch me! One! Two! Three! Four!' the strapping soldier called out. His charges looked at him in disbelief. They could hardly hold themselves up let alone bend their bodies to rhythmic counts. One man who didn't have the strength to perform the feat was made to crawl the length of the field and yell 'Exercise is play, exercise is play.' Pramoedya was put in charge of supervising the punishment.

Following callisthenics, the men received their first decent meal since they left the mainland. A handful of rice and dried fish was all they had to eat but again no one complained as they were just happy to be able to eat. Rice and salted fish was all the food they had until they could grow and harvest their crops, which could take several months. A quick calculation of the supplies showed that each prisoner was allowed only 600 grams of rations a day.

The *tapols* were then assigned their first job, clearing the elephant grass so that a road could be constructed. The only problem was that no tools were available. The six foot spine-covered blades lacerated their hands and by the end of the week reduced their palms to a swollen and bloodied mess so that they couldn't even hold food.

Slowly, rations were reduced to 500 grams, and the salted fish eventually disappeared. Again, the prisoners had to resort to eating anything they could catch off the land including rats, snakes and monitor lizards. A few days later some equipment arrived, consisting mainly of small tools such as machetes, hoes, crowbars, saws and axes, which made their work mercifully easier. The prisoners were divided into 18 units that were assigned different tasks: some built roads, others tilled and planted, and the rest hauled supplies.

Under watchful gun barrels, the prisoners laboured from daybreak until nightfall to build homes for themselves, because they no longer had homes on the mainland. Their lives now belonged to the New Order, which determined where they would live, who they would see, what kind of work they would do and how long they would live; the arbiters were young corporals with little or no formal education.

Home for Pramoedya was now in the Wai Apo valley in the northern part of the island. The barren plain was surrounded by hills and the only way out was the river from where the boats came. The loose topsoil and infrequent rains made the conditions even more unsuitable for agriculture. The intense heat during the day would quickly drop to uncomfortably cold levels at night. Insects added to the daily dreariness and malarial mosquitoes worsened the plight of their newly arrived food stock.

With climatic conditions the way they were, how the men were going to grow enough food for themselves was a puzzle. Without farming equipment, they needed a miracle. The miracle did come, however, with the arrival of a new commander, Daeng Masiga, a former adjutant to Sukarno, who, unlike his comrades, showed a spark of humanitarian spirit. Unfortunately, weather conditions were not as sympathetic. The cassava that was planted did not take root and the sugarcane showed no sign of growth, despite being nursed by an inmate who had been in the cane cultivation business back in Java.

The men started to search for seed. They scavenged the fields left behind by the natives of Buru Island, nomadic tribes practising subsistence farming. Their staple was sago, which they harvested from sago palm swamps, with wild boar and deer meat as supplements. As a result, very little was left behind for the prisoners to use. The men turned to the forest in search of more arable soil. They felled trees and burned undergrowth. Just when the situation seemed utterly hopeless, the rains came and gave life to the ground. In the next few days the rice started to grow, which meant that at least there would be no mass starvation.

Since 1950, writing had been the sole source of Pramoedya's income and the only type of work he had been capable of doing. It was his lifeline, both economically and spiritually. While he was imprisoned between 1965 and 1969, his reputation as a writer traversed the archipelago. Before his arrest Pramoedya had already written ten novels, three collections of short stories, three volumes of socio-political analyses (*Socialist Realism and Indonesian Literature*, *The Intellectual Community in the Third World*, *The Chinese in Indonesia*) and 15 translations of classic works into *Bahasa*, including those of Tolstoy, Steinbeck, Shokolov, Pascal, and Gorky. But extensive and intensive as these works were, Pramoedya had yet to write his most outstanding composition.

His early writings were published and widely circulated in Indonesia. Interest in his works began to permeate bookstores and classrooms. Wary of their influence, Suharto banned the publication and sale of Pramoedya's books.

On Buru Island, writing had become all but impossible for the author. In the four years since his arrest, all the writing he had done was on the dotted line in his detention papers. But wit, sardonic and cruel as it might have been, was not beyond the soldiers, who joked that Pramoedya could write all he wanted. He just did not have pen and paper. On one occasion a commander unexpectedly presented him with a fountain pen, some ink and a writing pad. The officer was obviously conscious of his captive's substantial ability and thought it cruel to deprive the artist of his tools. On the top of the writing pad he had scribbled: 'For personal greatness or the greatness of Indonesia.'

Pramoedya was thrilled about the prospect of being able to write again, but the years of incarceration and beatings had left him unable to focus his thoughts and the continuous deprivation of food had robbed him of the alertness and mental acuity. He found it difficult just to recall the names of some of his children. Every day was a struggle just to stay alive. His weight, like many of his fellow inmates', had fallen to below 40 kilograms. Even squatting down to defecate had become a strenuous exercise, as his legs had difficulty supporting his body.

To ease the situation, Pramoedya turned to eating whatever animals he could catch. Without fruit and vegetables, his health continued to deteriorate, as his body was in dire need of vitamins and minerals. He began to experience dizzy spells, especially when he was out in the padi fields, where the pools of water swirled around him. One day, a guard caught him resting when he was supposed to be planting rice and immediately took him to the guard room.

The guard gestured him to take a seat. Before anyone could say anything, he struck the prisoner across his jaw with the back of his fist.

'What were you doing?' the lieutenant asked.

Stunned by the blow, Pramoedya didn't respond.

'You're an old man,' the lieutenant shouted, 'old enough to be my parent. When he has to, a young man must send a reminder to his parents; that's if they'll hear him. For *Pancasila*...'

Before the officer could complete his sentence, a sergeant leapt up and started to strangle the writer. 'Belief in God! Belief in God!' he raged, oblivious to the incongruity of his exhortation and deed. As he screamed his fingers tightened around the scrawny neck. Pramoedya's face turned puce and his eyes bulged. The sergeant finally released his grip and pushed his victim backwards, causing his head to hit hard on the floor. The guards then pulled the gasping prisoner up and started punching his face. When it was over, the writer picked himself up and limped back to the barracks. When his bunk mates saw his swollen face, they bowed their heads and said nothing.

Weeks later the pain in his left ear grew worse. The smash from the soldier's rifle on the night he was arrested had left his hearing partially damaged. Now his ears started to swell and liquid seeped out. A high fever developed and his hearing deteriorated to a point where he could only hear his own heartbeat and voice. In the days that followed, the swelling lessened and his fever subsided. But the hearing loss, though not complete, had become permanent. 'Even now,' he told me, 'my ability to catch low frequency sounds is only about 25%. There is this constant ringing sound in the background.'

The crops that the detainees planted were repeatedly stolen by the guards. One morning during roll call, the soldier on duty noticed an odour that was particularly offensive.

'What's that bad smell?' he half-accusingly enquired.

The *tapols* said nothing, for they knew where the smell was coming from.

'It's you, isn't it, you filthy lot,' he said, 'Don't you know anything about cleanliness?'

The men by now had learned that questions were not meant to be answered.

'Get down and give me 50 push-ups!' the young soldier ordered.

In the condition they were in, the best the men could give was way off the target, the strongest managing only 15. They were grimy because they hadn't been able to bathe the day before. The pool of water in which they usually took their baths came from upstream where the guard house was. That day, apparently suffering from a bout of diarrhoea, a soldier had contaminated it with yellow watery stool. From the colour of the excrement, the prisoners suspected that he must have eaten too much of the unripe sweet potato that he had stolen from the prisoners.

Late in 1970, Commander Daeng Masiga was transferred back to Java. He left Pramoedya a goodbye note as well as a towel and a pair of briefs. Deprived of such provisions, Pramoedya treasured the hand-me-downs. With the sort of labour they had to perform, the *tapols'* clothes quickly wore out. Many of the men worked naked in the fields during the day saving their clothes for the nights. What Pramoedya longed for was a hat to shield him from the uncompromising sun. In the end, he traded his fountain pen for a large, cone-shaped bamboo farming hat.

Masiga's replacement was a pint-sized lieutenant named Sudjoso Hadisiswojo. 'I may be small but not my rank. Don't try anything with me,' was how he introduced himself. His first act of cruelty was to dismantle the cooperative that the men had put together, where surplus crops were sold whenever they were available. With the token sums of money collected, the *tapols* had bought some chickens, which they reared to get a supply of eggs and meat. As long as they remained entombed on Buru Island, no gesture, however well intended, could restore the self-worth of the prisoners, but the cooperative had helped to give to the detainees a degree of control over their lives. As a result, crop production increased as did the number of chickens and eggs.

Permanence was never a feature in the cursed camp. Not only did the new commander do away with the cooperative but, like some pipsqueak latter-day feudal lord, he also demanded that three chickens and 15 eggs be brought to him daily. The prisoners did their sums and figured that the supply of chickens would be depleted in a matter of months. They began to encourage the chickens to lay more eggs to ensure that the commander received his supply of the birds, and they their sanity. Hadisiswojo bundled the chickens to the harbour and sold them for a tidy sum. The lucre ended up financing an affair that he was having with another man's wife. A few weeks later, he ordered the prisoners into the forest to cut wood to build a house for another woman with whom he was also indulging in trysts.

Not only was the lieutenant corrupt, he also possessed a sadistic streak. He would come by the barracks in the morning to see if he could pounce on any of the men waking up late. Whoever was caught was given plenty of time to rest; for three days and nights the offenders had to sleep at the foot of the Commander's bed, allowed to move only to go to the toilet.

If anything remain unchanged under Hadisiswojo's command, it was the beatings. One of his first victims was a *tapol* named Kayun. A good natured young man in his early twenties, Kayun had graduated from a teachers' college before his arrest and was one of those rare souls who brought cheer into others' hearts, no matter how dreary conditions were. He was always ready to pull more than his share of the burden, especially if it meant easing the workload of older prisoners. His death was therefore especially distressing to the men.

Kayun had fallen ill from malaria and found himself unable to work. For months, he had to be washed and fed by the other *tapols*. Guilt soon got the better of him and, as his conditioned worsened, neurosis crept in. This was more than Hadisiswojo could tolerate. Not only was the prisoner unable to work, but he had the nerve to be neurotic. When he was caught wandering in the fields one day, the commander took the young man to the guard house and proceeded to administer a vicious beating. Two days later Kayun was found dead in a field hut, his body blue and his mouth frothing. Everything in the hut was in disarray, as if someone had been struggling in hysterical pain. Beside his body stiff from rigor mortis was a bottle of Endrine, an insecticide.

The work day lengthened until nine at night. Sometimes, the commander would order the men to hoe the field or saw wood out in the forest right through the night. Rice, vegetables, chickens, timber and just about everything the prisoners had in surplus were brought to the harbour and sold. No accounts were kept.

Meanwhile in the real world outside Buru, interest in Pramoedya's writings began to grow. The international press started to make requests to interview the author and the other prisoners. Under pressure from foreign governments and organisations, the Indonesian authorities opened up the penal complex to visitors, who were given guided tours.

Each time the tours came around, participating units would be spruced up, and healthy looking prisoners paraded in their khaki best. Prison ambience was enlivened by cultural shows performed by the prisoners. But the song and dance neither impressed nor inveigled the visitors, whose subsequent unflattering reports angered many a general in the Government and made some of the journalists persona non grata.

One of the journalists was Errol Hodge from Radio Australia who was able to interview Pramoedya. 'The People's Republic of China has now joined the United Nations. What is your opinion about this?' Hodge asked.

'That's China's business,' Pramoedya replied.

'Next year President Nixon will visit China. What do you feel about this?' he enquired further.

Pramoedya didn't answer. As always he was watched closely by members of the intelligence branch. The interviews were more for the reporters' benefit than for Pramoedya, who really could not say much. He remembered that Hadisiswojo had on various occasions commented that the interviews with the press constituted 'dangerous action'.

'During the time you've been here is there anything you've hoped for?' Hodge continued.

'During my time here I've had no hopes.'

'Then have you given up hope?'

'No.'

Hodge smiled sympathetically, knowing the restrictive circumstance his interviewee was in. As a form of encouragement, he told Pramoedya that many of his books were known in Australia and that his works were examined by research students in universities there.

Pramoedya was glad that his books had been circulating. The interview had done his confidence a world of good and the thought of his books being read in the English speaking world had been incalculably uplifting. The notebook and pen that one of the reporters left him came in handy as his writing spirit returned.

'What have you written in that notebook?' Hadisiswojo enquired after the journalists had left.

'I used it for cigarette paper,' Pramoedya lied.

'And the pen?'

'That too,' came the confused reply.

That night Pramoedya quickly burned the notes that he had written. He could not risk another beating.

Then came the break that the prisoners had been praying for. Commander Hadisiswojo was to be transferred back to Jakarta. But the lieutenant's worst act of depravity was still to come. At his final roll call with the prisoners, he lined up the men so that they could witness the thick black smoke rising from the field huts which contained the seed stock for the next season. Hadisiswojo had ordered them burned. The men were baffled by his anger. They soon discovered why. The commander had contracted ascites, an unusual but deadly condition that causes fluids to collect in the abdomen, resulting in painful cramps. He was to die before he could make it back to Java.

For the good of Indonesia

On one occasion, Pramoedya and five other prisoners—scholars and academics—were instructed to travel to Unit 4 for an interview. The reason for the exercise was not made clear to them. After three days of trekking through the forest, climbing hills and wading across swamps they reached their destination. The six were met by the Inter-University Psychology Team headed by a Dr Fuad Hassan. Hassan pointed out that their job was to interview the prisoners and he encouraged the men to talk freely, assuring them that the team was not part of the military.

'What would you think of having your family brought out to join you here?' Hassan started off. The Government encouraged married men to have their families brought to the island, but few would wish upon their loved ones the curse they had to endure on Buru.

'It would be impossible for me to consider such an offer,' Pramoedya replied. 'First of all, my wife is ill. And second, while my contribution to the cultural development of this country might be small or insignificant, I still feel that my children should have the right to partake in the national culture. That would be impossible for them here on Buru.'

Of course, what Pramoedya didn't say was that his wife and daughters would end up serving the soldiers as maidservants and sex toys. As much as he was deprived of intimacy with his wife, Pramoedya could not bear to bring her to Buru Island.

Maimunah, through the years, had remained a ballast for the family. When Pramoedya was imprisoned by Sukarno in 1960, she never failed to show up on visiting days to bring food, even when she was in the last stages of her pregnancy and suffering from tuberculosis. Before he left for Buru, Pramoedya had asked her to remarry; she was still young and needed someone to help care for the children. She refused, and continued to hang on to the hope that one day her husband would be returned to her.

The years of isolation cruelly altered the personal lives of the prisoners. Young men who were brought to Buru were condemned to a life of sexual deprivation. Inevitably the prisoners turned to each other for sex. When dramas were performed for the soldiers' entertainment or for visitors, the prisoners who played female roles attracted sexual overtures from some of the men.

Prisoners in a unit which was located on the outer fringes of the complex, and therefore closer to the local inhabitants living in the forest, resorted to the risky practice of sneaking away for a quick sexual tryst with the tribeswomen. The women soon began to enjoy the novel experience as lovemaking with their own husbands was always performed in a predetermined position: the women would go down on their hands and knees and the men would copulate from behind. With the *tapols*, a whole new world of sexual experiences had opened up. Of course, there was the problem of the husbands. Under the law of the Buru jungle, the women were obliged to confess (which was not unheard of within their own community) and matters would be considered settled after a fine was paid to the husband.

Seeing that Pramoedya was adamant about not bringing his family to Buru, Hassan changed the subject: 'What do you think would be the best way to develop this island?'

'That's a difficult question to answer. But let me give you an example. My friend Dilar Darmawan was a professor of English literature at Gadjah Mada University. He has been here for eight years, a period during which he might have produced several scholars of English literature. But what he does here is till fields.

'As to the development of Buru itself, I look at the problem from the point of view of the detainees who are developing it. The answer is simple. Free the political detainees. That would make for the development of a much better Indonesia.'

'But you must see the situation from an objective point of view,' interjected one of the interviewers.

Objective? Pramoedya thought. 'During the eight years that I have been detained, all I know is the experience of being detained. That is objective. I don't know what has happened outside of this place.'

'Aren't you aware that you are here because of G30S and the violent murder of the generals?' another asked.

'My answer to that is the same as the one I gave to the investigative team: I know nothing about the incident whatsoever.'

The team asked a few more questions about the G30S incident that led nowhere.

'The writings of yours that I've read indicate that you are a Marxist,' commented one.

'Which writings would that be?' Pramoedya asked.

Unable to come up with an intelligent answer, the interviewer quickly turned to other prisoners.

Later, Hassan came back to Pramoedya. 'Can you see any kind of justification for your presence here?'

'I feel that I've not been treated in accordance with the law. I've never been tried and never been sentenced. I'm a writer who writes under his own name. If there are errors in my writings, if I make mistakes, then anyone may…criticise them especially the Government, which has its own Ministry of Information. So you tell me why I'm here. If I were guilty of something, I'd willingly accept the sentence imposed on me.'

Pramoedya related how he was arrested that night in 1965 and how the soldiers destroyed all his manuscripts, documents and books.

'It had taken me 20 years to build up that library and documentation. I said that if the Government wants it, take it, but don't destroy it. Regardless of my own personal interest, the library would be of great value to the nation. But what happened? It was completely destroyed. Was this good for Indonesia?' This was the first time that Pramoedya had been able to show his feelings about the senselessness of the regime's actions.

'At any rate if I'm wrong then dole out the appropriate punishment. But if I'm not, then let me go. The treatment that has been shown me has not been educational and will not contribute to the development of a better society. What is the use of studying freedom if one has no guarantee of freedom itself? And for those of us who are here, what can an education in the principles of freedom mean but greater suffering from the knowledge of loss of that freedom.

'I have a story to tell you about this. One day a mother asked her son, a primary school student, to go out and locate their father. And so the boy left home and went from one detention centre to another until he finally found his father. Yes, his father was a *tapol*. Because he loved his father and didn't want to leave him, he stayed with his father. He became a child *tapol*. Sometime later the boy's father was released, but not the boy himself. Not only that, the boy was sent to Buru.

'Based on this little story of mine you might try to define the meaning of "justification". All I'm saying is that this place provides no support for the development of a better Indonesian society. Think of that boy who has been here for years and think of the harm that has been done to him.'

Looking a little sheepish, another team member challenged, 'How would you define a better society?'

Pramoedya looked him in the eyes and deadpanned, 'A democratic society.'

But a democratic society was far from Suharto's mind. After the proclamation of the New Order, the President bore down on political parties. Leaders of the PNI who remained loyal to the former President were arrested. Those who paid homage to Suharto were elevated, usually to key positions within the bureaucracy. The full import of Suharto's designs became clear when political parties were 'streamlined' into the Development Unity Party and the Indonesian Democratic Party. Again, the junta weighed in with initiatives, constitutional or otherwise, to ensure that leaders in both these umbrella parties remained less than enthusiastic in their opposition to the President. The *Golongan Karya* (Golkar), or 'Functional Groups' was set up which Suharto insisted was a movement, not a party, and therefore free of the shackles of ideology. Politicians whose guiding principal was to not antagonise the President found the new organisation a safe haven. To enhance political conformity, Suharto decreed that there was to be no contestation of political ideas during elections; only competing development programs could be put forward.

And in case he missed plugging any loophole, Suharto packed the legislature with Golkar members. Only the *Dewan Perwakilan Rakyat* (Parliament) was open to elections which was crafted to favour the President's men. The *Majelis Permusyawaratan Rakyat* (People's Consultative Assembly) was filled with high-ranking officers from the armed forces and representatives of the political parties whose appointments the President had the power to regulate.

But if the junta's political manipulations seemed disingenuous, its corruption was downright reprehensible. After Sukarno was deposed, Western aid poured in to revive the country's economy. Instead of using it for developmental projects, state owned enterprises often had their largesse frequently, and often crudely, creamed off by the military brass for personal consumption. The generals built huge mansions in the midst of squalid slum areas, establishing small private armies, purchasing luxury cars and throwing lavish banquets.

Chinese business *towkays* courted these powerful generals in order to obtain easy credit from banks to start up their own ventures, with little or no accountability about how the funds were to be used. The generals in turn 'adopted' these businessmen as *cukongs*, or financiers, to underwrite their own forays into the corporate world. It was a cosy symbiotic relationship. Fake documents were often issued to get loans. Embezzlement—large and small—raised few eyebrows, cases of whole-sale swindling went uninvestigated, and bribery became the norm. Leading the pillage were Suharto and his family members who owned or were involved in anything from banking to car manufacturing industries worth billions of dollars. Financial unscrupulousness became so endemic in Indonesia that within a matter of years, the country acquired the reputation as one of the most corrupt nations on earth, a status for which it paid dearly during the Asian financial crisis in 1997.

Those involved in the scams were often protected by the junta and remained largely immune from prosecution unless the case was overwhelmingly indefensible even by the system's degenerate standards. And then the sentences meted out were disproportionately light. Critics were often made to pay for their audacity, the most outstanding one being Mochtar Lubis, who ran a scathing campaign against the rich and corrupt in the weekly, *Indonesia Raya* magazine, of which he was the editor. For his outspokenness he was arrested on several occasions and imprisoned.

The behaviour of the top brass permeated right down to the rank-and-file soldier, as was the case in Buru Island. The malaise was poignantly captured by Brian May:

> 'How much [rice] went to Kedokanbunder?' I asked, not telling [the official] I had been there. 'About two tons,' he replied...'No, it didn't,' I said pulling out a handful of small, mean-looking grains of the substitute from my pocket. 'All they have received is seventy-five kilograms of this.' He giggled; and I left. It was clear what had happened: rice had been misappropriated down the line. Twenty tons disappeared in Bandung, the provincial capital, and Indramayu. Most of the rest was to be put in store to be sold for the benefit of the officials. It was the same with the vitamin B that was supposed to be administered to 5,000 beriberi sufferers. I was told that mass injections were taking place in an area that nobody dreamed I would visit; I went there and found that it was fiction. Eventually an official admitted that only thirty-five injections had been given. The rest could have easily been sold in Singapore.

A true sign of kindheartedness

'Let me first say that I am happy to be here, to meet you and engage in a direct dialogue with you here on Buru. I have along with me the Inter-University Psychology Team as well as a number of senior journalists and top news-people, editors from several Jakarta newspapers.' General Sumitro was addressing five *tapols* who were selected to attend the briefing. International pressure had been mounting on the regime, which was trying to show some compassion by sending a high-ranking officer to have a dialogue with selected prisoners. It turned out to be more of a soliloquy.

'You have been here for some time now, in isolation since 1965. For that reason you are probably unaware of many developments in the outside world. Or maybe you are up to date?' It was 1973, and the General proceeded to give a run down of the political developments that had occurred during the years Suharto had been in power.

Sumitro went on to tell the five men that they would be allowed to go home one day. 'But while you are waiting for the resolution, here in this calm and peaceful natural environment, find enjoyment in your suffering. And later, when you are happy, exercise caution,' Sumitro turned philosophical. The men listened with concealed incredulity.

Then he turned to Pramoedya. 'I learned that Pram's documentation was destroyed. I know that for him, as a writer, his documentation was a source of pride. I ask you to make an inventory of the books and supplies that you need, and I will send them to you. I will also send newspapers so that you can keep up with outside developments and with President Suharto's important political speeches.

'To Pram I convey greetings from your friends. It appears that on the outside world you still have a lot of friends.

'Think about what problems you have and, at another time, we will discuss them.' And as suddenly as he entered the room, Sumitro disappeared. That release 'one day' did not happen until years later, the discussion at 'another time' never took place, and Pramoedya never received those 'books and supplies.'

About a month later, another general visited the penal complex. This time a group of 13 *tapols* were called to the unit commander's office.

'Whenever the President summons me to Jakarta, he's always sure to ask me, "How are our brothers on Buru Island?" And I always answer that our brothers on Buru are doing well,' the General started off. Like Sumitro, he rambled on about how good Suharto had been for the nation and how ideology was no longer necessary for Indonesian politics.

He concluded, 'I've also brought with me a letter from President Suharto that is addressed to you. Though it is addressed to a particular individual it is intended for all of you here on Buru.

'This letter should be an incentive. I'd say it's rare anywhere in the world that a President would take the time to write a letter to detainees like yourself. The President is constantly busy with the job of governing the nation, yet he still takes the time to write a letter to you. It is a great honor that President Suharto has shown you, a true sign of his kindheartedness. And after you have read and digested what this letter says, I would like you to write a reply.'

The President of The Republic of Indonesia
Jakarta, November 19, 1973
To: Pramoedya Ananta Toer
Tefaat Buru Island

I received a report from the Commander for the Restoration of Safety and Security and General of the Indonesian Armed Forces on the condition that you detainees are in.

For every person a mistake in judgment is common, but that must of course be followed by its logical consequence, that being 'Honesty, courage and the ability to rediscover the true and accepted road.'

I pray that God the Most Powerful and Most Loving provides protection and guidance to you in finding that route. Amen.

Strive for and pray to Him for His guidance.

Soeharto
President, the Republic of Indonesia
General, Indonesian Armed Forces

When the General said that he 'would like' the prisoners to reply, he was, of course, speaking euphemistically because the men were ordered to draft a response which was given a makeover before it was sent to the President:

> To the President of the Republic of Indonesia
> General Soeharto
> Respectfully,
>
> I was both surprised and moved to receive your letter for I had never imagined that a political detainee would ever be shown such a great honor. I express my sincerest thanks and my greatest respect for the valuable time and attention that you have bestowed on me.
>
> There is obvious truth in your letter of November 10, 1973, i.e., in that 'every person a mistake in judgment is common,' and that 'that must of course be followed by its logical consequence.'
>
> To you, the honorable President of the Republic of Indonesia, I would like to say that my parents, as with, I assume, most other parents, educated me to always cherish truth, justice and beauty, as well as a knowledge of our nation and our people.
>
> It was with this education as my provisions that I made my way into the world. And the mark that I leave behind, the traces of my footsteps, are there to be judged by anyone. For that reason, in your letter, when you asked me to seek 'Honesty, courage and the ability to rediscover the true and accepted road,' I read that as a call from my own parents who held in high esteem the message that the magnanimous soul will forgive mistakes just as the strong will extend their hand to the weak.
>
> I extend to you my deepest thanks for your prayers to God the Most Powerful for there is no true protection or guidance outside of His own.
>
> I shall forever strive and pray. With the deepest regards and greetings, I am...
>
> Political Detainee No. 641
> Pramoedya Ananta Toer

Notwithstanding the 'true sign of [Suharto's] kindheartedness,' the prisoners were to meet with a situation so grim that any pretence of humanity the regime had towards its detainees was irrevocably exposed.

It happened a year later on 12 November 1974. The men were asleep in their barracks when they were awakened by the shouts of the guards. The sky was dark, as dawn was still some hours away. The prisoners were half asleep and confused at the orders to assemble for a roll call at such an hour. The vicious edge in the guards' voices told them that something terrible was about to take place. Their hearts started to beat hard, their naked feet pounding the earth as they ran to the assembly area. When they got there, more soldiers were shouting more orders. Before they could catch their breaths, bamboo poles, iron pipes and wooded clubs came crashing down on their heads and bodies. Howls of pain pierced the night air as the soldiers drew blood.

As other prisoners streamed in from the surrounding barracks, guards were on hand to hurry them along with metallic butts and leather boots. If a *tapol* tripped, the soldiers would descend upon him with such brutality that he would remain bloodied and motionless on the spot where he had fallen. The men knew not to try to ward off the blows, as that would mean instant execution.

When all the prisoners were assembled, the officer on duty called the roll. Other soldiers walked around swinging their truncheons and rifles indiscriminately as they cursed the frightened men. Whenever a weapon found its target, the dull crack of bones would be followed by loud screams as the men crumpled to the ground. The guards were so violent that the wooden poles also broke.

Then a military chaplain addressed the *tapols*. 'Even a dog knows the hand that feeds it!' he yelled, 'If you're supposed to be men, how come you don't? Tonight, you're going to be skewered.' The prisoners were still unaware of their crimes to warrant such a crazed beating. No one dared ask. Everyone looked on in terror, trying to avoid making eye contact with their tormentors lest more blows come their way.

The prisoners were then ordered to stand on one leg with their hands behind their heads. The soldiers continued their bludgeoning. Another group of prisoners arrived. They were late because no one had informed them of the roll call. The new arrivals were lined up in front of their fellow *tapols* and each one was thoroughly beaten until none was left standing. Many lay unconscious, covered in blood, but no one dared to help them.

Still hungry, the guards turned back on their earlier targets and continued the orgy of violence. It was one full hour before the madness abated—not because the prisoners were by then half dead, but because the soldiers themselves were exhausted. The ground was littered with broken bodies and the smell of blood pervaded the air.

But the end of the detainees' ordeal was still far away. They were ordered to take off their clothes. As many did not possess underwear, the scene was one of naked men cowering in front of a group of thugs who, before the night's end, would determine whether their captives lived or died. The men were then ordered to lie prone on the ground. The cold night made their bruised bodies even more painful. An hour later, they were told to roll over and go to sleep. Machine guns were placed around them. Thinking that they were going to be shot, some prisoners started to cry uncontrollably. Others started to think about fighting back. After all what did they have to lose? In the end, calmer emotions prevailed.

Hours after assault started, the *tapols* were still no closer to finding out what had brought it on. Just before daybreak, several barrack-leaders were called to the command post. 'It was your men who staged the uprising wasn't it, and who got one of our men killed?' accused an officer.

The two events had indeed occurred that evening, yet the officer was only half right. It was true that a group of prisoners had planned to overpower the guards to stage a revolt. It was also true that a guard had been killed. But one event had nothing to do with the other. The soldier had not been murdered by the prisoners, but by his comrades, possibly because of disagreements in splitting the profits from the timber trade. The incident had taken place in a hut-turned-mini-casino where the soldiers frequently gathered. The guards who had killed him reported to the commander that the men in Unit 2, which happened to be near the gambling den, had rebelled and killed their colleague, unaware that a rebellion was actually taking place.

Earlier a group of about 50 or more prisoners had gathered at midnight to make their way to the command headquarters.

Their plan had been to overpower the guards there, grab their weapons and release all the prisoners in the other units. Armed with handcrafted sturdy bamboo staves and potboiled hardy eggs (for eating), the group of *tapols* set out to confront their torturers.

Before their eggs could even cool, shots were heard coming from the direction of Unit 2. The startled prisoners abandoned their plan to capture the headquarters-everyone just ran for their lives into the jungle. Helicopters hovered above while a full battalion of soldiers combed the area; within a week all the escapees had either been shot or captured or had voluntarily returned. Meanwhile, the other prisoners, who were unaware of the plans to revolt, had borne the full brunt of the soldiers' fury.

When dawn came, the guards ordered the men to stand up and a fresh round of beatings commenced. One soldier ran amok, brandishing a semiautomatic rifle wildly. He kicked and punched those who remained standing, screaming obscenities and working himself into a frenzy. After a while, he abruptly calmed down and walked away. He hadn't gone very far when he suddenly turned around and resumed his hysterics. Only this time he picked up his rifle and was about to open fire when another soldier yelled at him, alerting a few guards, who quickly wrestled their comrade to the ground. The raving rifleman was apparently related to the murdered guard.

A couple of hours passed before the commander of the Buru prison arrived at the scene. Acutely aware of the attention of the international community, he knew that he could not afford to have such an awful spectacle exposed. He castigated his subordinates and duly explained to the prisoners what had happened the night before. He did, however, concede that it was a mistake to assume the escapees had killed the soldier. The admission brought little comfort to the prisoners. The 'mistake' had left 27 of them dead and hundreds severely crippled. Not sure what else to do with the surviving prisoners, the commander dismissed them and allowed them to return to their barracks. The rampage was by no means an isolated incident on Buru Island. Scores of prisoners were killed by the soldiers, often with little provocation.

Word of the incident leaked out and before long the international media began to run stories on it. Requests by foreign journalists to visit the island increased, and the Indonesian Government came under renewed pressure to release the detainees. Reports of forced labour in the complex also began to surface. Trade for the commodities that the prisoners were forced to produce had until then been controlled by corrupt soldiers with little or no remuneration being paid to the *tapols*. Construction of roads and buildings was carried out by the prisoners, often for the personal benefit of the prison officials.

Unable to do without foreign economic aid, the army was forced to treat the prisoners of Buru Island more humanely. The detainees were, henceforth, paid for the goods they produced that were marketed in the command's welfare store. Eggs, simple tools, handicrafts and small furniture were some of the items for sale. A cut of the proceeds went to paying for medicines for sick prisoners. With whatever money they earned, the *tapols* could buy their own supplies.

The introduction of stricter rules regulating the relationship between guard and prisoner resulted in a little less hellish life for the *tapols*. The movement of soldiers among the prisoners was restricted, and the detainees could now report beatings directly to their commander. But in a market where all the wheeling and dealing goes was restricted to chickens and chairs, the only commodity to invest in was corruption. As long as there was money to be made off the backs of the prisoners the soldiers were not going to ditch the well-worn practice of making money without making sweat.

The relative calm that now prevailed gave Pramoedya the time that he needed to write. In the past, when tensions ran high in the camp, the prisoners often lived in a state of terror. To help the inmates relieve their psychological torment, Pramoedya would extemporise a story about Minke, a native of Surabaya who lived under Dutch rule at about the turn of the century. The intense young lad is no ordinary citizen. Attracted by the allure of Western learning but fiercely Javanese in his roots, Minke sets out to galvanise his people against the colonial caste. At the height of his power when he becomes a god-like figure to his people, Minke is banished to a small island where he lives until his return to Java, a forgotten but unbroken man.

Pramoedya would tell the story when the prisoners had some quiet time. He took them on a meandering stroll through his mind, and weaved and wandered his way to a mammoth 1,500-page tetralogy that would eventually win him international acclaim. Now that he was free to write again, Pramoedya set about it like a man possessed. His four chickens gave him a continual supply of eggs which he sold to buy paper and cigarettes. He wrote without attention to place and time. In his own words, it was like 'a dam breaking and the words just poured out without control.'

'Pram never rewrites his text,' an associate of the writer told me. 'I've seen him write, usually on student notebooks, and there are no cancellations or scratches on his notes.' Friends volunteered to undertake his chores so that he could write uninterrupted. They even built him a shack so that he could be alone to compose his epic tale. When he was done, Pramoedya had written the story of his life, both figuratively and, to a degree, in the literal sense, for the story of Minke is peppered with his own experiences.

In four volumes—*Bumi Manusia* (This Earth of Mankind), *Anak Semua Bangsa* (Child of All Nations), *Jejak Langkah* (Footsteps), and *Rumah Kaca* (House of Glass)—the *Buru Quartet* tells of heroes and villains, plots and counter-plots, repression and freedom, magnificent triumphs and crushing defeats, betrayals and love affairs, court room battles and conspiracies. The dozens of characters span religions (including a new Eurasian Muslim convert and a native Indonesian Catholic), nationalities and professions (there is the *agent provocateur* from the Chinese Kuomintang, a Dutch governor-general, and a Japanese prostitute), and cultures (Minke himself is married at various stages to a Shanghainese, a French, and a Melanesian with Portuguese blood).

The manuscripts were smuggled out of Buru Island by a priest. Written in *Bahasa*, Pramoedya's writings have been translated into 20 languages. They have been the subject of study and research by graduate students all over the world, and have been used as texts in Malaysian schools. The *Buru Quartet* has been through five reprints in the United States. Pramoedya's works have been variously compared to those of Solzhenitsyn, Dickens and Conrad. 'Hugo and Dostoyevski are the writers Pramoedya resembles at his best,' wrote the

New Yorker. His name has been on the lips of the literati for a Nobel Prize since 1983. In 1995 he won the Ramon Magsaysay Award, the most distinguished literature prize in Asia. As he was not allowed to travel to the Philippines, his wife accepted it on his behalf.

When it was announced that Pramoedya was awarded the Ramon Magsaysay Award, other Indonesian writers, including Mochtar Lubis, also a recipient of the Award, protested that the Foundation dishonoured the memory of Magsaysay because, during the Sukarno years, Pramoedya 'led the oppression of the creativity of non-communist writers who happened to be on the other side of the (political) fence.'

Pramoedya did not deny that he had opposed his literary opponents in the 1960s but defended that the conflict was merely a polemic. 'It was indeed fierce, but it didn't lead to murder, did it?' he wrote. 'And isn't polemic a way of arriving at the truth...?'

Ironically, the biggest tribute was paid by Suharto himself. Described as 'poisonous', the President banned Pramoedya's books and imposed severe penalties on anyone found possessing them. That anyone was Bambang Subono, who attended a play and found it opportune to conduct a sale of Pramoedya's books by word of whisper.

The murmuring found its way to a man who lumbered up and greeted him with an impolite, 'These are banned books, bastard!' With six copies of *Rumah Kaca*, three of *Gadis Pantai*, one of *Anak Semua Bangsa* and a bunch of lottery coupons in his bag, there was little Subono could offer as defence. He duly found himself in jail with a seven year term. Two more Pramoedya admirers and prominent activists, Bambang Isti Nugroho and Bonar Tigor Naipospos, were also caught selling his books were promptly sentenced to eight and eight and a half years imprisonment respectively. Yusuf Isak, Pramoedya's publisher, was also jailed. University of Indonesia students who had invited the writer to speak were arrested and expelled.

Since then, the Buru books have been through 11 reprints in Indonesia. *Bumi Manusia* alone sold 10,000 copies within two weeks of its release. Ten months, five reprints and one ban later, the number hit 50,000. The Government kept a lookout for the contraband and denied torching as many as 10,000 copies.

Opening doors to dead ends

Talk about the impending release of the prisoners was rife. There were press reports that the first batch of 1,500 prisoners was going to be released in December 1977. 'Your name is on the list, Pram,' one of his unit mates said excitedly.

Pramoedya remained calm, even indifferent. He had learned that the Government had the habit of opening doors and ushering people to dead ends. His mind went back to the evening when the mob attacked him at his house and the police had told him that they would take him to 'safety'. Time and again, he had been told that there was a chance of release whenever the guards told the prisoners to prepare to leave the prison; they always ended up in another facility. And when they told him that he was finally going to be released, he found himself on Buru Island. No, he was not excited.

His friends came by his shack one after another, some to say goodbye, some asking if they could have his room and some just to be remembered. Many were in their fifties, skin and bones after years of food deprivation. Their shirts and trousers were pieces of rags torn in a hundred different places, some stained permanently in blood. They didn't wear shoes and their eyes were empty, spiritless. 'And to think we were all scholars and thinkers once,' Pramoedya sighed.

Despite all the excitement and activity, Pramoedya still resisted the idea that he was going home after all these years. The information coming in was conflicting. Some said that they had just received confirmation from TVRI, the state owned television station, that his name was on the list, others said that it wasn't. There was no way of knowing and the officials were not telling.

Fellow *tapols* continued to visit Pramoedya to say goodbye. One hugged him and started to cry. So did he. Through the more than ten years they had spent on Buru Island—all the beatings, punishment and humiliation—they had come to depend on each other for strength in times of despair, calm in times of terror. Through the agony and hopelessness, all they had was each other. They had become family.

'It makes me happy just to think that someone out there who has been freed is thinking of me,' one said. For many of the prisoners who had come to accept that they were never going to leave Buru Island, to live vicariously the freedom enjoyed by other *tapols* was all the pleasure they could afford.

A reporter from *Kompas*, a local newspaper, then came to Pramoedya's room and asked for an interview: 'I was just at your home before I came here. Your daughter asked about you. "Are you really coming home, Papa? Is it true what the newspapers are saying?" your daughter asked.' He seemed genuinely sympathetic and continued to relay the questions Pramoedya's family asked.

Maimunah said to the reporter, 'Twelve years have passed and I hope that the children and I won't be disappointed again. After I heard there was to be a release, two more weeks of waiting seems so long. I don't know what I'm supposed to do. I'm so confused. But the children are beaming and happy and are making their own plans. All sorts of things. They're all so sure that your name is on the list. All I do is pray day and night that this time my prayers will be answered.'

The youngest child added, 'I really hope that this month we'll all be together again.'

Pramoedya broke up inside. It had been such a long time since he had seen his family. A myriad of thoughts and emotions ran through him and he didn't know which one to respond to.

'How is it at my home?'

'It's good, very good in fact. Your wife is working hard selling ice snacks. The children are doing well. Your daughter Titiek plans on going to university,' the reporter replied.

'But do you think my wife and children really want me to come home?'

'Of course, of course they do. They love you,' he reassured.

'Someone told me that my wife had remarried.'

'That's a lie, just a lie.'

'It would be all right if she did, she has the right,' Pramoedya said, more to himself than to his interviewer.

'But it's not true,' the reporter responded.

'My wife, is she still beautiful?' Pramoedya smiled.

'She is, just a little older is all,' he smiled too.

'Who looks older, me or her,' Pramoedya asked cheekily.

'You—a little,' the reporter answered tactfully.

Pramoedya was not released with the rest of the prisoners in 1977. His wife and children had to wait for another two years.

When Jimmy Carter was elected President of the United States, he immediately brought pressure to bear on the Indonesian Government about its human rights record and threatened to cease economic aid to Indonesia if political prisoners were not freed. Unable to live their enchanted lives without American funding, the regime bowed to the pressure and released a token number of detainees in 1977.

Carter was not moved. Special Deputy Secretary of State for Human Rights Affairs, Patricia Derian, made clear the President's unhappiness over the delay of the release of Pramoedya and the remaining prisoners. The Indonesian Government said that Pramoedya was not ready for release because the answers he gave during interviews conducted by military officials were 'unacceptable'. The White House continued its pressure on Suharto and demanded the release of the prisoners in the shortest time possible. In 1979 the Indonesian Government gave in and on 12 November the last batch of prisoners left Buru Island.

When the men arrived back in Surabaya, Pramoedya and 40 others were separated from the rest and whisked off by bus to a prison in Magelang in Central Java. Among them was Hashim Rachman, former editor of the influential *Bintang Timur* newspaper. Pramoedya and Hashim had known each other for a long time. Hashim was one of those who had been able to hold the men together in times of crisis. 'At Tangerang, Hashim saved many lives,' recalled Pramoedya, 'I don't know how, but he managed to get medicines from outside, and many friends were saved by him. I'll always remember that.'

Hashim Rachman was a dignified looking man with a silvery mane and a sandpapery voice. We sat in his modest study as he recalled his days in Buru and the eventual return to Java: 'Right until the last minute those guys were still trying to prevent our release. They were just lawless.'

When the Catholic Church came to find out about the 'kidnap', it started to campaign for their release. Washington applied more pressure and, after another month, Suharto finally released them. Pramoedya returned to his family in

Jakarta. He was still very much a prisoner under city arrest. 'I'm still living under the boots of the New Order,' he said to me as he picked up another cigarette. The New Order ran his life: he had to obtain permission to travel out of Jakarta, could not be employed in government services, was banned from publishing his writing, and was not allowed to vote. Another open door, another dead end.

Bonar Tigor Naipospos, or Coki, as his friends call him, bounced in the driver's seat as we sputtered along in his battered mini-jeep on our way to Pramoedya's house. It had been a few years since he was released after his imprisonment for selling Pramoedya's books.

In his mid-thirties, Coki speaks with a grin permanently sliced across his cherubic face, which made him look more like a master chef than a human rights activist. He was slowly bringing to boil his people's frustration of Suharto's dictatorship through his activist work which was giving Jakarta's generals plenty of indigestion. A couple of months after we met and just before the military regime crashed, Coki was arrested along with several other Indonesian democracy fighters.

The Indonesian rupiah had been flying at dizzying altitudes before plummeting with other Asian currencies in the 1997 financial fiasco. Suharto, too heavy in his authoritarian seat, could not eject in time and crashed with the currency.

His political demise started on 12 May 1998 when Trisakti University students gathered in their campus in downtown Jakarta, demanding the President's resignation. The riot-squad was called in. Soon, students and soldiers stood facing each other in a tense stand off. Suddenly a shot rang out and the soldiers charged. More shots were fired followed by tear gas and swinging batons. Four students were killed that day.

During the next few days, mobs ravaged the city: stores were looted and burned, vehicles overturned and torched, and innocent people terrorised. The ethnic Chinese were particularly targeted; hundreds of women were raped and killed. Evidence suggests that the rioters were set loose by officials within the military to create a situation chaotic enough so that martial law could be declared.

Students took to the streets to demand Suharto's resignation. His effigies were bludgeoned and burned, and caricatures likening him to Hitler were gaily paraded, one placard screaming: 'Suharto wanted for crimes against humanity!' The scenario was eerily similar to the one he had orchestrated against Sukarno more than 30 years earlier. Like a boomerang, events had come full circle and were heading straight for the dictator. Unable to duck in time, Suharto took a direct hit and announced his resignation as President of Indonesia on 21 May 1998.

After what seemed like an interminable journey of twists and turns down back alleys, through which Coki adeptly manoeuvred, we reached a cluster of houses. Not far away sat a group of shirtless young men playing guitars that had obviously seen better days. Beside them some goats were tethered to a dilapidated fence. Further down the narrow road was a middle aged man standing behind a pushcart selling ice snacks. Someone had told me about Pramoedya's house being watched by some street vendor who reported the comings and goings to the authorities. The ice-snack man? Big Bung comes in many forms, why not a snack seller? As part of the political opposition in Singapore, I'm used to being under surveillance. In the world of autocracy, some things never change.

Pramoedya looks older than his 72 years. He walks with a slight stoop and is as thin as his books describe him to be. As we talked, he repeatedly cupped his ear to hear better. His smile reflects none of the bitter experience of his years of imprisonment and his spirit for Indonesia remains aglow.

His views on democracy remain as clear as ever: 'man was not born to be oppressed or muzzled. Let human beings live with dignity as human beings. Surely that is better than being cattle that have to carry out orders without their own consent.' But he also told me that the he feels that the struggle for a democratic society, not only for Indonesia but for other parts of Asia as well, must now be passed on to the younger generation: 'Don't think that democracy is just an idea. The young must fight for democracy, not only with their minds but their whole body, arms, legs, everything. Whether you are at home or outside, do not fail to publicise democracy.'

He continues to compile notes for the encyclopaedia of Indonesian literature which he started to write more than 30 years ago, before he was so rudely interrupted. 'I spend about five hours a day just to collect clippings for the compilation,' he said dryly. 'The pile has grown to about four metres but I don't have the energy to finish this project.'

In the *Buru Quartet*, Minke, Pramoedya's alter ego, returns to his home town after exile without achieving his goal which was to rid his people of the Dutch. He died tragically leaving behind 'only the imprints of his footsteps'. Pramoedya was born a writer and he will die one. He will leave behind more than footsteps; he will leave a treasure trove of experiences and ideals which will inspire many for generations to come.

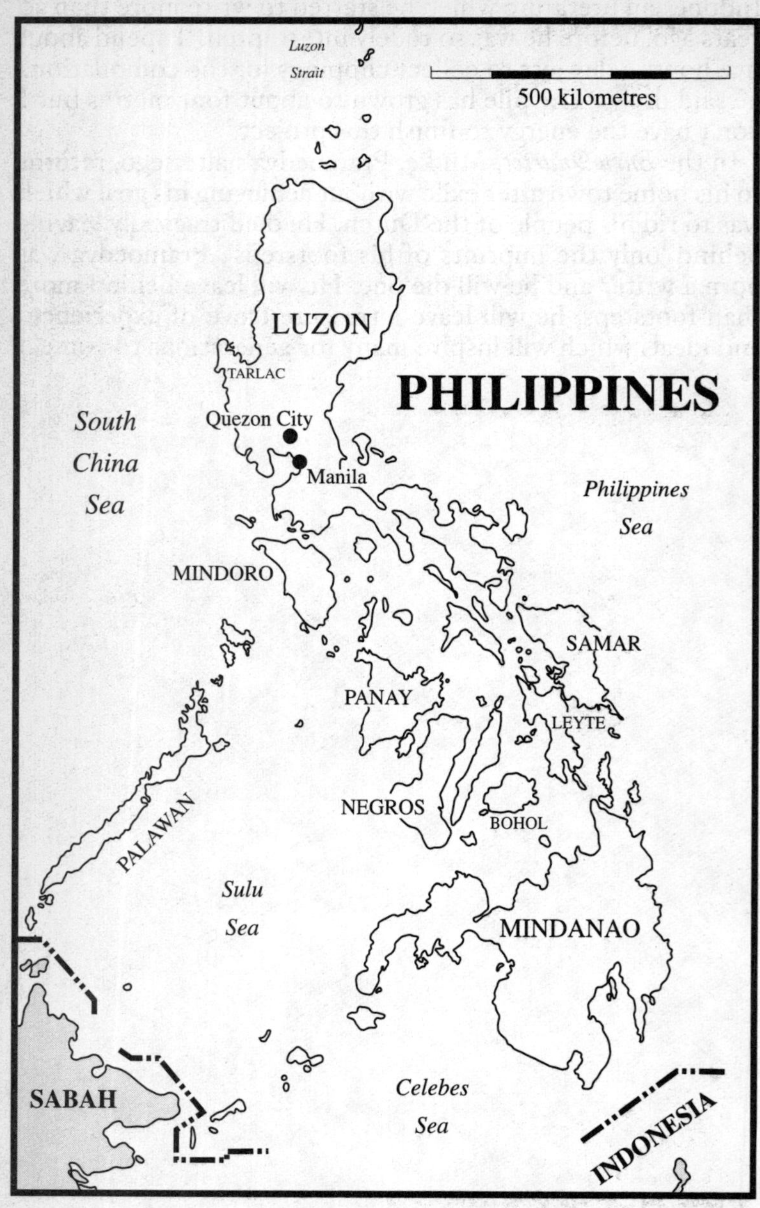
Luzon
Strait
500 kilometres
LUZON
TARLAC
PHILIPPINES
South
China
Sea
Quezon City
Manila
Philippines
Sea
MINDORO
SAMAR
PANAY
LEYTE
NEGROS
BOHOL
PALAWAN
Sulu
Sea
MINDANAO
SABAH
Celebes
Sea
INDONESIA

4
The Philippines

Benigno S. Aquino Jr

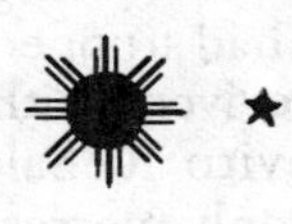

Guns, goons and gold

It was Saturday night in the teeming city of Manila. A huge crowd of almost 10,000 people had gathered at the Plaza Miranda for a political rally organised by the opposition Liberal Party. The contest was for eight seats in the Senate and the Liberals had lined up an impressive slate of candidates. The election campaign had been a bruising one so far, with government and opposition hurling charges and countercharges at each other.

The crowd cheered as the band struck up a carnival tune. Fireworks added to an atmosphere which was already pregnant with anticipation of fast talking politicians firing their entertaining one-liners straight from the hip. The candidates, feeling the pulse of the throng, raised their hands to acknowledge the applause.

The rally did not start in earnest until a little past nine, when the party leader stood up to introduce the candidates. Suddenly, a fragmentation grenade was tossed onto the makeshift platform and, within seconds, an explosion rocked the stage. People close to the front were tossed into the air and fell lifeless to the ground. Mangled pieces of flesh and bone were everywhere. Pandemonium broke out, with people screaming and stampeding to get away from the carnage.

For a moment, the scene on stage was total chaos and confusion. After some minutes, the injured crawled to their feet crying for help. There were altogether 98 of them. Nine others, including a news photographer, lay motionless on the ground, all dead from the blast. All the candidates were wounded. The mayor of Manila, Ramon Bagatsing, lost his foot. Councilor Ambrosio Lorenzo was walking to his seat when the first blast caught him. Before he could fall to the ground, shrapnel from the second grenade tore into his body. Grenade fragments ripped through Senator Sergio Osmeña Jr and pierced his lungs. He was bleeding profusely when his aides picked him up. His heart had stopped beating when he arrived at the hospital but was revived on the operating table. Of all the injuries, Senator Jovito R. Salonga's was worst. Both explosions had gone off only metres from where he sat. The shrapnel took his left eye and three fingers. His left cheek was shattered as was most of his right arm. 'He looked like a frog on a dissecting table,' the surgeon said later. His chest and limbs were all blown open, with blood spurting from quivering tissue and metallic fragments protruding from torn musculature.

The date of the massacre was 21 August 1971. Twenty-six years later, I sat across the table from Salonga, who was now in his seventies.

'I still have more than a hundred pieces of shrapnel in my body,' he said blandly.

I kept silent.

'The doctors told me that I was dead—clinically at least.'

My eyes darted to a deep scar on his right wrist. It was more like an elongated hole about an inch in length, covered by a layer of skin.

'They're all over my body,' he said. And as if to make sure that I didn't have any doubts, he rolled up his sleeve and revealed an entire arm of gaping old wounds. 'My eye was blown off too.'

'Yes, I noticed,' I replied. His left eye was replaced by a glass piece.

'What's that?' he asked, cupping his hand to his ear. His hearing was also affected by the impact of the blast. His left index finger was reduced to a stump where the surgeons had reattached a portion of the digit to the knuckle.

Not wanting to seem as though I was staring at his injuries, I quickly moved on: 'That was a very dark period, wasn't it?'

For a moment, he looked lost. 'Yes,' he resumed, 'at that time, things were going from bad to worse...'

Even before nerves could recover, accusations erupted as the opposition pointed the finger at the ruling Nacionalistas and accused the regime of trying to wipe out its political opponents. President Ferdinand Marcos was just as predictable in his indictment of the communists, charging them with trying to seize political power through violent means. He went on television and condemned the bombing as 'an unmitigated crime against the Filipino nation and people' and accused some mainstream politicians of working hand in glove with the communist New People's Army, including Senator Benigno Simeon Aquino Jr.

But Aquino was the secretary-general of the Liberal Party and those on the stage were his party mates. Yes, Marcos countered, and he was trying to eliminate them so that he would have no rivals when the presidential election came. Besides, why was he not present at the rally that night? Aquino replied that he had planned to attend but was held up at a wedding reception for his god-daughter. He was on his way to the rally when his driver reminded him that he did not have his bulletproof vest on, so he went home to get it. He heard of the bombing while he was in his car. With gun in hand, Aquino rushed to the rally site and then to the hospital to see his colleagues.

The opposition and the press questioned Marcos's theory. If the communists wanted to seize power, why did they attack an opposition rally instead of a government one? Unmoved, Marcos went on television from his office in Malacañang Palace and fired another salvo accusing Aquino of instigating the violence and of collaborating with the communists. For good measure, the President had beside him two men who claimed they knew Aquino well but who had distanced themselves when they discovered what he was up to. Both stood silent and poker faced in front of the camera until the President motioned them away. The public was, understandably, confused. Aquino had the chance to clear the air when he was invited to debate Defence Secretary Juan Ponce Enrile on television. Enrile expectedly pressed on with the conspiracy theory of the Aquino-communist alliance.

Aquino hit back and accused the Marcos of raising the Marxist bogey as an excuse to perpetuate his own rule by imposing martial law.

The television appearance seemed to help Aquino; according to a public opinion poll, only 3% believed that the Senator was behind the massacre. Marcos didn't come off badly either as only 8% believed that he had planned the bombing. Almost half believed that it was some foe of the opposition, unseen and unknown, who did the killing. It was this frightening loom of an incorporeal enemy in the people's minds that Marcos exploited so skillfully and ruthlessly to bring an entire nation, long known for its colour and ebullience, to its knees.

Why did Marcos single out Aquino? After all, the Philippines was never short of opposition politicians who were eager to vent their vitriol on the powers that be. But Aquino, in Marcos's eyes, was not just another opposition politician. The President instinctively recognised that the Senator possessed qualities which made him a threat to his own power, and pursued his rival with a ferocity that set the stage for a titanic struggle.

The match reminded one of the wicked witch who found out that Snow White was the fairest one in the land and then set out to rid herself of the young creature. With the qualification, of course, that Aquino was not quite the wide-eyed and maidenly lass whose chastity charmed everyone. Critics charged that Aquino was the other side of the same ruthless coin as Marcos, attracted to the three 'Gs' that ran Filipino politics during that period, goons, guns and gold. Like the President, Aquino had also been accused of not hesitating to hit below the belt. And as with all coins, one side would end up flattening the other.

Those closer to him described Aquino as a veritable snake charmer who used rhetoric like a flute. As one Filipino politician told me, 'Ninoy could not only talk a bird down from a tree, he could make it sing on his shoulder.' Nicknames are commonplace, even customary, in the Philippines, and Ninoy was the name given to Aquino.

Ninoy Aquino was everything that both his adversaries and admirers said he was—and more. He was disarmingly cunning and garrulously implacable; a die-hard debater and a joker who never passed up an opportunity to entertain people with his tongue of sugar and wit of red hot chilli. Aquino attracted crowds wherever he went. He made them laugh, gave them hope and, most importantly, won their loyalty and affection.

'Ninoy could talk to anyone,' said his sister, Tess, now a congresswoman herself, as we talked in the House of Representatives in Quezon City. 'What endeared him to people was that he made you feel important when he talked to you. He grew up with a very religious mother who believed in him and that gave him the confidence he needed.'

However one saw him, it remained a fact that Aquino was a politician who had the people in his heart. This was to be the principle by which he conducted his politics—a principle for which he lived and, ultimately, died.

As a 17-year-old journalist, Aquino was despatched to Korea to cover the war for the *Manila Times*. He then travelled through Indonesia, China, Malaysia, Thailand, Vietnam and Burma, reporting the political turbulence that was ravaging East Asia at the time.

This caught the eye of Ramon Magsaysay, the Defence Secretary. Aquino quickly worked his way into his confidence and plunged into Magsaysay's election campaign when he decided to run for president. He was put in charge of devising a campaign strategy and defining the candidate's platform. When Magsaysay won the elections (he later died in a plane crash in 1957 while holding office), Aquino eased into Malacañang Palace as Special Presidential Assistant. This was not the first time that he had been to Malacañang. As a child, he was a frequent visitor to the President's office. His father, Don Benigno Aquino Sr, who himself was a senator, often visited President José P. Laurel and took Ninoy along.

Malacañang seemed to beckon him, and Ninoy likewise felt that it was a matter of course for him to one day be in the palace, not as a child or an adviser, but as the most powerful man in the country. But the path he chose to get there was arduous.

From senator to prisoner

Aquino senior died when Ninoy was still a teenager. He suffered a fatal heart attack at the ringside of a boxing match and collapsed into the arms of his son. He had been accused of being a collaborator during the Japanese occupation, and this reputation eroded Aquino's self-confidence when his friends teased him about it and ostracised him at school. With his father's death, Ninoy was determined to redeem the family name.

He joined the Nacionalista Party in 1955 at the age of 23 and became the youngest mayor in the country's history. His cherubic physique and thick rimmed glasses did not cut a figure of a dashing and dapper national hero, but it wasn't looks that the young politician counted on for political victory. It was the indefatigable personality and commitment that drove him to do what came naturally—leading from the front—that won him his battles. Six years later, he waged and won a fierce fight to become governor of his home province of Tarlac.

Meanwhile, Diosdado Macapagal had become President on the Liberal Party ticket. Fresh from victory, President Macapagal was in no mood to tolerate a young upstart as a governor. At least, that was the impression that was given publicly. What Macagapal really wanted was to have Aquino on his side. The message was clear: join the Liberal Party or face the consequences. Aquino stood his ground.

At least for as long as resources held out. In the months that followed, pressure was brought to bear on him. Tarlac was shorn of all funds for services and facilities: roads remained unpaved, teachers were dismissed, and medical supplies for the public health service slowed to a trickle. Seeing that the people were the ones to bear the brunt of realpolitik, Aquino finally relented and crossed over to the Liberals, amid accusations of being a turncoat. It was not an easy decision but he knew it was a decision he had to make for his people in Tarlac.

The Liberal Party was founded in 1946 by the first Philippine President, Manuel Roxas. It quickly grew to become the main rival of the Nacionalista Party. In 1963, President Macapagal reneged on his promise not to run for a second term. On learning this, another young politician by the name of Ferdinand Edralin Marcos stormed out of the Liberal camp. Within months, he joined the Nacionalistas and unerringly pocketed the Party's nomination for president in the 1965 elections. With the same frightening efficiency, Marcos routed

Macapagal in a bitterly fought campaign to become the sixth President of the Republic of Philippines.

No sooner had Marcos settled into office than he started planning for his re-election in four years. He initiated a systematic campaign to subjugate institutions such as the press and the judiciary that were hitherto relatively independent. Like his predecessors, he 'persuaded' those who held elected positions in the opposition camp to switch sides. Unlike his predecessor, however, Marcos was not content to let things remain the way they were. He knew that Aquino, through his years as mayor and governor, had built up a substantial army of followers. He had to move fast to curb the power of the nettlesome Governor.

And what better way to achieve this than by encouraging anti-Aquino factions to wage guerilla warfare in Tarlac, which did wonders to kill confidence in the young governor's leadership. As the situation deteriorated, the people grew increasingly terrified and weary of the violence. Again, as with President Macapagal, Aquino found himself caught in the middle of a political tug of war, with the head of state on one side and the state of hundreds of lives on the other. Only this time the President didn't see the need to play tic tac toe. He wanted Aquino out of politics entirely. To avoid further chaos and bloodshed, Aquino decided not to seek re-election. Marcos's will had prevailed, at least for the time being.

Aquino realised that Marcos would always have the upper hand as long as he remained a governor running a province which ultimately depended on the President for resources. As a senator and less encumbered by provincial blackmail, he would have a great deal more political latitude. There were only two problems. One was that after he left Malacañang to become mayor and governor, which added up to about ten years, his popularity had waned at the national level. The other was that he was just 13 days short of the required age to run for a senate seat. But to him, these were minor irritations.

Firstly, he had to convince his party colleagues that he was their ticket to power and glory. That was the easy part. Then he turned to the voters. He took to the streets, putting up billboards and filling the airwaves with his message 'Youth! Experience! Hope!' ('YEH!') to capitalise on the 'Beatlemania' that was sweeping the country. He ranted and raved against

President Marcos, blaming him for everything from running up prices of goods to running down public services. He campaigned across the country, not resting until all the speeches were made and all the hands were shaken.

It worked like a charm. When the results were announced, he was the only Liberal candidate to win out of a slate of eight. Marcos's Nacionalista Party won the rest. When the campaign began, only 6% of Filipinos had known who Aquino was. Yet he polled the second highest number of votes among all the candidates. It was a triumph well won. Tragically, it was also to be his last.

Once in office, Aquino knew that the question of his age eligibility would surface. As his term in the Senate could be cut short, he would make every day count, firing volley after volley of political charges at the President. One of them concerned a covert military operation in the East Malaysian state of Sabah. A small and secret army had been assembled by the Philippines in territory over which both they and Malaysia claimed sovereignty. The objective of Operation Jabidah was to disguise Filipino soldiers (mainly Muslims) as Malaysians to infiltrate Sabah. The soldiers would kill town dwellers to create the impression that things were out of control, and hopefully pave the way for a Philippine invasion and occupation.

As with most dubious real estate takeovers, this one ended in a terrible mess. Some of the soldiers, apparently unhappy about harsh conditions, staged a murderous mutiny in which several of the men were killed. Aquino heard of this and set out on a personal investigation. When Operation Jabidah was exposed, the intermittent skirmishes between Muslims and Government forces in the southern Philippines erupted into widespread fighting. Relations with Malaysia deteriorated to a significant low.

Marcos never forgave Aquino for the humiliating exposé. Aquino felt it his duty to call attention to the unsanctioned military operations that had jeopardised national security. Not only had he offended Marcos, but he had also trod on the toes of the army generals.

Still, he continued to barbecue Marcos with his speeches. And for dessert, he picked on First Lady Imelda Marcos, who, in 1969, had taken it upon herself to build a cultural centre as an ostentatious monument to her husband's (and her) era. Incensed by this total disregard for national priorities, Aquino launched a diatribe against the Marcos administration in a senatorial speech entitled 'Imelda's Pantheon'. The attack raised even the eyebrows of his party colleagues. To risk Marcos's ire by attacking his presidency was one thing, but to incur his wrath by taking aim at his wife was political daring, kamikaze style.

The Senator doggedly maintained that millions of impoverished Filipinos needed government aid just to survive. 'But no,' he fumed, 'a 50 million peso cultural centre must be constructed so the bejewelled elite, the nation's first one hundred families, can enjoy the Bernsteins and the Bolshoi.' There was method in his mania, however. The presidential election was drawing near, and as the Liberal standard bearer he had to dampen Marcos's chances of winning another term. This was not to be, as the incumbent drew on all his resources—personal, party and public—to secure an unprecedented second term.

The expensive campaign exacted a heavy toll on the national economy, which went into a tailspin immediately after the elections. Discontent with the administration was as widespread as it was deep. Social and economic unrest drove Marcos to take refuge in Malacañang Palace. From there the President defiantly pointed the finger at the communists for causing the chaos, a charge he would make repeatedly. Rather than seeing himself as under siege, Marcos secretly welcomed the angry actions of his countrymen. At that time, the Philippine constitution didn't allow anyone to run for the presidency for more than two terms. The longer the unrest persisted, the stronger the case he could make for his long-held plan to extend his rule by imposing martial law. The President had written in his personal diary on 17 February 1970: 'We should allow [the protesters] to gather strength but not such strength that we cannot overcome them.' He later added: 'A little more destruction and vandalism, and I can do anything.'

The charges and counter-charges of the politicians in the midst of a deteriorating economic situation only added to the confusion, which gradually led the people to lose faith in the existing political order. Demonstrations and protests escalated into open violence, and riots broke out in the cities and townships. With the midterm senatorial elections looming, Marcos and Aquino stepped up their invective against each other, with the President dropping hints that martial law was not far away.

The violent confrontation between the political forces came to a head at the Plaza Miranda bombing. Following the massacre, Marcos suspended habeas corpus and pledged that the perpetrators would be swiftly tracked down and justice meted out. Like much of Marcos's airy bombast, nothing came of the investigations and no arrests were ever made. Meanwhile, the Liberal Party continued to campaign and ended up with its candidates—lives in the balance and limbs in bandages—trouncing Marcos's by winning all the seats.

Despite their overwhelming victory, the opposition could not cool down the political tension, which was not helped by the widespread student protests against the war in Vietnam. The Filipino people continued in their state of nervous agitation in the months that followed, clueless as to who the real enemy was. No one could be ruled out of masterminding the unrest, least of all the President himself, whom the United States State Department's Bureau of Intelligence and Research not so subtly hinted 'was trying to create an atmosphere of crisis in which martial law would be acceptable.'

At about the same time, Aquino had obtained information about Operation Plan Sagittarius, which detailed the President's plans to put Manila under the control of the Philippine constabulary and to later expand this to include the whole country. The Senator wasted little time in bringing the matter before congress.

Marcos retaliated. He not only continued his accusation that Aquino was sleeping in the same political bed as the communists, but also revealed how the sneaky Senator had once divulged information about the New People's Army to the Government. In one Machiavellian masterstroke, Marcos tagged his adversary as a double dealing demagogue who now not only had the state targeting him, but the communists as well. Seeing that his adversary was setting him up for the kill and that it might happen sooner than later, Aquino warned during a televison interview: 'Mr Marcos, if I die, my blood will be on your head.'

Then one night, while returning home, Defence Secretary Enrile's car exploded. The car behind driven by his bodyguards came to a halt. Everyone was aghast at the wreckage before them, and even more outraged by what appeared to be a cold and calculated assassination attempt. Enrile was not hurt, as he had been travelling in the second car with his bodyguards. It was a lucky escape, but suspicious minded Filipinos thought it too coincidental that Enrile just happened to be in another car at the time of the attack. They were right. Years later when he broke ranks with Marcos, Enrile admitted that the attack had been staged.

Citing the 'ambush' on one of his ministers as the last straw, Marcos finally set out to do what he had long planned. On 21 September 1972, he signed Proclamation 1081 decreeing the imposition of martial law. Claiming that the Government was 'imperilled by the danger of a violent overthrow, insurrection and rebellion', the President outlawed any opposition to his authority.

Two days later, Marcos went on television to announce to the nation his rule by decree. From now on, his word was law. He wasted no time in abolishing congress and taking over the broadcast stations and public utilities. Curfews were imposed, travel out of the country was prohibited, and public speaking was banned. Hundreds of people whom Marcos considered subversive were rounded up. Aquino, of course, was among them.

The 'New Society' at Fort Magsaysay

It happened on 23 September 1972, just past midnight. Aquino was in his room at the Manila Hilton after a senate committee meeting when Colonel Romeo Gatan, under orders from Enrile, called him on the phone: 'Martial law has been imposed. Please restrain your security.'

The Senator didn't say anything for he had been expecting—and dreading—this moment. To bring the message home that resistance was useless, Gatan pointedly added, 'I have 200 men surrounding this hotel.'

Aquino did not resist. He telephoned his wife, Cory: 'Martial law has been declared and they've come for me.' There was a pause. Then he continued, 'I want you to take the children and leave the country for a while. I've made arrangements with some of the embassies here.'

Corazon Aquino would have none of it. She said sombrely, 'If you are going to die, let's all die together.' Cory was always the stabilising half of the Aquinos. In her own quiet way, she was the rock on which Aquino launched his political fights. She always deferred to her husband when it came to politics, but would not allow anyone to tell her how to run her family matters. Through the next few years when Aquino underwent the most turbulent time of his life, Cory would always be there with him.

The days after the declaration of martial law were tense. Marcos quickly promised that after he had had time to reconstruct the republic into the 'New Society', he would restore parliamentary democracy.

With Aquino in detention, the President was at last rid of his worst nightmare. Although ten years Marcos's junior, the Senator never knew his place and had been audacious enough to challenge his authority. For Marcos, duels with Aquino had become more than a fight between two shrewd tacticians in a game of deadly power play; they symbolised his personal jealousy of his younger rival. Aquino led the more enchanted life; his entry into politics was never really a struggle. Marcos, on the other hand, had to fight for every scrap of success that fate had selfishly withheld.

From an early age, Marcos had learned that violence was not to be feared. When he was still a law student his father, Mariano Marcos, lost an election for a rural seat in Congress to Julio Nalundasan. Celebrations by the victors turned into contemptuous mockery of the Marcos family. Such display of in-your-face derision of the vanquished was not altogether unheard of in rural Philippines. Neither was retaliation. Ferdinand Marcos thought nothing of avenging his father's humiliation—he shot Nalundasan while the congressman was washing up to going to bed. Marcos was subsequently charged and convicted of murder. He appealed and, in his trademark attitude to 'die with armour on one's back', gave the most scintillating oratory of his life before a panel of judges who were so moved that they ordered his acquittal. This was Marcos's first taste of victory and it whetted his appetite for more.

Then came World War II. Marcos was drafted to defend Bataan. The fighting there against the invading Japanese army was fierce and bloody, and thousands of Filipinos and Americans died. Together with tens of thousands of soldiers, Marcos was captured and sent to a prison camp. He survived the ordeal and continued to serve gallantly throughout the war. At least, that was what he told everyone. Throughout his time at Malacañang Palace, the President never let Filipinos forget this episode in his life.

The months following the imposition of martial law saw relative calm returning to the Philippines. Marcos took this opportunity to deal with some chronic social problems. A report gave him credit for tackling the festering hostility between Christians and Muslims, initiating land reform by redistributing thousands of acres to tenant farmers, cracking down on rampant corruption, cutting the fat off the bloated civil service, and keeping the communist insurgents at bay. Economic confidence returned and foreign investors came back in droves. In the first three years of martial law, the economy was in the pink of health, registering successive increases of 7 per cent. Marcos became the darling of America's corporate bigwigs.

This so impressed everyone that accolades began to flow, with *Newsweek* magazine affirming that 'What is surprising is that Marcos has so far been a dictator with a difference. He seems bent on defeating his enemies by seducing them instead of shooting them.' Even President Nixon tacitly approved of Marcos's tactics when authoritarian rule was first announced. Falling over each other to praise, or at least make more palatable, Marcos's use of his self-styled 'constitutional authoritarianism' to bring progress to the Philippines, few foresaw the ruin that was to befall the country.

Aquino and the others arrested by Marcos were imprisoned in Fort Bonifacio. One afternoon, while he was doing his exercises on the basketball court, a guard came up and said, 'Put on your clothes, we're going somewhere.' Aquino asked where he was being taken to but the officer wouldn't say. After a shower, the guards led him to a van where he saw his friend and colleague Senator José Diokno already inside. They were taken to a helicopter which had the presidential seal emblazoned on its side. Both Aquino and Diokno were then blindfolded and handcuffed.

While airborne, Aquino counted in his mind to estimate the time that had lapsed. When he reached 900, which in his computation was about 15 minutes, the chopper was still flying. His heartbeat started to race. He had no idea where he was being taken, nor what his captors were going to do to him. To calm his nerves, he started saying the rosary. After about 35 minutes and what seemed like an eternity, the helicopter landed. Still blindfolded and handcuffed, the two were led to a pickup truck and driven to a building.

Ninoy found himself in a tiny cell about 15 feet square. The walls were completely bare except for a small barred window which was boarded up from the outside, leaving only a six inch gap for air to creep through. A small light burned day and night. The door had no knob; there were no switches, no tables, no chairs—just a steel platform for a bed. The guards stripped Aquino completely. Even his eyeglasses were taken away.

'Put this on.' A plainclothes officer handed Aquino a pair of briefs and a T-shirt. 'You can wash yourself and your clothes once a day in the morning.' He thrust a bedpan at his dazed prisoner.

Just before he walked out the officer barked, 'If there is an emergency, call for the guard.' With that, he slammed the steel door shut.

Disorientation set in. Everything had happened so fast. One minute he was a senator oozing confidence and congeniality, the next he was all alone and naked in a cell. He had never felt so humiliated in his life. For a man who enjoyed the attention of his followers, solitary confinement was especially cruel. And without his glasses, his head started to throb unforgivingly.

In the next few days, Aquino sank into depression and paranoia. He suspected that his food was being poisoned and refused to eat. Later the guards gave him six crackers a day and some water, which he accepted. Pictures of Cory and the children kept preying on his mind. There were times during the agonising solitude when he thought that he was not going to able to keep it all together. He paced around the room to exercise not only his body but his senses as well, recounting all his experiences from childhood up to his arrest in minute detail until exhaustion dictated that he slept, only to wake up few hours later to repeat the meaningless process. All this took place between bouts of uncontrollable weeping.

In the bitter depths of desolation where no one else is around, God is always an easy target: 'Would God allow me to die before seeing my family? Is this God's sense of justice? Maybe God is having a sound siesta. When he wakes up, I would be gone.' But if God was sleeping, He was also listening. Just before his last strand of mental fibre snapped, Aquino underwent a spiritual experience that threw him another lifeline. He dreamed about Jesus Christ admonishing him:

> With this realisation, I went down on my knees and begged His forgiveness. I know I was merely undergoing a test, maybe in preparation for another mission. I know that everything that happens in this world is with His knowledge and consent. I know He would not burden me with a load I could not carry. I therefore resigned myself to His will.

The families of Aquino and Diokno were not told of their whereabouts or even if they were still alive. Cory was handed her husband's glasses and clothes and told nothing. For one excruciating month, both she and Diokno's wife, Nena, tried to locate their missing husbands. Then one day, the army summoned Cory to Fort Bonifacio where she half expected to see her spouse again.

She was met, instead, by an officer: 'Mrs Aquino, have you been writing to your husband?'

When Cory said yes, the officer then taunted that 'Filipino men are not to be trusted', and that another woman had been writing love letters to her husband for a long time. 'Would you like to see the letters?' he teased. 'I also have letters from your husband to this woman.'

'Things like this I only discuss with my husband,' Cory replied curtly, and asked to be excused. Although she did not show her emotions in front of the officer, the brief encounter tortured Cory, for she had been aware of Ninoy's trysts with other women. But she was not one to succumb to the psychological warfare that the army was waging. It was an especially difficult time for her. Friends and former associates started to distance themselves, partly out of fear and partly from pressure that Marcos had brought to bear upon them.

Some had even turned informants and later testified against the Senator in court.

Eventually, Cory and Nena were brought to Fort Magsaysay, where their husbands had been imprisoned. Aquino was weak and barely recognisable after being held incommunicado for 41 days. When he saw Cory and the children, he broke down and cried.

I would rather die on my feet with honour than live on bended knees in shame

Aquino was taken back to Fort Bonifacio where prison life was just a shade more bearable. It took a full 11 months after his arrest before Marcos brought charges of illegal possession of firearms, arson, treason and murder for which the penalty was death. On 27 August 1973, he faced a military tribunal in a room packed with friends and supporters. As the tribunal read out the charges, Aquino stood and kept his peace until the head of the commission asked him how he pleaded, upon which he let loose:

> Sirs, I know you to be honourable men. But the one unalterable fact is that you are the subordinates of the President. You may decide to preserve my life, but he can choose to send me to death. Some people suggest that I beg for mercy. But this I cannot in conscience do. I would rather die on my feet with honor, than live on bended knees in shame.
>
> My friends and relatives have been harassed. Some have been detained. The witnesses I intend to call are all afraid. I want to save all from further agony.
>
> I have therefore decided not to participate in these proceedings: first, because this ritual is an unconscionable mockery; second, because every part of my being—my heart and mind and my soul—yes, every part of my being is against any form of dictatorship. I agree we must have public order and national discipline, if the country is to move forward. But peace and order without freedom is nothing more than slavery. Discipline without justice is merely another name for oppression.
>
> Mr President, Honorable Members of this Commission, I fully realize the consequences of my decision. You have

your own duties to perform, I have my sad fate to meet.

I have chosen to follow my conscience and accept the tyrant's verdict.

May God have mercy on all of us!

It was a rebuke aimed right at the solar plexus of the tribunal and it packed a heavy wallop. As the crowd cheered, the winded commissioners groped for a response, for they had not expected that the lead character in their play would refuse to go along with the storyline even in the opening scene. With the performance unable to continue, the curtains fell and the case was suspended for the next one and a half years. It took another four years before a verdict was reached in 1977 after an on-again, off-again trial.

In the meantime, Aquino refused to cooperate with the commission. He continued to raise objections against the injustice of such a trial. Feeling increasingly helpless, he decided to go on a hunger strike. In a letter to his family, he explained that his action was:

> in protest against a procedure that is intended to humiliate and dehumanise me, considering that all they wanted was for me to be identified as a common criminal and not only for myself but on behalf of the many other victims of today's oppression and injustices. I know I have caused my loved ones immeasurable anguish and sorrow. But there comes a time in a man's life when he must prefer a meaningful death to a meaningless life.

Even as he continued his fast, the tribunal proceeded with the hearing. Every morning, the Senator was dragged out from his cell to appear before it.

As the days passed, Aquino grew weaker. He suffered from dizzy spells, and his body's defence mechanisms started to break down. He became so weak that his wife had to help him out of bed to go to the bathroom to wash. His body developed a foul smell because of the acids produced in a stomach deprived of food.

Marcos knew that he could not allow Aquino to die. But the prisoner was also watching the President's moves, and the two stared at each other through the walls of palace and prison to see who would blink first. Marcos did. After about a month, as the Senator lost weight at a dangerous rate of one pound a day and his conditioned reached a critical level, the President ordered that Aquino be quietly transferred to a hospital. His family and closest friends decided that they had to prevent him from fasting to death. Apart from wanting to keep him on earth for a while longer, everyone agreed that Aquino was still their best hope in their struggle against Marcos. On the fortieth day of his fast, Cory finally managed to convince her husband that the Filipino people needed him alive to continue the fight.

Not long after, the Senator received a message that the commission had finally reached a decision. He was taken before the tribunal for the judgement. Verdict: guilty on all charges. Sentence: death by firing squad.

By then it was late at night. Aquino was led back to his cell. Again, as when he was first thrown into solitary confinement at Fort Magsaysay, he felt that crushing sense of loneliness. This time, he was calm and in control of his emotions. In the days that followed, he turned to the Bible more and more for comfort and strength.

The death sentence was not carried out. Few expected that it would be. The United States Congress had threatened to cut off economic and military aid, and that seldom fails to convince impecunious autocrats. Marcos calculated that he was better off having the sentence hanging over Aquino's head than executing his arch-foe and making a martyr out of him.

International pressure became so intense that Marcos had to quickly call for a retrial. The same pressure also forced him to hold elections and bring about an end to martial law. In one of those strange compromises that eventually leads to the status quo, Marcos was obliged to conduct elections, although he was adamant that he should continue to rule by decree. Thus in 1978 he called for the election of an interim parliament in which 200 seats were up for contest. Marcos even allowed Aquino to stand for election from his prison cell. Only 20 other opposition candidates joined in the race, with the rest carrying out a boycott. The President began the political song and dance by playing his favourite tune, accusing Aquino and his supporters of being pro-communists, unworthy of national office.

The candidate with a cell for a campaign office formed his own political party, *Lakas ng Bayan* (People's Power), which when shortened to *LABAN* meant 'fight'. Eighty-year-old former Senator, Lorenzo Tañada, Aquino's close friend and mentor, became his campaign manager. The candidate was even allowed one television appearance. The years behind bars had done nothing to dull his cutting wit. By the end of the debate, his supporters were convinced that the good old Senator was back.

On the eve of the election, Tañada and other opposition leaders organised a noisy rally and encouraged Manilans to make a din that the city would never forget. When the appointed time of 7 p.m. struck on 6 April 1978 with car horns, pots and pans, musical instruments and whistles—the people, in a rare show of unity, created a barrage so deafening that even the opposition was surprised. Drivers tooted their horns and dragged empty petrol cans tied to their bumpers, residents banged on pots and pans, pedestrians blew whistles, musicians played instruments, and churches all over the city sounded their bells. Even the police took part by revving the engines of their motorcycles.

When the results were announced, to everyone's disappointment but no one's surprise, Marcos's candidates won every seat. Oppositionists led by Tañada took to the streets, infuriated by this blatant manipulation of the election results. The President had not expected the noisy challenge of the people nor the subsequent disquiet of the international community when it came to know of the electoral fraud that his henchmen had carried out. He responded by sending Tañada and the protesters to Bicutan prison. A humorist drew a cartoon of Marcos scolding a truckload of prisoners: 'Ingrates! Let them vote, and the next thing they want their ballots counted!'

Exile in America

Aquino returned to the drudgery of existence at Fort Bonifacio. The days grated on his mind like sand on silk, and his body responded accordingly. Suddenly, blessing came in the unrecognisable form of chest pains. He started to experience shortness of breath as his heart went into uncomfortable palpitations while he was out in the yard doing his exercises. He was taken to the Philippine Heart Centre for examination, where doctors agreed that he had suffered a heart attack. The cardiac problem worsened to a point where a coronary by-pass operation was necessary.

Being operated on in a land where one word from the perverse President could see his life conveniently come to an end was not on Aquino's list of solutions. If he was going to die, he wanted Marcos to be left holding the weapon. The President deferred. Arrangements were quickly made for the ailing prisoner to be sent to the United States. Even Imelda Marcos visited Aquino at the hospital and relayed to him the message that after his operation he would have to return to the Philippines and go straight back to prison. In addition, while he was in America he could not make any statement criticising the Marcos regime.

Aquino agreed to both conditions. This surprised many political observers who thought that the Senator was giving up his struggle. Even his supporters were confused by his rather quick departure from the Philippines. Before he left, Aquino told Imelda that he held nothing against the First Lady and that he took back all the nasty accusations he had hurled at her. He even gave her a gold amulet which he had worn through the years in prison to give to Marcos as a going-away present. 'It helped me these last seven years,' he told her. 'It will help him.' All this led some people to suspect that the Senator had seen the last of Filipino politics and may have struck a deal with the President to leave the country for good.

Aquino left with his wife and children on board a Philippine Airlines flight. He wore a white safari jacket with his initials embroided on the shirt pocket and a matching white pair of jeans. He looked tired but his mood was buoyant. All he cared about was that after seven mind mutilating years in jail, he was reunited with his loved ones. 'A week ago I was in my cell dreaming about the real world,' he said, unable to conceal his excitement when he arrived at the airport in Dallas. 'Now I'm here. Pinch me. I can't believe it.' He checked into Baylor Medical Centre where he underwent a successful triple by-pass operation.

Aquino then went to Boston where he accepted fellowships at Harvard University and the Massachusetts Institute of

Technology. The family bought a spacious house in a lush suburb. Life returned to normal with the children around the house, Cory going back to being a housewife, and the former prisoner driving off to work at Harvard and MIT. He gave a series of lectures and worked on a couple of manuscripts for his book. Slowly, Cory nursed her husband back to the health which he had lost during the years in prison. Aquino regained some weight but not his pre-prison chubbiness. He looked very much the statesman that he had become.

Those were days that Corazon Aquino cherished. Life was a beautiful dream, far away from the nightmare years at Fort Bonifacio. Ninoy had even promised her and the children that he would give up politics and not go back to the Philippines. Deep inside she knew that her dream would not last and that her husband would yearn to return to his homeland. The thought of returning to the Philippines and having her husband go straight back to the stockade depressed her.

Back in Manila, a storm was brewing. Marcos found out that the economy was not as easy to rig as elections. The annual GNP growth dipped from 7% to 5%, inflation soared by 26%, foreign debt ballooned to US$12 billion and real wages declined by 30%. The President was also suffering from a kidney ailment, *lupus erythematosus*, which, if left untreated, would become fatal.

Aquino was keeping his political seismograph close to the Filipino ground. Various groups of politicians as well as non-politicians who had fled the country visited his home. They kept him abreast of what was going on and the plans they were making to challenge Marcos. The National Concord for Freedom was an umbrella body formed to unite all the mainstream opposition groups to force the President to transfer power peacefully through genuine elections. Either that, the leaders declared, or face a revolution.

In concert, the Liberal Party, Aquino's Laban Party, José Diokno's Civil Liberties Union and even Marcos's own former Nacionalista Party initiated the 'Dump Marcos' movement. The more militant groups were also sharpening their knives. They, unlike the moderates, had long passed the point of negotiating with the dictator. One such group, a militant faction of the Social Democrats, persuaded Aquino to join them and lead them in their struggle. The President, they said, only understood power through tanks and grenades, a viewpoint which was later vindicated. They claimed that unfortunately warfare was necessary to topple the tyrant.

As a cocky young senator, Aquino would not have hesitated to join these militants, but his ideas had changed. 'He was profoundly influenced by Gandhi's philosophy and the civil rights leader's approach to resisting tyranny,' his sister Tess told me. 'When we watched the movie in Boston, he was very much affected, so much so that he had decided to dedicate his fight through non-violence.'

It seemed that his goals had changed as well. Getting to Malacañang was no longer the be-all and end-all of his struggle. 'No more,' he said when asked whether he would still seek high office. 'I believe that unfortunately history has passed us by, my generation anyway. We'll have to fade out with Mr Marcos. We must now build the new leadership.'

Nevertheless, the fact that so many were ready to pick up arms against Marcos disturbed Aquino. On the one side were Marcos's men armed to the teeth, and on the other was the guerilla movement which was busy multiplying its arsenal. He ventured to Saudi Arabia to see whether he could raise funds to buy arms for the moderates as well as to meet exiled Filipino Muslim guerilla leader Nur Misuari. He also visited Nicaragua at the invitation of President Daniel Ortega to take part in the second anniversary celebration of the Sandinista revolution. After his visits, Aquino grew more convinced than ever that an armed revolution was not the answer to his country's ills. Yet, secretly, he knew that Marcos would not hesitate to fight. Violence seemed unavoidable.

In August 1980 Aquino broke his promise that he would not criticise the regime when he was in the United States and accepted an invitation to speak at the Asia Society in New York. He called on Marcos to return the Philippines to democracy and put an end to martial law. Pre-empting any attack from Marcos about his promise not to criticise the President while in the United States, Aquino argued that 'a pact with the devil was no pact at all.' He urged reconciliation between government and opposition, and made it clear that he wanted no violence:

> I have decided to pursue my freedom struggle through the path of non-violence, fully cognisant that this may be the longer and the more arduous road. If I have made the wrong decision, only I and maybe my family will suffer. Only I will suffer solitary confinement once again, and possibly death by firing squad.

Aquino also issued a stern warning to Marcos, saying that the situation had deteriorated to such an extent that violent revolution by forces within and outside of the country was imminent. He cautioned: 'I've met with men and women who are determined to launch an urban guerilla movement. They've read all the manuals and all the books. They are prepared and ready to go.'

Barely a month later, bombs started exploding in Manila's government offices, private companies and commercial buildings. All told, 45 people were wounded and two killed. Marcos himself came close to being a victim when a bomb went off only 50 feet from him while he was attending a public function hosted by the American Society of Travel Agents. Far away as he was, Aquino was accused of being behind the attacks and was called the 'Mad Bomber.' Mad Bomber or no Mad Bomber, the terrorists vowed that they would continue their campaign until Marcos stepped down—or was dead.

That same year, Ronald Reagan replaced Jimmy Carter as United States President. Under Carter, Marcos had a rather stormy relationship with Washington while Aquino enjoyed a warm relationship with the American President. When Reagan came into power, things changed. Reagan looked upon Marcos more benignly than his predecessor ever did, and alienated Aquino in the process.

Ever the tactician, Marcos immediately played up the situation to his own advantage. Like an abstract artist with an expansive brush, Marcos painted the formless villain of communism and plastered it on Aquino. By accusing his foe of masterminding the bombing campaign, Marcos managed to taint Aquino in the eyes of the White House. At the same time he scared Reagan, who seemed a willing victim, into believing that if the communists succeeded in their campaign, the United States would lose its military bases in the Philippines. Marcos also attempted to negotiate an extradition treaty to bring back those in exile in the United States, claiming that they were criminals who had to be tried in Philippine courts.

'Carter refused,' Raul Manglapus, former Philippine foreign affairs secretary and one of the exiles during Marcos's rule, said to me. 'But the minute Reagan was elected, the Secretary of State, Alexander Haig, came here and signed the treaty. Fortunately, that time, the Senate was still in the hands of the Democratic Party and it signalled the State Department that it might as well not submit the treaty because it would not be ratified.'

Instead, Washington continued to apply pressure on Marcos to lift martial law, which he did on 15 January 1981, calling for presidential elections. Wary Filipinos were not impressed. With all the institutions under tight control and the ever vigilant secret police keeping a close tab on all political movements, nothing had really changed.

When elections came, Marcos announced his candidacy for the presidency, ignoring the constitutional limit of two terms. The opposition boycotted the election, saying that Marcos had done nothing to reform the system so that the polls would, at the very least, be free and fair. Unfazed, Marcos went through the process of counting the ballots—real and faked—and proclaimed himself ruler of the Philippines for another six year term. Meanwhile, the Reagan administration seemed content to be charmed by Marcos's political shenanigans. Vice-President George Bush attended the inauguration ceremony where he praised the dictator for adhering to 'democratic principles and to the democratic process.'

Realising that the longer he stayed in the United States, the greater the havoc Marcos would wreak back at home, Aquino made up his mind to return to the Philippines. Friends and relatives naturally cautioned him against this move. There was still an outstanding death sentence on him. What was certain was that the President would have his old foe locked up again at Fort Bonifacio, very possibly for good this time.

Aquino had not come to this decision lightly. He weighed all the political ramifications of not returning and found them unacceptable. Foremost in his calculations was that Marcos was unaware of the pressure building up against him and was not entirely in control of the situation. If and when the lid popped, Aquino contended, 'violence would develop into a momentum of its own and we will all be sucked into the vortex.' He also predicted that Marcos would not live much longer, given his fight with the kidney disease, leading to a power vacuum. Aquino predicted one of two scenarios: either the military under Marcos's right hand man, General Fabian Ver, would engineer a coup and establish junta rule, or the communist New People's Army would make a successful grab for power.

He was convinced that either outcome would plunge the country into greater misery. Ironically, he concluded, Marcos was the only one who could tame the beast that he had himself created, and the only way this could be done was for the President to restore democracy. Repeatedly, Aquino called for dialogue with Marcos, with the objective of initiating such a transition. This, however, could not be achieved as long as he stayed away: 'I think my usefulness in America has come to an end. And I think I'll be able to help the opposition from there more effectively than from the safety of America.'

When Marcos got wind of Aquino's intention to return, he quickly despatched his wife Imelda to the United States to try to change his mind.

'Since you were the one who got me out of prison, I want to tell you that I am coming back,' Aquino said to Imelda, who pretended she did not know of his intentions. The two met at her request when she visited New York City in 1983. Imelda told Aquino that her husband had extended his medical furlough and that he should stay in the United States a little longer. Aquino replied that his fellowship was coming to an end, and that he had no intention of seeking political asylum in the United States.

'You realise that if there is a conflict of interest between you and Marcos, he would be stupid to let yours prevail,' Imelda said. It was a threat—subtle, but nonetheless very real.

Aquino responded with a matter of fact 'Yes.'

Sensing that she was not getting anywhere, the First Lady pushed on and told her obstinate opponent that if he went home, he 'must be jailed'.

Aquino feigned innocence. Imelda then pointed out that if Aquino were permitted freedom in the Philippines and harmed, her husband's interests 'would be hurt'. It was a classic match of shadow boxing, of which Imelda was a worthy exponent.

Aquino asked her who would want to kill him.

'Many people,' she parried, adding that he had 'many enemies' and that the communists would kill him and 'blame it on my husband'.

When she saw that he was undeterred, shadow boxing suddenly turned into seductive bribery. She promised that she could obtain funds from wealthy financiers for his personal use provided he did not return to the Philippines.

Aquino remained adamant and insisted that he had to go back.

The journey home

On 13 August 1983, Aquino left Boston to make his journey back to his homeland. The previous night, Cory told her husband that she felt helpless and scared, very much like the day he was arrested when martial law came into effect. Aquino wasn't sure what to say. All he knew was that it was tearing him up having to leave his loved ones behind. He also knew that he had a mission to fulfil which could not be postponed. They had arranged for Cory and the children to wait a couple days before joining him in Manila. That night they held each other, afraid of what lay ahead.

Next morning, people came to the house to wish Aquino well and to say goodbye. After attending mass at a nearby church, he made his way to the airport. At the departure gate, Cory said goodbye and reminded him to call at every stop. He smiled and nodded, and then walked away into the passenger ramp.

The flight took him to Los Angeles. Both Manila and Washington, for very different reasons, were keeping a close watch on his movements. He left Los Angeles and flew to Singapore with a brief stopover in Tokyo. His plan was to travel around various cities in Asia to confuse Marcos's surveillance. He would move from Singapore to Malaysia, then back to Singapore, then to Taiwan and, finally, from there to Manila.

He was travelling under a fake passport and fictitious name, Marcial Bonifacio, a cheeky combination referring to martial law and Fort Bonifacio. He kept his promise and called Cory wherever he stopped. They had a pre-arranged code that would indicate to her where he was without him having to say so over the phone. Each time he called, Cory would read a Bible passage to her husband, which had a great calming effect on him. Tipped off about his departure from Boston, the Philippine Government also started making calls, trying to find out what the man was up to.

When he arrived in Singapore, Aquino was greeted by a son of the Sultan of Johor, whom he had come to know when the prince was studying in Boston. With several bodyguards, the prince took his very important but very furtive guest across the causeway which linked Singapore to peninsular Malaysia. From there they proceeded to the Malaysian capital, Kuala Lumpur, where Aquino met with government officials behind closed doors.

Up until then, Aquino had managed to travel relatively undetected by Marcos's secret police who, unexpectedly, received some help when he arrived back in Singapore. As he was passing through customs at Changi Airport, his passport caught the attention of the immigration officials who took it away for several minutes. When they returned, he was handed back his passport and allowed to proceed. Meanwhile, Singapore's own secret police had informed the Filipino authorities that the man they were looking for had just been through the country. En route to Taipei, Aquino made a brief stopover in Hong Kong. Marcos's agents had already flown there from Manila.

While in the British colony, the former Senator stopped to make his call to Cory. As before, Cory read a Bible passage to her husband. He spoke briefly with each of his children and, as he did so, tears ran down his cheeks. After he hung up, he wrote each of them a letter.

At Taipei's Chiang Kai-shek International Airport, he passed through immigration uneventfully. Just as he was about to clear customs, two Taiwanese military officials took him aside. They only wanted to confirm that everything was all right with him. Aquino was joined by his brother-in-law, Ken Kashiwahara, a newsman from the American Broadcasting Corporation, who would accompany him on the final leg of the journey to Manila.

Aquino had organised the international media to meet him in Taipei and join his flight to the Philippines. He thought that this would make it less likely that his enemies would attempt anything rash. In the event that they did, the situation would, at least, get maximum coverage. He was, tragically, only half correct.

Throughout his journey from Boston to Manila, Aquino was on an emotional roller-coaster. One minute he was chatting excitedly with friends and journalists, the next he was racked with fear and gloominess. He held Cory and his children close in his mind. He knew that he was walking straight back into the arms of a treacherous enemy who would just as soon see him removed from the face of this earth.

The question was just a matter of the *modus operandi*: would he be jailed again or assassinated? More than once he considered calling the whole thing off and returning to Boston, but each time his sense of mission got the better of him.

On the morning he was to leave Taipei for Manila, Aquino woke up early and put on his white safari jacket and jeans, the same clothes he had worn when he left the Philippines three years earlier. He was quietly proud of the fact that he could still fit into them. Together with the journalists and cameramen, he made his way to the airport. Preceding him were some of Aquino's old acquaintances who had gone to check in his baggage and obtain his boarding pass. Still fearful that the Taiwanese authorities might change their mind and prevent him from leaving, he wanted to get on to the plane as quickly as possible.

He even tried to disguise himself as a tourist on vacation with his girlfriend. For the part, he chose *Time* correspondent Sandra Burton. In her book, *Impossible Dream*, she gave a first hand account of her experience at the airport with her hastily arranged 'boyfriend':

> I put on a big smile and did my best to look infatuated and on vacation. Soon we were laughing about this weird 'honeymoon' on which we were embarked.
>
> Suddenly a voice behind us boomed, 'Are there any Filipinos here?' I continued to smile and chat, pretending not to hear the question.

'Turn around and keep talking,' Ninoy instructed me under his breath.

His back was still turned to me, and he was staring at the window wall to his far right, behind which a man in a beige uniform stood staring back at him.

'There's my guardian angel,' he whispered, excitedly.

Indeed, the Taiwan security connection on whom Ninoy had been counting appeared to be in place. The security man's eyes met his again for a split second. By now the agent, who just seconds ago had been searching for Filipinos, was nowhere to be seen, while the 'guardian angel' appeared to be positioning himself to help Ninoy through the passport checkpoint, should there be any questions about his papers.

He passed behind the glass, where he was greeted cordially by his contact. When I reached them a few moments later, they were engaged in conversation. We were given full VIP treatment through the line for the hand luggage check. Just as we caught sight of our departure gate, number 6, the guardian angel halted in response to the crackle on his walkie-talkie. He held the device to his ear, then spoke into it in Mandarin. 'Wait one moment,' he said to Ninoy. 'My boss wants to meet you.' Ninoy froze, and no wonder. We had gotten to within yards of our plane without incident, only to be stopped in the stretch. Observing our discomfort, our escort smiled. 'Don't worry,' he said.

The uniformed personnel near the luggage scanner stepped back and bowed as a thin Chinese man, dressed in a Western suit and obviously well known to them, strode in our direction. Our escort also bowed, then introduced Ninoy. The thin man pumped Ninoy's hand energetically, then pulled him aside to say a few words. They shook hands again, and I heard the gentleman wish him 'Good luck.' He and the guardian angel then turned and walked away, while Ninoy and I went to the gate.

'Who was that?' I asked Ninoy.

'The head of the Taiwan Garrison Command,' he answered.

It was 11.15 a.m. when China Airlines flight 811 cleared the runway in Taipei.

Aquino found his aisle seat on row 14. Ken Kashiwahara was seated across the aisle from his brother-in-law. A few passengers stared curiously at the man in white, not quite sure if he was really who they thought he was. Everyone in the party looked tense as the plane climbed towards cruising altitude. Aquino, after the anxious moments at the airport terminal, was visibly fatigued.

When the seat belt sign was switched off, he relaxed a little. The newspeople, who had hitherto acted as if they did not recognise Aquino, went straight to work with their cameras, tape recorders and notebooks. Never one to disappoint the media, Aquino duly held an in-flight press conference. He reiterated that he was going home to try to forge a reconciliation between Marcos and the moderate opposition so that a peaceful transition of power could be effected through democratic elections. He also knew that Marcos was in no mood to negotiate a transfer of power, at least not a peaceful one, and acknowledged that he was putting his own safety on the line, but added that it was a mission he was determined to see through. When lunch was served, Aquino went back to his seat but did not touch his food.

Burton had taken the seat beside him and they sat chatting:

> His gaze had turned to the window, where the lush green landscape of the northern Philippine island of Luzon suddenly hove into view beneath the clouds. Ninoy was ecstatic.
>
> 'I'm home. All I have to do is kiss Philippine soil, and that will be enough, don't you think?' he asked.
>
> For the first time during our short acquaintance, I voiced a personal opinion about what he was telling me. 'No,' I said impulsively, 'that's not enough. You have so much more to do.'
>
> He had been through so much, and he spoke with such clarity about what his country needed. He was the underdog, and he was full of such passion. I was the American, and I believed that people like him made a difference. What had seemed to me a fruitless mission only yesterday now appeared to be a rare convergence of the right leader at the right time.

As the plane started its descent, Aquino strode over to the aft toilet where he pulled on a bulletproof vest and then put on his safari jacket over it. He told Ken that he didn't think they would assassinate him, but he couldn't take the chance. 'But if they hit me in the head, I'm a goner.' He then took off his gold watch and handed it to his brother-in-law: 'I want you to have this.'

Then he added, 'Don't forget to go to my house as soon as we land and have someone take my belongings to me in prison.' He had no doubt that he would be going straight to Fort Bonifacio.

The flight attendants came over to Aquino to wish him luck. Some of the passengers wanted to have their photographs taken with him. After the brief fuss, he went back to his seat. As the pilot made the final approach to the runway, he took out his rosary beads and prayed silently. He thought of his wife and children.

It was one o'clock in the afternoon when the plane landed at Manila International Airport. 'Ninoy,' Ken called out softly, 'we're home.'

Aquino looked at him and smiled.

'We hope you've enjoyed your flight and will fly again soon with China Airlines,' the stewardess announced as the pilot taxied the aircraft to its berth. Outside there were machine guns and tanks in close proximity. Sharpshooters were strategically perched on top of the terminal building. Then a blue van with the insignia of the Aviation Security Command (AVSECOM) pulled up beside the plane. Soldiers armed with magnums and M-16s jumped out and surrounded the aircraft, pointing their weapons away from it, ready to fire upon any intruder.

Inside the terminal, a huge crowd had been gathering since morning. It was a mass of yellow shirts, dresses and hats. The buses that had ferried them there were decked with yellow ribbons. They were welcoming home their hero in the spirit of the song *Tie a Yellow Ribbon Round the Old Oak Tree*. Among them was Aquino's 73-year-old mother, Doña Aurora. His siblings, relatives and close friends who had organised the homecoming party were packed into the VIP lounge. The arrival lounge and even the carpark outside were filled with thousands of supporters. From where he was sitting, Aquino could not see them, and anxiously asked if anyone had come to greet him.

Back in Boston, it was a little after midnight. Cory was still awake. She had an ominous feeling that something terrible was going to happen. Then Ballsy, their eldest daughter came into her room. She, too, could not sleep. And so mother and daughter sat up and talked, trying to comfort each other. Cory calculated that her husband would just be arriving in Manila.

When the plane came to a complete halt and the seat belt sign was turned off, everybody stood up to disembark. Suddenly, the pilot announced that all passengers were to remain in their seats for ten minutes. A few seconds later, the drama began.

Three men entered the aircraft: one was wearing the Philippine Constabulary uniform while the other two were in khaki AVSECOM outfits. Immediately, the television crew and journalists crowded round Aquino. The Constabulary man walked down the aisle, obviously uncomfortable with all the cameras trained on him, straight past Aquino. The first AVSECOM officer also missed him. The third man spotted him and came up to shake his hand. Aquino smiled and accepted the offer. Then the officer made a cursory body search and felt the bulletproof vest that Aquino was wearing.

Cory looked at the clock. It was a little after 1 a.m. She became increasingly anxious and went to the bathroom to pray.

As he stood up, one AVSECOM officer took Aquino's bag and the other grabbed his arm. The third man gripped his wrist. Aquino, who had been smiling all this time, suddenly became tense. His lips were pulled taut and a grim look came over his face. Ken Kashiwahara stood up: 'I'm coming with him. I'm his brother-in-law.' An AVSECOM officer turned round and replied coldly, 'You sit down.' With that, they led Aquino down the aisle. A few more officers had gathered at the entrance of the plane. Some were in plainclothes, wearing the customary *polo barong* shirts, while others were in uniform.

The press crew rushed after Aquino who was led out of the plane and on to the passenger tunnel. The officers at the entrance suddenly formed a human barrier and cut them off. Sensing that something was amiss, the newspeople tried to break through the cordon, but it held firm. They then poked their cameras, microphones and tape recorders above and below the officers, trying to catch an electronic glimpse of what was happening. The security men responded by placing their hands over the lens of the cameras.

Noynoy, Aquino's son, was also awake. He was watching television and tuned in to a cable channel to see if there was word of his father's arrival in Manila.

Instead of taking Aquino into the terminal, the AVSECOM personnel suddenly swung him towards a doorway on the left where a stair ramp had been placed to take them down to the waiting blue AVSECOM van. Aquino disappeared from view as he was led down the stairway.

Halfway down, one of the officers shouted, 'Ako na, ako na! (I'll do it!)'

'Kanila na, kanila na! (They can have it!)' came another voice.

'Eto na (Here he is),' someone else shouted.

Then a female voice cautioned: 'Manong magigiba ito—magigiba ito! (It will collapse!),' apparently referring to the ramp.

'Get down, get down!' someone shouted in English.

The ramp began to shake dangerously as the commotion grew.

At that moment a voice was heard, 'Pusila! (Shoot him!)'

Another voice echoed, 'Pusila!'

A woman inside the plane screamed.

'What happened? What was that?' Burton shouted.

It was a single gunshot, followed seconds later by another five. Passengers scrambled for safety, screaming and crying. The media crew were hysterical, scrambling to the plane windows.

A man kept shouting, 'Inside, inside, inside.'

Another volley of shots rang out.

Aquino slumped forward; the bullet had pierced the back of his head and came out through his chin. The guards, unable to prop him up, let him fall a few feet from the ramp. He crashed heavily, scraping his face on the ground.

Just then, a man wearing a blue shirt suddenly appeared from out of nowhere. A hail of bullets from the armed AVSECOM personnel riddled his torso. He spun round and collapsed onto the ground. Another soldier ran up, pointed his M-16 at the dead body and unloaded several more rounds into it.

Sandra Burton shouted, 'The soldiers...they put sixteen shots in him. They shot Ninoy...they're dead, he's dead out there.'

Aquino lay face down on the tarmac, arms outstretched, with blood spurting from the bullet hole in his head. His white safari suit was stained red.

An eerie silence followed and for a few seconds the world seemed to stop. The date was 21 August 1983, exactly 12 years since he had escaped death at the Plaza Miranda bombing. At the age of 50, Aquino had finally come home. He had paid the ultimate price for the freedom for his people.

Finding the facts

The room was packed with onlookers who had come to hear the testimony of the soldiers. Presiding over the hearing was the Fact-Finding Board (FFB) commissioned by Marcos. Naturally, the FFB carried the odium of being another of Marcos's instruments to whitewash the affair. Chaired by a former Court of Appeals judge, Corazon J. Agrava, the only woman on the five member panel, it was an improvement on an initial investigative body led by Supreme Court Chief Justice Enrique Fernando. The Fernando Commission, as it came to be known, was so hopelessly compromised by Fernando's close relations with the First Family that it bowed to intense public ridicule and relinquished its authority after only two sittings. Unlike its predecessor, the FFB was determined to prove that it was capable of carrying out an impartial and fearless inquiry.

Even before the process could begin, Marcos unleashed a predictable torrent of charges against the communists, laying the blame for the assassination of Ninoy Aquino squarely at their feet. The decision to eliminate the former Senator, Marcos claimed, was made by none other than the general-secretary of the Philippine Communist Party, Rodolfo Salas. He was referring to his earlier claim that Aquino had befriended and subsequently betrayed his communist comrades.

'The protection of a public official's life against a determined killer who is ready to die in the attempt at assassination will always be one of the most difficult, if not impossible, tasks of security men in the world,' the President tried to explain. He promised that no resources would be spared to bring the perpetrators to justice 'in the quickest possible time.'

But all was not well with Marcos. His kidney problem had deteriorated to a point where an emergency transplant operation had to be carried out in secret. His absence from public view only fuelled talk that he might be directly responsible for the Aquino's slaying. Many at that time believed that the President could not have ordered—or even wished for—Aquino's assassination, especially as it was done so brazenly. The cunning of the man, they argued, did not match the clumsiness of the murder. Still, most Filipinos were convinced that the President was deeply involved in Aquino's death.

In Washington, officials were scrambling to make sense of the situation and to chart its course for the coming weeks. The Reagan administration did not want to do anything to jeopardise its agreement with the Philippines over Subic Bay and Clarke Air Base. So strong was the prevailing mood in the White House that it was not even prepared to consider the involvement of the AVSECOM security men in the assassination, let alone Marcos's hand in the affair.

Back at the FFB hearing, the military officials were called to testify first. One by one, they repeated their well drilled story that they had seen a man wearing a blue shirt, later identified as Rolando Galman, come from behind the service stairs, pull out a gun and shoot Aquino in the head as the former Senator was led across the tarmac to the van. It was then that the officers opened fire at Galman. A total of 41 officers testified that Galman was the killer; 82 eyes, surely, could not hallucinate in unison. No one else, at least no one who would come forward to testify otherwise, was witness to those few crucial seconds.

If the soldiers' words tallied, logic didn't. First, there was the issue of the security cordon that was thrown round the plane as it docked at the terminal. With all the security personnel deployed at the scene, how did the gunman get so close without being spotted?

Second, audiotapes and cameras of the journalists who had been with Aquino had recorded the moments from when he stepped out of the plane to the time the first shot rang out. A total of ten seconds had elapsed, too short a period for him to have reached the ground and stride to the point where the soldiers claimed the shooting took place.

Third, the trajectory of the bullet was downwards through Aquino's head, entering the occipital region behind the left ear and exiting through the chin. The alleged assassin would have to be much taller than Aquino to fire the gun at such an angle. Galman was only one centimetre taller than the man he was supposed to have killed. The bullet through Aquino's head would have to have been fired from an elevated position such as the service stairs.

Fourth, why was Galman shot repeatedly after he had fallen? Before he even hit the ground, he had already taken five direct hits, including one in the head. Another soldier then came up and killed him some more with his M-16. Why did the soldiers want to make sure that Galman didn't live?

Fifth, photographs showed that Galman's body was lying in front of Aquino's. If the gunman had come up from behind and had been shot immediately after he pulled the trigger, as described by the soldiers, it would have been impossible that he could have fallen in front of Aquino.

Sixth, how did Galman know that Aquino would be disembarking at that particular terminal and, for that matter, taken down the service stairs instead of going through the passenger ramp?

Seventh, what motive did Galman have? To be sure, he was not exactly Manila's model citizen. He had been convicted of several crimes including murder, robbery and illegal possession of firearms. But there was no evidence to link him to the communists whom the Marcos regime so badly wanted people to believe were responsible for the assassination. Only Galman himself knew what he was doing at the murder scene, and he was not telling.

Contrary to the military's testimony, all the evidence pointed to the fact that the shot had not been fired by the blue-shirted lone assassin on the ground, but by one of the military escorts while Aquino was still on the service stairs. Unless an eyewitness could testify to this, little more could be said about the incident.

The breakthrough came when Ramon Balang, a member of the airport ground crew, plucked up enough courage to tell the FFB what he had seen. As the China Airlines plane pulled up to the terminal, he had gone about his routine of checking the aircraft. That was when he noticed a stranger wearing a blue shirt amongst a group of uniformed airport service personnel. Then he heard a shot and saw a man in white fall to the ground with blood coming out of his neck. The blue-shirted man was surrounded by the AVSECOM soldiers. He was smiling at them as if he knew them, and at one point, was waving to them. Suddenly, the soldiers shot him repeatedly.

Balang intimated that he had kept this information to himself because he feared losing his job and the harm that would befall his family if he spoke up. On hearing this, Defence Secretary Enrile, who by now was becoming increasingly disenchanted with the President, immediately ordered guards to be posted to protect Balang.

Balang's account confirmed the suspicion that the FFB and almost everyone else had all along: Rolando Galman was recruited to be the fall guy, and had been set up by the conspirators to be present at the time Aquino arrived at the airport. His specific role still remains unclear, but he was probably told that Aquino's assassination was going to take place and that he was there to kill the assassin. The FFB was now convinced that they had uncovered a plot within the ranks of the armed forces. The question that remained was, how high did the conspiracy go?

The FFB members surprised everyone when they went all the way to the top and called General Fabian Ver before them. The General had been a longtime ally of Marcos, entrusted with the responsibility of commanding all military, police and intelligence units in the Philippines. Wielding such authority, Ver was a much feared man. Even Imelda Marcos had learned to defer to the General, as she harboured ambitions to become president herself. Knowing that the position required the patronage of the powerful armed forces, Imelda was aware that Ver was an indispensable source of support.

Taking the stand, Ver conducted himself well and gave away nothing that might incriminate himself or the President. Then he stumbled when asked about his knowledge of Aquino's arrival date. At first, he said that he had no knowledge of the Aquino's movements. This had to be the story if he was going to protect himself and his men from being implicated in the shooting. But this was also the story that revealed the vermin in Ver.

When the board expressed disbelief that the man in charge of the country's overall intelligence had no idea of how or when a returning fugitive would arrive in his own backyard, the General knew that he was cornered. After intensive questioning, he finally conceded that he had known Aquino's movements after he received the tip-off from Singapore that the former Senator was travelling on a fake passport en route to Taiwan.

Other pieces of evidence began to come out which made it increasingly unlikely that Aquino had been assassinated by Rolando Galman. As the FFB began to wind up its investigations—which had lasted for almost a year, recorded more than 20,000 pages of testimony given by 193 witnesses, and examined nearly 2,000 photographs and exhibits—word got out that General Ver was among those who would be indicted.

Marcos resorted to intimidating the members of the board when he failed to persuade them not to cite Ver. Chairperson Agrava crumbled. She filed a separate report from her fellow members in which she left out the General's involvement and so became the lightning rod for public anger. The other four members pressed on. To them, Ver could not have been innocent of the whole sordid affair. They presented their report to Marcos and called a press conference to announce their findings. They needed to go public as quickly as possible as bearers of bad news often bore the brunt of Marcos's bellicosity.

A horde of media personnel and onlookers had congregated for the event; the boldness of the remaining FFB members created an atmosphere of tense expectancy. After months of questioning and listening, action was at last forthcoming. One of the FFB members rose and announced: 'In the light of all the foregoing considerations, we find the following to be indictable for the premeditated killing of Senator Benigno S. Aquino, Jr and Rolando Galman at the Manila International Airport on August 21, 1983.'

Cheers erupted in anticipation.

'General Fabian C. Ver.'

The audience went wild. It was the one name they wanted to hear. A total of 25 military personnel and one civilian were indicted. Among the uniformed officers named were a major-general, a brigadier-general, two colonels, three captains, a lieutenant, twelve sergeants, two police officers and two airport officials.

Marcos knew that he was beaten. Under mounting public pressure, he was forced to relieve Ver of his post. Ver was subsequently charged in a civilian court with his co-conspirators. The President, always looking ahead, promised his trusted aide and longtime friend that he would be reinstated at a later time after he had been acquitted. True to his word, Marcos reappointed Ver and his men when the appropriately named Graft and Corruption Court acquitted them. The General was back in business.

But even without the conviction of Aquino's killers, the FFB had inflicted a wound that would eventually prove fatal to the President and his regime.

The revolution begins

Cory Aquino remained unimpressed by the proceedings. She believed that Marcos was responsible for her husband's death and she said so openly. When she first learned of her husband's assassination through a phone call in Boston, she called her children around her. They prayed and cried together.

In Manila, when they heard that Aquino had been shot, his family and supporters made their way to the nearby Baclaran Church to pray for him, not knowing that he was already dead. At the camp where Aquino's body had been taken, officials only allowed the immediate family to enter the premises. His body was wrapped in a green sheet and placed on a knee-high shelf. Tess pulled open the cover, and the family was shocked to see the bloodied corpse. Doña Aurora let out a long, piercing scream, holding her son's head to her bosom. When the officials came to remove the body, Doña stared at them: 'Just give him back to me. I don't want you to touch him—I want the world to see what they did to my son.'

Cory took the lonely flight back to Manila. She knew that she had to repress her own pain, at least for the few mind numbing days ahead when personal and national decisions had to be made. First she wanted to be alone with Ninoy to say her last goodbye. When she saw her husband's body, tears overcame her tired eyes. She bent over and planted a kiss on his forehead. His closed eyes were red and swollen. Lacerations on his face were still clear. A dark hole in the chin where the single bullet exited remained untouched. His proud jacket had turned blood red. The image of a once effervescent senator now lying in a bloody mess was a powerful symbol that would focus the world's attention on Marcos's ruthless dictatorship. She had no intention of letting her husband's death be in vain.

To be sure, Cory was not always that sanguine about her fellow citizens. During the days of Aquino's incarceration, she would often complain to him that Filipinos were apathetic cowards, forever willing to roll over and play dead to Marcos's bullying. She was not the only one to feel this way. José Diokno, who had been in solitary confinement at Fort Magsaysay with Aquino, once said that, apart from those arrested, the Philippines was made up of '49 million cowards and one sonavabitch.'

As Aquino's body lay in state in their home in Quezon City, thousands came to say farewell to their martyr. There was an outpouring of grief as people openly wept. Street vendors, clerks, factory hands, janitors, bus drivers, housewives, teenagers and old people formed lines that snaked through the streets. Slowly, the middle class joined the line. Then the rich and furious came as well. Cory saw how her husband's death had breathed life and courage into the people again, and her confidence returned. She made a pledge to her husband that she would continue the struggle to bring freedom back to the people—a pledge that she made good when she rallied them to overthrow Marcos in a bloodless revolution.

On 31 August 1983, the cortege left for Santo Domingo church. Two million people stood in the rain to say their personal goodbyes to Senator Aquino. Before the casket was brought to the church, the procession headed for Tarlac, the province that launched the young governor on his career. Along the way, villagers poured out in the hundreds of thousands to pay their respects. Metro Manila came to a standstill as teachers, students, expatriate workers, nuns, public servants and corporate executives came out to witness the event.

At one point, emotions started to get the better of some of the marchers, who shouted that Aquino's body now belonged to the people and not just to the family. It seemed that the casket was going to be snatched away to become the centre of an explosive riot. Fortunately, the masses kept their cool and the procession continued in an orderly fashion. Shopkeepers brought out water, sandwiches and biscuits for the marchers who formed a protective cordon around the casket and the family cars, breaking into chants of 'Ni-noy! Ni-noy!'. The police were so outnumbered that their presence became meaningless.

Inside the church, Aquino's coffin, draped in the national flag, was surrounded by his family. Cardinal Jaime Sin, the popular Archbishop of Manila, read mass. When Cory rose to deliver the final message, her voice cracked with emotion. The people responded with an impassioned standing ovation. With each reminder of Aquino's love for his homeland and the sacrifices that he had made, the applause grew more thunderous. And when she finally thanked the people for demonstrating that her husband had not died in vain, the week-long funeral reached an emotional climax. The revolution had begun.

As Cardinal Sin said the final prayers and committed Aquino's soul to eternity, a crescendo of weeping filled the hall. 'The mass has ended,' Sin bade farewell. 'Go in peace. Goodbye, my friend.'

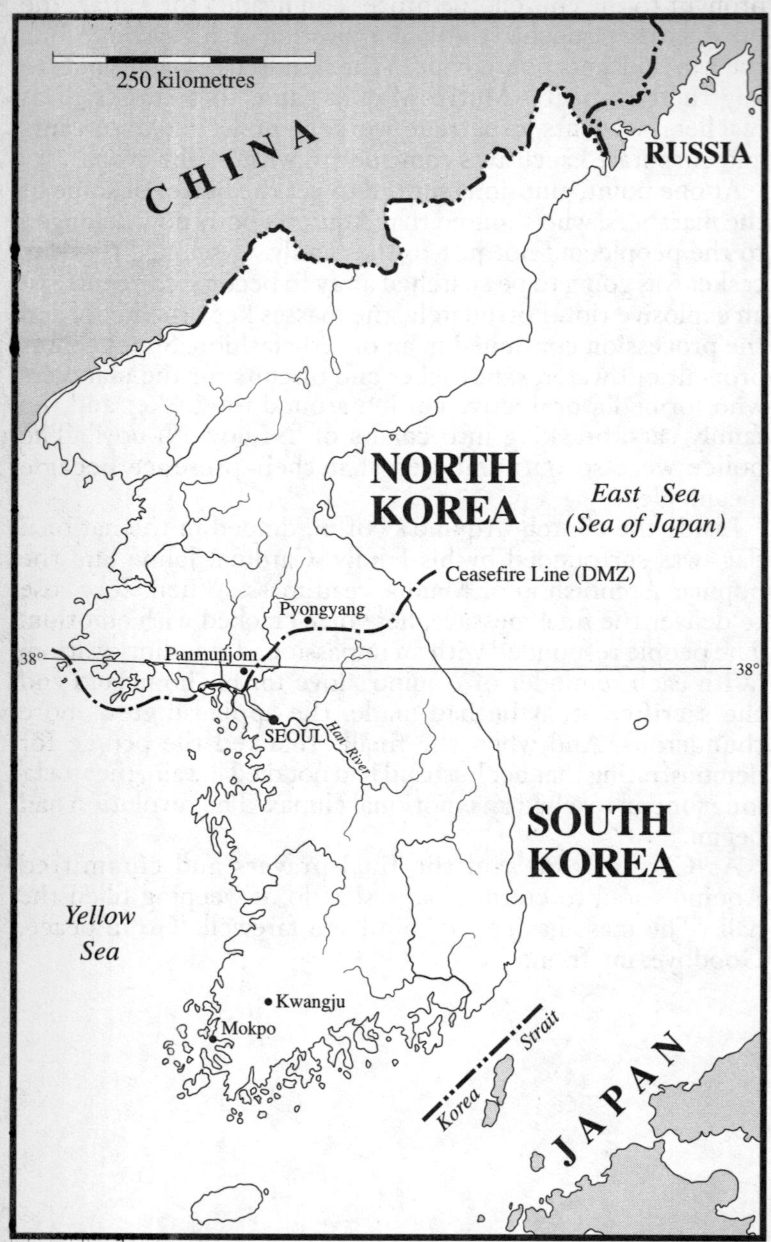
250 kilometres
CHINA
RUSSIA
NORTH KOREA
East Sea
(Sea of Japan)
Ceasefire Line (DMZ)
Pyongyang
38°
Panmunjom
38°
SEOUL
Han River
SOUTH KOREA
Yellow Sea
Kwangju
Mokpo
Korea Strait
JAPAN

5
South Korea
Kim Dae Jung

Getting a seat

This is a story about a Korean politician who survived two assassination attempts, a kidnapping, numerous house arrests, years of imprisonment, a death sentence and exile, to finally become the President of his country. His name is Kim Dae Jung and his journey through the brutal world of Korean politics is one that has been driven by a singular goal: democracy.

Kim was born in 1925 in a remote village on Ha Eui, an island off the south-western coast of the Korean peninsula. A few years later, his family moved to the port city of Mokpo in the Cholla province on the mainland. He was always close to his parents who had a strong influence on him. His father was a kindly man with a penchant for the arts, but it was his mother, an 'iron-willed lady and yet magnanimous', who gave him the endurance and persistence that he was going to need for his political career.

Politics stirred in Kim even as a child. As the village chief, his father would receive a free copy of the newspaper; at the age of 8, young Kim was already taking an interest in political events. By his mid-teens he had decided that he would pursue a career in politics.

A mountainous country on a peninsula, Korea is surrounded by the Yellow Sea to the west, the Korea Strait to the south, the Sea of Japan to the east, and China and Russia to the north.

The history of Korea's monarchical rule can be traced back to 18 BC. Five Kingdoms, the Paekche, Koguryo, Shilla, Koryo and the Choson, ruled the peninsula until 1910, when Japan colonised it. The Korean culture is heavily influenced by Buddhism and Confucianism brought about by migrations of the Chinese, Mongolian and Japanese peoples through the centuries. Christianity, in particular Protestantism, bloomed in South Korea in recent decades, attracting almost 20% of the population. It remains the fastest growing religion in the country.

When Emperor Hirohito announced Japan's surrender at the end of the Second World War in 1945, the Soviet Red Army had just begun advancing into Pacific Asia. Even before the Japanese could get out of the Korean peninsula, the Americans and Russians moved in to claim their positions. Two colonels, Dean Rusk and Charles H. Bonesteel, were entrusted with the task of dividing the peninsula so that the regions could be administered independently by the Soviets and Americans. Within half an hour, the two colonels returned with the proposal that the 38th parallel be used as the divider—any line closer to the Equator would have conceded Seoul to the Soviets.

When the communists, surprisingly, made no objections, the Americans drew the line through Panmunjom and ended Korean civilisation as it had been for centuries. The ideological animosity between the communists and the capitalists continued, however, and resulted in skirmishes between the two armies.

In June 1950, the North Korean Army launched its assault on the South. With its disciplined infantry, it outnumbered and overpowered the South Korean and American forces. Two months later Seoul fell to the Democratic People's Republic of Korea (DPRK; North Korea), and its army was poised to push further south.

General Douglas MacArthur rallied his troops and managed to repel the North Korean assault. In September the Americans, in a daring amphibious landing on the western city of Inchon, recaptured Seoul, surprisingly, without much resistance. Buoyed by the success, the Americans pursued the North Koreans back over the 38th parallel and marched northwards towards the Yalu River on the southern border of

China. By then 250,000 soldiers had been killed on both sides.

But the communists were making their own plans as well. Seeing North Korea's army faltering badly, China volunteered to help. When China was fighting its own war between the nationalists Kuomintang and the Chinese Communist Party, Kim Il Sung, leader of the DPRK, had sent tens of thousands of Korean soldiers to aid Mao's forces. With the Chinese communists' victory in 1949, Mao saw it necessary to fulfill his obligation to North Korea. In October 1950 China entered the Korean War.

With a massive Sino-North Korean army, the communists reversed the gains made by the South Korean and American troops, hammering MacArthur's men back across the 38th parallel. Like a ping-pong game, Seoul was again in danger of falling to the North.

Alarmed at China's involvement, Washington escalated its involvement. American President Harry Truman warned that 'it looks like World War III is here.' In November 1950 he threatened to use atomic bombs; General MacArthur submitted plans to drop 26 of them.

Fortunately, the bombs were never used as the fighting receded. With the war locked in a stalemate for the next two years, and after more than two million deaths and the complete destruction of almost every city and town on the Korean Peninsula, someone stumbled upon the brilliant idea that peace was the only solution. In 1953 an armistice was agreed upon; the truce line was drawn through the Demilitarized Zone, where until today Korean brother stares hatefully at brother.

South Korea, or the Republic of Korea, has its form of government modelled on that of the United States, with an executive presidency and the legislative National Assembly. Its first president was Syngman Rhee (Yi Seung Man), a long-time opponent of Japan's occupation of Korea. Rhee had spent almost 40 years in the United States, where he married an Austrian woman and obtained his PhD from Princeton University. After the war he returned to Korea, and with General MacArthur's support, Rhee quickly established himself as America's choice for President of the Republic of Korea. When the election was called on 10 May 1948, he won decisively.

Democratically installed but despotically inclined, Rhee entrenched his rule through police brutality, press censorship, mass arrests of political opponents, and rantings against the communists (mainly for the benefit of the Americans). He cheated, threatened and murdered his way through three elections until 19 April 1960, when some 100,000 students and youths gathered outside the Presidential Palace calling for him to desist from his outrageous behaviour. He greeted the protesters with gunfire, killing more than one hundred and injuring another thousand.

More protests followed. By that time, the inexhaustibly belligerent octogenarian had even tried the patience of his American minders, who urged him to resign. After some tepid remonstrations, the President and his wife packed up and unceremoniously left office in April for retirement-cum-exile in Hawaii. The Government was left to Prime Minister Chang Myon who did not possess the strength to steer the political truck—already sputtering with a choking economic engine—and allowed it to veer to the left.

Then in the early morning on 16 May 1961, Major-General Park Chung Hee, after positioning senior army officers and 3,500 soldiers at key points all over Seoul, woke up Prime Minister Chang Myon and told him that he was no longer in charge. Park had taken over the wheel, and in so doing gave it a sharp yank to the right.

Park Chung Hee was a stony faced army general (the people called him stone face) with a trim, diminutive physique. His hair was greased in a permanent pompadour which made him look even more austere. In his younger years, he could easily pass for a pugnacious bantamweight Korean boxer.

Park joined the Japanese army when he was young and was deployed in Manchuria during Japan's occupation of the region. He won an award from Emperor Hirohito, 'which may have included tracking down Korean guerillas who resisted the Japanese'. He switched to the Korean Military Academy after the Japanese defeat, graduating in 1946.

Immediately after the coup, Park introduced the unctuously named Political Purification Law, which, among other things, prohibited all politicians from running in future 'elections' for a minimum of eight years. All, of course, except those in the Democratic Republican Party, which he was about to form.

Kim had become the spokesman for the Democratic Party when Park came to power, and was arrested by the General. He was later released and asked to join Park's Democratic Republican Party, which he declined.

Park formed the Supreme Council of National Reconstruction, and pledged to rid Korea of all 'social evils'. With almost messianic zeal, he suspended the constitution, banned the National Assembly and dragged more than 15,000 politicians, military personnel and civil servants to camps for 'purification'. A year later in 1962, thousands more were arrested and almost all of the daily newspapers were shut down. Pressure from the United States, however, forced Park to rescind his Purification Law and to reinstate free and fair elections.

When World War II broke out, Koreans were forcibly recruited into the Imperial Army. In order to avoid conscription, Kim Dae Jung worked for a Japanese shipping company. When the Japanese left at the end of the war, its owner abruptly returned to his nuclear ravaged homeland. The Korean employees then got together to elect a new head. At 22, Kim Dae Jung became their manager. The post-war Korean economy picked up superbly, and so did the business under Kim's management. A few years later, he started his own business, which also flourished and allowed him to venture into shipbuilding. With trade booming, Kim made enough money to take over the *Mokpo Ilbo* newspaper.

Business and the call of the corporate wild could not hold Kim; politics beckoned, and he succumbed. In 1954 he ran unsuccessfully for a seat in the National Assembly as a Democratic Party candidate. He ran again four years later in a different district. The ruling Liberal Party, led by Syngman Rhee, tried to get Kim's candidacy invalidated by pressurising his seconders to endorse the Liberal candidate instead. Since endorsers could only nominate one candidate, Kim suddenly found himself without any seconders. He scrambled to look for new endorsers and luckily found some willing supporters. Always one artful step ahead, the Liberal Party had the police take away his endorsers' wooden seals—which were used in place of signatures—leaving them unable to endorse anything. The frantic candidate then stumbled upon some pumpkin peelings and, in a moment of innovative desperation, proceeded to carve the seals on the skins.

With the fruit imprinted nomination papers, Kim rushed to the registration centre, only to find the officials unyielding. When he refused to accept their decision, the police were called to drag him out of the building. Kim's expostulations did not end there but were simply raised to a higher decibel—in the Supreme Court. He finally managed to get the election results nullified. At the by-election, the ruling party merely replaced crass deception with sophisticated trickery and Kim lost again. And then again. By 1960 he had lost a total of four elections and was beginning to feel very cheated.

In 1961, after Syngman Rhee was forced out of office, Kim finally succeeded in his ten-year campaign for a seat in the National Assembly. His supporters were ecstatic and revelled in the victory. Three days later Park Chung Hee staged his coup. When he heard about the military takeover, Kim jumped into his car and sped seven hours to the capital, only to find the Assembly door shut and his seat out of reach yet again.

In 1963, when Park reinstated national elections, Kim was again elected, this time in his hometown of Mokpo. He immediately hurried to Seoul to claim his slippery seat in the National Assembly.

From businessman to assemblyman, riches to rags, Kim now had difficulty providing for his family, as his campaigns had used up most of his funds. Meanwhile his wife Cha Yong Ae had given birth to two boys and the family had to eke out a very modest living. Cha remained steadfastly by her husband, and in the midst of his difficulties encouraged him to continue his struggle: 'Be brave and fight! Even if you are arrested, I will take care of the children.' But she couldn't. Cha Yong Ae passed away not long after the birth of their second child.

In 1962 Kim married Lee Hee Ho, who bore him another son. Lee was herself a stout-hearted campaigner for democracy, holding the post of secretary-general in the National Council of the Young Women's Christian Association in her youth. She, too, abided by Kim as he struggled through the years.

The late 1960s saw relative progress in South Korea's economy under Park, and this translated into popular support for the President. But with cash came corruption. The state allocated huge sums of foreign capital and resources to selected entrepreneurs (it helped if you were related to the official handing out the cash) in selected industries. Many of the giant Korean businesses called *chaebol* (family-run conglomerates) were developed in this manner and grew ever deeper within the country's corporate culture.

Meanwhile, Kim Dae Jung was working to build his support base and edging closer to challenging Park for the presidency. In 1971, when the presidential election was due, Kim decided to apply for the job.

With the Cholla Province secure, Kim focused his campaign on the north of the country. Put on a stage with a microphone, Kim 'could work a crowd better than any other politician'. He smudged the image of the President with his barbs on corruption, which had become embedded in Park's system and, apocalyptically, warned his listeners that the President was fiddling with the idea of perpetuating his one man rule through a 'generalissimo system'.

But the country's economic buoyancy—and not a little vote buying—carried Park to his third presidential victory. Even so, Kim reddened the President's rigid face when he insolently grabbed 46% of the vote. 'The opposition has charged that I intend to be President for life,' Park told the voters during the campaign. 'I wish to make it clear to you today that this is the last time I shall appeal to you to elect me again.' He kept his word to the very letter. One year later, he suspended the constitution, emasculated the National Assembly, and declared the Presidency to be his as long as he lived.

Kidnap in Tokyo

Following the suspension of the constitution, Kim Dae Jung moved to Japan, where he continued his attacks against Park. On 8 August 1973, he was having lunch at the Grand Palace Hotel in Tokyo with two of his politician friends. After the meal, the three were walking back to Kim's room on the twenty-second floor when they were suddenly accosted by five Koreans. Two of them held Kim's friends while the other three pushed him into an adjoining room.

'Who are you, guys?' Kim asked, his pulse racing.

'Keep quiet!' one of them warned as he slammed the door shut.

'What are you doing?' the terrified Kim shouted.

The answer came in the form of kicks and punches. The pain radiated through his body as he tried to struggle free. Then all three grabbed him and before he could fight back, he felt a cloth covering his face and then the overpowering smell of chloroform.

'Hold him still!' one of the men shouted.

When they finally let go of him, Kim was dizzy and weak. Everything became a blur and he had difficulty trying to focus his thoughts. As he lay on the floor, the men got ready for the kill. The modus operandi was simple—cut the body into small pieces.

'In the bathtub,' one said. 'Where are the knapsacks?'

'Make sure the pieces are small enough so that they can all fit into the knapsacks,' another one instructed. 'We'll get rid of them later.'

With whatever might he had left, Kim screamed for help. When they couldn't quieten him, the abductors became jittery. They blindfolded their victim and dragged him downstairs. Kim couldn't resist as he was limp and in a daze; the pain from the beating was excruciating. He was pushed into a car and quickly driven off. His ordeal was just beginning. Worst of all, death seemed certain—the only question was how gruesome it was going to be.

'Why is this happening?' Kim kept asking himself. 'Does anyone know that I've been abducted? It'll probably be too late by the time anyone finds out.' Kim prayed for his life as the car continued its journey.

Just when it seemed like the ride was never going to end—it had been about five or six hours of driving—Kim felt the car coming to a halt. The party had arrived in a small port town, and Kim was taken inside a two storey house. There they removed the blindfold and taped up his entire face, leaving just a small gap around his nostrils so that he could breathe. They strapped his hands and feet, leaving him completely immobilised. In darkness, in pain, and in bewildering terror, Kim lay there at the mercy of his captors.

Before long, he was tossed into the car again. This time the drive was much shorter, about an hour or so. As they took him out of the vehicle, Kim could hear the waves. Soon he was on board a boat. The engine started and he felt the bobbing of the water as the vessel moved out to sea. After a while, the engine quietened down to a purr and then stopped. He was picked up again and transferred to a bigger vessel.

His kidnappers removed the tape and untied him. It was already nightfall. The large boat bounced up and down as it made its way across the sea. He still hadn't a clue where he was being taken to. All he could feel was the after-effects of the chloroform, but this was nothing compared to the fear that clung to him. He continued praying and hoping that everything would end soon and that he would be back on land and—more importantly—remain alive. The day's trauma had taken a toll on his mind and body and he soon drifted into sleep.

He woke up with a start as someone grabbed his hands and trussed them behind his back. It was daylight again and his nightmare was real after all. Another man came round to the front, shoved a piece of wood into Kim's mouth and taped it up. His nostrils were now flaring as he tried to take in air. His heart was pounding hard. They tied their trembling captive to a wooden plank, and secured concrete slabs to his arms and legs. Kim tried to move them and quickly found that they must have weighed between 30 to 40 kilograms.

The thought of being dumped into the ocean burned through his mind. The wood in his mouth made breathing all the more difficult; to heighten the terror, his eyes were taped shut. Then he felt the men haul him into a crate the size of a coffin. 'Don't bother to ask for water,' one of them growled, 'you are going to die soon.' With that the lid slammed shut.

The silence was only broken by the sound of his heart pounding against his chest. On the verge of hysterics, Kim started to imagine his death. 'If they throw me into the sea, I would struggle for three or four minutes and then die. This tormented life of mine would then be over. At least that's good,' he tried convincing himself. 'Maybe the sharks would eat up my lower parts and leave my upper body intact.'

'No! What am I thinking?' he recoiled. Kim found himself sinking from terror into desperation. 'I don't want to die!' He writhed and turned inside the crate, trying desperately to break free Houdini style. But this was no illusion, and the people who had tied him up were not his assistants.

He twisted and kicked and jerked in the hope that those wretched knots would come loose. He started to gag; his body needed more oxygen than his nose let in. After several minutes, he was too tired to continue and his breathing was perilously short. Then suddenly, he saw the image of Jesus Christ. In desperation, Kim tried to reach out and grab Christ's robe. 'Please save me!' he pleaded. 'I still have much to do. This is not the time for me to be killed!'

When the American CIA's Seoul bureau heard of the kidnapping, its chief, Donald Gregg, immediately swung into action. He called up his Korean counterparts to find out as much as he could. Ambassador Philip Habib quickly went to see Park Chung Hee and warned that the relationship between the two countries would be gravely jeopardised if anything were to happen to Kim. Habib was sure that 'if [the United States] didn't say anything Kim will be killed.'

There was suddenly an explosion. Kim heard a commotion on deck as the men scrambled about. Someone shouted, 'It's a plane!' Kim felt the boat picking up speed as if it was being chased. The men scrambled frantically and it was a while before things calmed down.

'Aren't you Mr. Kim Dae Jung?' a voice came through as someone opened the crate. Kim nodded nervously.

'I voted for you in the election two years ago,' the voice continued. It was the most delightful thing to hear and Kim nodded again with gratitude, not for the vote, but for a friendly voice at last. 'You seem to be saved now,' the voice reassured.

The aircraft which intercepted the boat had managed to stop Kim's abductors from tossing their captive overboard. It is uncertain whether the aircraft was Korean, Japanese or American.

'Don't move for three minutes,' a voice hissed. Kim Dae Jung, still blindfolded and trembling, stood alone in the sultry night air. Then he heard the car speed away. Everything was quiet again. After a couple of minutes he slowly reached to undo his blindfold. He stumbled to the door and frantically rang the bell. When his wife appeared, they hugged each other in a tight and tearful embrace.

It had been five days since he was kidnapped in Tokyo by the Korean Central Intelligence Agency (KCIA).

Life under a dictator

The KCIA agents who were involved in the harebrained plot included the first secretary in the Korean embassy in Japan. The agency was a product of the American CIA. In the 1950s, when the war with communism was at its height, the U.S. State Department instituted a 'counter-subversion' plan called the 1290-d Program, which provided equipment and training for the agency. As with most cases of bad parenting, the KCIA grew up to become an uncontrollable, thuggish brute, far transcending its parent's intentions.

If the United States was the negligent mother of the KCIA, Park Chung Hee was its authoritarian father. Having been part of the Japanese army's Kempeitei, he was a master of torture techniques. At its most fearsome, the agency—supported by funds from business interests in casinos and hotels as well as 'unbudgeted funds'—employed more than 50,000 agents across the world, keeping an eye on Koreans wherever they might be and occasionally spiriting them back to Seoul. When kidnapping posed too high a risk, lying was used. One dissident student was lured back from overseas to receive an award from the President himself; when he arrived in Seoul, gift in hand for the President, he was ferried straight to prison. And if the disobedient could not be bamboozled perhaps they could be bought. With the promise of easy loans for their enterprises and even easier sex for their entertainment, Koreans were persuaded to desist in their dissent. For the recalcitrant, the final destination was the So Bingo, a centre where Koreans are taken not to gamble, but to engage in something altogether less enjoyable—torture.

After Kim was released outside his house, soldiers moved in to cordon off the street. Agents informed him that he was being placed under house arrest. A year later, he was charged with various offences ranging from 'campaigning prior to the official election period in 1971', to 'making a false charge' that Park was going to institute a 'generalissimo regime'. To Kim (and everyone else who knew Park's vindictive streak) the trial was political revenge. He told the court before judgement was passed, 'I am not afraid of the outcome. History will prove that this trial was illegitimate.' He was sentenced to a one year term.

In the 1960s, Park instituted successive five-year plans to industrialise the country, demanding diligence and obedience from the people in return for rapid economic growth. The strategy worked—for a period, anyway. South Korea's per capita income tripled and the GNP bounded to $7.2 billion (from $1.8 billion), prompting the President to promise that 'every straw-thatched home in Korea will have its roof replaced by shiny tiles.' A Korea watcher told me that 'the massive project was then awarded to cronies and friends'. Indeed, the speed with which South Korea industrialised was so stunning that observers began to describe its capital, Seoul, as the miracle on the Han (river).

While the country grew economically, Park continued to retard its political development. By threatening to cut off economic aid, the Kennedy administration pressured Park to ease up on his dictatorial methods. He relented and held presidential elections in 1963, 1967 and 1971, all of which he won. In 1971, after he beat Kim Dae Jung, the economy began to show signs of middle-aged flabbiness, and Park feared that he might lose his hold on the country. As a knight cannot justify his chivalry if there is no dragon to slay, a ruler in Asia cannot defend tyranny without communism to crucify. And Park was no novice when it came to raising the communist bogey. He cited the raging conflict between North and South Vietnam, and warned that if his authority was questioned, North Korea would see it as a sign of weakness and invade.

Of course, as with all great cons there was a 'but': the people had to sacrifice their liberties. And, as with most repressions, some meretricious name had to be coined to give the dictatorship a sense of benignity. Park christened his the '*Yushin* system'. *Yushin*, or renewal, is derived from the Japanese word *issin*, referring to the Meiji period, when the emperor was restored to power over the central government.

Unable to bear the annoyance of having to subject his rule to the existing constitution, Park wrote his own. In it he told Koreans that rules restricting his tenure in office no longer applied, that he would appoint one-third of the members of the National Assembly, that political rights and civil liberties had to be removed and, most important, that whatever he decreed was good and right—the most wholesome being Decree no. 9 of 1974 which, in a nutshell, stated that criticism of his regime would be seen as a violation of national security, the penalty for which was death. Park knew that he could mollify Washington and get away with his authoritarian rule as long as he showed that he hated communism more than he hated democracy.

Newspapers were not spared. In November 1974, the Government issued guidelines prohibiting the reporting of sensitive news, ranging from student demonstrations to coal briquettes (the Government was concerned about the unhappiness generated by complaints about the poor quality of the coal caused by the addition of clay). The *Dong-A Ilbo*, a national daily with a reputation for jealously guarding its editorial independence, decided not to comply with the restrictions. The Government sent in the KCIA. Tired of typing with the goons looking over their shoulders, the staff called a strike and demanded that the agents be withdrawn from their offices. After a few days, the agents duly withdrew and the newspaper went back into print.

Then suddenly, clients started to cancel their advertisements. Businesses from department stores to car dealers came under pressure to do so, and it looked like the publication would soon print its last page. But help came from a most unlikely source. The Kyungdong Presbyterian Church bought an entire page and printed its support for the newspaper. One good ad, as it turned out, deserved another. And another. Soon the *Dong-A Ilbo* was flush with one-line personal ads.

'I skipped my daily glass of wine to support freedom,' read a tiny advertisement bought by a cab-driver; 'Better to stand and die than bow your head and live,' ran another which was placed by a group of female textile workers; yet another paid for by a physician warned, 'A bad doctor kills his patient and a bad government kills the people.'; '*Dong-A Ilbo*, if you capitulate, I will emigrate,' a student wrote; 'Let's pull out rotten teeth,' a dentist quipped. The newspaper found itself doing much better without corporate advertising, and the daily circulation leapt from 600,000 to more than 800,000 copies.

The bud of such indiscipline had to be quickly nipped. The owner of the paper was forced to fire his staff, and KCIA agents were sent in to rough up the more defiant journalists. Soon things were under control again. One of South Korea's most independent and fearless dailies had been brought to its knees and transformed into a government mouthpiece. Meanwhile, the corporate advertisers returned.

A month after Park declared his new constitution, he staged a monstrous play that involved a cast of thousands, including a Catholic bishop, Chi Hak Soon, a former President, Yun Po Sun, Christian workers and clergymen, and university students. Unlike most dramas, however, there were only villains in this play, with eight men being assigned the lead roles of communist scum whom Park accused of heading the People's Revolutionary Party.

In a most unwatchable performance where confessions—tortured out of the accused at KCIA centres—were read out, military judges sentenced all eight to death. Suh Seung, a student at the Seoul National University, appeared in court with his face mottled with acid-burned tissue; his eyelids and ear had disappeared, and his fingers were fused into an ugly stump of charred flesh.

They were allowed to appeal to the Supreme Court, which upheld the sentences after a closed-door session lasting all of ten minutes. Next morning the wives were told that they could visit their husbands in prison. Upon arrival at the gate, they were informed that their spouses had been hanged at four o'clock that morning. The bodies were then cremated without the consent of their families. 'This time we'll scare the hell out of [the people],' Park had said after he read a letter from Cardinal Stephen Kim pleading for clemency for the eight.

In the years that followed, anyone who openly objected to Park's 'Korean-style democracy' was taken to torture centres. Prisoners were electrically shocked on the genitalia, hung from the ceiling and spun around, whipped on the soles of the feet, stripped naked in subzero weather and doused with water, forced to face a white wall for days without sleep to induce hallucination, burned with lighted cigarettes, deprived of sleep, and poked under the finger nails with pens. The torture often resulted in ruptured eardrums, abscessed lungs, prolapsed anuses, broken bones and heart attacks.

One detainee was taken to a basement cell that was ankle-deep in water. The guards knocked him to the floor and stood on him, forcing his face into the murky pool until he stopped struggling. He later described the macabre treatment:

> Returning to consciousness after the water torture, I looked around the room confused, and noticed various strange-looking machines. I was stripped naked and hung upside down. Then with a knife they slashed my heels; the blood flowed profusely down my body and even went into my nose. Shortly, they attached something to both my temples and to my fingertips. At that moment, upon receiving the electric shock, I felt my eyes roll backwards and I passed out...

During winter, water was poured into the cells so that it formed a sheet of ice. The prisoners were then forced to sit or lie down on it. KCIA agents would call up the victims' families and let them listen to the screams of their loved ones while they were beaten or electrocuted. A concert pianist was so traumatised by the shrieks of her husband that for years, she was unable to play the piano. After he was eventually released, her husband could only get to sleep at night after numbing himself with whisky.

If Park was a monster to the Korean people, he was an angel to corporate America and Japan. In partnership with wealthy Korean families, United States and Japanese businesses poured millions of dollars into Korean industries, many of which were dependent on cheap female labour. In 1978 about 70 textile workers banded together to protest appalling work conditions. When a group of female workers walked into the hall to elect their union leaders, government-engaged gangsters lined up the women and stripped them. The dung-wielding thugs, wearing rubber gloves, then proceeded to pelt the women with faeces, smearing their bodies and faces. Some were even forced to eat the human waste. Those who resisted were pulled by the hair and kicked.

Foreign investments continued to pour in, not a little of which was used to fund Park's 1971 campaign against Kim Dae Jung. The 'largest single gift'—US$4,000,000—came from the Gulf Oil Company in the United States. As long as there was money to be made, most people cared little about Park's handling of his opponents. But by the late 1970s, the South Korean economy had begun to tire, with the growth rate falling by 5% in 1979. The surge in oil prices caused by the revolution in Iran, over-capacity in the heavy industries, rising labour costs and a heavy foreign debt all conspired to drag down the country's economy. Events began to grumble ominously about Park's authoritarian control.

Park Chung Hee was delivering his speech at the National Theatre on the morning of Liberation Day, 15 August 1974, when a man made his way to the front of the auditorium. As he got close to the stage, he suddenly pulled out a Smith & Wesson revolver and aimed it at the President. Two shots rang out, and pandemonium erupted. Security agents sprang to the aid of the President, who had taken cover behind the bulletproof lectern. They returned fire, missing the assassin but hitting a 16-year-old choirgirl who died instantly. While the screaming audience scrambled for cover, police pounced on the gunman and wrestled him out of the theatre.

When the shaken Park regained his composure, he motioned for calm; after getting his nervous audience to retake their seats, he continued with his speech. When he finished and turned to sit down, an aide whispered to him that one of the bullets had hit his wife, who was also seated on stage. The bullet had pierced her temple and there was little surgeons could do to save her. The 48-year-old First Lady died a few hours later.

Like the gunman's bullet, fate seldom discriminates between the good and the bad. The First Lady was the humane half of the Parks and had been a softening influence on her husband. With her death, Park was deprived of a compassionate counterweight, and it only made him more determined than ever to crush his opponents. When you only injure a tiger, you make it more dangerous as well, and oppositionists braced themselves for a mauling.

The gunman was 22-year-old Mun Se Kwang, a Korean born in Japan, who told the police that he had stolen the revolver from a police station in Japan and smuggled it into Seoul. While most Koreans grieved, the more suspicious minded wondered how the killer had managed to steal the gun, get it through the tight airport security and, even more surprisingly, past the KCIA agents at the National Theatre, especially when only invited guests with identification badges and assigned seats were permitted into the hall. The ballistic records were never made public, prompting questions about whether it was actually Mun's bullet that had killed Mrs Park.

Theories started to breed. One said that she had begun to grow increasingly vocal about her husband's savagery, while another suggested that the President was having an affair with a movie starlet who 'jetted back to Seoul before the earth was even dry on Mrs Park's grave.' In both instances, it would have been expedient to get rid of the First Lady.

The less salacious rumours posited that Park had to stop the outcry against his kidnapping of Kim Dae Jung, which had angered the international community. Tokyo had accused the Korean Government of violating Japanese sovereignty and insisted on an investigation into the abduction. Under pressure, Park obliged and sent his Prime Minister to deliver an embarrassing apology to Japanese Prime Minister Tanaka Kakuei before the matter was dropped. With the attempt on his life, Park could turn the tables by accusing the Japanese of being lax on Korean terrorists operating from their country. At the same time, he could avoid the discomfiture of having to explain Kim's abduction. Cannily, the regime informed the Japanese Government on 14 August 1975—the day before the anniversary of Mun's attempted assassination—that the Korean police had not been able to identify Kim's kidnappers and were thus calling off their investigation. To make sure that the smokescreen was realistic, anti-Japanese feelings were whipped up in a stomach churning demonstration in Seoul. Thirty-two protesters, calling themselves the 'Anti-Japan Suicide Squad', chopped off their fingers with butcher knives and sent the dismembered digits wrapped in the Korean flag to the Japanese Prime Minister. As with most violent demonstrations, there was a price for this one. The demonstrators (later found to be convicted criminals) 'were paid by the Seoul government for their theatrics at a rate of $125 to $375 per finger.'

Whatever the truth, the country—and the world—wept for Park and, in so doing, poured more iron in his fist.

Challenging the dictator

1 March is celebrated in South Korea as the day when Koreans began the revolution against their Japanese colonial

masters in 1919. More than half a century later, the struggle for independence was still in progress, but the anger was now directed at the Korean dictators who ruled the country with just as much truculence.

On 1 March 1976, more than 500 people gathered at Seoul's Myong Dong cathedral to remember the struggle of the Korean people. Word about the mass had been spread quietly in order not to arouse the KCIA. But as worshippers arrived at the cathedral, the agents were already out in force and surrounding the building.

At the start of the mass, the congregation glanced nervously at the security men milling outside. Fear melted away as prayers began, and even turned into courageous hymn singing as the service, which lasted for almost three hours, progressed. Lee Woo Jung, a member of the Christian Professors Association, read out the Declaration of Democracy and National Salvation, which had been compiled by a group of political and religious leaders led by Kim Dae Jung. The six page human rights manifesto launched a bold attack against the *Yushin* constitution. As the supportive congregation listened intently to the message, becoming more edgy with every criticism of Park Chung Hee, the security agents were preparing to make sure that the message didn't get beyond the walls of the church.

As she closed the service, Lee called for the President to 'resign from power'. 'Long live democracy!' shouted the wife of a political prisoner. As they left the cathedral, the KCIA officers were on hand to show the two women that Park was still very much in dictatorial control and placed them under arrest. A week later the security police surrounded Kim Dae Jung's residence and took both him and his wife to prison. After two months, Kim and 17 other signatories of the declaration were charged with organising a 'nation-ruining plot'.

More than 200 family members and friends turned up to attend the trial but were not allowed into the courtroom. While they jostled with riot police, the defendants and their lawyers threatened to boycott the trial. Kim's wife, released earlier, shouted, 'Democracy in Korea is crucified!'

During the trial itself, nerves were rubbed raw and the defendants began to lash out at each other. One of the priests complained to Kim, 'We've all been arrested because of you.

If we had made the same statement on our own as religionists, there would have been no problem. But because of your involvement, the Government attacks us for participating in politics.'

'Your accusation is not true,' he replied after some consideration. 'I thought about what you said. I'm a politician and politicians can adapt to various conditions. If I weren't a Christian, I could, no doubt, cooperate with Park Chung Hee and continue my political life. But you ministers and priests always say, "Man does not live by bread alone. Follow Christ." That seemed reasonable. So that's why I came to be put on trial now. So you're the one who's responsible. I don't hold a grudge against you for this. I'm happy to be here. But the responsibility is yours.'

Another minister intervened, 'No, you're both wrong. It is not we or you who are responsible, but Christ himself.' But the tribunal wasn't interested in convicting Jesus. When it came for him to testify, Kim told the court, 'I want an opposition party which will unite in dedication to true democratic principles and will be able to engage in dialogue with the Government. I have said—and now say again—that we will work for our ends in legitimate democratic ways.' With that confession, Kim was sentenced to five years imprisonment.

Koreans in all walks of life defended democracy in whatever way their skills allowed. One such talent was Kim Chi Ha, a poet and Roman Catholic, who unfailingly poked prose at the President and gave the people the courage they needed so desperately to oppose him. He was arrested on the usual charge of being pro-communist. The President did not know how to handle the writer, repeatedly releasing him, then arresting him again, torturing him, condemning him to be hanged, commuting his death sentence to life imprisonment, then releasing him, only to start the process all over again. 'Whenever Chi Ha's mother visited him in jail, she collected his clothes to wash them,' a friend remarked to me. 'She told me that, on many occasions, his briefs were stained with blood.' Through the more than ten years of contending with the dictator's fickleness, Kim Chi Ha continued to pen his dissent through poems, often reflecting on the darkness of Korean society under Park:

Your Blood

Let us meet.
Your red blood, the hot breath,
resonant voice, the burning glance, all
scattered and gone, worn down to the bone,
nothing left now, but let us meet.
There, on Puyong Mountain.
There, in a hole in the red earth.
There, where arrowroot screamed at the skies.

Sorrow, heart-piercing.
The gunshot, the pounding at the door,
the heavy sound of steps following, heart-piercing.
Let us meet as well under the clubs,
your blood, bright red and pine fragrant.

You were in the sleeping child's smile,
in the song fading away, in the breath, and in each
night after long night;
you were there
and so your blood lives,
even now within me leaping up.

Let us meet, and though the handful of earth
that absorbed your bones
be scattered in the wind,
there on Puyong Mountain,
on the red, red earth,
on the dazzling, scalloped ridge,
there we meet
and again it flows,
your blood, bright red and pine fragrant

in my life
in the earth
in the clear eyes of children
who fall asleep in rags
and there, in the light of the sun.

Kim Chi Ha's ultimate sin was to have been associated with Kim Dae Jung. He was suspected to have written a poem about Kim's kidnapping in Tokyo. The regime was extremely nervous about the influence of Kim Chi Ha's powerful writings. Combined with his unbending will to rid the country of the dictatorship, they could, in Park's calculation, incite unrest. Even as he languished in solitary confinement, the poet was smuggling out his words:

> I want to identify with the oppressed, the exploited, the troubled, and the despised. I want my love to be dedicated, passionate, and manifested in practical ways...
>
> Those who fear the people, who find the masses despicable, are not democrats. When the going gets rough, they will stand at the side of tyranny. What is democracy? It is an ideology opposed to silence, a system that respects a free logos and freedom of speech. It encourages the cacophony of dissent. A political system where everything is not revealed to the public is not a democracy. I believe that the truth, only the truth, will liberate people. ...Only when people struggle out of the darkness, driven by the very chaos of their opposition to tyranny, will they reach the sun-drenched fields...This is my dream, my faith.

On 26 October 1979, Park Chung Hee slipped out from his official residence at the Blue House to have dinner with his KCIA chief Kim Chae Gyu. Park was accompanied by his secretary Kim Kae Won and his bodyguard Cha Chi Chol. Dinner was served with the usual delectables, including a model and a singer for entertainment. Halfway through the meal, dinner turned into din as the KCIA chief got into an altercation with Cha, one of those squat-looking toughs whose head seemed comfortably ensconced on his compact trunk without the need for a neck.

One man's bodyguard is, it appeared, another man's bug. 'How can we conduct our policies with an insect like this,' Kim Chae Gyu growled as he drew his .38-calibre revolver and shot Cha. As the President sat stunned, Cha tried to crawl to the door but was shot again, this time fatally. Then the KCIA head turned to his boss and shot him from under the table, killing him instantly. As security agents rushed into the room, more shots rang out and another four men were killed.

Kim Chae Gyu then ran out of the building to meet General Chung Seung Hwa, who went with him to another KCIA building, promptly placed the intelligence chief under arrest and ordered an inquiry. Accounts of the assassination were varied, however, depending on who was telling the story. It was hard to conclude whether the event was a conspiracy (and if so, who was the mastermind?) or whether Kim Chae Gyu had acted alone. Was Chung Seung Hwa a co-conspirator, only to doublecross his partner after the murder? Whatever the speculation, one thing remained clear: Park Chung Hee was dead and the bloodstained baton would now be passed on to whoever could attract the most goons and guns.

General Chung was convinced that he could, and immediately moved his army units into position. He called for Kim Chae Gyu's trial and sentenced him to death (and his lawyer to jail). He announced that martial law would continue. The General, in keeping with the best of dictatorial traditions, castigated Kim Dae Jung as a communist who was unfit to 'be given the post of commander-in-chief of the armed forces.'

Such boldness, however, has a strange way of angering other would-be dictators which spawns more coups. A month later Chun Doo Hwan, a powerful major-general, sent crack units to Chung's residence for a shootout which ended in the General's arrest. Again, troops were despatched throughout the city to take over key installations. When putsch came to shove, Chun was not willing to let tyrant Park be toppled only to be replaced by despot Chung. He wanted the pleasure for himself. Following his grab of political leadership, Chun sprinkled a couple of stars on his epaulette and became supreme commander of the armed forces.

Weeks after he took control, Koreans took to the streets and demonstrated. 'It is time to Koreanize democracy,' Chun declared and proceeded to close down everything he could think of, including all political activity, the legislature and the universities. Anything he couldn't ban, he arrested; thousands of political activists were rounded up during the midnight hours of 17–18 May 1980. The press was not spared either. More than 170 newspapers and periodicals were shut down.

And like his predecessors, he found it necessary to condemn Kim Dae Jung. But Chun was even more determined to rid himself of the democrat who just would not lie down and die.

Life under another dictator

The unrest which followed Chun Doo Hwan's takeover spread to cities all over the country, including Kwangju, Chonju, Suwon, Taegu and Inchon, with university students taking the lead. In Seoul, almost 50,000 people assembled in the streets calling for Chun to step down.

Kim Dae Jung had been released in a general amnesty for 105 prisoners declared by Park Chung Hee just a few months before he was shot. American President Jimmy Carter had been leaning on his Korean counterpart to ease up on his opposition decimating style and clear the way for democratic governance. Limping, with a cane in one hand and a Bible in the other, Kim Dae Jung walked out of the Seoul University Hospital into a cheering crowd and, immediately, denounced Park's rule.

On 14 May 1980, some of the student leaders approached Kim and asked him to endorse a statement calling on soldiers, workers and businesses to support the movement to overthrow the Chun regime. Kim's eyes widened when he read that soldiers were being asked to join in the revolution. Kim thought that Chun and his generals would see the challenge as a threat to national security and crush the student movement instantly. In the eyes of the public, that would not be unjustifiable because if North Korea sensed any kind of weakness within the military, the Southern despot could very quickly be replaced by the Northern one.

Kim told the students not to proceed with their statement. For him to endorse it would only make him a prize catch for Chun, who would not lose much sleep calling for his execution. Besides, Kim explained, any soldier leaving his post in the Demilitarized Zone would be shot on the spot. He urged the students to press instead for the resignation of Chun Doo Hwan and the reinstatement of the democratic process. The students were adamant, however, and were determined to go on with their campaign with or without Kim's support.

When the demonstrations threatened to spin out of control, civilian officials within the Government urged for calm. So did Kim, who appealed to the students 'to leave politics to the politicians for the time being.' This time the students heeded his call and the protests abated. As soon as they did, the military swooped in and rounded up Kim and other key dissident figures.

The fact that he had declined to sign the students' statement may have spared his life. 'If you had not scrapped the draft statement, Mr Kim, you might not be a living man any longer,' his interrogator told him. For Chun, whether the dissident did anything or not hardly mattered; the General wanted his opponent dead. But Chun had to find a reason to execute him. It came in the city of Kwangju on the day after Kim was arrested.

In Kwangju, the struggle against Chun had been particularly fierce. It started on the night of 17 May, when paratroopers stormed the Chunnam University and broke up a group student demonstrators. Many were placed under arrest and hauled away in army trucks. When morning came, more students joined in the demonstration. Several hundred marched to the city centre waving banners: 'Chun Doo Hwan must step down!', 'Free Kim Dae Jung!', 'Martial Law must be immediately lifted!'.

The soldiers ploughed through the streets firing teargas and indiscriminately battered anyone who crossed their path. Those who were arrested were stripped and made to hold their clothes while their hands were bound. While they knelt on the ground, rifle butts and bayonets were brought down mercilessly on them. Some were made to lie on the road and roll. Five high school girls were tied up and had their breasts repeatedly cut by bayonets until gaping holes were left in their chests. As they writhed on the ground, the soldiers kicked them until they were motionless. One student was tied to the back of an armoured personnel carrier and dragged across town. By the time the gruesome spectacle ended, no skin remained on his lifeless body.

Weeping residents watching the carnage from their homes were ordered to shut their doors and windows. Onlookers who screamed at the soldiers were chased and shot. Parents and the elderly who ran to protect the students were gunned down. When the demonstrators ran into buildings to seek refuge, the paratroopers chased them and tossed them over the balconies. As the hospitals filled up with the injured and the dead—a pregnant woman was carried in with a bayonet sticking out of her torso—the soldiers ransacked the premises and destroyed the equipment, and even killed the injured as they lay on the trolleys. The soldiers were then organised into teams to conduct house-to-house searches. Anyone who looked younger than 30 was arrested. Screams of parents and children filled the air.

Even the local city police were warned not to interfere. 'If you try to hide the students or let them escape, we will treat you in the same way as the demonstrators,' the commander warned the officers. Caught in the middle, the police could only help by pleading with people to go indoors. 'Please, please leave this area at once,' a trembling officer, in tears, yelled through a megaphone. 'If the Martial Law troops catch you they will kill you.'

But war had already begun. Now, instead of just the students, the people too joined the fight. Shaking with disbelief and anger, bystanders picked up wooden staves and iron bars that they had dismantled from railings, bus-stops and construction sites.

Like a matador, but with the brains of the bull it teases, the army enraged the mob even more by firing straight into the crowd. People fought back clubbing wildly at the soldiers. Some of the paratroopers who were caught later revealed that they had not eaten for days prior to their assignment to Kwangju. The day before they were sent out, they were fed *soju* (rice wine) which was laced with a drug, and told that they were being sent to put down communist insurgents.

After two days of violence, the commanders finally sensed that they were not going to put anything down, least of all the fury they had incited. They sent two helicopters to announce: 'Students and citizens, if you lose your sense of reason, the commotion will only get worse. Quit your futile resistance and go home at once!' But the crowd, which by then had grown to nearly 200,000, was way beyond restraint. Some protesters commandeered trucks and drove them into lines of soldiers. The troops knew that the situation was out of control, and they retreated into a government building.

Meanwhile the Munhwa Broadcasting Company and the Korean Broadcasting Station, two government run television and radio stations, claimed that 'Northern spies' were inciting the riots and spreading 'Northern propaganda'. They were soon burned down. Armouries in the police headquarters were raided and the people made off with sizeable weapon stockpiles. Thereafter, they traded bullet for bullet. After three days of intense fighting leaving thousands dead and thousands more wounded, the soldiers fled the city in helicopters.

As Kwangju burned, Chun Doo Hwan fumed. He had not expected the people to fight back so tenaciously. Local reports from all over the country condemned the rioting and placed the blame on the protesters. Chun needed someone to blame for the blood and anger of Kwangju. He charged Kim Dae Jung, whom he had already arrested, for fomenting the riots in Seoul and for organising the Kwangju riots from behind the scenes in an attempt to overthrow the Government. If found guilty, Kim would face the death penalty.

For six days after the troops retreated, the citizens ran Kwangju. Vigilante groups were organised to prevent further chaos. A sign outside a building that had remained unscathed read: 'This police station is our own property. Any damages mean further taxes for you. Defend it.' Banks, schools, churches, granaries and supermarkets were left undamaged by the protesters and were now protected by armed civilians. Food was rationed and distributed, survivors lined up to donate blood, and medical treatment resumed. The captured soldiers were tended to as well.

Then the soldiers returned. Helicopters warned the residents to disarm and return home. With lessons learned and firepower enhanced, Chun's men swept into the city from all directions in the early hours of 27 May, methodically cutting down armed civilians and arresting hundreds of students. Within two hours, the military overran the ravaged town and ended the Kwangju rebellion.

Prosecutors triumphantly hauled Kim before a panel of five military judges, who read a 156 page indictment charging him with all manner of political evil, including being pro-communist and organising the Seoul and Kwangju uprisings. A two hour documentary was aired on television showing how he was linked with groups in North Korea. Local newspapers were not allowed to mention his name except when libel accompanied it: the *Korea Herald* screamed 'Kim Dae Jung Masterminds Kwangju Riot' and convicted the man and his co-defendants of organising students to 'agitate for disturbances and violence' with the aim of overthrowing the Government in a 'bloody mass revolution'.

Meanwhile, in an underground cell, Kim Dae Jung was stripped naked and interrogated 15 hours a day for two months until he finally broke down and signed confessions to instigating the Kwangju uprising. Twenty-three other dissidents had also been arrested and forced to incriminate Kim; it was either that or be tortured by having their fingers crushed or sticks shoved up between their legs in between bouts of beatings. Sometimes the prisoners would be hung upside down and beaten with a pole, other times the guards would jam the detainees' heads on the floor with their boots and pour water into their nostrils. Shrieks and cries for mercy tormented those who were being interrogated in adjoining rooms.

For more than two weeks, a prisoner by the name of Kim Keun Tae was given the water and electric shock torture. Each session lasted for about five hours. His interrogators stripped him, tied him to a table and blindfolded him. 'This is the Last Supper for you. Today, there is going to be a funeral for you,' his torturer warned. With that, water was poured on his head, chest and groin to aid electrical conductance. Electrodes were clipped to his fingers and the shocks were administered in short and light episodes. As the detainee's screams grew louder, the torturers turned up the radio to drown them out. Gradually, they increased the intensity and duration of the shock. The prisoner's muscles contracted painfully every time the current went through. After several episodes, he passed out.

When he came round, he could not eat or sleep for days. Sometimes the torture sessions were not necessary as the terror induced by threats was enough to reduce the prisoner to crumbling fits. 'I will torture this guy myself,' a burly guard smiled at Kim Keun Tae. He carried a bag that clanged with tools. 'Our undertaking business is about to start. Do you know how Lee Jae Mun died here? He died when his internal organs burst. Now it's your turn. I'll allow you to retaliate after you achieve democracy. Then I'll be on the torture rack instead of you,' he sadistically offered.

'I don't know how my newly-wed daughter is doing these days,' one torturer would say to his colleague as he prepared to administer another bolt of electricity. 'I'm sure she's fine. I wonder how my son did in his college entrance exams,' another one said as he turned on the switch. After these sessions, they made their victim crawl naked on the floor while they kicked him and forced him to beg for mercy.

As the prisoner was lying in a semi-conscious state, one of the guards remained behind. 'I hate what I'm doing,' he said to Kim Keun Tae. 'Get out of here as soon as possible. Why don't you confess everything we ask? Otherwise you are going to die here.' He wiped his tears as he left the broken prisoner.

Kim Dae Jung was spared the torture only because the international community had their eyes fixed on his case.

The Government wanted Kim's trial to be as quick and as painless as possible. Dragging it out would only provoke the hostility of the public. But on the first day, Kim insisted that he would not answer any questions, and on the second, he repudiated all his forced confessions. In prison, his interrogators repeatedly made offers to entice him out of the opposition. There were vague references to an offer of the vice-presidential post. The alternative was death, the guards reminded him, for the trial was just a formality.

'I am a Christian and I believe in free democracy,' Kim said during the trial. 'I have always supported the Republic of Korea and never formed an anti-state organisation. I have never plotted to overthrow the Government.'

This, according to the judges, was all well and good, except that the verdict had already been written. Kim, 'an agitator-politician' who had to be 'eliminated from this land for good',was found guilty of sedition and sentenced to death. He later recalled:

> When I stood at the bar on the day for sentencing in my trial, I stared intently at the lips of the judge. If he started to protrude his lips, he would utter '*mu*' for '*mugi*' for 'lifetime', but if he would lengthen his lips on both ends, it would be to pronounce the words '*sa*' for 'death'. I had hoped that President Jimmy Carter would have saved my life, since he tried so hard, but then he was defeated in the presidential election before this verdict of the Korean Supreme Court.

'Even if I die,' Kim said to the judges as he steadied himself, 'I hope that a political retaliation like this incident will never again happen in our land.' As the judge retired, those in the gallery rose and sang *We Shall Overcome*.

Back in his cell, Kim was less defiant. 'As my death seemed to draw nearer, I became somewhat uneasy,' he remembered. The tension was more than he could bear and he began to cry. As the days wore on, he had to steel himself and to constantly remind himself that God was with him and that 'even if I were killed by Chun Doo Hwan, history would remember me as victorious because I had been on the side of my people and of justice. God would never abandon me.'

The Supreme Court upheld the tribunal's decision. Kim's life now depended on clemency from Chun, which was exactly what the General had been scheming for. The local press, robbed of all its independence, started on a vilification campaign to press for the prisoner's execution. Meanwhile the international community, especially the United States and Japan, urged Chun not to hang Kim. Pressure was mounting on Chun, and he loved every minute of it.

Meanwhile, Washington was having its own battle over Kwangju; hardliners pushed for silence in consideration of the larger picture of national security, while those concerned with human rights abuses urged the White House to call the Chun regime to account. Richard Holbrooke, the Assistant Secretary of State for East Asia and Pacific Affairs, successfully urged Carter—who had threatened to withdraw American troops from South Korea if the Chun junta continued in its repressive ways—not to make too much of an issue over the massacre. Years later, he landed a plum appointment as a consultant to Hyundai Corporation.

When Ronald Reagan defeated Jimmy Carter in the 1980 elections the scenario had changed, for the President-elect was not enthusiastic about the role human rights had played in Carter's foreign policy. Carter recalled in his memoirs:

> We talked about what was being done to save opposition leader Kim Dae Jung's life in South Korea, and I thanked [Reagan] for sending a message to Chun Doo Hwan urging that Kim's life be spared...[Reagan] expressed with some

enthusiasm his envy of the authority that Korean President Park Chung Hee had exercised during a time of campus unrest, when he had closed the universities and drafted the demonstrators.

Richard von Weizsacker, President of the Federal Republic of Germany, added to the pressure that the international community was bringing to bear on the Korean dictator. The German foreign minister, Hans-Dietrich Genscher, leading the European Economic Community, also demanded that Kim's life be spared. Japan warned that relations between the two countries would be severely strained if Kim was executed.

Only weeks earlier, 2,525 electoral college delegates dourly marched up to the ballot box to cast their vote for the new President of South Korea. When it was announced that Chun had been elected by 2,524 votes to one spoiled ballot, he smiled wryly and stepped onto the podium to acknowledge the stilted applause that passed for acceptance of the new tyrant.

Chun quickly got down to doing what he knew best: curtailing activities of politicians and government officials, and throwing anyone he thought could ruin his day (including more than 35,000 journalists, students, teachers, union leaders and workers) into 'purification camps', where they were starved and beaten, many to death. *Paekkol* (White Skull) thugs, trained to break bones and dressed in protective gear, were sent into crowds to execute their deadly knowhow. The President seemed in a remarkable hurry to become Korea's most hated dictator since World War II, and by his first year in office he had rivalled Park Chung Hee for the title.

As pressure mounted to pardon Kim, Chun remained unmoved. After a meeting with the President, the CIA chief in South Korea, Donald Gregg, was convinced that 'Kim Dae Jung was a dead man.' But Chun also knew that repercussions both within Korea and internationally would be very serious for him if he went ahead with the execution. Needing a way out, he sent his KCIA men to apply pressure on the prisoner to sign a petition of clemency. At first Kim Dae Jung rejected the idea, so he was told that a repentance would also help his fellow prisoners. He finally relented and, after haggling over the words, signed the letter expressing his sorrow that he had 'created controversy both at home and abroad and adversely affected national security', and promising to 'never again engage in politics'.

Chun promptly declared that it was the Government's nature 'to treat magnanimously anyone who repents of his wrongdoings' and commuted Kim's death sentence to life imprisonment. Chun's behaviour was motivated by many factors, but magnanimity was not one of them. He had lobbied hard to be Ronald Reagan's first foreign visitor, and 'shrewdly used Kim's death sentence as a bargaining chip to coax an early state visit out of the incoming Reagan Administration and thus shore up his (non-existent) legitimacy.' Within 48 hours of Reagan's agreeing to invite him to the White House, the dictator announced the stay of execution and reduced Kim's life sentence to 20 years. He also announced that presidential elections would be held on 25 February 1981.

The local press made sure the people would not forget the fact that Kim was a 'tough' not suited for national office, a 'radical' opposition politician who threatened to tear the country apart, and a 'dangerous' collaborator with communist North Korea. Kim likened the situation to someone putting up 'a bloody fight with an intruder who breaks into his home' only to have his family rebuke him for 'being tough and radical...instead of thanking him for saving the situation...' It was a depressing episode. 'Whenever I was an object of misrepresentation...,' he lamented, 'I used to feel like collapsing in despair.'

Dreaming of freedom

Kim was incarcerated in Chongju Prison where, like any other criminal, his head was shaved. As he sat there while his hair was shorn, tears welled up in his eyes. They weren't tears of anguish, but relief after weeks of uncertainty about whether he would live or die. He was taken to a cell that had three compartments. The guards occupied the first, Kim stayed in the middle, and a metal bucket for washing was placed in the third. Two wardens would always be on duty at any one time.

A little window, covered by a thick wire mesh in the rear of his cell, gave him a glimpse of the sky. The compartment was bare and Kim had to sleep on the floor, which during the winter months became unbearably cold. His arthritis only made conditions worse. The guards provided him with a little electric heater that was no match for Korea's frigid winter. At night, drops of water from the pipes turned into ice. Meal times proved no more comforting for 'edible food' in the prison was loosely defined.

He found it difficult to sit on the floor because of a leg injury that he had sustained during a car crash in 1971. A few weeks after his unsuccessful run against Park Chung Hee for the presidency, Kim and his three colleagues were on their way to a meeting when a truck coming from the opposite direction suddenly veered into the path of their car. The truck driver seemed intent on a deadly head-on collision, and at the speed with which the 14-tonner was hurtling, the result was going to be unimaginably bloody. Kim's driver swerved desperately, causing the truck to sideswipe it and bear into the car behind. The crash killed two people. Kim managed to crawl out shaking with fright and pain. His arm and pelvis were broken, and he still walks with a limp.

His arthritis plagued him throughout his imprisonment, and he repeatedly asked for treatment, which was denied. He soon developed a painful and constant ringing in his ears, for which he was allowed to consult an obstetrician who came into the prison only every once in a while. 'I don't think I could have gotten pregnant in my condition,' Kim later joked.

Perhaps not, but insanity was always lurking about in prison, looking for infirm minds. Totally cut off from civilisation and with time seemingly on hold, one begins to sink into despair and confusion. Kim started to carry on imaginary conversations with himself, his wife and his sons, just to keep his wits about him. During his darkest moments, he repeatedly turned to the Bible. 'My faith in God helped me overcome loneliness,' he later recorded. 'I knew that God was with me. I often had dialogues with him, and in that way I escaped from the surroundings.'

He decided to make life as miserable for the guards as they made it for him. He demanded reading material, letters from his family, visitation rights and paper to write to his loved ones. Rights in prison are hard to come by; when you get them, they become absolute treasures. For Kim, there were four. One was reading which he did liberally. Newspapers were banned but he was allowed ten books a month. His family brought him books about theology, politics, economics, history and literature, including Bertrand Russell's *A History of Western Philosophy*, Arnold Toynbee's *A Study of History*, Plato's *Republic*, Augustine's *The City of God*, and some of the theological works of Pierre Teilhard de Chardin, Reinhold Niebuhr and Harvey Cox. He also soaked up Asian classics such as the *Analects of Confucius*, *Mencius*, Sima Qian's *Records of the Historian*, and the writings of various other Korean philosophers and Buddhist scholars. Tough as prison life was for him, the agony was compensated for in 'spiritual fulfilment and elevation'.

His second right was the monthly ten-minute visit from his family, which was 20 minutes shorter than the legal minimum. Kim weighed in with his usual tenacity and managed to lengthen the meetings to 20 minutes each, twice a month. He would talk to his wife through the glass partition on a three-way telephone, with the authorities on one end. The moment his family left, he counted the number of days till he would see them again.

The third pleasure was receiving letters from his wife and relatives. Kim's wife, Lee Hee Ho, regularly wrote to him during his years of imprisonment, totalling 640 letters by the time he was released. The letters and photographs were retrieved by the guards when he finished reading them. In return, Kim was only allowed to write one postcard a month. Having succeeded in extracting more time for his family visits, he now launched into battle to secure one piece of normal sized writing paper for his letters. No luck. If the paper size didn't increase, his handwriting would just have to decrease. He was able to fit 14,000 characters 'half the size of a grain of rice' into each card, which his wife savoured with the help of a magnifying glass.

Not everything passed muster as far as his prison editors were concerned. On one of his birthdays when his family visited him, his sons, in traditional style, knelt on the floor and bowed. The gesture affected him so much that he decided to write a poem to his wife:

> On the wooden floor of the meeting room
> My three sons bowed deeply,
> Congratulating me on the New Year
> And on my birthday, moving me deeply.

My dearest, be not sad,
For we are blessed with these sons.

I long for my family and friends.
I long for nature outside and my fellow beings as well.
Let us embrace when the bells peal.

Kim was banned from sending the poem to his wife because the authorities felt that it might draw an emotional reaction from readers.

The last of the four pleasures was to tend a flower bed, almost 30 metres long and two metres wide, outside the cell. Kim used his hour of exercise after lunch every day to care for his petunias, azaleas, dandelions, daisies, salvias, and vinca roses. Watering and pruning them became a focal point of his days. Conversation with his colourful companions helped immensely to ease the reproach of the silent walls. Even spiders and ants became subjects of intense observation. Kim soon found himself feeding his arachnoid acquaintances with flies that he would stun (because 'they do not like to eat dead flies') and carefully hang on the web.

In prison, one can only dream of freedom, or anything that can secure it. A story floated among the inmates that if one dreamed of a clock, release would follow soon. And so Kim, as with many of the prisoners, set his mind on clock dreaming. But the tormenting timepieces just would not appear, no matter how hard he tried. One night, however, it finally came, and with a timely vengeance. He dreamed that he was in a store 'filled with dozens and dozens of clocks'. With the hard-earned breakthrough, Kim anticipated the promised release, which, of course, didn't happen. He smiled a wistful smile and sank back into his lonely life. Anything was worth a try.

But if the clocks didn't bring him release, his azalea did. He had dug up the plant, re-potted it into a container and brought it into his cell, which was a little warmer than the yard. Every sign of life in solitary confinement was solace for the soul, and Kim wanted to keep the plant alive for as long as he could. He shifted the pot every day so that it obtained maximum sunlight. When it bloomed unseasonably in the middle of December, Kim was stunned, and showed it to the warden. 'That this flower has bloomed in the middle of the winter like this is a good omen!' he boasted. That afternoon, 19 December 1982, he was transferred to the Seoul National Hospital. He had spent more than two and a half years in prison.

Kim was still under heavy guard at the hospital. On the day before Christmas Eve, he was taken by ambulance to the airport, accompanied by scores of KCIA men to make sure that there were no detours enroute. He was put on a plane with his wife and sons for a flight to Washington DC, ostensibly for treatment of his arthritis. Hours later, the Chun regime announced a general amnesty for 1,200 prisoners, most of whom were common criminals.

Within days of his arrival in the United States, Kim was making plans to return to Korea. 'The main object of my stay is treatment of my illness,' he insisted. 'I don't have a plan to stay here for long.'

And finally—President

As Chun Doo Hwan stood beaming on the White House lawn, Ronald Reagan reaffirmed the close relationship between the United States and South Korea—an announcement that all but killed any hope of South Koreans escaping the brutality of their dictator. Not only did Reagan ignore the matter of Chun's torturing of his people (the State Department had asked Congress to delay the publication of the report of South Korea's human rights abuses until after Chun's visit), he also assured his guest that the United States would not withdraw any troops from the country. Every South Korean dictator who wanted Washington's support, it appeared, could not omit bringing up the threat from North Korea; the louder the rantings against the communists, the bigger the smile on the American president's face.

But from the vantage of the people, two dictatorships cannot a democracy make, and South Koreans saw little sense in the United States supporting one and not the other. While grateful to Carter and Reagan for pushing Chun to release him, Kim insisted that the United States had not done right by democracy: 'Even if I couldn't come out, America should justly defend the principle. Human rights issues should not be a transaction between governments but should be supported by the voice of world consciousness and by the power of our people. I would like to see an America which defends the principle even if I were not released.' He argued that American presidents advocated and supported the practice of democracy internationally. 'In reality, America has helped dictatorial regimes in the name of anti-Communism, security and economic rehabilitation.'

Parts of the United States Government has always maintained that, in order to fight communism anywhere in the world, strong governments were needed. Kim agreed, but added that such strength could not come about without the people's backing, as would be the case in a democracy. Besides, in the case of South Korea, 'we must have peace with North Korea first. And the only way we will achieve peace and unification is to return to a democratic system in the South. If we do not have that, we cannot differentiate ourselves from Communism in the eyes of the North Korean people.'

Whilst in the United States, Kim also accepted a long-standing invitation from Harvard University, where he wrote his first book, *Mass-Participatory Economy: A Democratic Alternative for Korea*. Although the short stint in the United States was a comfortable one, he longed to return to his country. Besides, he jested, 'my wife believes in the same ideals and she is a fighter. If I gave up and chose the comfortable life, she might divorce me and I am too old to live alone.' His critics had a different interpretation: Kim's egotistical nature did not allow him to stay away from the centre of South Korean attention for long. Whatever one thought, his return to South Korea was not without danger.

Although Kim repeatedly appealed to Washington to address the question of democracy and human rights in South Korea, Chun Doo Hwan continued to have his way. In 1985 Kim made up his mind to return home. He had asked his government to validate his passport—which had permitted him to travel to the United States only—for entry into Europe as well. Otherwise he would be forced to return earlier. Chun was not thrilled by either option. Allowing the dissident to go to Europe would mean even wider criticisms of his regime, as Kim wouldn't just be visiting the scenic spots. But if his nemesis were to return before the National Assembly elections scheduled for February that year, which would be taken as a referendum on his rule, his chances of a good showing might be jeopardised.

Kim had seen his friend Benigno S. Aquino Jr gunned down when the Filipino politician returned home from Harvard University (Aquino had presented his typewriter to Kim before he left for the Philippines, a gift he still treasures). No one believed that Chun would allow a similar assassination, especially after witnessing the wrath that President Ferdinand Marcos faced when his arch-foe was murdered. Nevertheless, Kim knew that he would walk straight back into jail to finish the remaining 18 years of his 20-year jail term, the amnesty Chun granted notwithstanding.

In the end, the South Korean junta agreed to let Kim return early. Despite the United States Government's hope that Kim's 'return will be trouble-free', he took no chances and cobbled together an entourage to accompany him. One of those in the group was Korea observer, Bruce Cumings, who wrote:

> Kim Dae Jung returned in February 1985, and I was fortunate to be part of an American delegation that accompanied him back to Seoul from exile in the United States, in hopes that our presence might prevent another airport murder like that which cut down Benigno Aquino on the Manila tarmac...The Koreans were too smart to do that, but stupid enough to cause a huge fracas at Kimp'o International Airport; a phalanx of KCIA thugs in brown windbreakers pummeled and threw to the floor prominent Americans (two congressmen were on the delegation), while roughly snatching Kim and his wife into a waiting car and subsequent months of house arrest.
>
> When we got to the bus that would take us into Seoul, hundreds of Cholla people in tattered winter clothing milled around us, exclaiming that Kim was their 'great leader'. On the left side of the road leading into Seoul were thousands of riot police. On the right side were enormous numbers of Seoul's common people—workers in denims, students in black uniform, mothers in long skirts, little kids wrapped tightly against the wind, old men and women in traditional dress—with placards hailing Kim's return. It seemed as if the whole population had divided between the riot police and the demonstrators.

But Kim faced opposition not only from the President. Through the years, he had remained steadfast in his call for unification with North Korea, which, in his opinion, is the only way lasting peace can be brought about on the peninsula. The hawkish generals always saw Kim as a civilian who knew little about the tension with the North and who was willing to blow kisses to the communists even as they remained a threat to South Korea. To commanders who knew might only through guns, those advocating a system where power is fought for without violence (and then relinquished after a few years) made little sense. Besides, many of the generals, including Park Chung Hee, had been part of the Imperial Japanese Army, where firepower meant everything.

If the military saw Kim as poison, feelings of South Korea's business world towards the dissident were even more miasmic. Staunchly championing workers' rights and advocating free labour movement, Kim never endeared himself to the *chaebol* chieftains. 'I will have earth cover my eyes before a union is permitted at Samsung,' founder Yi Pyong Chol once swore. *Chaebol*—business conglomerates such as Hyundai, Daewoo, Lucky-Goldstar, and Samsung—started off as small family businesses; and sweated and toiled their way to fabulous wealth. They have an oligopolistic control of the country's economy, with the top 30 companies accounting for 80% of the GNP; with networks (reinforced by intermarriages of the children) reminiscent of the *zaibatsus* in Japan, they have cornered Korea's commerce to a point where 'ten families control 60% of the miracle on the Han.'

No guts, no glory; no chicanery, no *chaebol*. The business sector through the years grew hydra-like into the Government, and started a comfortable nexus with politicians that eventually bloomed into a corrupt complex which ended in two Presidents, Chun Doo Hwan and Roh Tae Woo, as well as several big business tycoons, being convicted for massive corruption. Worse, the system contributed massively to South Korea's economic meltdown in the 1997 crisis. In those dark years when wages and welfare of workers were way down the management checklist of must-do items, Kim Dae Jung was heretic number one whose eyes the *chaebol* would sooner have earth cover.

On the other hand, students and Christians were firmly behind him. University students have always been highly regarded by Koreans as moral guardians of society, and the people seem willing to lend them support, tacit or otherwise, in their battles. Their strength is drawn from a rich tradition of Confucian heritage that, as the people interpret it, insists that scholars have the responsibility of moral leadership. In 1919, it was students who sparked the movement to drive the Japanese from the peninsula, and in 1960 students drove Syngman Rhee into exile. They have often been described as Korea's 'best organised and most articulate pressure group'.

Together with the students, Christians were in the thick of leading the 1919 resistance movements. During Park's regime, Protestant and Catholic churches, whose followers comprise almost a quarter of South Korea's population, defied the KCIA. Church leaders were often jailed and tortured, but continued to lend support to the democratic movement, especially the people at the bottom of the *chaebol* foodchain. They did this through the Urban Industrial Mission (UIM), which helped Korea's poor and working class against the onslaughts of government and business. The KCIA retaliated by branding the UIM as communist inspired, waging a brutal campaign against the religious organisation. For Kim, support from the Christian community and the labour movement never waned.

Through the 1980s, Korea continued to simmer under Chun Doo Hwan, and was brought to the boil on 10 June 1987, when a student was tortured to death by the Agency for National Security Planning (ANSP), an alias for the KCIA. Demonstrations broke out all over the country. Having amassed a kingly fortune for himself, Chun nominated his friend and army colleague, General Roh Tae Woo, as his successor, trusting Roh to continue the dictatorship and to protect him after he stepped down as President.

As protests grew, the United States pressured both Chun and Roh to ease their armlock on society and to call for elections. Sensing that he stood to lose more than Chun if he continued the repression, Roh pulled the rug from under his comrade and announced direct presidential elections in December 1987. He freed Kim Dae Jung and other political prisoners, and promised to fully restore their political rights. Laws curtailing press freedom were abolished, bans on labour unions lifted, and the ANSP brought under greater control.

To make sure that he did not submerge himself in the political sandtrap with Chun, Roh announced that blame for the 1979 coup (in which he himself had participated by pulling his division from the Demilitarized Zone to reinforce Chun's troops in Seoul) as well as the Kwangju massacre should be laid squarely at the his predecessor's sinking feet. Roh did throw his old friend a lifeline, however, by shielding him from prosecution and allowing the despot to seek refuge and repentance in a far-off Buddhist monastery. Roh, to be sure, was not a revolutionary bent on democratising the country. He still packed the deadly ANSP under his political cloak and repeatedly unleashed it on dissidents and labour leaders.

With his new found freedom, Kim Dae Jung made an emotional journey back to his home Cholla Province on 8 September 1987. He visited Kwangju city and paid tribute to those who died during the massacre in 1980. He was greeted by tens of thousands of supporters who believed that he was their only hope for the presidential election to be held in December that year.

While he enjoyed overwhelming support of the people in the southern province, Kim was much less popular in the northern parts of South Korea, traditional strongholds of Park Chung-hee, Chun Doo Hwan and Roh Tae Woo. Politics in the Republic is driven by intense regionalism where it is not surprising to find support for a constituency's candidate to reach above 90%. In the 1987 presidential elections Kim polled 95% of the votes in Kwangju, but could scrape only 2% in North Kyongsang. While he was almost God-like in southern Cholla, he was attacked by stones, eggs and other flying objects when he visited the northern city of Taegu. His critics described him as a vain and uncompromising individual, and 'a power seeker who maneuvres and manipulates others'.

In the meantime, Roh's political savvy not only saved him from going down the path of previous junta leaders, it also boosted his chances of being legitimately elected as President, which he duly did when he defeated his two challengers, Kim

Dae Jung and Kim Young Sam in December 1987. Kim Young Sam had also been a longtime democracy campaigner in the opposition and a rival, as well as a blander version, of Kim Dae Jung. The contest between the two Kims split the opposition vote and allowed Roh to win.

Constitutionally barred from seeking a second term, the President knew he had to be cautious lest he end up like Chun Doo Hwan. He calculated that, by forming an alliance with the one most likely to be the next president, he could secure a safe retirement. Roh had been bruised by the National Assembly elections in 1988, where the opposition won a majority of the seats. A merger with Kim Dae Jung's Party, the President figured, would help him reassert his control over the political scene.

Midway through his term, Roh invited Kim Dae Jung to the presidential Blue House. 'President Kim, don't you want to stop your suffering?' (Kim was the president of the Party for Peace and Democracy). It was a strange question, to say the least, and Kim wasn't sure how to respond. 'Let's merge parties!' the President suggested, going on to explain the benefits of the merger.

'I'm sorry but I can't do that,' Kim replied after some thought. He told the President that he had been elected to the National Assembly to oppose the ruling party's platform, so to join it now in a merger would not be right. 'Instead of proposing a merger, just rule the nation in a thoroughly democratic way. Then I'll support you openly without any hesitation. That's not only good for you but also good for me. Most of all, this is the way to show your respect and reverence to the people.' Roh kept silent as his guest continued his lecture: 'You mustn't attempt to change the balance of power in the National Assembly simply because you can't always have your way.'

Roh Tae Woo turned to the other Kim and successfully organised a merger with Kim Young Sam's Reunification Democratic Party, which proved to be the clincher for Kim Young Sam during the 1992 presidential race against Kim Dae Jung. Not long after he stepped into the Blue House, Kim Young Sam ordered the arrest and trial of both Chun Doo Hwan and Roh Tae Woo, who were convicted for their roles in Chun's unconstitutional grab for power in 1979 and in the killings in Kwangju. President Kim subsequently commuted Chun's death sentence to life imprisonment. Roh's 22 years were reduced to 17 on appeal.

In December 1992, Kim Dae Jung's house was crammed with his aides and supporters, sullenly following the election results. Throughout the campaign, Kim was repeatedly accused of being a closet communist, an accusation that had all the properties of a rainbow—colourful but illusory. Still, it was an effective tool in scaring the voters.

As the results filtered through, Kim was trailing his rival and the gap never closed. He retired to his bedroom and lay down. Closing his eyes to get some sleep, he could hear the voices in the living room. Then he heard his wife crying. He turned to her and said, 'I narrowly escaped death several times. Can't the mere thought that I am alive today comfort you?'

A few hours before dawn, he decided to retire from politics. 'Didn't somebody say that the right time to retreat is when you want to stay around just a little longer?' he thought in the darkness. 'A man should finish clean. However great one's achievements, one cannot be favourably evaluated if the finish is ugly. How many others ruined their reputations and faded away, tarnished because they were compromised in the end. My time is over.'

Kim then went on a brief visit to Cambridge University but, once again, he was not able to keep away from Korea for long. He returned in 1994 and immediately re-entered the political arena. He was no longer the fire breathing dissident. He started taking a broader perspective on democracy in Asia, and initiated the formation of the Forum for Democratic Leaders in the Asia Pacific (FDL-AP), which he used, among other objectives, to campaign for the release of Aung San Suu Kyi and the Burmese people from the rule of the junta.

'I hope he runs again,' a National Assemblyman told me over dinner during an FDL-AP conference in Seoul in 1995. 'We've come so far to achieve democracy but the political system is still very shaky. One slip from an uncommitted president and the generals will be back in the Blue House again. Kim Dae Jung is the only one truly committed to democratic ideals and determined enough to fight the generals back.'

The next day, Kim shuffled into the seminar session where I was speaking. After my presentation, a Korean woman stood up and recounted the turbulent times when the KCIA pounced on anyone they thought harboured democratic aspirations. Her husband was arrested then and she hadn't seen him since. Silence followed. Kim, who had quietly taken a seat behind, pulled out a handkerchief and wiped his tears.

When the session ended, he limped over. 'Sorry I walk so slow. An old injury,' he said with a smile. At the end of our brief conversation he said to me, 'I know Singapore. Persist. Those on the side of liberty and justice can never fail.'

On 25 February 1998, as he stood on the podium as President of the Republic of Korea, Kim Dae Jung promised his people: 'I will consult you on all issues. You, in return, must help me if only for one year—this year—when the nation is standing on the brink of disaster.' Kim pledged, as he always had, to help the country recover from the years of ruthless authoritarian rule and to reconcile the Southerners with their Northern brothers. True to his promise not to resort to retaliation during his presidency—he had in earlier years visited Park Chung Hee's grave in a sign of reconciliation—he pardoned Chun Doo Hwan and Roh Tae Woo, citing Abraham Lincoln: 'Malice toward none, charity to all.'

Each line on Kim's face told the story of his struggle which had been borne out of an unstinting love for freedom—a love that he never questioned. And as I read an interview that the President gave after his inauguration, one sentence caught my eye: 'Someone who stands for liberty and justice can never fail.'

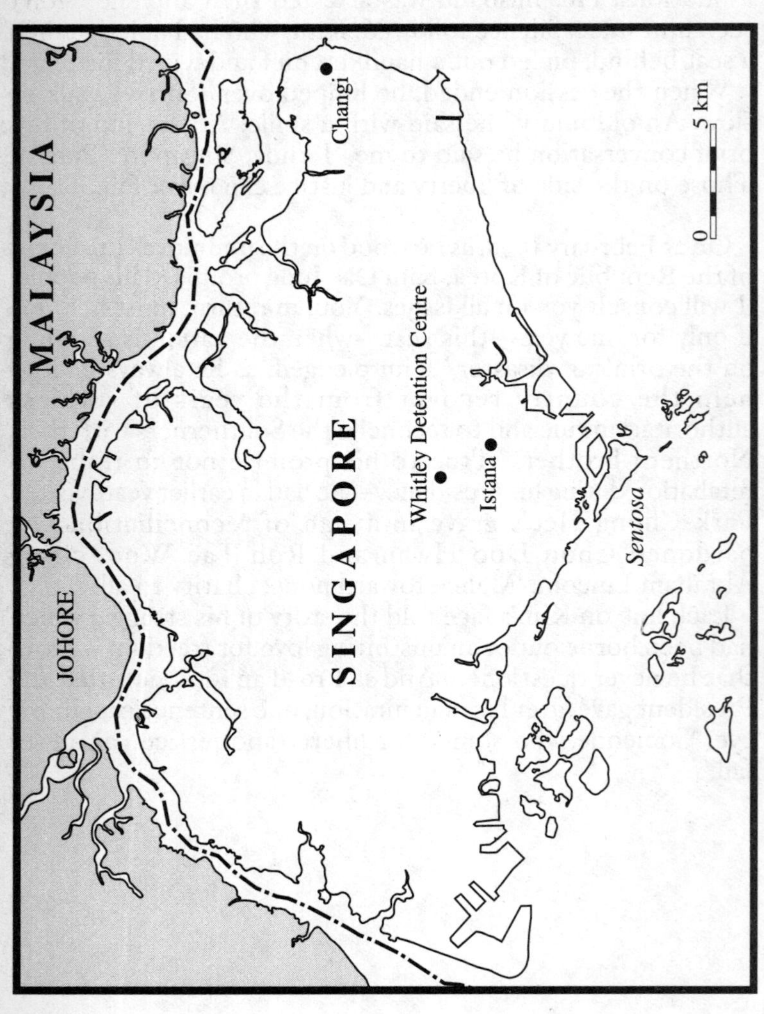
MALAYSIA
JOHORE
SINGAPORE
Changi
Whitley Detention Centre
Istana
Sentosa
0
5 km

6
Singapore
Chia Thye Poh

How are they going to jail democracy?

Berlin, Germany, 1997.

I made my way to the counter at the train station. 'What's your destination?' the attendant asked.

'Hamburg,' I replied.

As the train rolled across the expanse of a soporific Sunday morning German countryside dotted with indolent cows, I thought of the curious manner in which the man at the counter asked me for my destination.

The question was as simple as it was recondite. We all have places to go. When we arrive there's another destination to look forward to and then another. Unless we die, or sit and refuse to move, an ultimate destination will never come to pass. Yet goals, and that maddeningly philosophical preordained course that we call destiny, are also destinations.

I was heading to meet a fellow Singaporean who seemed to have neither goal nor destiny. For nearly a quarter of a century he had sat in prison, and now that he was released, he seemed devoid of any real purpose in life. Where was he going?

I made my way to the huge Philips billboard where we had arranged to meet. I found him waiting, with his unmistakable grin and thick-rimmed glasses. We shook hands heartily as if we had known each other forever, giving away little that this was our first encounter. He had been in jail a total of 22 years, six months, two weeks and four days, most of it in solitary confinement. 'As long as Nelson Mandela,' a political activist had once remarked. But Mandela was a member of a banned political party, had admitted to breaking the law, and was given his day in court, however execrable its process. He is now a free man and President of his country. Chia Thye Poh, on the other hand, was an elected opposition member of parliament, has never been charged with any crime, and was never allowed a trial. While South Africa was afflicted with apartheid, Singapore was gallantly building 'a democratic society based on justice and equality'.

Chia was elected in 1963 as a candidate of the Barisan Sosialis (BS), or Socialist Front. Accusing the ruling People's Action Party (PAP) of harassing its leaders, the BS staged a boycott of Parliament. Three weeks later he was in the party headquarters one afternoon when the police walked in. 'Chia Thye Poh, you are under arrest,' one of them said as he slapped his hand on Chia's shoulder. With that he was taken away to prison, where every right he had as a human being was taken away. He has lost the best part of his life, been separated from his loved ones, and was never able to start his own family. The best things in life are free, so people say, but even those were taken away from him.

In 1989 he was released onto Sentosa, now an island resort just south of Singapore. There, he was kept in a small house near a fort which has been turned into a tourist attraction. Tourists peered into the house whenever the window-shutters were open. So Chia kept them shut. He was allowed to go onto the main island to work in Government approved jobs. The money he earned had to be stretched to pay for rent and utility bills that the Government charged him. Everynight by 9 p.m. he had to be back in the house.

In 1991 he was allowed to be reunited with his family. He is not allowed to issue any public statement. He is banned from writing or publishing. He cannot be a member of any organisation—'not even a chess club'. He is barred from travelling overseas without Government permission. In short, he continues to live like a criminal on parole.

The Government told him that he would be released from prison if he would leave Singapore and never return. Chia declined. The PAP has finally allowed him to take up a long-standing invitation for a scholarship from the Hamburg Foundation in Germany for one year.

One day he decided to visit his old constituency, where he was the member of parliament, and talk to some of the people there. He was trailed by the police who questioned the residents about the visit after he left.

Having had nowhere to go for nearly a quarter of a century, where is he headed now? 'I can't say very much,' he told me as we walked around the deserted town square on a chilly morning. 'They served me another restriction order.' He fished a letter from his pocket:

> To: The Commissioner of Police, Singapore, and all other police officers and all others whom it may concern.
>
> WHEREAS the President of Singapore is satisfied with respect to CHIA THYE POH, [address], that, with a view to preventing him from acting in any manner prejudicial to the security of Singapore, it is necessary to impose upon him certain restrictions:
>
> NOW, THEREFORE, I, WONG KAN SENG, Minister for Home Affairs, in exercise of the powers conferred on me by section 8 (1)(b) of the Internal Security Act, hereby order that the said CHIA THYE POH be subject to the following restrictions for a period of 2 years with effect from 28 November 1996:
>
> I that he shall not issue public statements, address public meetings or hold office in, or take part or in any way assist in the activities of or act as adviser to, or be a member of any organisation or association, or take part in any political activity without the prior written approval of the Director, Internal Security Department, Singapore; and
>
> II that he shall not knowingly associate or be in communication with any person who currently is or has previously been detained under the Emergency Regulations of the Federation of Malaya or of the Colony of Singapore, the Preservation of Public Security Ordinance, 1955, of Singapore or under the Internal Security of Malaya, Malaysia or Singapore Ex-political Detainees' Association, provided he is also a member of the Association.

Made this 7th day of November 1996
By Order of the President
(signed)
WONG KAN SENG
MINISTER FOR HOME AFFAIRS
SINGAPORE

These 'Dear Commissioner of Police' ministerial missives are never easy reading. All the mumbo-jumbo about the 'Colony of Singapore', 'WHEREAS' and 'NOW, THEREFORE, I' makes one wonder why this archaic lingo is still used. The officious tone aims to strike awe in the population but, more insidiously, to masquerade iniquity. It is also the ruling party's way of saying, 'Don't look at us, the British started it first.'

Then there is the 'manner prejudicial to the security of Singapore'. The Government has never defined this, except to insist that Chia was in some conspiracy to use 'force and terror' to overthrow it. Evidence? None needed. Reason? Because Singapore is different. More about that later.

In a bizarre twist, Chia was suddenly accused—19 years into his imprisonment—of being a member of the Communist Party of Malaya (CPM). He pointed out during an interview that the 'allegations were deliberate fabrications to absolve the Government from the blame of human rights violations...I have never been a member of any communist party and I have never advocated violence, let alone been charged in court for any offence of violence.' Chia also wrote to the Government in 1985:

> I joined the Barisan Sosialis and took part in the general elections and became a member of the legislative assembly. I did so solely out of my own intention to fulfill my obligation to society and the people, and needed no other person...to direct me. Inside the legislative assembly I spoke with facts and policies. Outside the legislative assembly I made petitions on behalf of people. Isn't this what a legislative assembly member should do?

By this time, the leader of the CPM, Fang Chuang Pi, all but considered his movement to be terminally non-functional, Gorbachev's Soviet Union had dolefully hobbled to its final resting place, and Lee Kuan Yew was hobnobbing with Deng

Xiaoping in every conceivable manner except, perhaps, playing bridge. Yet Chia was still in prison, with the Government insisting that he had to confess to being a communist and renounce the use of violence.

Even if he was hellbent on blowing up the country, how was Chia going to procure arms, who were going to be his foot soldiers, and where was he going to set up base? One of his colleagues joked that in Malaysia the communists could retreat to the jungle, but in Singapore there was only the Botanic Gardens.

The reference to Chia's detention 'for a period of 2 years' is as restrictive as boxer shorts. At the beginning of his imprisonment, the security agents promised that, until he confessed, the detention would 'go on year after year' and sooner or later they would find the 'means to break' him. More than two decades later, these means were still eluding them and the initial show of political might had fermented into mulish sadism. The ruling clique knew that its pretext for continuing the detention was wearing thin but it could not find a way to release their captive without loss of face. After he was released, Chia said:

> They tried very hard to break prisoners, to extract confessions from them, to have them confess on television. They made me pay a very high price for not kowtowing to them.
>
> In 1966, they put me in a dark cell and said some people had gone insane under such circumstances. Sometimes you could hear people kicking the doors as if they had gone insane. I went from one prison to another and was in solitary confinement several times. Sometimes I was deprived of reading material for months at a stretch. They said that there's no end to this, that it will go on year after year if I don't confess, that even if I'm made of steel, they have means to break me.
>
> I told them that I had nothing to confess, and that if the government had the evidence it should try me in an open court, where I could see the evidence against me and defend myself.
>
> There were day-long interrogations in a freezing cold room. They pressurised my family. But I always thought,

no matter how long they keep me in this way, some day they will have to release me, because I'm innocent and I have support. It's part of the broad struggle for democracy all over the world.

When you are in solitary, there is nothing in the cell. But you can explore, and see faint scribblings from previous prisoners. I still remember one of them. It was a poem in Chinese:

Ten years behind bars
Never too late
Thousands of ordeals
My spirit steeled.

When you were alone and helpless, and you saw things like that, you were encouraged.

Through the long years in prison, Chia remains unbeaten. He continues to hang on to the prospect that the international community will not forget him because he says that the Government is hoping that he 'will succumb to psychological fatigue'.

'This is not about a personal battle,' he explained, as we sat down for lunch at a Turkish fast food outlet. 'The struggle for democracy is much more than personal battles. I don't feel bitter towards anyone. Democracy is not about violence. They can jail me, but how are they going to jail democracy? One day, I'll get there—we'll all get there.'

I had been wrong in the train. Chia Thye Poh knows his destination.

Among the various countries I've written about in this book, the part on Singapore has been the most difficult. One reason is the reluctance of former political prisoners to openly relate their experiences for fear of being rearrested and imprisoned by the Internal Security Department (ISD), Singapore's answer to the KGB. Apart from the secret police, the PAP has many potent weapons at its disposal when it comes to dealing with its opponents. What is related in the following chapters is a truncated version of an even more disturbing story, a full revelation of which would allow the PAP to identify its victims and punish them further.

The veneer of a modern city—replete with skyscrapers and stockmarkets, condominiums and country clubs—masquerades something altogether more corrupt in the city state. As a citizen, I am subject to the laws that the PAP manipulates and interprets to its own advantage. I would be lying if I said that the tendency to self-censor did not occur time and again. But reality must also be told; the reality of how fearful and repressed the Singaporean society is and of how the ruling clique continues to deny the people the ideals that inspire the human race—freedom and justice. It must not be relegated to an asterisk in the Singapore story.

The toothless tiger

Legend has it that a young Indonesian prince was out at sea one day when he spotted a strange looking creature. As with gossip, legends have the tendency to inflate. This creature soon grew to mythical proportions, becoming a magnificent lion (never mind the fact that the felines were not indigenous to Southeast Asia), and so the name Singapura (lion city) was coined.

For centuries the lion seemed more interested in taking a siesta than roaring about its potential, and Singapura remained a quiet fishing spot. That was until a young English officer from the East India Company, Thomas Stamford Raffles, arrived in 1819. He recognised that the tiny island was strategically placed between the Indian and Pacific oceans, blessed with deep seabeds and natural harbours, and immediately envisioned it as a main trading post.

With minimum fuss and maximum wile, Raffles went to Johor and negotiated a deal with the sultanate, ceding the island of just 225 square miles to British administration. With this acquisition and the subsequent Anglicisation of its name, Singapore became the third shining tack on the map, joining Penang in the north and Malacca in the middle, through which seafaring traders had to pass through in an interminable loop. The Straits Settlements became the collective, if somewhat prosaic, name for the three cities.

The colonial government ruled uninterrupted for nearly 150 years. Chinese immigrants arrived in ever greater numbers, eventually becoming the predominant ethnic group in the

Straits Settlements. The indigenous Malays, migrants from the Indian subcontinent and various peoples from the Middle East made up the remaining 25% of the population.

Trade flourished and the lion began to stir. The *ang moh kows* or 'red-haired monkeys', whom the locals called their overlords (most times out of earshot), were the British masters. With their wisdom and power, 'Fortress Singapore' was too well defended to be threatened by anybody. When war broke out, everyone knew that the warriors from the land of the bulldog would have little problem in beating back those from the Rising Sun.

By February 1942, the Japanese had taken the Malayan Peninsula and were advancing on Singapore. When the marauders arrived, British guns were pointed every which way except at the enemy, who rumbled into the city, not in armoured cars and tanks nor in blazing battle ships as anticipated, but on those infuriatingly slow bicycles. After that modest entrance, the Japanese demonstrated their brutality by lopping off a head or two to show that their madness was not to be trifled with. After the fall, some of the Allied troops were marched off to Changi prison; others were taken to build the Railway of Death in Burma.

When the British returned after the war, they were none too pleased about the dispossession of their colonial spoils by the Japanese. But to the locals, the difference between the Japanese and the British was about as significant as that between arsenic and cyanide. Independence movements developed all over Southeast Asia, with Singapore pouring forth its own band of freedom fighters. The British Government knew that its running of Singapore, which by then had developed into an energetic entrepot city, had the expiry date stamped all over it.

As pressure mounted, London agreed to conduct elections in 1955 that would sanction limited powers to a local assembly. The Governor, however, remained in supreme command over internal security, defence and foreign affairs.

The elections were won handsomely by the Labour Front, whose leader, David Saul Marshall, an effervescent lawyer and a liberal of Jewish ancestry, became the Chief Minister. His priority was to rid the island of its colonial chaperone, but Britain was reluctant to grant immediate self-rule. The Chief

Minister led a motley delegation of political aspirants to London to negotiate a full transfer of power, which was doomed even before the propellers of their aeroplane started to whirl. For their own reasons and agendas, not everyone wanted the talks to prosper. The impetuous Marshall threatened to resign if his mission failed. After protracted and tortuous negotiations, he came back with no more than when he left. Exasperated and honour bound, he quit, and was replaced by Lim Yew Hock, who proved much more malleable to British dictates.

Marshall then formed the Workers' Party, and was the opposition leader for a period before retiring from politics. He later accepted the post of ambassador to France when Lee Kuan Yew became Prime Minister. I met him at a birthday party many years later, when he was in his eighties. In his animated fashion, he entertained those around him with his extraordinary tales. I could never quite figure out which parts were real and which, if any, embellished. Everyone loved them just the same.

Once, he took me aside and, with fiery eyes and flaming eyebrows burrowing into me, said, 'Don't trifle with this man Kuan Yew. You're better off away from here. Go to Malaysia, Kuala Lumpur or Penang, and come back only after he dies.' I thought it curious counsel but didn't doubt its seriousness. A year later, Marshall passed away.

Even with Lim Yew Hock in charge, the independence movement continued apace. The people wanted to be the Queen's subjects no longer, and their impatience quickly turned into obstreperousness. Strikes and riots flared up in the city. The influence from mainland China, which had recently succumbed to the might of the communists, was inescapable. With the British administration determined to keep the leftist and pro-communist groups at bay, and the local educated Chinese equally resolute to get rid of the colonialists, a collision seemed certain.

From amongst the rebels there emerged a young man whose homely demeanour and quiet nature hardly conjured the image of a rabble-rouser. Yet, when Lim Chin Siong took to the stage, his flair and mass appeal was patent. His speeches rarely ended without an untamed ovation. An admirer recounted, 'At the height of the struggle, I remembered how Chin Siong got up on stage and told everyone: "Saya masuk first gear, lu jangan gostan!" (When I get into first gear, don't you go into reverse!) The crowd loved it!' Another recollected, 'In his heyday, Chin Siong's political rallies were packed. They were memorable events. At one rally he said to the crowd sitting on the ground, "The British say that you cannot stand on your own feet. Stand up!" The crowd rose to a man.' Idealistic, socialistic and, above all, un-Westernised, Lim was the embodiment of everything the embryonic nation aspired to. He spoke their language, lived their lifestyle and had an unquestionable regard for their interests.

To the extent that Lim was idolised by the people, such was his downfall. He was on the wrong side of power and time. The British wanted to ensure that the region remained communist-free. Singapore, being of vital importance to their commercial interests, could not fall into the wrong hands. Lim Chin Siong's political ideals never bore fruit, as he was repeatedly arrested during the country's fomenting and formative years.

Britain was looking for someone whom they could trust to continue their legacy on the island. A young, British-trained lawyer, who spoke impeccable English but whose command of the Chinese language was lamentable, seemed to fit the bill. Harry Lee Kuan Yew was a rapier tongued, lightning witted and thoroughly Westernised Oriental, once toasted by the British foreign secretary, George Brown, as the 'best bloody Englishman east of Suez.' While these qualities found favour with the colonial government, they left Lee floundering when it came to his being the fisher of the local folk.

Lee was also deeply involved in the agitation for independence. Upon returning from studies in the United Kingdom, he acted as the legal adviser to unions and organisations that were battling the British at every conceivable opportunity. With nationalistic fervour, the young lawyer sprang to the defence of his clients, invoking the virtues of individual liberty and freedom.

Lee saw Lim Chin Siong's power. He knew that if he was going to make any political headway, the younger Lim was going to be indispensable. He not only defended that if Lim 'were a communist, then I would say I agree 75% with him', but also declared that 'I cannot in all honesty say that communism is a diabolical evil' and that 'if I have to choose communism and anti-communism I will chose [sic] communism...if you hate something because you do not like some aspects of it, you can work yourself into a state where anything said or done by the communists must be wrong and evil.' In 1954 they formed the People's Action Party (PAP). A year later Lee, Lim and another candidate won their places in the national assembly at the elections. Marshall was still in charge, and the PAP became the opposition.

The alliance between Lee and Lim was as uneasy as it was treacherous. Differences in political disposition and personality meant that their relationship was doomed from the beginning. T. J. S. George compared the two in his book, *Lee Kuan Yew's Singapore*:

> Lim Chin Siong had qualities that made him a formidable political rival, and he was superior to Lee as a human being. First, his charisma and mass appeal were embellishments evidently beyond Lee Kuan Yew's reach. Second, his interest in general reading despite his lack of Westernisation was in marked contrast to Lee's inclination then and now to avoid everything that was not immediately and directly relevant to his job...Third, Lim was widely recognised as being utterly selfless.

Things came to a head in 1956 when the PAP's all-powerful central executive committee was due for an election. Lim Chin Siong proved to be the mainstay of the Party, and his Chinese speaking, left-leaning faction seemed indomitable. Suddenly, the British ordered an island-wide crackdown on communists. Lim Chin Siong and his associates were detained without trial under the Preservation of Public Security Ordinance (PPSO). Lim vehemently denied being a communist, but the authorities paid scant attention. With the arrest of his comrade-adversary, Lee was able to establish his control of the Party.

But the 'threat' from the left was far from over. A year later, several of Lim's supporters were elected to the PAP's governing body. Again, the British authorities ordered a communist purge and arrested most of them. As George wrote, 'Repeated government intervention to ensure Lee Kuan Yew's political survival confirmed the feeling that Lee was by now Britain's chosen man for Singapore.'

Lee Kuan Yew knew, however, that he needed the support of his jailed comrades, whom the masses looked to for leadership, in the general elections in 1959. He visited them in prison and wanted them to sign a statement pledging their allegiance to him before he would campaign for their release. They did. In return, the prisoners wanted him to sign a statement that if he won the elections he would free all political prisoners. He didn't.

In the meantime, Lim and the rest of the detainees had been shipped to an even tinier island in the southern waters of Singapore. In one of their discussions, Lee had arranged for the meeting to be carried out on board a boat. The prisoners were out the entire day. That night when they retired, one heard a hissing sound coming from the ceiling. Thinking that it could be a snake, the prisoners got up to investigate. What they found was much more chilling: snugly planted in one corner of the roof was a microphone. The detainees immediately suspected that Lee was building up a dossier on them for later use.

In the lead up to the elections, the PAP's campaign received a boost. Thomas Bellow, another Singapore observer, described how 'Lee used information against the Labour Front to which only the Council of Ministers were supposedly privy' to enable the right-wing PAP faction to suddenly 'seek an absolute majority of the seats in the May 1959 elections.' It was a thumping victory: the PAP won 43 out of the 51 seats.

The PAP had fought the elections with clear policies on education, the economy and health, which observers remarked were so far left that they sounded furtively communistic. The PAP leaders were unconcerned. They knew where the support was coming from, and nothing was going to stop them from taking advantage of it. Lee Kuan Yew also knew that hardheaded policies were not enough. The heartstrings of the people had to be given an unmistakable tug. The spectre of their hero Lim Chin Siong languishing in prison was too delicious not to be exploited.

Before the elections, Lee had called for the release of his comrades and challenged the Lim Yew Hock government's democratic credentials:

> But either we believe in democracy or we do not. If we do, then we must say categorically, without qualification, that no restraint from any democratic process, other than by ordinary law of the land, should be allowed. If you believe in democracy, you must believe in it unconditionally. If you believe that men should be free, then they should have the right of free association, of free speech, of free publication. Then no law should permit those democratic processes to be set at naught.

He even pledged that, if the PAP won the elections, it would not take office until all its leaders were freed. The words were music to the ears of the Party's left-wing supporters.

Love is like many things—according to Lee Kuan Yew, even repression. 'I'm told it is like making love,' he romanticised in 1956. 'It's always easier the second time around.' This sensual homily was an outpouring of angst against a repressive system where first 'you attack only those whom your Special Branch can definitely say are communists. Then you attack those whom your Special Branch say are aiding the communists. Then finally, since you have gone that far, you attack all those who oppose you.' At that time, Lee was waging war against the introduction by the British Government of detention without trial:

> All you have to do is to dissolve organisations and societies and banish or detain the key political workers in these societies. Then miraculously everything is tranquil and quiet on the surface. Then an intimidated press and some sections of the press and the government controlled radio together can regularly sing your praises and slowly and steadily the people are made to forget the evil things that have already been done. Or if these things are referred to again, they are conveniently distorted, and distorted with impunity, because there will be no opposition to contradict.

It was a bold denunciation against dictators of any hue or colour. It also turned out to be his blueprint for control over Singapore when he became Prime Minister.

When Marshall was Chief Minister and the PPSO was introduced, opposition leader Lee warned, 'What he [Marshall] is seeking to do in the name of democracy is to curtail a fundamental liberty, and the most fundamental of them all—freedom from arrest and punishment without having violated a specific provision of the law and being convicted for it.' He berated that, 'If the Government can prove its case, let us have a public inquiry, let us have evidence laid before some political tribunal and let the allegations be proved.' Thirty years later, Prime Minister Lee said: 'It is not the practice, nor will I allow subversives to get away by insisting that I've got to prove everything against them in a court of law.'

Such political somersaults are not rarities. When the British required the people to carry identity cards, Lee opposed it: 'I wish to point out as one who...believes in a liberal way of life, that [the identity card] is a marked departure from the normal traditions of a liberal civilised society.' Today, Singaporeans are photographed, finger-printed and bar-coded on the identity cards that they have to carry.

The British had pressed for the arrest of more than 300 pro-communist elements in 1956. It was David Marshall who rebuffed the proposition and arrested only seven, an action which the PAP criticised as 'soft headed'. This tactic of publicly identifying with its leftist comrades, while quietly working with the British to arrest them, kept the PAP's opponents nonplussed.

In 1959 when he took over the Government, Lee Kuan Yew felt that the surreptitious dual role of the PAP could be dispensed with. Another Lee surfaced. No more did he need to pay homage to democratic canons and parliamentary politesse. In came the first musings about Lee's brand of democracy—Asian democracy. As early as 1962 he said, 'At a time when you want harder work with less return and more capital investment, one man one vote produces just the opposite. This system is not held in esteem anywhere in Asia.' He conveniently omitted telling his audience that it was precisely this system that had enabled him to become Prime Minister. It was vintage Lee.

Meanwhile, many of his colleagues whose release he campaigned for during the election remained locked up. Among those who were released was Lim Chin Siong, who was relegated to being an ordinary member of the PAP. Lim was barred from the Party's cadreship, an important appointment which gave a member the right to vote for, and be elected to, the central executive committee. Lim was also not granted his citizenship papers. Instead, he was offered a job in the Ministry of Finance, the Siberia of Singaporean politics. To top it off, he was put under intense surveillance.

Lim had promised, however, that he would continue to support the PAP if it would abolish detention without trial. Firmly in power, there was no need for the Prime Minister to negotiate with his foe, and he decided to go public with their hitherto arcane feud. Lim Chin Siong, Lee charged, had embarked on this 'reckless adventure of trying to make Singapore a Cuba' and 'took instruction from the communist underground.'

Lim, piqued by the treatment, made a formal break with the PAP and formed the BS in 1961. A substantial chunk of the Party—seven out of the ten branches—defected with him. Overnight, the PAP appeared to be in tatters, with only a couple of men staffing its headquarters. But the Party was unruffled, for it had an infinitely more powerful body from which it could fight its battles—the state machinery.

In August 1963, when Malaya gained independence from British rule, the PAP fought for inclusion in the new Federation of Malaysia. Lee Kuan Yew called for Singaporeans to decide on the matter in a referendum. On the ballot were three choices—or rather 'three ways of saying yes to [inclusion] and none of saying no.' The people were told to choose one of three conditions under which they wanted merger with Malaysia. As voting was compulsory, the BS told the voters to cast a blank vote to signal their opposition to joining the Federation. The PAP announced that all blank ballots would be counted as votes in favour of inclusion. There were no surprises when the results were announced. Lee boasted that when his opponents 'lost the referendum...and the overwhelming majority of us—the people—voted decisively for merger... they knew that their fate was sealed.'

With Singapore part of the Federation, the PAP set its sights on the Government in Kuala Lumpur. In a space of two years, relations between the two governments became so abrasive that it finally proved untenable. Lee's insistence of using the title of Prime Minister did little to soothe tempers between Singapore and Kuala Lumpur. 'There can never be two prime ministers in one nation,' Tunku Abdul Rahman, Malaysia's Prime Minister said. In August 1965, Malaysia expelled Singapore from the Federation and the island city became a sovereign nation.

'For me it is a moment of anguish,' Lee lamented during a television interview, soon after he told Singaporeans about the breakup with Malaysia. 'All my life...my whole adult life...I have believed in merger...' He started to cry.

The Tunku was more surprised than he was moved: 'I don't know why Mr Lee acted like that...he was quite pleased about [the split].' Lee had gone to Kuala Lumpur to see the Malaysian Prime Minister about Singapore's stormy relations with its neighbour. A day later, he called some of his colleagues and arranged so that they did not travel together so that they could not discuss the matter. 'I don't know why he was crying,' said Toh Chin Chye.

Since its inception, the BS had maintained a steady drum beat, loud enough to keep the PAP on edge. The leftists appeared strong enough to make a major demonstration of strength at the polls. Trouble was also brewing elsewhere. Indonesia's President Sukarno was breathing fire at Malaysia and Singapore, and stoking the sentiment of *konfrontasi* to a feverish pitch. Indonesian volunteers were being trained to be 'deployed' in Malaysia to fight the British. In February that year, a blueprint was drawn up by the Internal Security Council (ISC), the British intelligence outfit, to nab suspected communists. While the British were ostensibly the protagonists, the PAP was the prime mover behind the operation.

'Lord Selkirk was then the British High Commissioner,' a friend who had intimate knowledge of the goings-on within the ISC revealed to me. 'Lee Kuan Yew charmed Selkirk with his silky smooth English, replete with "you know" and "old chap" and such like.' Selkirk agreed to detain pro-communist agents who were deemed a threat to the national security of the Federation of Malaysia, of which Singapore was still a part.

Maurice Williams, the British security liaison officer, was initially reluctant to proceed with the crackdown but acquiesced after some persuasion from the Singapore branch. George Bogaars, who was then director of the Singapore

Special Branch (SSB), had commented that 'basically the initiative for action came from Lee Kuan Yew.' After some persuasion Williams came around and later suggested the name Operation Cold Store. 'Let's "coldstore" the chaps for a period of time,' was how it was put.

The SSB went to work, with Lee Kuan Yew taking a personal interest in the affair. Dossiers and case histories were prepared. The list was submitted to the Kuala Lumpur Special Branch and was in turn handed to the ISC for final approval. But Williams had become increasingly wary. He did not want the British to be used to provide respectability for the PAP's political cloak-and-dagger manoeuvres. The MI5 agent was also unhappy about the list of people to be arrested, as he considered it too long, with many of the targets not even remotely communistic. He suspected that the operation was politically motivated and that it would be undemocratic to arrest some of them. After considerable wrangling, a list of 150 names was finalised.

David Marshall later charged that the order for arrests 'came from [the PAP] Government and it is cowardly to seek to hide behind the skirts of the ISC.' Marshall said that even he was described as a communist: 'It is easy to call people subversives, to damn them as communists. I know myself that I am as communist as the Pope, but that has not prevented the Government and its stooges from seeking to paint me red. I speak from experience.'

Meanwhile word leaked out, and the BS leaders readied themselves for the crackdown. Lim Chin Siong took to attending late night movies, knowing that the PAP and its henchmen were at their best under the cloak of nightfall. On 2 February 1963, the order was given and the hunt began. Days before the operation, intense surveillance was mounted on the targets, tracking the BS leaders' every move. Five hundred police officers assembled in Senai, Johor, so as not to arouse suspicion in Singapore. In the dead of night, 100 teams crept into the slumbering island. Lim and company didn't stand a chance. Before the night was over, most of the PAP's opponents were captured.

'We were riding a tiger and we knew it,' Lee later claimed melodramatically when he talked about his fight with the left. Someone had forgotten to tell him that the British hunters had already declawed the cat and rendered it toothless before he mounted it. But squeezing out braggadocio from bellicosity has always been the hallmark of the PAP.

After his arrest in 1963, the once spirited Lim Chin Siong finally cracked under the might of the PAP. While imprisoned, he came close to taking his own life. In 1965 when he was at the Singapore General Hospital, Lim hanged himself from a pipe in the toilet. He was discovered just in time and rescued. After he recovered, he was sent back to prison. Four years later, he penned an abject capitulation to Lee Kuan Yew and told the Prime Minister that he had 'finally come to the conclusion to give up politics for good' and repudiated the 'international communist movement'. With that, Lim was given a one way ticket to the United Kingdom and allowed to return only on the say-so of the Government.

In 1995, he was silent as we ate our dinner at a friend's house. Throughout the evening, as the conversation became vivacious when politics was the subject, Lim sat stoic and sullen. At times, he stared blankly into space as if reminiscing about the days when he walked tall and proud among his people.

'This is not the Lim Chin Siong of the 1960s,' another dinner guest remarked. 'He's now so diffident, subservient and seems to have lost the cause. Even his handshake, which was firm and uncompromising, has become limp and unconvincing. There's a lot of speculation as to why this is so: drugs, prolonged solitary confinement, torture—nothing has been confirmed.' At the end of the evening, just as we were about to take our leave, Lim suddenly turned to me and, in a low rasping voice, uttered his first words: 'Don't give up.'

In February 1996, Lim Chin Siong passed away. At the crematorium, his former comrades said their last goodbyes and eulogies in a hall which overflowed with family and friends. As the casket was pushed into the furnace, a thunderous and defiant applause resounded.

With the leaders of the opposition out of sight and action, the PAP called for elections to be held in September 1963. Its victory was not to be doubted; the only question was how the playing field could be careened so that gravity became the coach, player and referee against which the opposition would have to fight. The minimum of nine days was given for campaigning, which included festive holidays to distract voters. Printers were pressured and blocked to minimise the publication of opposition literature, while PAP material had been prepared months ahead by overseas presses. Permission for public meetings was delayed and denied, opposition bank accounts frozen, and non-government organisations de-registered.

Even today, with the progress of technology, elections continue to be fought on the PAP's terms. In the 1997 general elections, opposition video tapes were banned while the PAP made full use of the television network. When the Singapore Democratic Party put up information of its candidates on its website, the Government ordered it removed. Sites for public rallies were designated at remote swamps that quickly filled up during the monsoon rains. Voters were bribed with construction of public amenities and refurbishment of their Government-owned apartments if PAP candidates were elected in their constituencies. Otherwise, the PAP threatened, such municipal upgrading would be delayed or withheld. Voting slips, which are numbered, add to the apprehension of the voters. Nothing gets past the ruling party.

The universities came under the Government's hammer as well. In the late 1960s, students applying for places had their applications scrutinised by the intelligence unit and were issued 'suitability certificates', based not on their academic performance and aptitude but on the political leanings of their families. When the Vice-Chancellor of the University of Singapore resigned in disgust, the Government appointed the Deputy Prime Minister, Toh Chin Chye, to the position. Toh later grew increasingly disillusioned with his colleagues and left the Government: 'As a minister, I had to go around defending certain policies I didn't believe in, I'm glad I don't have to do it any more.' The PAP leaders didn't even bother with political niceties with the Chinese language Nanyang University—they just closed it down. Through the years, academic staff have been intimidated, sued, sacked, and charged whenever they speak up against the regime.

Lee Kuan Yew best summarised his overpowering of the opposition when he said, 'The British may be a little bit squeamish about having to do in somebody they had made use of...But let me say...that nationalist governments all over the world, when they assume power and they face opposition which is irresponsible, deal summarily with it.'

Indeed. In the years that followed, the opposition was hounded, arrested and beaten into submission. 'That time, 1963 to 1966, the opposition had 13 members in the 51 seat parliament—too strong for the PAP,' Chia Thye Poh recalled. 'Immediately after the 1963 general elections, five of the elected opposition MPs were arrested. And after a few years, I was in. Over the years there were more arrests, and the opposition was very much weakened.'

Chia Thye Poh stood in defiance throughout the decades, and has come to symbolise the opposition's fight for democracy, signalling to the regime that the struggle for freedom and justice will go on.

I confess

Originally set up to deal with triad gangs and communist insurgents, the ISD now focuses its attention on the PAP's political opponents. Political prisoners at the Whitley Detention Centre, a drab building camouflaged by leafy trees in the heart of the city, are left to languish in dark and airless cells. Peng (not his real name) is one such victim.

'When they first brought me into the detention centre, I was blindfolded and didn't have a clue where I was,' Peng recalled.

He was led to a hall where his blindfold was removed. As he adjusted to the light, he heard a voice telling him to remove his clothes. He was given a set of khaki prison wear and told to change. As he turned to look for a restroom, a guard shouted, 'Change here!' There must have been at least ten security agents lolling around. 'Remove everything, and I mean everything,' he ordered.

It was the first of many humiliations that Peng had to endure. He was fingerprinted and put before a photographer who somehow had the knack of capturing a victim at his most dishevelled. Two Gurkha soldiers then dragged the prisoner down a flight of steps.

'It was dark and I prayed that this was all just a nightmare,' Peng recalled.

The basement seemed like a long corridor with walls painted black, the non-colour that is used to induce depression. A series of doors lined the walkway, above which flashed green light bulbs. 'Interrogation in progress,' they say to no one in particular.

The door was opened and Peng was thrust into a freezing room. His body temperature plummeted and within seconds, he started to experience involuntary spasms.

'Come on, Peng, it's not that bad,' a corpulent officer taunted. But they were all fat from the thick winter clothing they wrapped themselves in. It was hard to make out all of their faces as two blinding lamps bore down into his eyes.

'Come here, sit down.' Peng hesitated, and the officer dragged him to a chair which was directly under a massive blower that ejected unforgiving gusts of bone aching cold air. As Peng sat down, his body underwent another frigid paroxysm and his eyes started to close involuntarily. 'Uhh!' he heard himself utter as his body desperately tried to warm itself. He coiled up his feet.

'Stand up,' the interrogator said as coldly as the air from the blower. He knew that standing up would force his victim to make contact with the cold floor.

'You are involved in communism, you are a communist, are you not?' the interrogator started off with one of those accusations clothed in a question's skin.

'No, I'm not.'

Without warning, his open palm struck Peng's face. It wasn't an ordinary slap—the interrogator knew his martial arts. He lined up another blow from the opposite direction, using the back of his fist. The strike emitted a grisly crack as knuckles smashed mandible.

'You are a communist!' the interrogator hissed.

Peng was reeling from the pain. His cheeks were stinging and his eyes were unable to focus. Stunned, he left the indictment unchallenged. The interrogator repeated his pattern of blows.

'You are a communist!' he repeated. 'Say you are a communist.'

'No, I'm not,' Peng mumbled. His mouth began to bleed where his teeth cut the inside of his cheeks. Another two blows shook his head.

'You are a fucking communist!' his accuser said again.

'No, I'm not,' came the stubborn reply. He shut his eyes and braced for another onslaught. As sure as the interrogator would later deny that he ever touched his hapless victims, the blows landed with pronounced malice.

The fight, far from being isometric, continued, with one exponent using all the might his well-fed body could ram across, while the other countered with everything his inexorable spirit could hang on to. The rest of the officers leaned against the wall and watched. The beating continued for what seemed like hours. Blood dribbled down the side of Peng's mouth, and his jaw was a distended purple. His head throbbed from the punches and slaps, and the table in front of him looked like it was standing on jelly.

Another interrogator walked in: 'Did he confess?' 'No.' With that salutation, the officers changed shift.

The second interrogator was even more well versed in pugilistic persuasion, with an even more unedifying vocabulary. 'Fucker! You better confess!' he loosed, even before the assault. He punched into Peng's back, causing the bruised victim to lurch forward and crash into the table.

'Get up! You communist fucker! Confess!'

'No. I told you, I'm not a communist. You can kill me.'

'You think you're so smart, you bastard? You want to be like Nelson Mandela? Look at Chia Thye Poh, no one gives a damn. This is Singapore, my friend. In here, you're mine and no one cares about you! You understand, you fucker?'

With all his strength he ploughed into Peng's chest with his fist and forearm. Peng crashed over the chair behind and landed gasping several feet away. He started to cough uncontrollably. The beating ceased for a while as the assailant grew exhausted. In frustration, he walked out. Some food was brought in for Peng. With his mouth swollen from cuts and his jaw close to breaking, it was impossible to chew. An hour passed and Peng sat under the cold blast, his body trembling.

Then the interrogator returned. Like an overextended gambler knee deep in debt, the interrogator wagered desperately that his next smash would yield the payoff.

'Say you are a communist!' came the familiar hounding. The officer wound his arm back like a softball pitcher and brought it into Peng's stomach with so much fury that he crumpled like soft drink can. After a few minutes, Peng straightened up. The interrogator smashed into the same spot, and Peng keeled over again, pain pumping his face red.

'Say you are a communist!'

Unable to get up for more, Peng finally yielded: 'OK, I'll say it.'

'I want you to write about your life story, Peng,' the interrogator said, after delivering his final punch. 'Start like this: "I joined communism to overthrow the Singapore Government".'

'But I didn't,' Peng retorted.

'But you just confessed.'

Peng knew that he had no way out. As he hesitated, the interrogator repeated the line, slowing down in case Peng didn't hear every word, 'I-joined-communism- to-overthrow-the-Singapore-Government.'

Peng bowed his head and started to write the ISD's version of his life.

'Here, Peng, have something to eat, you must be hungry,' the interrogator offered, as he put on the table a plate of steamed pastries which looked like they had been in rigour mortis forever.

Peng didn't even bother to raise his head. Another former detainee who was imprisoned for almost 20 years said to me:

First there must be an understanding that 'confession', the basic requirement for release, is not an attempt to present the truth, or the facts. It is image building. It is implication, often used as grounds for further arrests. The process of bargaining leaves horrible scars. The 'price' keeps on slowly escalating. The detainee is made to feel that release is just round the corner. Finally he feels cheated, he feels betrayed. But he has unwillingly written and signed what is required of him, in slowly increasing instalments. There is deep depression, a loss of self-respect. He avoids friends, he is 'neutralised'. He wants justice but there is no way, unless he makes a press statement on his own. We know those who did were rearrested.

Day after day, Peng was forced to write and rewrite his confession. After the third day, he passed out, whereupon the officers took him to his cell and allowed him a two hour respite.

Then he was forced to write again for twelve hour stretches every day, for months at a time.

When the interrogators were finally satisfied with the confession, the detainee was made to rehearse his lines. The local media was then called in. 'Smile,' a journalist encouraged as he interviewed Peng whose minders sat just out of camera range. 'Place your hands on the armrest', 'Cross your legs', 'Relax your shoulders', 'Look happy.' Several takes were necessary to capture the right mood for the cameras. The following day, headlines screamed: 'I CONFESS', 'THE RED PLOT', 'POLICE SMASH UNDERGROUND CELLS'.

But Singapore's media was not always that obedient. Through the years, the PAP arrested and detained without trial many of the island's leading journalists. Said Zahari was a prominent reporter and editor of the Malay language *Utusan Melayu* until he was imprisoned for more than 15 years without trial. In 1971, four senior staff members of the *Nanyang Siang Pau*, a Chinese daily, were arrested and the newspaper banned for 'stirring up racial issues and glamorising communism.' The newspaper countered that all it was doing was to 'bring to the attention of the government (since there is no opposition in Parliament) the wishes, criticisms and legitimate grievances of the general public.' If the Chinese daily was 'glamorising communism', the English language *Singapore Herald* and *Eastern Sun* were engaged in 'covert subversion'. They were closed down that same year. In 1976 editors of the *Berita Harian*, another Malay daily, were arrested. Some of the journalists had their citizenship revoked, which rendered them stateless.

With the local press sanitised, the foreign media was the next target. Any publication that ran unflattering stories of the Government was taken to court and sued for huge sums of money, as well as having its circulation curtailed. What remained after the massive surgery on the media was, and still is, a press with a well endowed central nervous system but without a cerebrum.

Peng measured his cell—exactly eleven footlengths. The humidity of Singapore's unchanging climate left a constant film of perspiration on his skin which, from time to time, collected into droplets and reluctantly dripped onto the floor, moisturising a patch of dried blood. 'Did he vomit the blood or was it a result of beatings?' Peng wondered about the last guy who was in there. He recalled having seen dents in the wallboards in the interrogation room, and shuddered as the thought of a prisoner smashing into it flashed through his mind.

Some nights he heard an eerie wailing, and someone kicking at the iron door of the cell. Peng felt like screaming himself and would sometimes begin to hyperventilate and wail. Such times, he would curl up on the hard bunk and try to calm himself down. The ISD had 'staff specially trained in producing mental breakdown in political prisoners.' Chia Thye Poh described:

> The Singapore Government's policies on political detainees have always been tough, harsh and ruthless. Once you are in there, the whole repressive machinery is bearing down on you. First, they try all means to exact confessions—mental and physical torture. After that, they will keep you in jail, solitarily, to brainwash you. And if you don't confess, they will keep you in jail for as long as possible. During these years you will be subjected to all sorts of pressures. They call it psychological fatigue, to grind you down and to reduce you to vegetables or irrelevant non-persons.

After the beatings and interrogations, prisoners were usually led to cells the size of toilet cubicles. Solitary confinement, which can last for weeks, was aimed at breaking down resistance to the interrogation process later on. A light burned continuously so that the prisoners never knew the time. At regular intervals, heart jolting thunderous claps were blasted through speakers to disorientate the victims and induce auditory and visual hallucinations. With the full cycle of sleep repeatedly interrupted, the effect further wore down the detainee.

The ISD officers conduct their own election campaigns within the confines of the detention centre. Texts feting the PAP's policies and lionising its leaders were often read ad nauseum to the prisoners. Morose melodies are played over and over to help incapacitate the healthy mind.

Deprived of all means of communication, prisoners looked for signs of intelligible life in the most improbable places. Toilets, though reeking of urine and vomit, afforded the prisoners a tiny measure of privacy, where blood from squashed mosquitoes provided precious ink for scribbling rudimentary messages.

The beatings, sleep deprivation and fear inducement were all designed to bring about a state of helplessness and would 'continue until all the prisoners are broken down or try to commit suicide'. Once resistance had been eliminated, the prisoner was easily led to whatever outcome the state required. Those who could not be broken were left to rot in prison. The prisoners developed behavioural symptoms such as pacing, talking to themselves, hallucination and depression.

A prisoner who withstood such torment was Poh Soo Kai. Poh, a medical practitioner, was arrested during Operation Cold Store in 1963. He was released unconditionally after the ISD tried for nine years to extract a confession from him and failed. When he was freed, Poh and other former political prisoners founded a civil rights organisation to publicise Singapore's detention laws, which were already suffering an unlovely repute in the international community. Although it ended with horrid consequences, the endeavour was not altogether unsuccessful.

The PAP was called up by the Socialist International (SI), of which it was a member party, to account for its ill behaviour. Party stalwart Devan Nair, who was later appointed the President of Singapore by his boss, Lee Kuan Yew, and later yet sacked by Lee, trooped to London in 1976 and upbraided the organisation for 'the absurd allegations of ill treatment, torture, and inhuman conditions in our prisons and detention centres.' With diatribe delivered, there was one last swagger to render. Pre-empting the unceremonious boot that the PAP was about to receive, Nair announced his Party's resignation from the SI.

'I am obliged to eat a good number of the words I uttered in London in 1976,' Nair wrote 18 years later. In a humbling *volte face*, the fallen comrade admitted that he had been 'all too gullible' when he had accepted that prison conditions of the PAP's captives were 'humane and civilised' purely on the words of the Government.

Within a week of the humiliating London episode, Lee Kuan Yew ordered the rearrest of Poh Soo Kai and his fellow activists in June 1976. Someone whispered 'Marxist!' and Poh was pronounced guilty by the PAP of being part of a communist network. Coerced confessions accused him of providing medication to a Malayan Communist Party member who had been injured while attempting a bombing mission. Poh's wife was also arrested and interrogated. She was released 27 days later when the ISD goons failed to 'persuade' her of anything. Poh remained incorrigibly steadfast, receiving another six years, including two in solitary confinement.

We were sitting in a clubhouse, sipping on cool lime juice and nibbling on barbecued chicken wings. Wearing a pair of black-rimmed glasses cerebrally nestled on his nose, Poh spoke with a voice that was as self-effacing as his words. Throughout our conversation in 'Singlish', the local patois, the dissident who had spent 15 years of his life behind bars maintained an air of humility. His serenity told me that all was well with him—it was the PAP that needed help. Like Chia Thye Poh, he held no grudges against those who ruined his life. He has separated from his wife and now lives in Canada. Like Chia, he was unable to talk about his experience lest someone whispers 'Marxist!' again.

We don't do these things in Singapore

Throughout the PAP's reign, numerous Singaporeans who opposed it were arrested and suffered horrendous beatings and torture. Each time, however, the Government would deny any wrongdoing.

In 1970, the authorities decided to subject prisoners to harsh labour. The detainees refused to cooperate on the grounds that they were political prisoners, and staged a hunger strike to protest against the ill-treatment. After a few days, the guards decided to force feed them, administering vicious beatings at the same time.

Ho Piao, secretary of the now banned National Seamen's Union, who was arrested in Operation Cold Store, related his ordeal: 'This whole day I was tied to a wooden chair. They pulled my hair, pressed my nose and poured water through my nose and mouth.' One of the interrogators then grabbed Ho by the throat and drove his fist into his stomach. With his hands tied, his torturers continued punching his stomach. As he gasped for air, another officer laid one more punch—only this time he didn't pull back, but let his fist bear into Ho's aching gut, cutting off his breathing. When the prisoner came close to passing out, the officer pulled back, only to have others come in to smash their knuckles into his rib cage. Another delivered a karate chop to his chest while a third hurled himself at Ho and threw the prisoner to the floor. Ho curled up as his torso and chest heaved in pain. While on the icy floor, his interrogators poured cold water on him, causing his body to go into a painful contraction. Before he could recover from the shock, the thugs bore down on him yet again, kicking and punching his head.

'This is how we treat animals,' one of them snarled. 'This is an introductory gesture.' Ho later said:

> Their torture made my body feel like a corpse. I could not move. They pulled me up from the floor and tied me to the chair. Another group came to torture me. I would recognise them. They used the same method. They poured water over me 64 times. This torture went on for four days. My body was drenched and shivering. They shouted in my ears and prized open my eyes. I did not sleep or eat or drink for four days.

As he lay on the ground, one officer lifted Ho's chin with his shoe. 'This is a strange man, when we poured water over him, he did not shiver,' he said. 'But when we stopped, he started to shiver.' The assaults stopped only when he finally lost consciousness.

Other prisoners were similarly tortured. Chua Hock Hua was thrashed so badly that his health deteriorated rapidly. His fellow inmates repeatedly asked the guards to release him for medical treatment. For four years Chua's condition worsened and for four years the Government refused him proper treatment. In March 1978, his situation became dire and the authorities finally agreed to send him to the Singapore General Hospital, by which time it was too late. Days later Chua died, according to the hospital, from carcinoma hepatitis. His family was convinced, however, that it was not cancer that killed him, but 'a lacerated liver caused by beatings.' His death was so politically sensitive that 'no newspaper in the Republic was willing to carry an obituary notice from his family.'

Prisoners had their jaws broken and teeth knocked out during the torture sessions. Their hearing was often damaged as a result of blows to the ears. Their genitalia would often be attacked as well. The more sadistic officers would hook up the detainees to electrodes and pass electrical currents through their bodies. They poured urine on the prisoners' heads and dragged them straight to their cells without a chance to wash away the stench. Prisoners had filthy rags jammed into their mouths and red ants liberally sprinkled on their mattresses. Often they were interrogated naked, and made to walk to and from their cells without a stitch of clothing on them.

Wong Kui Inn, a detainee herself, was brought in to watch as the interrogators bashed her husband until they broke his jaw. Later he tried committing suicide by banging his head against his cell wall.

'The Government does not ill-treat detainees...We don't ill treat people. We don't beat people,' said Lee Hsien Loong, Lee Kuan Yew's son and Deputy Prime Minister.

'We don't do these things in Singapore,' S. Jayakumar, the Home Affairs Minister, repeated.

Goh Chok Tong, the Prime Minister, went even further, 'In Singapore, we believe that leaders must be honourable men, gentlemen or *junzi*...' The *junzi* is Confucius' categorisation of the class of enlightened scholars and noblemen whose sole purpose in life is to seek wisdom and the truth.

Not only is there no torture, as Lee Kuan Yew assures, but his foes 'live comfortably in prison with butter and eggs and meat according to special rations which the rules of the game lay down upon us.' He had earlier averred that he and his colleagues 'abjure violence as a method of achieving political ends', and exhorted that: 'There is one thing we must prize above everything else. If we condemn the communists for being hypocrites, for being thugs, for being rogues who intimidate other people then let us be honest Democrats.'

When confronted, the Government tries to downplay the gravity of its abuses by assuming a paternal role. The PAP reprimands that its detractors will feel the firm smack of the government. It is this ability to play to perfection the wise and fatherly ruling elite, while keeping its repressive lid on the populace, that has enabled the PAP to get away with so much for so long.

Much of the cover-up is fobbed off on the people. Mortified by the rowdy protestations of a group of Chinese nationals when they were inadequately served at a check-in counter at Changi Airport, one Singaporean wrote to the newspaper that 'it should be made clear to these people that such behaviour is unacceptable here. They can behave any way they want in their country. But please, not in Singapore.' It may be difficult to accept rowdy behaviour in orderly Singapore. After more than three decades of authoritarian control where the media has been thoroughly domesticated, Singaporeans find it hard to contemplate that unlawfulness is still very much a part of life in their island republic.

A government intimidating and duping its own people is one thing. To convince the less fearful and gullible, especially those from the West, is another; for them a second line of defence has to be invented. By disingenuously dragging in Confucius, the PAP at once arouses a local reaction against cultural colonisation by the West (read as the overbearing and imperialistic white race) on the East (read as people who find the democratic process an indigestible Western profligacy) and branding its local critics as traitors to their own origins. The idea is to create a smokescreen where cultural barriers between East and West remain permanent and unbreachable. 'We are a different society...,' said Lee Kuan Yew in 1988. 'We are a different society,' Goh Chok Tong parroted in 1997. What one cannot comprehend, the PAP hopes, one cannot criticise.

In Lee's vision of a different society, youngsters can be trained to be good people as 'even dogs can be trained as proved by the Police Training School where dogs, at whistle, jump through a hoop, sit down or attack those who need to be attacked.' It is also necessary 'not only to train every boy but also every girl to be a disciplined and effective digit in the defence of their country.' Both dogs and digits need to be taught what to eat, how to wash and when to defecate. In the code of conduct for the Vigilante Corps Members, the PAP tells the people that they must 'eat natural food' which must be 'non-fattening'—but not too much, because 'fasting occasionally is good'. They must also bathe because 'bathing in hot water is good for bodily cleanliness'. And not only must the outside be clean, but one's entrails must be kept spotless by 'regular moving of the bowels'.

Just in case the people forget, the Party reminds them that 'the State provides our basic needs' and that 'the Government is responsible for the organisation of our society' because 'it is through the efforts made by the Government, on our behalf, that we are able to obtain our basic needs.' It orders everyone to 'Be Tolerant', 'Be Civic Minded' and 'Observe the Law'. In other words, do as the Party says, not as it does.

From falling in love to investing in shares, from how and what language people should speak to how many children they should have, from how they spell their names to what time they should arrive for dinner, from how to keep public toilets clean to why they cannot chew gum, the teachings drone on endlessly. Dependence on the Party is of ultimate importance.

The Marxist bogey

In the mid-1980s the secret police had tailed several young professionals over a period of months, sometimes degenerating into car chases. That was a curtain-raiser for the arrests in May 1987 of 22 young professionals whom the Government tiresomely claimed were engaging in 'communist united front tactics with a view to establishing a Marxist state'. Tan Wah Piow, a former student leader exiled in the United Kingdom, was said to be behind the conspiracy, plotting with Marxist ideologies to bring about the Government's downfall.

To be certain, Tan had never been an admirer of the PAP. In 1974, when he was a student and life still stirred in the university, he had hazardously tangled with the Government over the plight of retrenched workers. He won a heated verbal joust at a union meeting with Phey Yew Kok, a PAP member of parliament and leader of the Pioneer Industries Employees' Union (PIEU).

A week later at the Union's headquarters, Phey was scheduled to address the laid-off workers. Tan showed up with workers and students, but was confronted by a union office with windows shut, doors closed and leader nowhere to be seen. A commotion suddenly erupted inside the meeting room and everything on the premises was smashed.

The riot was pinned on Tan who was duly convicted and sentenced to a one year jail term. Upon release, he was called up for compulsory national service in the army. Because 'circumstances surrounding the call-up were most extraordinary and improper', Tan quickly left for the United Kingdom. With him went the last vestiges of an independent labour movement in Singapore.

Unions were speedily brought under the control of the National Trade Union Congress, headed by a cabinet minister. At a conference in 1997, the Namibian Prime Minister related that his Singaporean counterpart, Goh Chok Tong, had told him that should the African premier encounter any churlish trade unionists, he could send them to Singapore. Without exception, the participants all turned and looked at me, smiling one of those amazed-but-also-sympathetic smiles.

While the 22 were in prison, the PAP produced a labyrinthine Marxist conspiracy involving an ill-assorted cast of communists and Catholics, solicitors and social workers, directed by networks stretching from Belgium to Britain. Tan Wah Piow, who had by then taken up law at Oxford University, and another Singaporean, Paul Lim, who lived in Brussels, were supposed to be the masterminds. The *Straits Times*, the main English language newspaper, faithfully reproduced every accusation the Government made and even helped its readers by printing a chart complete with arrows and boxes to show who was connected to who.

Locally, Vincent Cheng, the executive secretary of the Catholic Justice and Peace Commission, was alleged to have used unsuspecting church helpers, lawyers and social workers to 'incite disaffection and urge for revolutionary change'.

Even Washington D.C. and the Christian Conference of Asia (CCA) were dragged into the cabal, accused of interfering in Singapore's politics. An American diplomat was expelled because he was trying to 'manipulate and instigate Singaporeans in order to bring about a particular political outcome.' The office of the CCA was closed down and its staff deported.

Like ghost stories, there was no logic in this one. How the head was joined to the tail, and how the body was to wreak the havoc, the Government didn't care to explain. But ghost

Pramoedya in 1957.

Tapols on Buru Island taking a lunch break.
Courtesy Pramoedya Ananta Toer

Pramoedya reuinted with his wife in 1977.
Courtesy Pramoedya Ananta Toer

Pramoedya in 1997.

Benigno Aquino, 1981.
Courtesy Ninoy Aquino Foundation

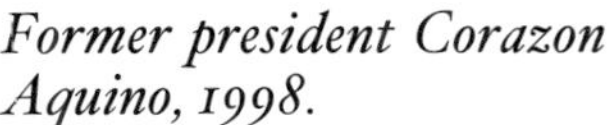

Former president Corazon Aquino, 1998.

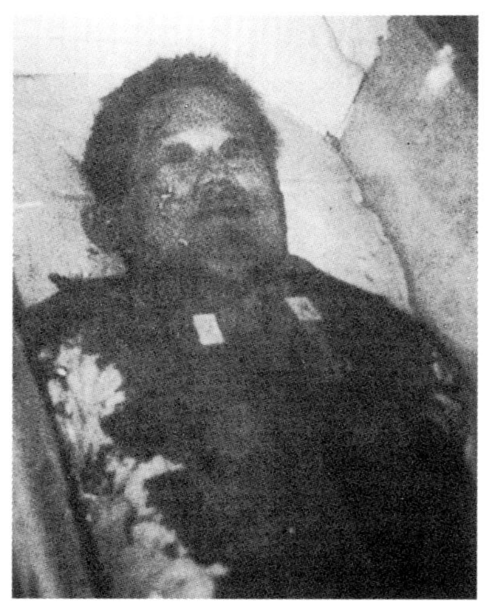

Benigno Aquino in his coffin.
Courtesy Fact Finding Board

Part of the crowd at Benigno Aquino's funeral.
Courtesy Fact Finding Board

Korean student Suh Seung (right), whose face was burnt with acid.

Courtesy Korea Communiqué

Kim Dae Jung during a presidential campaign.

Courtesy FDL-AP

Kim Dae Jung addressing a crowd during the 1987 presidential campaign.

Courtesy FDL-AP

Kim Dae Jung and his wife Lee Hee Ho at his presidential inauguration, 1998.

Courtesy FDL-AP

Burmese General Khin Nyunt (right) with drug lord Lo Hsing-han (left).

Courtesy SBS Australia

General Khin Nyunt (left) being presented to Singapore President Ong Teng Cheong (right).

Courtesy SBS Australia

Anti-government protest by university students, Singapore 1976.

Chia Thye Poh (right), with the author, Germany 1997.

stories are not meant to make sense—just to frighten, and the illusion of a shadowy communist plot achieved excellently the PAP's purpose of unnerving the Singaporean people.

But what were the reasons for the intimidation? Some say that the PAP was feeling nervous about the contagious effect of the increasing influence of the Catholic Church through 'People Power' in the Philippines, to the less spectacular notion that Lee Kuan Yew was testing the younger generation of PAP leaders' capacity for violent confrontation. The less imaginative asserted that it was just timely to bring out the ISD as a gentle reminder of the ruling elite's power and glory. Like a buffet, it was perhaps a little of everything.

Those arrested were taken to the Whitley Detention Centre where, like others before them, confessions were extracted. Even the female detainees were not spared. When Tang Fong Har, a lawyer who had been lending the opposition Workers' Party a hand and is now living in exile, was first arrested, she was ordered to remove her clothes, underwear and shoes in exchange for the prison get-up:

> In the midst of the accusations being hurled at me, I retorted 'Now look here' or words to that effect. I never completed my sentence: one of the interrogators slapped me across my left cheek, not with a flick of his wrist but with the full force of his body. I fell to the ground and my glasses landed on my chest. I was completely shocked by the assault and wished that I could faint as I felt that I could not take any more. I had never felt more humiliated in my life...The female Chinese officer then made a show of helping me to stand and said something like 'It's OK, take it easy, why don't you cooperate?'This was the first time I was bra-less and I stooped whenever I walked to hide my breasts. My posture was a permanent curve soon after. I could not stop the trembling. I vomited countless times, and by the morning of the third day I had my period and I stained my prison pants.

When the detainees were subsequently released, the regime made no apology 'for the [ISD's] effectiveness in uncovering the truth without torture'. The prisoners were repeatedly challenged to seek legal representation if they felt that they had been unjustly treated. Lee Kuan Yew had earlier guaranteed that 'any officer who assaults a person under interrogation is liable to civil as well as criminal actions.'

Lee had even challenged Chia Thye Poh to sue him for calling him a communist. 'But [Chia] has never accepted the challenge,' Lee told his listeners during a visit to Australia. Behind the scenes, however, his ISD officers worked tirelessly to make sure that the prisoner had no illusions about taking up legal proceedings. '[The officers] told me never dream of going to court,' Chia said, 'because [I was] detained under the Internal Security Act.'

In its present form, the Internal Security Act (ISA) doesn't allow the judiciary to intervene on behalf of a political prisoner. When Chief Minister David Marshall first passed the Preservation of Public Security Ordinance in 1955, he also set up an Appeal Tribunal consisting of three judges who had the authority to order the release of any detainee if it felt that there were no grounds for such detention, thus lessening the chances of abuse of the Ordinance. When the PAP came into power, it abolished the Appeal Tribunal and replaced it with an Advisory Board. The new body has no power to override the detention orders as its capacity is only, as the name suggests, an advisory one.

Months after their release, nine of the 22 detainees issued a press statement in 1988 to rebut the Government's accusations. (Tang Fong Har, one of the nine who signed the statement, had left Singapore after her release.) They first qualified that they did not 'intend to challenge the Government', nor were they seeking to make 'political capital' in issuing the statement. They only wanted to state their 'position for the record'. They revealed that they were 'hit hard in the face', some not less than 50 times, while others were 'assaulted in other parts of the body'. They documented that they were threatened with the 'arrests, assault and battery' of their spouses, loved ones and friends, and that the ISD had repeatedly invoked the image of the grandfather of Singaporean political prisoners, Chia Thye Poh. As for Lee Kuan Yew's assurance that violent interrogators are liable to 'civil and criminal actions', the detainees said that the ISD officers had 'actively discouraged' them from seeking legal action.

The eight were promptly rearrested.

The Government announced that it would appoint a commission of inquiry to 'get to the bottom of these allegations by the nine that they were innocent and that they had been abused and assaulted during their detentions.'

The prisoners had not been very obedient, now they were going to be very sorry. The ISD had to prove that the Government was not lying when it vowed that political prisoners were not tortured. They got down to work. The eight prisoners were told that they would not be released until they signed statutory declarations repudiating their press statement. If any of them had the idea of refuting their second confession after release, they could then be charged with making a false declaration, which was itself a criminal offence.

After suffering more sleep deprivation and other 'disorientation techniques', all the prisoners eventually signed the statutory declarations and withdrew their press release. Before she signed the declaration, however, Teo Soh Lung sought the legal services of Francis Seow, former Solicitor-General turned critic of the Government. When Seow arrived at the Centre to meet his client, he was ushered into the interview room. After some moments, an ISD officer motioned him into a courtyard where some 15 plainclothes officers were gathered. One of them stepped up to him: 'Mr Seow, I am arresting you under the ISA.'

Seow was detained for 72 days, during which he was forced to confess that he was also involved in trying to overthrow the Government. The officers didn't bother to conceal the fact that they were there to keep Lee Kuan Yew and the PAP in power. 'So you think you can take on and bully the second-generation leaders?' one interrogator screamed at Seow. 'Well, our job is to make sure you do not succeed. We are here to neutralise you...For your information, Lee Kuan Yew is running for another term...So where will you be? You can give up all your ideas of going into politics.'

Following his release from detention, investigations into Seow's income tax records began, during which one of his employees was threatened with tax charges if he did not make incriminating statements against Seow. He did, and Seow was subsequently convicted, fined and sentenced to jail. Before the trial began, however, Seow had gone to the United States for treatment of his heart condition and has remained there since.

After further confessions and statutory declarations were extracted from the eight prisoners, the Government claimed victory, released three of them and imprisoned the rest for another year. It also conveniently announced that it would not proceed with the commission of inquiry.

First communism, then democracy

'I am a firm supporter of the democratic system,' said Lee Kuan Yew. The support would have been firmer if his victims did not also include democrats.

On 29 June 1988, Singapore was shocked as Lee Kuan Yew revealed in Parliament that Singapore's former President, Devan Nair, was an alcoholic who, during one of his state visits to the Malaysian state of Sarawak, had downed one too many whiskies, misplaced his scruples in the process and began indulging in the ways of the fancy-free. Everything from the President's fondling of nurses to beating his wife to disguised dalliances with a German woman were poured out during the speech. All this, it seemed, had taken place in 1985, and Nair had then resigned and gone to the United States for therapy.

Lee and Nair's alliance goes back to the freedom fighting days when screams of 'Merdeka!' (independence) raised the hackles of the local people and inspired many to militant action. They also delivered Nair, who was then a strident trade union leader and whom the British considered a communist sympathiser, into jail. Then, Lee had pointed his guns in the other direction and had campaigned tirelessly for his comrade's release. In the latter years of the relationship, however, the two had gradually grown apart in their political vistas.

After stepping down as President, Nair had become increasingly critical of Lee's regime, issuing public statements denouncing his former friend and ally. Thus incited Lee conducted a parliamentary roasting of his foe in 1988. He peeled off Nair's skin layer by excruciating layer carving out every sordid detail of his inebriated stay in Sarawak 'so that Singaporeans can understand his motives and see through his statements.'

In an open letter to 'Kuan Yew', Nair denied that he was an alcoholic and bitterly refuted every allegation, letting fly with his own barrage of revelations. His 'erratic conduct' had not been a manifestation of drunkenness, but came about after 'heavy sedation' from '125 mgs of valium daily' for ten days, administered by his medical staff, enough medication 'to dope an elephant'.

Nair also charged that his friend and travelling companion on the Sarawak trip, Kalu Sakar, an Indian national, had been quietly whisked away by the ISD in the middle of the night from the the Istana, the President's official residence, and forced to make disparaging statements about him.

Deep as the arm of the ISD is in reaching into the heart of Singapore's presidency, wider still is its span. When Francis Seow visited the United States after he was released, the Singapore Government engaged American private investigators to spy on him. These agents, employed by the incongruously named All Integrity Investigation and Security Inc., tiptoed behind the unsuspecting Seow from one end of the country to the other, stealing into his hotel room in search of anything that could be used by their Singaporean bosses.

A similar matter was reported by the *Sydney Morning Herald*. An American academic, who had been helpful in obtaining a fellowship for oppositionist-in-exile Tang Liang Hong at a Californian university, found himself under surveillance. Apparently more attracted by computers than cash, some intruders had broken into his home and tried to access computer records listing 'people interested in Singaporean affairs'.

Following the clumsy break-in, the scholar said he had been put under two weeks of even clumsier surveillance. Out on a stroll one day, he suddenly noticed a nearby tree shaking. Thinking that an animal might be stuck on its branches, he stepped up for a closer look. What he spotted was a human sized creature of Chinese ethnicity who released a fusillade of camera shots at him before scampering away. On another occasion in the same park, a man suddenly turned his video camera on him.

In Singapore, surveillance of the opposition is conducted by the almost invisible ISD paparazzi. Photographs and tapes seldom make it to the tabloids, but continually grace the pages of plump secret dossiers. Conversations of mine are routinely recorded by my ISD minders. One particularly memorable occasion happened during dinner at a coffee house. As my fellow diners and I took our seats at a table in a quiet corner of the room, we were joined by a couple at the next table who apparently wanted some privacy as well but inexplicably felt the need to be intimate with us. The man carefully placed his briefcase on a seat, taking care to point the tiny aperture in its side in our direction. His demure date, with the nonchalance of a stilt walker, unromantically placed her opened handbag in the middle of the table, hoping to capture our conversation on tape.

We placed our orders; our shadows, faithfully, did likewise. Our coffee arrived a little before their food. As we sipped our beverage, the couple tucked in to their dinner. The man was dining in a most awkward position, with one hand trying to feed himself and the other maladroitly perched on top of his briefcase. When we abruptly decided to change venues for our discussion and got up to leave, the startled agent fumbled for his handphone and called his colleague stationed at the entrance, frantically trying to make himself intelligible while his tongue struggled with the pesky strands of noodles in his mouth.

In recent times, however, the PAP has found it preferable to employ legalistic means to deal with its opponents, as the use of the ISD tends to leave behind a messy residue of soured international relations. The ruling clique believes that suing an opposition member or two will keep the masses well and truly silenced. *The Guinness Book of Records* would do well to note Joshua Benjamin Jeyaretnam, the leader of the Workers' Party, holds the record for being the most sued politician of all time.

Jeyaretnam was elected Secretary General of the Workers' Party in 1971. The following year he stood for elections and lost. For another ten years and five elections, he tried and failed to get elected. Then in 1981 he entered Parliament in a by-election, the only opposition member after more than ten dissent-free years in the House. His tenure was not to be for long.

In 1984, Jeyaretnam and his co-accused, Wong Hong Toy, then the Chairman of the Workers' Party, found themselves before Judge Michael Khoo, charged with four counts of making false statements and fraud. The judge acquitted the accused on three of the charges and convicted them of one. A year later, the Chief Justice reversed the acquittals and ordered a retrial for one of the charges, and transferred Judge Khoo from the bench to the Attorney General's Chambers. Lee Kuan Yew justified the transfer by pointing out that Khoo had made 'a series of misfindings of fact and two misfindings of law in one simple case.'

Jeyaretnam and Wong were finally fined and jailed. As the two left in a police van for prison, scores of supporters crowded outside the courthouse in a defiant but helpless mood. Following more fines imposed on him by Parliament, Jeyaretnam lost his seat.

Both men then appealed to the Privy Council in London. The Council was then Singapore's highest court of appeal and, according to the the PAP Government in 1986, the 'litmus test' of the judicial system in Singapore. In 1988, the Council opined that the Chief Justice 'patently exceeded the proper function of an appellate court and wholly ignored the advantage enjoyed by the trial judge [Khoo] who had heard and seen the witnesses. This amounted to a serious error of law which vitiated the Chief Justice's decision.' The Council also registered its 'deep disquiet that by a series of misjudgments [Jeyaretnam] and [Wong] suffered a grievous injustice. They have been fined, imprisoned and disgraced for offences of which they were not guilty.'

Within months the Singapore Government abolished the right of appeal to the Privy Council citing that their Lordships in London were 'out of touch with local conditions'.

In the 1997 general elections, Jeyaretnam's colleague, Tang Liang Hong, was similarly taken through the legal laundry and cleaned out of more than two million United States dollars for remarks he made during an election rally. The case was bizarre as it was instructive. Tang had made the allegation in a police report that the PAP leaders were 'instigating criminal violence against him and his family' by saying that he was an anti-Christian, anti-Islamic Chinese chauvinist. Goh Chok

Tong, the Prime Minister, wanted a copy of the report as soon as it was lodged, and was duly handed one by his Minister of Home Affairs. Within hours a writ was served on Tang by eleven PAP leaders, all suing him for defamation based on the statements he made in the police report.

In all the excitement, few stopped to ask why a police report was handed to the PAP politicians. Goh was not acting in his capacity as Prime Minister in a matter regarding the business of the state because all the PAP politicians sued Tang in their personal capacities.

If the line is blurred between the ruling party and the civil service, it is redrawn, underlined and highlighted when it involves the opposition. On polling day, 'no person', according to the Parliamentary Elections Act, 'shall loiter in any street or public place within a radius of 200 metres of any polling station'. During the 1997 elections, I was stopped by the police from entering a voting centre even though, as a candidate, I was authorised to visit any of the centres in the district I was contesting. The police recognised me but told me that I had to wear my identification card before they could allow me in. Commendable adherence to orders, undoubtedly. After putting on my authorisation label, I made my way into the building. To my amazement, Goh Chok Tong swaggered out. He was not a candidate in the contest, wore no identification card and certainly had no authority to enter the premises. In other constituencies, PAP politicians were photographed and filmed going in and out of polling stations where they were not candidates.

Together with other opposition members, I lodged a police complaint against these violations. I was subsequently called up by the police to give a statement which, oddly but not surprisingly, resulted in a complaint being lodged against me. I asked to see the report but the officer declined, conscientiously citing that police reports could not be released to the accused. If he is right (and he is) then somewhere up in the chain of command someone wasn't paying attention when the report that Tang made against the PAP leaders was passed to them.

What followed was even more bizarre. The Attorney General said that he was not going to proceed against the PAP leaders because they were 'loitering inside the polling station', as opposed to loitering outside it, and therefore not in breach of any regulation. If logic can be stood on its head, this was an exquisite handstand.

On 24 April 1996, Singaporeans woke up to a curious headline: 'HPL rapped for delay in disclosing condo sale at discount.' What Singaporeans had been whispering on the Internet had slowly seeped onto the front pages of the local newspapers. HPL, or Hotel Properties Limited, is a property development conglomerate that had built two opulent condominium projects in the heart of the city. A number of units had been sold to Lee Kuan Yew and his family members with attractive discounts worth millions of dollars. The units were sold during a 'soft pre-launch' before the apartments were released for public sale.

The problem arose when HPL's shareholders came to know of the deals and registered their unhappiness by trying to block the sales. The company was listed on the public trading board of the Stock Exchange of Singapore (SES) and under the rules was bound to seek the consent of the shareholders before proceeding with such transactions. The board of directors, for reasons only they knew, did not comply. As the saga lurched on, it surfaced that Lee Suan Yew, the younger brother of Lee Kuan Yew, was one of HPL's directors.

Eleven months belatedly, HPL applied to have the requirement of obtaining the approval of the shareholders waived. By this time, unhappiness within the company was threatening to explode into the public domain. Lee Kuan Yew stomped into Parliament and roared that there had been no wrongdoing. Parliament cleared him. Meanwhile, Lee Suan Yew resigned from the HPL board.

Clearly, regulations laid down by the SES were breached, but there was no investigation to determine the accountability of those involved. If the shoe had been on the opposition's foot, the story might not have ended so uneventfully. For even in a situation as trifling as a forum conducted by the Singapore Democratic Party overrunning its allotted time by 22 minutes, or so the undercover police officers claimed, Party organisers were called up to explain the alleged misdeed.

Even the calling for an investigation into the matter was against the rules. When the *Yazhou Zhoukan* (Asiaweek) published Tang's question about why the matter was not handed to professional government agencies, Lee Kuan Yew sued him and the magazine. The *Yazhou Zhoukan* apologised and ended up paying Lee half a million United States dollars in damages.

'Peace on earth and goodwill to all men.' The message, splashed across an angelically painted board, caught my eye as I drove past Singapore's famed Orchard Road where Christmas—or at least Christmas shopping—is celebrated like in no other place.

The enormous shopping centres were delightfully decked out in their Santa Claus best, complete with Rudolph and adorable little elves. Right down the boulevard, tiny lights dangled from chic looking street lamps, creating a phantasmal shimmer. Insouciant mannequins gaily dressed in shop windows seduced their admirers, their come-hither look beckoning shoppers to reach for their Visa and American Express cards.

Midway through the crowded street, a choir further sweetened the mood with familiar Christmas melodies. Enchanted passers-by paused in their bargain hunting to listen. The hymns soothed tired souls (and feet): *Gloria in Excelsis Deo!* The audience applauded appreciatively, even though not many knew its meaning.

As in most public events, the country's ruling elite was not far away. Weeks before Christmas Day itself, the official celebration began—the operative expression here being 'official', for in Singapore nothing happens without sanction from officialdom. Of course, that's an exaggeration—but only slightly. Even the act of expressing one's patriotism, the displaying of the national flag, is regulated. Citizens are encouraged—strongly—to fly the flag. They are allowed to do this only in August, when the National Day is celebrated. A public notice reminds everyone to remove the flags after the period of official celebration is over.

The President was on hand to perform the customary Christmas light-up, where one flick of the switch transformed Orchard Road into a virtual fairyland. The underlying message is that the Government spreads good cheer—and economic progress as well, the PAP always reminds. From being a third world backwater hovel in the 1960s, Singapore now has a per capita GDP of well over US$20,000. Everything, according to PAP logic, could not have happened without Lee Kuan Yew.

Leaving the tinsel behind me, I turned into the Marco Polo Hotel to meet Tang Liang Hong. It was late and there was hardly anyone around. I had just come from the counting centre, exhausted from the day's events. It was 2 January, the day of the 1997 general elections and I had been a candidate of the Singapore Democratic Party. As I sank into the plush upholstery, I looked around and saw that the hotel was also bedecked with the infectious Christmas cheer. 'Peace on earth, and goodwill to all men!' The sign kept flashing through my mind. If imitation is the highest form of flattery and not the basest form of hypocrisy, then Singapore, a society Westernised to its very core, is at least not bereft of the hope that ideals will not just be consigned to sleigh-belled slogans. For barely a mile away from all the yuletide revelry stands the Whitley Detention Centre.

As an opposition candidate, Tang had electrified the crowds at his rallies with folksy barbs shot straight at the PAP. They caused a stir and not a little political mirth.

When he arrived, he was accompanied by two Malay men, Azmi and Mohammed (not their real names). They were employees in his law firm, now doubling up as his bodyguards. After the formalities, we sat down and recounted the events that led up to the balloting. The opposition, as before, had not done well. We parted after an unanimated discussion, agreeing to meet again in a few days. It turned out to be the last we saw of each other in Singapore.

'Drop me off at home and you guys can take the car with you,' Tang said to his escorts. 'We'll meet later.' It was way past midnight.

Barely hours after the votes had been counted, the chanting was over and the excitement dissipated. Everyone was asleep.

That's when the PAP strikes.

As his car turned into Hua Guan Avenue where he lived, Tang noticed that Azmi, who was driving, was becoming increasingly agitated: 'Mr Tang, there are a few cars following us.'

Tang turned around. Azmi was right, there were three or four cars trailing them. When his car approached his residence, he told Azmi to drive on: 'Turn into one of these lanes.' The cars followed.

'Where do we go now, Mr Tang?' Azmi asked.

'I don't know, just drive on, I'll think of something,' Tang replied, not sounding very convincing.

'Why don't we go to the police?' Mohammed asked. The two stared at him incredulously.

'You bodoh (stupid) or what? They *are* the police!' Azmi shot back. 'Why don't we drive to my place in Woodlands,' the driver continued. 'Maybe we can shake them along the way.'

As they drove for the next hour, the cars kept up.

'We can't go on driving like this,' Tang said. 'See if you can duck into a small lane. Then slow down and I'll jump off.'

They had driven back into downtown Singapore. Azmi turned into a narrow road not far from the grand old Raffles Hotel. Tang jumped out and the car drove away.

He ran towards a cluster of old shophouses, taking gigantic gulps of air. His 61 years were catching up with him. He turned to see if anyone was chasing him—no one, the cars hadn't noticed the evasion. It was still dark and Tang slowly made his way to the Mandarin Hotel on Orchard Road where he sat in the lobby until daylight.

When morning came, Tang called his family and arranged to meet his wife and daughters. When they got together, his daughter showed him letters which they had received over the last few days. 'Death Sentence. God's Will,' one said. Another less cryptic one read: 'We know where you work, we know where your children study. So think carefully.' 'We will know how to deal with bastards like you,' threatened a third. 'May you be damned until your dying days, which shall not be far off!,' screamed another.

He knew then that it was time to leave the country. That afternoon Tang escaped to Johor Bahru, Malaysia. Some things in Singapore never change.

As the carriage pulled away, I saw Chia, now 57, straining his head like an old uncle to make sure that I was safely on board, his boyish smile permanently plastered on his face. He didn't see me, but he was waving all the same. As the train rolled away, his hand was still up.

Throughout the few hours that we talked, our conversation was peppered with him asking me 'Are you warm enough?', 'Did you have enough to eat?', 'Have you got your ticket with you?' For a moment, I wondered if I had mistaken him for a different man from the one that Lee Kuan Yew had accused of using force and terror.

Appearances can be deceiving, one must admit. All the avuncular warmth outside could easily cover a terroristic cold inside. That's how Lee sees it, anyway. 'Chinese communist style,' he sneers at Chia's deferential manners, 'that is the ideal communist. You must be humble, you must be very frugal and Spartan, not flashy, not trying to awe or impress people. They impress people by their humility and self-sacrificing manner, a certain exaggerated understatement of themselves, but a steely determination.'

A 'certain exaggerated understatement'? After having met Chia, I found that description hard to accept. But Lee was right on another count; Chia had a steely determination. 'I always thought, no matter how long they keep me in this way, some day they will have to release me, because I'm innocent and I have support,' he had said. The world did not hear him for almost a quarter of a century. No one knew who he was, no one cared. Which forces the question: how is one able to impress with humble innocence if there isn't an audience?

Lee Kuan Yew, on the other hand, has never had any problem attracting listeners. When asked by a foreign correspondent in a television interview whether Singapore was a police state, Lee, with an icy laugh, said, 'Do I look like a policeman? A 73-year-old man? But I don't need the police. All I need is the administration of the law.'

A 'certain exaggerated understatement' perhaps?

'It is in the nature of a guilty suspect,' Lee Hsien Loong explained about political detainees, 'that he will build up defences around himself and present himself in the most innocent possible way.' He could easily have been referring to his father.

Guilt and innocence are terms that Lee Hsien Loong has chosen to use in a political game where his Party now stands as the judge, jury and jailer. As events around the world, and particularly in Asia, begin to unfold, one judge towers far above the strongest of strongmen, unflagging in its impartiality and unfailing in its consistency, in delivering its verdict—truth.

The PAP continues to hang on to the delusion that freedom and justice can be replaced by might and money. History does not concur. As the human race evolves, freedom will come, and together with it, peace on earth and goodwill to all men.

7
Conclusion

The Struggle Continues

The democratic revolution in Asia

The cab lurched along in the Roxas Boulevard traffic jam. Ramon had his eyes fixed on a girlie tabloid propped up by his steering wheel, looking up only every now and then to avoid hitting the car in front. 'We are bimbo girls, living in a bimbo world,' a pop group warbled over the radio with surprising conviction.

Suddenly Ramon looked to his right and performed the customary sign of the crucifix. 'That's the Baclaran Church,' he offered. 'You know Ninoy? Ninoy Aquino?'

'Yes.'

'We all came here to pray after he was shot.'

'That was terrible,' I replied.

'Yeah, but this is the Philippines.'

Yes, this is the Philippines—more than 7,000 islands sprinkled in the South China Sea, largely inhabited by ethnic Malays, commercialised by Chinese settlers, conquered by Spain and 'ruined by America' (as a local activist sourly remarked).

With a *lingua franca* of Tagalog and American English, Filipinos have carved out a uniquely colourful world, semantically and visually, for themselves. Where else would one find a deposed dictator's wife running for president against 70 other candidates, one of them a Jesus lookalike complete with thorny crown and shepherd's staff; or a prominent and deadly serious democracy fighter named Joker with an equally distinguished counterpart in the establishment named Ding-Dong; or cigarette puffing security guards with shirts unbuttoned, toes poking out of their weathered sandals and M-16s casually slung over their shoulders, watching over cash laden vehicles parked outside a bank; or passengers clinging onto jeepneys gaudily painted with the Virgin Mary on one side and Donald Duck on the other; or devout entrepreneurs christening their businesses the Holy Infant Trading Hardware Store? A 'tutti frutti' country, as someone once said.

All this belies a pain that Filipino society feels, a pain that is just beginning to heal after long years of misrule and mismanagement. It took the death of Benigno 'Ninoy' Aquino to stir his fellow countrypeople to rise against Ferdinand Marcos. His picture is now etched on the country's 500 peso bill alongside the words 'The Filipino is worth dying for', a phrase Aquino uttered when he was alive and one that he fulfilled.

Following his assassination at the airport that now bears his name, Aquino's wife reluctantly agreed to challenge Marcos in the presidential elections of February 1986. The results did not surprise anyone: Corazon Aquino won, but Marcos claimed victory. Independent foreign observers were left with no doubt that he had rigged the elections. But Marcos refused to vacate the Malacañang Palace, threatening to drag the country through another six years of tyranny.

On 22 February Defence Secretary, Juan Ponce Enrile, in an 'act of contrition' for his role in the dictatorship, walked into Camp Aguinaldo, a military base which had been taken over by officers opposed to the dictator, and announced that he no longer recognised Marcos as President. Vice-Chief of Staff, Lieutenant-General Fidel Ramos, later joined him.

Over the next couple of days, Marcos tried to negotiate a way out, while Enrile and Ramos repeatedly conducted headcounts to make sure that they could back up their challenge. When Cardinal Jaime Sin, Archbishop of Manila, entered the fight and called for support for 'our two good friends', one million Filipinos massed on the highway surrounding Camp Aguinaldo and Camp Crame to defend the two bases commandeered by Enrile and Ramos.

As tanks rumbled towards the camps, Marcos spoke to Enrile on the phone to urge the rebels to surrender. Enrile insisted that the President withdraw the tanks and said he needed time to discuss the matter with his men. Marcos, feeling increasingly uneasy about the high stakes that he suddenly had to deal with, assured him that he did not wish to see bloodshed, but added that his troops were 'not able to stay from forceful action for very long.'

The rebel camp then gave the signal to block the path of the advancing tanks, and the massive school of human fish responded immediately—a spontaneous welling of emotion waiting to erupt on just such an occasion. When the tank commanders found themselves besieged by human bodies praying and pleading, chanting and cajoling the soldiers to listen to their hearts instead of their headsets, Marcos's power ebbed momentarily.

Then the command came for the tanks to press ahead. The engines restarted and the vehicles inched forward. The firepower was there but the hearts weren't, and when the commanders refused to roll over the people who had readied themselves for a steely death under the tanks, Marcos's battle was all but over.

As the masses cheered the victory, the President called a press conference and charged Enrile and Ramos first with 'stupidity' and then with something altogether far graver—treason. The faithful General Fabian Ver had meanwhile manoeuvred his tanks to another location in the dead of the night and was ready to strike at the two camps at dawn. When the time arrived, the General ordered his helicopters to swoop down to provide cover for the infantry attack. As the 15th Strike Wing took off, the rebels braced themselves for the onslaught.

All the rebels could do was pray. It worked. The pilots landed their choppers inside Camp Crame and ran out to join the rebels, white handkerchiefs in hand. If Ver was stumped by the defections, Marcos was left with a presidency that controlled nothing, save for a few aides and a getaway team holed up in the Palace. That also was to be taken away from him, as his personal pilots deserted Malacañang into the open arms of the rebel camp.

With vital forces under their control, it was now the rebels' turn to scare Marcos as they started bombarding the Palace grounds with mortar rockets. The First Family was under siege and cowering within walls that for two decades had kept them in safety and luxury, away from the long-suffering masses. Frantic calls were made to Washington for help. Marcos also conducted one last, lonely press conference during which he declared a state of emergency and ordered a curfew to be imposed. But no one was listening.

Without sleep, and deteriorating from *lupus erythematosus* (an illness that usually attacks the kidneys), the President was 'babbling and incoherent'. His family urged him to make a run for it with help from the United States embassy but he had refused. Then at 5:30 in the morning on 25 February, after a final phone call to Senator Paul Laxalt in Washington who told him to 'cut and cut clean', Marcos knew that it was useless to hang on. He climbed aboard a United States marines helicopter to leave the Philippines with his family.

A little earlier, Corazon Aquino had taken the presidential oath and, in a television address, declared: 'We are finally free.'

'*Mabuhay*!' the President greeted an award ceremony at the Philippine International Cultural Centre. It was eleven years since Ramos had helped depose Marcos, and five years since he had succeeded Aquino as President. 'The global tide of re-democratisation in many parts of the world begun in the earlier 1970s,' Ramos told his audience. 'Our own People Power revolution in February 1986 was a dramatic precedent in that time and it is said to have inspired some of the subsequent democratic impulses in Eastern Europe.'

Not to mention Asia. The democratic revolution in Asia started with a man so powerful that he crushed a mighty empire that spanned the world, and invented a weapon so lethal that it even toppled a Javanese king half a century after his death. This conqueror was more scrawny than he was brawny, he wore not armour but a piece of white cloth that he spun himself, and he packed not a cannon but a crooked staff which he used to prop up his crooked body.

Mohandas K. Gandhi achieved his conquests without beating up a single person or firing a single bullet. His weapon was *satyagraha*, or 'truth force', a concept that encapsulated his ideas of waging war on oppression and injustice by seeking the truth and advocating non-violence. The *Mahatma*, or 'great soul' as he is often called, is one of humanity's greatest political and social reformers. The enormity of Gandhi's task to rid India of her British colonialists was lessened, and the endeavour ultimately made possible, only because he steadfastly believed that 'if a government does a grave injustice the subject must withdraw cooperation, wholly or partially, sufficient to wean the ruler from his wickedness.'

Not only did Gandhi call for non-cooperation with dictators, he continued through his entire political life to instigate civil disobedience and civil resistance to authority. Respect for the law remained the Mahatma's creed, but disobedience of unjust and immoral laws through non-violent means, Gandhi argued, was an even weightier duty of every citizen:

> Civil disobedience is really a synthesis of civility and disobedience, i.e. non-violence and resistance. Resistance to bad laws is essential for man's moral growth, while civility is the demand of a stable social order without which man's life and growth are not possible. Disobedience is in itself destructive and anti-social. But obedience to an immoral law is even worse and can never be a duty. Disobedience to immoral laws of the state is really obedience to a higher moral law, the law of truth and justice. Civil disobedience is thus an effort to reconcile the demands of freedom and law.

Many have argued that Gandhi's approach to modern-day politics is too simplistic, and his methods workable only against the British, who knew that their colonial rule was on its last legs, and whose brutality was significantly constrained by their own consciences. Malcolm X, the slain American civil rights leader, did not embrace the non-violent approach to political action and believed that 'it's a crime for anyone who is being brutalised to continue to accept that brutality without doing something to defend himself.'

Yet, Gandhi's call to active but non-violent resistance so inspired Ninoy Aquino while he was exiled in the United States that he made a conscious effort to model his fight against Marcos along Gandhian principles. 'According to Gandhi,' Aquino wrote, 'the willing sacrifice of the innocent is the most powerful answer to insolent tyranny that has yet been conceived by God and man.' How much of the philosophy of *satyagraha* was accepted by Aquino is open to question, but he was certainly steeled by Gandhi's quest for non-violent struggle. But unlike Gandhi, who was assassinated towards the end of his fight, Aquino was killed before he could begin his post-exile work. The irony was that it took the fatal attempt on Aquino's life to spur the people to a non-violent revolution of their own.

The revolution did not end after Marcos's downfall. Nor was it confined to the shores of the Philippines. Soon after Aquino's tragi-triumphant return, Kim Dae Jung was inspired to return to South Korea to face Chun Doo Hwan. The leadership of the *Mahatma* was also a model for Kim, who described Gandhi as 'a saint and a superior strategist.'

Taiwan's democratic leaders also drew inspiration from the revolution in the Philippines. Hsu Hsin-liang, also in exile in the United States, decided to follow in the footsteps of Aquino and Kim, and returned to his own country to lead the opposition movement that eventually achieved full democratisation on the island.

In 1988, the Burmese revolt against Ne Win's dictatorship was also inspired by the Filipino People Power. Although it was brutally crushed, the movement compelled Aung San Suu Kyi, who herself had acquired a 'lasting admiration for the principles of non-violence embodied in the life and philosophy of Mahatma Gandhi,' to come forward to serve as the country's democratic leader.

The contagion spread to China a year later, when students conducted their own revolution against the communist dictators, and repeatedly cited the successful overpowering of the Marcos tyranny during their ill-fated protest in Tiananmen Square.

What failed dismally in China, however, proved to be a most unexpected and astounding success in Indonesia. Many experts and academics had predicted that this would never happen because, according to one Western observer, 'Indonesians are so different from Filipinos.' In just a matter of weeks, the once invincible Suharto, God-like to many of his supporters, came crashing down to earth.

And all because one scrawny Asian said enough was enough and decided to confront injustice and tyranny all over the world.

The courage to lead—and forgive

Many factors contributed to the demise of autocracy in Asia and set the necessary conditions for democratisation. Distressed economic conditions in the Philippines, Burma and Indonesia proved to be Herculean forces that provided the people the wherewithal to rise against the dictators. In Taiwan and South Korea, the burgeoning educated middle-class grew increasingly intolerant of the military regimes. Some observers contend that the sheer force of Hegelian thesis-antithesis evolutionary process meant that the changes were inevitable.

Whatever the reasons, the revolutions that occurred across Asia were not a result of spontaneous combustion. There were years of relentless campaigning and sacrifice by individuals who saw the need and found the courage to offer themselves as leaders of the people—and targets for their governments. Their fellow citizens remained in fear of the regimes, making the struggle of the dissident leaders an even lonelier toil.

The reticence wasn't because people couldn't tell right from wrong. For one reason or another, they didn't see the need to act. As nineteenth century philosopher Henry D. Thoreau, an eminent man of letters and ideas who greatly influenced Gandhi, said of his fellow Americans, 'There are thousands who are in opinion opposed to slavery and war, who yet do nothing to put an end to them. There are nine hundred and ninety-nine patrons of virtue to every virtuous man.' The late Senator José Diokno echoed Thoreau's anguish, when he said, somewhat less poetically, that the Philippines under Marcos, was inhabited by '49 million cowards and one sonavabitch'. Even Corazon Aquino at one point questioned whether Filipinos were worth her husband's sacrifice because they only bent further and further with each repressive act that Marcos forced upon them. They seemed willing to trade the lives of their democratic leaders for peace of mind, however fleeting it might have been.

The scene was hardly any different in Taiwan. At the height of the struggle between the *dangwai* and the Kuomintang Government in 1988, when *Freedom Times* editor Cheng Nan-rong had immolated himself in protest at the Government's banning of his journal and trying to arrest him for treason, an activist lamented that she would never 'encourage anyone to sacrifice for the 20 million Taiwanese because sometimes when I see them, I feel like giving them one big slap.' That slap, presumably, was to jolt Taiwanese out of their apathy and the hypnotic pull of materialism.

An Indonesian academic once told me that every time Indonesia seemed on the verge of a massive protest against Suharto's dictatorship, society's angst would quickly fizzle out and die. 'Sometimes, I think Indonesians don't deserve democracy,' he said.

In Singapore, I've been told more times than I care to remember by my fellow citizens that Singaporeans are basically a selfish and materialistic lot concerned only about cars, credit cards, condominiums and cash, and not worth agonising over.

If history is any guide, however, the keys to freedom and democracy turn ever so slowly—sometimes indecently so. Without the few who are willing to lead their peoples, justice and freedom will always remain out of reach. Warned of the danger of returning to the Philippines, Aquino told those around him, 'I have carefully weighed the virtues and the faults of the Filipino and I have come to the conclusion that he is worth dying for because he is the nation's greatest untapped resource.' Aung San Suu Kyi recognises that 'not everyone is brave enough to participate' in the initial fight for freedom and that 'it is usually the minority who always struggle' before the masses find the courage to follow. Taiwan's Shih Ming-teh wrote from his lonely cell that 'freedom fighters crawl along a narrow path. But in the end, those who follow will broaden the path into a broad avenue.'

And it is always the few who are willing to defy the autocrats and engage in acts of civil disobedience that keep the delicate flame of democracy kindled. Whether it is Shih Ming-teh helping to organise election campaigns for his colleagues although expressedly forbidden by the Kuomintang, or Kim Dae Jung defying Park Chung Hee by issuing the Declaration of Democracy and National Salvation, or Aung San Suu Kyi trudging out to the villages in 1989 to campaign for her party despite repeated warnings by the Burmese generals (and more recently, camping out in her vehicle when the authorities blocked her way), or Pramoedya Ananta Toer continuing to write his criticisms of the Suharto regime despite a nationwide ban on his books ('Every book that is banned is a badge of honour,' he said), deliberate non-violent acts of disobedience have always been at the forefront of the democratic fight.

Although engaging in civil disobedience, Asia's dissidents have always made it their guiding principle not to engage in bitterness and revenge, no matter how abominably they were persecuted by their opponents, even if the persecution affected the lives of their families. Shih's wife spent 12 years, sometimes campaigning, sometimes pleading for her husband's release from lifelong imprisonment. She separated from him when all else failed. As fate would arrange, Shih's sentence was reduced to 15 years in an amnesty announced six months after his wife left him. His brothers were also arrested and imprisoned, one of them fasted to death. Lin Yi-hsiung's mother and twin daughters were gruesomely murdered by his political opponents during his trial for the riots in the Kaohsiung Incident in 1979.

Pramoedya's wife abided by him through the years of imprisonment, trying unsuccessfully to rein him in: 'I always tell him not to be so stubborn, because the family has to suffer with him. But he is still so defiant against Suharto. I know he is right and I support him, but it is so difficult for the family.' Today she lives with her husband and a throng of descendants in their modest house in Jakarta.

Kim Dae Jung's two sons and youngest brother were also arrested and imprisoned. Hong Il, his eldest son, walks with a limp sustained during torture sessions.

Aung San Suu Kyi has been separated from her husband, Michael Aris, and their two sons for nearly a decade. They are still seldom allowed into the country to see her.

Chia Thye Poh didn't even have a chance to marry and start his own family. Arrested at 26, he was kept in jail continuously until he was almost 50. His girlfriend waited for him, but with no charge, no trial and no sign of release, she went her way after eight years.

Armed with only their spirit and their courage to withstand the pain, the loneliness and the humiliation, these freedom fighters always appealed for forgiveness for their adversaries and consistently sought reconciliation. 'I cannot intentionally hurt anything that lives much less fellow human beings even though they may do the greatest wrongs to me and mine,' Gandhi wrote. 'Whilst, therefore, I hold British rule to be a curse, I do not intend to harm a single Englishman or any legitimate interest he may have in India.'

When Kim Dae Jung walked out onto the stage in front of thousands of guests during his inauguration, one of his first acts was to turn to Roh Tae Woo and Chun Doo Hwan, who had sentenced him to death in 1980, and shake their hands. He had earlier granted them clemency for their atrocities during their dictatorships. He had even visited Park Chung Hee's grave after the despot was assassinated in 1979, an act which Kim considered as finishing his 'long overdue homework' because, to him, 'to forgive is to win truly'.

If hell exists on earth, Shih Ming-teh went through it and lived to forgive those who inflicted it on him. Tortured, hounded and imprisoned for most of his adult life, Shih stands a proud and humble man today, 'grateful to God' for the gift of forgiveness for, and the lack of bitterness towards, those who nearly killed him. 'Anyone who carries bitterness in his heart,' he told me, 'cannot do any good for society.'

Singapore's Chia Thye Poh, locked up for almost 23 years without ever given a day in court, shows absolutely no hatred towards his tormentors. 'Twenty-three years is a long period, a quarter of a century, half of my lifetime has been spent in prison,' he said, 'but those individuals that have perpetrated the wrongdoings unto myself, I bear no grudges.'

While the persecuted offer their hands in reconciliation, the persecutors have rejected them and shown no remorse for their brutality. Worse, they often elevate themselves to the realm of the wise and the humane. Goh Chok Tong, Singapore's Prime Minister, sees himself and his colleagues as Confucian *junzi*, 'upright and morally beyond reproach', even as the secret police torture political detainees. Lee Kuan Yew mused, 'Our tragedy is that we know that if our foe wins we will die, and die painfully, but then when we win our foe lives comfortably in prison.'

Suharto never failed to enquire about his 'brothers on Buru Island' and praised the virtues of 'honesty, courage and the ability to rediscover the true and accepted road' while he starved and killed them.

'We, the government, are totally against human rights abuses,' Burma's Trade Minister swears even as children are forced into labour, political prisoners tortured and women raped.

And in the Philippines, it took Marcos to clarify that his country 'has been one of the strongest advocates of human rights both in the United Nations and in our traditions and history.'

It is difficult to argue that autocrats do what they do to their opponents for the sake of peace and stability, because the mere physical incarceration of these persons was considered inadequate; torture and humiliation often accompanied the detentions.

Why the need to resort to such sadism? Perhaps it is the perception that aggression is the only means to convince their opponents of their views that drives authoritarians to such violent hate. Or perhaps it is the notion that, as Lee Kuan Kew said, 'if our foe wins we will die', that spurs autocrats to physically overpower their opponents. The reason could also be as uncomplicated as James Minchin suggests in *No Man Is an Island: A Portrait of Lee Kuan Yew*: 'Power removes the humiliation of being bested.'

This still leaves the denials of torture unexplained. As Aung San Suu Kyi questions, 'If they think that it is all right to do the things that they do, they should just say: "Yes, we do that. So what? What's wrong with it?" Why won't they say it?' The most plausible reason is that they are unable to reconcile their deeds with norms of internationally acceptable behaviour.

But more than their inability to come to terms with their own actions, perpetrators of violence also find it difficult to reconcile with their victims. 'The tormentor finds it difficult to forgive the victim,' Aung San Suu Kyi offers, 'because he knows he has committed an act of shame. That makes it harder for him to forgive.'

Whatever the motivations of the bullies and the bullied, a consistent pattern runs through the preceding six chapters: the ability to not only not hate their opponents but to forgive them as well, remains the abiding feature of those who advocate freedom and democracy, as opposed to the vengeful and violent nature of their opponents. Such is the single most distinguishing attribute between the oppressors and the oppressed, between cruelty and courage.

By drawing such a conclusion, one runs the risk of being accused of over-simplification, indeed, of being naive. Needless to say, democracy fighters are not beyond criticism. But having to go through the torment (in Aquino's case death) that these individuals did, and seeing one's loved ones tortured and murdered, and still be able to preach forgiveness and reconciliation is a virtue worthy of acclaim—and emulation. The intent is not to paint a story of good versus bad but rather an attempt to re-underline Lord Acton's oft-cited observation that 'absolute power tends to corrupt absolutely'.

It would be wrong to reduce authoritarian behaviour to mere deficiencies of character, for there is calculation in their cruelty. The perpetration of violence against their opponents has a specific purpose, including the age-old tactic of terrifying the masses into submission. While terminology may differ—if used by triad gangs or the Mafia it is called organised crime, but when used by governments it is blessed as national security—the principle is unmistakable: fear is one of the greatest, if not *the* greatest, modifier of human behaviour. Politicians, either by instinct or through training, recognise this fact and use it repeatedly. Those with a violent streak go a step further and use it to terrorise their peoples. Political scientists call this 'state terrorism' which:

> involves deliberate coercion and violence (or the threat thereof) directed at some victim, with the intention of inducing extreme fear in some target observers who identify with that victim in such a way that they perceive themselves as potential future victims. In this way, they are forced to consider altering their behaviour in some manner desired by the actor.

This is usually carried out by intelligence organisations, which often operate unrestrained by the law. Their members, whose value systems often do not differ significantly from those of the underworld, commit abductions and acts of torture that invariably instil dread in the masses. Whether it be the Korean Central Intelligence Agency, the Directorate of Defence Services Intelligence in Burma, the Taiwan Garrison Command or Singapore's Internal Security Department, the secret and unsavoury arm of the police has always been at the fore in keeping autocratic regimes in power.

Lee Kuan Yew knows the efficacy of fear in maintaining political power. He brags: 'Between being loved and being feared, I have always believed Machiavelli was right. If nobody is afraid of me, I'm meaningless.' One dreads to think of what he would do to induce fear if he were to gain control of a larger country where obedience is not as easy to extract as in tiny Singapore. Compared to the kind of power that Gandhi wielded—where hundreds of millions were willing to do his bidding, not out of fear but through love and respect—the hollowness of Lee is revealing, if not tragic.

In Indonesia, Suharto also knew how to use fear in his political game, and was happy to administer his murderous 'shock treatment' on the people, the effects of which might still come back to haunt him as the country begins to open up after his fall.

Park Chung Hee never hesitated to use his secret police to 'scare the hell out of' Koreans, a tactic which, ironically, contributed to his own assassination.

Aside from brute force, fear is induced in the population by the raising of an external threat, almost always in the form of communism. The headless, formless phantom has been used repeatedly in scare campaigns. As Richard Barnet and Maurice Raskin once observed:

> The bigger the crisis, the bigger lies people could swallow, because their dependence on their leader grows in time of crisis. Leaders have always protected their power by hinting at mysteries which only they know and only they can control. The effect of official secrecy is to make the citizen doubt his own judgement and his own best instincts. 'If you only knew what I knew,' his leaders continually tell him. The official pretence at knowing more than what a conscientious newspaper reader and television viewer would know disarms the citizen, makes him more dependent on the keepers of the secrets and permits the government to play on his hopes and fears.

And if the threats are not real enough, they can always be created: Marcos staged the bombing of Enrile's car to give himself the pretext to impose martial law, South Korea's army intoxicated its soldiers with *soju* before sending them to Kwangju for the massacre so that Chun Doo Hwan could later point his finger at Kim Dae Jung for masterminding the unrest, Taiwan's riot police attacked and provoked the crowd until riots broke out during the Kaohsiung Incident for the Kuomintang to justify its ban on opposition rallies, Burma's security agents were drugged and sent out to loot and plunder during the unrest in 1988 so that the SLORC could have a reason to continue its repression, and most recently, the May riots during the revolt against Suharto may have been instigated by the army so that martial law could be declared.

But as people learn to see through the tactics of the scaremongers, dictatorships have begun to crack and their champions wither, Suharto being the latest to join the ranks of deposed despots. Even the Singapore regime is becoming aware of the staleness and obsolescence of the communist bogey, and has of late kept the state thugs at bay by not ordering arrests under the Internal Security Act. This does not mean an undoing of the repressive apparatus, for the ruling elite knows that the general population may have been intimidated to such an extent that, at least for a time, no indelicate demonstration of force is needed. For one thing, the use of the secret police against its often imaginary communist foes attracts the unwelcome ire of the international community. Besides, observers point out:

> The most effective use of coercion reveals itself by its apparent absence. Conflict has been suppressed. People know what they can and cannot do. In essence, the behavioral terror process has become part of the political structure. As structure it is no longer observable as a behavioral event, except at those times that lessons are forgotten or the regime decides that greater numbers of people or additional categories of persons need to be more tightly controlled.

When that time comes, some story about internal security would have to be woven and a fresh round of arrests ordered, regardless of international opinion.

Terror campaigns by themselves are insufficient for regimes to exert the kind of control they do on society. The mass media must also be subjugated. In order to portray dissidents as menacing criminals, 'officialising' newspapers and broadcast stations is a must. Korea's *Dong-A Ilbo*, Indonesia's *Jakarta Post*, Singapore's *Straits Times* and Taiwan's *Central Daily* were all dragged through obedience school at one time or another, and after training were put on extremely short leashes.

For control to be complete, the legal system must also be incorporated. Ninoy Aquino, Kim Dae Jung, and Shih Ming-teh all faced military tribunals where they never stood a chance of getting a fair hearing, let alone winning. Chia Thye Poh and Pramoedya Ananta Toer were simply locked away, and Aung San Suu Kyi placed under house arrest. Alternatively, using legal system to induce fear among the populace by suing opposition politicians for debilitating sums of money, as in the case of Singapore, works just as well. Tactics may differ, but the results are equally effective.

With the unholy trinity of the intelligence unit, the local media and the legal system under lockstep control, society's will to resist their regimes becomes as resolute as putty.

The problem with myths

'If we are able to weather this storm in Southeast Asia today,' Ramos said to his people, 'if we are better than the others in terms of surviving the speculative attacks against our national currency, it is because we have gotten on a path of sustainable development with the participation of all citizens, especially the least and the poorest among us.' The 'quality of Filipino democracy,' he added, was the 'cutting edge of Philippine competitiveness.'

The country, an economic pancake during the Marcos years, is finally beginning to recover. But it wasn't so long ago that Lee Kuan Yew lectured that discipline, not democracy, was the key to economic progress. With Asia knowing nothing but one party rule up till the late 1980s and registering locomotive-like progress on its economic front, Lee's observation seemed particularly insightful.

Then the Liberal Democratic Party, the only ruling party Japan had known since World War II, lost the elections. Long-suffering oppositionist Kim Young Sam became South Korea's President, Taiwan's Democratic Progressive Party inched ever closer to dethroning the ruling Kuomintang, Thailand's ambitious army generals were forcefully beaten back by protesting civilians and students, and Marcos ended in forced retirement (and died) in Hawaii.

Even then, so impressive was the economic advancement of countries in the region that the argument of doing things the 'Asian way' suddenly became the most exciting discovery since penicillin. The 'Asian century', 'Asian millennium', 'Asian renaissance', 'Asian democracy', 'the New Asia' and the all encompassing but incomprehensible 'Asian values' burst forth like overdue raindrops to quench the world's thirst for intellectual and moral guidance.

Few would argue that some of these Asian values are worth upholding. The problem begins when we think of them as uniquely exclusive to Asians or that just because their proponents call these values Asian, Asian peoples actually practise them. For example, advocates of 'Asian' values believe that the family is the all important unit without which society at large cannot function effectively. Yet, infanticide and child prostitution are problems frequently found in Asian societies. In Singapore where the leaders profess a Confucianistic approach to family life, laws are passed to enable elderly parents to sue their children for financial support.

Asian autocrats would also like to think of the region as largely conservative in its social mores. Facts don't bear this out. In Japan pornographic flicks are readily available on the air after midnight, and sex houses, promising gratification for every fantasy for the sexually bored, abound. Cities in Thailand are not exactly frequented for their splendour in pottery and painting. Steamy sex scenes in Hong Kong made movies no longer raise eyebrows. The Indian *Kamasutra* and the Chinese *Golden Lotus* depict sex that leave nothing to the imagination. In clean and green Singapore, prostitutes parade themselves in darkened cubicles along alleys lined with peddlers hawking every contraption, gizmo and potion, promising to heighten and prolong sexual pleasure.

What authoritarians claim and how Asian societies actually operate don't necessarily coincide. Often, they are at complete variance. The contradictions (more will be highlighted throughout this discussion) notwithstanding, Asia's autocrats insist that it is adherence to such values that enabled the region to prosper. Ironically it was Singapore, the most westernised Asian society, that led the way to enlightenment. Tommy Koh, its ambassador at large, concluded that 'East Asia will overtake North America and the European Union in the year 2000,' presumably because its governments have developed 'their own concepts of good governance' so much so that 'a cultural renaissance has begun.'

Then someone in Bangkok turned off the lights. In June 1997, the Thai Government was forced to float the baht and Asia has not been the same since. Currencies came tumbling down, businesses went belly-up, and foreign investors took the nearest exit from the region.

What took years to build up—homes and hopes, and not a little hubris—suddenly became nothing but broken dreams and deals. Savings were wiped out, the owing many found it difficult to pay to the owning few, investors reaped none of the wild dividends their neighbours kept talking about, food and medicine became as unaffordable as Ferragamo and Mercedes, and retailers and tourists had to unhappily end their marriage.

Everyone gave their views on what had gone wrong. From defective banks to deceptive practices, every fault was dissected, examined and castigated ten times over.

It seemed that 'Asian values' no longer had a part to play. Singaporean leaders were not talking about 'overtaking' Europe and America any more. Lee Kuan Yew and Goh Chok Tong started calling on the West to 'extend its help' and 'rescue' the troubled region. Lee Hsien Loong, Lee Kuan Yew's son and Deputy Prime Minister, trotted to the United States to tell whoever would listen that Singapore is not like other Asian countries, in the hope that when Americans think of Asia, 'they think of it as different features, not all one uniform shade of dark grey.'

When it was pointed out to Lee Kuan Yew that accountability and transparency were part of how the West went about its business, he replied that if that was the best way then 'it doesn't matter where it comes from.' It seemed like a change of heart.

It wasn't. Lee was referring only to commercial businesses and not to 'whether a government was more democratic or upheld human rights ideals.' And so 'Asian values' now take on a new twist—they apply, it seems, only to politics and not economics. But wasn't the once booming Asian economy possible only because Asian values were so uniquely wonderful? Now that the economies don't appear to be so different from the rest of the world, where does the 'Asian values' argument go? Remove the hyperbole and Lee's bastardisation of Asian values—more succinctly, the principles of Confucius, whose name he invokes from time to time to stymie his Western critics—and the argument falls flat, satisfying neither the intellect nor indigent pockets.

So are Asians like Westerners? No. Neither are we different. The last time anyone checked, Asians still had 23 pairs of chromosomes as did their Western counterparts, copulated just like any other man or woman, and possessed hearts which are programmed to stop after two and a half billion beats whether in Tibet or Texas. We all curse when angry and cry when sorry.

The differences are nevertheless striking. The Thais do a '*wai*', where palms are pressed together and brought to the forehead in a reverential greeting whereas Australians hug when they greet each other; the English would find it a trifle uncomfortable picking up rice and curry with nothing more than fingers (as would Chinese eating rice with forks); and German men might find the freedom afforded by the Burmese *longyi* a little too unrestrained.

The sharp knife of culture does not slice the world neatly into East and West, however. Koreans are just as ignorant as the Mexicans about the Malay tradition of touching one's chest after a handshake to signify a heartfelt gesture, while the Filipino knows not much more about the Japanese bow than, say, the French, and the Chinese are just as ill-informed as the Swedes about taboos in Buddhist Thailand. (There are, nevertheless, a few pointers that travellers would do well to remember, as Christopher Engholm advises in his book *When Business East Meets Business West*: in China one does not refer to Taiwan as the Republic of China, in Korea it is unwise to talk about the Japanese influence on the local culture, and in Singapore, 'avoid politics'.)

So what is to be made of Asian values? First we have to unmuddle the confusion between values and practices. Practices are behavioural responses which we perform out of imitation and persist with out of habit from which, over time, customs and traditions arise: the way we greet each other, eat or dress. Values, on the other hand, are principles, qualities and ideals which humanity considers worthy of achieving and maintaining. Values such as truth, non-violence and charity cut across cultures and religions.

Humans can't help being human. When they are fed, they look for shelter; when they are housed, they want to be loved; when they are emotionally secure, they strive to be competent; when they are proficient, they seek intellectual challenges, and so the struggle goes until, as psychologist Abraham Maslow describes in his hierarchy of needs, one reaches the pinnacle of self-actualisation.

Who or what is responsible for this process? The brain. The fact that the homo sapien brain is the most developed amongst living things suggests that there may be more to life than just existing. Complex behaviour is represented in the outer layer of the brain called the cerebral cortex. Stimulate one spot and we may become very aggressive, touch another and we may find it impossible to recognise the face of even a loved one. The centres of the brain need stimulation, and the ability to think, plan and calculate (which neuroscientists call 'higher' cortical functions) are just as important as the need to breathe, eat and sleep (the more 'primitive' functions). One way of stimulating these higher functions is communication. Take it away and you take away the human aspect of the human being. Freedom to think, to question and to disagree constitutes communication, and communication forms the basis of human life regardless of which society one belongs to.

Autocrats harping on the premise that Asian peoples are interested only in food and shelter run the danger of degrading the issue, according to Chinese dissident Han Dong-fan, to one of animal rights, not human rights. Wei Jingshen reiterated that, 'We, whether Americans, Africans, or Chinese, are people, not animals that care solely about the consumption of food.'

Of course, values and customs interrelate to produce the complex and confusing pattern of group behaviour that we call culture. More often than not, it is practices and customs, rather than values, that give rise to cultural differences. Ask an American how the handshake came about and you'll most likely stump him. He probably grew up seeing his parents, teachers and friends shake hands, and has customarily performed the behaviour, absorbing it from his cultural milieu. And yet, he knows that it is an expression of welcome and kindly regard—values that he wishes to extend to the person he meets. That value of courtesy and respect is also extended half a world away in Japan, but practiced differently in that culture.

Asian values are only as different from Western values as Asian children are from Western ones. Apart from the obvious differences in appearance, authority figures can encourage as many differences in outlook as they desire, and in the process erect barriers between peoples. Hong Kong's Tung Chee-Hwa, like his role model Lee Kuan Yew, never fails to invoke his sometimes Asian, sometimes Chinese values to dismiss foreign journalists whenever they ask one of those hard-to-answer-without-sounding-silly questions: 'You don't understand this. You are not a Chinese.' Given the similarity of the two cities, it is unsurprising that Tung looks to Singapore for political inspiration. His people seemed to understand Chinese values a lot better than Tung himself, and voted into the tightly guarded legislature 19 pro-democracy representatives out of a possible 20 in the 1998 elections (the rest of the 40 seats are appointed by Tung's Government).

But Tung is right. It is difficult to understand Asian values, but not only for Westerners. How does one comprehend the fracturing of values and deed in a place such as Singapore which enshrines 'nation before community and society above self' in its national Shared Values when that value had to be given a jumpstart by a Canadian housewife who had stopped her car to tend to a man who had jumped six floors to his death. When she pleaded for assistance, car after car (totalling about 20) stopped, stared and steered their way clear of the mess. Earlier two 11-year old boys had drowned off a Singaporean beach. While some tried to rescue the victims, most bystanders settled down with snacks 'as though they were watching a show.' Still others saw no sense in letting tragedy get in the way of that all important hobby of making more money, and reflexively took down the number plates of the police cars, which had subsequently arrived, for lottery.

While it may be difficult to understand such behaviour, it is hardly surprising that Singaporean society doesn't heed the nagging of the nanny state, if only for the simple reason that the Government itself does a commendable job of mastering hypocrisy. After all, the tightly-controlled society is simply a reflection of the Government, which has never been diffident about cashing in on others' miseries. 'While the other countries are ignoring Myanmar, it's a good time for us to go in,' an official of the Singapore Trade Development Board taught. 'You get better deals and you're more appreciated.'

No amount of warm pronouncements about Confucian ideals can mask the fact that, as the Burmese people continue to live under the murderous State Peace and Development Council or SPDC (formerly SLORC), Singapore's ruling party breaks formal agreements and insults public morality by selling rifles and rockets to Burma's generals who 'seem to have turned to Singapore for military training, intelligence advise and defence technology.' For a country which cannot even afford to feed its own citizens—a teacher in Rangoon earns about US$10 a month—it does a brisk business with its Singaporean arms-daddy to build a 'cyber war centre' to monitor and record telecommunications 'including the satellite telephone conversations of Burmese opposition groups.'

Then there is the Indonesian *Pancasila* which calls for, among other exhortations, a 'just and civilised humanity' though the former President lost not a night's sleep when his army went about the systematic slaughter of the people. If any one finds this a trifle jarring to the intellect, they can take comfort in the knowledge that only Suharto and his generals could comprehend the contradiction because, going by Tung Chee-Hwa's logic, one similarly cannot understand Indonesian values if one is not an Indonesian.

Nonetheless, Asian authoritarians will continue to play on the East-West divide of value systems, decrying democracy to give themselves the authority over the people, just like the big bully who steals the lollipop from a child and tells the dispossessed kid that candy causes cavities.

Cultural differences should be celebrated and savoured for what they are, because a world without colourful customs would be a maddeningly boring planet. Fundamental values, which transcend cultural boundaries and reach across humanity, remain indivisible. People, whether they eat with forks or fingers, wear Stetsons or *songkoks*, prefer ping-pong or Pavarotti, will not, given a free choice, deny themselves equality, hope and freedom—virtues which are embedded in democratic values.

If Asians and democratic values don't mix, geography is in serious trouble.

It has been a little more than ten years since martial law was lifted in Taiwan in 1987, but protesters are still fighting. The demonstrators, with caps, sunglasses and scarves pulled over their heads, still can not afford to reveal their identity. Only this time it was Taipei's Mayor Chen Shui-bian of the opposition Democratic Progressive Party on the receiving end; the police were out in full force, carrying not truncheons but tickets, and confronting not *dangwai* fighters but traffic offenders. The demonstrators, coy courtesans by night and articulate activists by day, were dogging the Mayor everywhere he went, demanding that he rescind a decision to ban prostitution in the city.

Then there was the television talkshow host who started off with: '*Wan ba tan* (egghead) Lee Teng-hui...' and continued to upbraid the President of Taiwan for praising Chiang Ching-kuo for lifting martial law. 'Who was the one who imposed it in the first place?' he bellowed. With just about every other commentator on just about every other channel in the dizzying array of options on the cable network, he was telling his fellow Taiwanese what he thought about anything from the German company Bayer's investment in a chemical plant in Taiwan to the safety and management (or lack thereof) of China Airlines.

'During the time when the Kuomintang was still very authoritarian, power failures would often occur when ballot counting was conducted,' my Taiwanese father-in-law told me. 'What happened to the ballot boxes then no one knew but the blackouts seemed too coincidental. Taiwan has come a long way since those days.'

Now the fighting in the streets has been transferred into the Legislative Yuan. A pristinely dressed female parliamentarian, speaking on the podium with manicured composure, apparently sullied the repute of another smartly clad lady legislator by chiding her for sitting immodestly with her undergarments seeing more light than they ought to. The offended member strode towards the lectern and, without a word, awarded her accuser the full impact of her palm across the face. With polish no longer a consideration, a most inglorious brawl followed.

Not to be upstaged, two male legislators, one hand grabbing a neck and the other clobbering a head, dragged each other from one end of the hall to the other and back, before falling to the ground to continue their disagreement there.

Democrats, especially those still unable to practice their beliefs, cringe whenever such unedifying spectacles erupt in fledgling democratic houses. 'The Kuomintang used to kill us, so what we're doing now is nothing,' an opposition official defended when I broached the matter. 'I'm kidding,' he added as he detected my chagrin. 'We're still a young democracy and we'll grow out of it. I'm sure of it.' Political manners do seem to be getting less brusque as democracy in Taiwan continues to mature.

So has Taiwan become less Asian by becoming more democratic? Shih Ming-teh never stepped outside Taiwan, let alone visited any Western country, until he was freed at the age of 49. Yet he waged a relentless battle against the Chiangs for Taiwan's freedom. Incredibly, it was Lee Kuan Yew, the 'best bloody Englishman east of the Suez' and whom Zhou En-lai, China's late premier, described as a banana—yellow on the outside and white on the inside—who would imply that someone like Shih is somehow less Asian.

'Those who think that Asians don't understand or deserve democracy, they show ultimate contempt towards their own people,' Shih expostulated during our discussion. 'Asian democracy fighters must be prepared to pay the price for achieving those ideals. One must be persistent and be prepared for a long battle. You may sacrifice today but you will win tomorrow.'

Lin Yi-hsiung said, 'The saddest thing about authoritarian governments is that they bring out the worst in human beings. They appeal to attitudes and values like selfishness, personal benefits and distrust of each other so that they can divide and rule. Democracy is not the best type of government, I know that, but there are no better alternatives. The trend of democracy in Asia cannot be stopped. It's not that Asians don't want it, they are simply oppressed.'

'Lee's [Kuan Yew] view of Asian cultures is not only unsupportable but self-serving,' wrote Kim Dae Jung. The Korean people recently elected the democratic minded politician to lead them.

Aung San Suu Kyi said, 'I think all the talk about Asian values is just to belittle us.'

Malaysia's former Deputy Prime Minister, Anwar Ibrahim, was able to see that:

> If we in Asia want to speak credibly of Asian values, we too must be prepared to champion those ideals which are universal and which belong to humanity as a whole. It is altogether shameful, if ingenuous, to cite Asian values as an excuse for autocratic practices and denial of basic rights and civil liberties. To say that freedom is Western or un-Asian is to offend our own traditions as well as our forefathers who gave up their lives in the struggle against tyranny and injustice.

Fellow Malaysian Syed Husin Ali, a scholarly and principled oppositionist who was himself detained without trial for six years, told me: 'As long as Asians are oppressed, we can never learn to be proud of our own heritage.'

But nowhere did the myth of Asian values explode more abruptly and violently than in Indonesia in 1998. For more than 30 years Suharto ruled without hindrance, save for the occasional protest here and critical commentary there. Since dumping Bung Karno in the mid-1960s, Pak Harto took the country's economy on a phenomenal flight, averaging 7% GDP growth a year. The President seemed to prove to the world that authoritarian governance could just about achieve anything once disciplined mind was imposed on democratic madness.

Suharto seemed to secure a place forever in history as the leader who turned the impecunious archipelago into the shining ricebowl of Asia. As skyscrapers sprang up next to slums, and banks burrowed into the corporate corpus, cheered on by the international investors, few said anything when Suharto started allowing plum projects to be channelled to his wife, sons, daughters, half-brothers, uncles, nephews and just about anyone who had that all important qualification—kinship. Servile subordinates were likewise given a generous greasing of the palm.

When family and friends siphoned off funds for a dubious national car project and wanted even more for an even crazier national aircraft project—and all this by a Government who couldn't find the means or the resources to put out fires in its own forests—few questioned them. Hardly anyone protested when critical newspapers were closed down, political leaders ousted from their own parties lest they became rivals for Suharto's job, and unrest quelled with brutal efficiency in Aceh, Irian Jaya and East Timor. The President had built himself an unchallengeable position.

Most people seemed convinced that, for Indonesia to maintain its stability, development was the answer. Few stopped to ask what seems like conventional wisdom now: development for whom? A year into the country's economic meltdown, it is not uncommon to find people—many who were salaried men and women—rushing to compost heaps, rummaging for anything from plastic bags for sale to left over food. By 1999, an estimated 140 million Indonesians, 66% of the population, will live below the poverty line—a level not seen since the 1960s. A villager summed up the matter when he said: 'After 30 years, nothing is changed, and we are sick and tired of it.'

The currency chaos in Asia uncovered a system that was rotten to the core. When investors lost their love for the rupiah, the ups (inflation, unemployment and riots) and downs (stockmarket, wages and the army's heavy hand) all came at once.

The situation created an international panic and, when everyone instinctively turned to the President for solutions, they very quickly realised that he was the problem to begin with. At one time, it seemed like Suharto's corrupt and obstinate ways could lead to a tumultuous implosion of the Indonesian society that would have imperilled the economic and social stability of the region, if not the world. International leaders and agencies implored him to institute reforms that would head off a political earthquake, to which the old despot responded by appointing his daughter and several cronies into his cabinet after his reappointment to the Presidency in March 1998.

Some maintained that Suharto was the only lifeguard who could rescue a drowning Indonesia. Aged 76 and ailing, confidence and energy were not the President's strongest qualities. What about replacements? There were, some analysts said, none—at least no one capable of holding the country together, let alone pulling it forward, in such a crisis. To come to such a conclusion about a country which has almost 70 times more people than New Zealand (which has three million citizens and which has never found itself in short supply of political leaders) seemed like a terrible racist imprecation on the Indonesian people. Nevertheless, it was a view that was held by many foreigners.

Suharto gambled on the assumption that the world would not do anything about his impudence because he had made sure that most of his opponents were either dead or detained. Either the inextricably interconnected world did things his way or not at all, the President calculated. And if the problem was not solved, he would go down with the rest of Indonesia and drag as many countries with him as possible. With 200 million people poised to rip the region asunder if there was dire political turmoil, it looked like the Indonesian President had the region by the throat. As the world watched anxiously, one unnerving fact kept coming up: no one knew how the crisis was going to end.

Then the Indonesian people stepped in to bring an end to Suharto's rule and the world breathed easier. Lest memories fade, one question that must be asked, and asked repeatedly, is: how did the international community get itself into such a quagmire in the first place and, more importantly, how will it prevent a similar occurrence in the future? Pretend, for a moment, that we could go back in time to 1965; knowing what we know today, would the international community still have looked the other way and allowed Suharto to establish his kingdom through murder, corruption and misrule? Would it not have made more sense to ensure that the former dictator had not been allowed, or even encouraged, to perpetrate his crimes on such a grand scale and for him to remain accountable to his people and, thus, to the world? Would the sacrifice of democracy at the expense of development still be looked upon so favourably?

Thirty years ago, letting Suharto unleash his fearsome tyranny without opposition didn't seem such an urgent matter for the international community to address. But time has a way of sneaking up on the callous and giving everyone a deserving kick in the backside.

Only the foolish would now say that democracy has no place in Indonesia. With what we know now, do we continue to allow other authoritarian regimes to flourish under the guise of economic progress without concomitant democratic development?

Opening up Asia

So where do we begin the democratisation process?

The Association of Southeast Asian Nations (Asean) is not a bad place to start. Asean will, if it hangs on to its hypocritical policy of the 'Asean way' of 'non-interference in the internal affairs' of its member nations, become an organisation deluding itself and its peoples. In the world of today, the nationalistic refrain 'It's none of your business' becomes increasingly untenable, even undesirable.

In a way, the impact of the present financial crisis might have been less if there was a greater degree of monitoring of systems and practices within Asean, and ultimately Asia. How the Indonesian president institutes political reform in his country affects the standard of living of the civil servant in Kuala Lumpur, what Ryutaro Hashimoto decides for Japan impacts upon the retailer in Singapore, and how the Beijing Government handles its *renminbi* determines whether the banker in Bangkok stays afloat or plunges into another round of pocket-emptying, life-breaking financial debacle. If the flight of capital thumbs its nose at national boundaries, then how are governments going to continue to argue that their ways and means should not be the subject of discussion or commentary by their neighbours?

As with capital, people will seek out safer havens when the political situations in their countries teeter on the brink of bedlam. Refugees from Vietnam, and more recently Indonesia, send sobering reminders to anyone who thinks that countries can continue to live free of 'interference' from each other.

Only months ago, if one were to ask shop-and-buy Singaporeans housed in highrise apartments what they have in common with the slash-and-burn farmers roaming the depths of the Kalimantan jungle, quizzical stares would probably be the average response. But how the subsistence farmers (not to mention the rapacious logging companies) burn the jungle brushes determines the conditions under which people in other countries live. When the health of the infirm and the young come under increasing threat from the smoke of these burning brushes, the 'Asean way' very soon becomes the absurd way.

And, as if to wake the club's leaders from their world of makebelieve, Cambodia's Second Prime Minister, Hun Sen, bombarded the First, Prince Norodom Ranarridh, out of the country and issued Asean with a testy challenge to admit his country into the organisation without conditions. Hun Sen poked at the most uncomfortable spot in the Asean belly by repeatedly reminding the Association of its hypocrisy in accepting the junta in Burma while rejecting Cambodia. The embarrassing episode caused a stir, with some Asean members voicing the obvious: a rethinking of the 'non-interference' policy was needed.

With India and Pakistan playing a deadly mine-is-bigger-than-yours nuclear game, Asean can 'non-interfere' no longer.

No one is suggesting that neighbouring countries intervene in one another's domestic matters everytime a problem breaks out. But if non-interference includes not commenting and not criticising each other, the premise upon which the United Nations is founded collapses. Ironically, it is Asean that has so egregiously interfered in Burma's affairs by not only recognising but also supporting the military junta that seized power from a civilian government overwhelmingly endorsed by the people in the 1989 elections. In particular, as noted, Singapore to date has ploughed more than one billion United States dollars into the country in trade and helps the military rulers continue their despotic rule. Lee Kuan Yew has said that Aung San Suu Kyi should leave the running of Burma to the SLORC (now SPDC).

Thai Foreign Minister Surin Pitsuwan broke ranks recently and urged, 'Perhaps it is time that Asean's cherished principle of non-intervention is modified to allow it to play a constructive role in preventing or resolving domestic issues with regional implications.'

These 'domestic issues' were brought sharply into focus in Indonesia in the aftermath of Suharto's downfall, when it was revealed that more than 4,000 shops and offices, 40 shopping centres and thousands of houses were burned down.

Approximately 3,000 people were killed and more than 450 cases of reported rapes. Most of the property and bodies belonged to Chinese Indonesians.

'Come out and face me!' a young man screamed and waved his fist at the Indonesian Consular in Melbourne, Australia. 'Come out, you bastard! Come out and tell the people here what you did to my family!' His voice cracked as he turned to the crowd outside the embassy, mainly made up of protesters from the Australian Chinese community. 'Please speak up for me,' he pleaded with the demonstrators as tears rolled down his face. A few of the protesters dabbed their eyes with their handkerchiefs. Similar demonstrations were taking place in Taiwan, Hong Kong, China, the Philippines, Malaysia, Germany, the United States and Canada.

Evidence that the killings and burnings were not random acts of violence started to surface: groups of thugs had gathered at specific points and were trucked to targeted areas; stones, fuel and readily-combustible material were conveniently available; orders of body bags from Taiwan in April 1998 suddenly increased; and houses were colour coded to tell the gangs whether to attack the occupants and how to do it.

The Food and Horticultural Minister didn't deny the atrocities. He justified that it was tolerable to have up to 5% of Chinese businesses destroyed to accommodate the people's anger.

But because of Southeast Asian 'brotherhood', Asean kept silent.

This is not surprising as authoritarian habits die hard. Many current Southeast Asian leaders will maintain their policy of interfering in other nations' affairs when it suits the occasion and scream in pain when other societies point to their shortcomings, all in a concerted effort to ward off democratic reform. Not surprisingly, only Philippine Foreign Secretary Domingo Siazon supported Pitsuwan's call for a review of the non-interference policy.

Lee Kuan Yew exemplifies this behaviour when he offers advice to all and sundry on how to conduct their affairs. He tells the Thais that their leaders have 'a natural reluctance to discipline' banks, the Japanese that their culture is 'not receptive of foreign influences', the Hong Kongers not 'to waste time talking about democracy', the Indonesians that 'the question mark on the successor' (hinting at B. J. Habibie being appointed Vice-President when Suharto was still the President) is 'a big problem', the Koreans that they have to 'change the nature in which [they] ran the *chaebol*', and East Asians that they need 'to strengthen [their] institutions of government'.

And Singapore? 'Nobody has the right to convert me,' he snaps.

With that notion firmly in mind, Lee teaches that transparency of economic information is vital for business. Doubtlessly. Since the advent of the Asian crisis, every economic pundit who has had anything worthwhile to say has not failed to mention the importance of transparency and accountability.

But where was the warning before Asia was beset with the mess? The Singapore Government was pouring billions into its neighbouring economies and calling on its people to go forth and multiply their businesses in the region, which was experiencing a money making miracle. There was nary a word of caution against the murky way that business was done in Asia. And even as he now excoriates his fellow Asian leaders for their 'stupidity and weakness', Lee showed his cleverness and strength by heaping one billion dollars into Burma to do business with a military regime which only an extra-terrestrial would describe as transparent and accountable. He chided Indonesia's erstwhile President Suharto, Malaysia's Prime Minister Mahathir Mohamad and Thailand's former Prime Minister Chavalit Yongchaiyudh that, had they 'been part of the information age, the end result [of their countries' economic crisis] wouldn't be half as bad.' But if Lee had been so sophisticated with information, why did he invest so much of Singapore's public funds in these economies in the first place?

Now that things have gone sour, Singapore's investments in other Asian countries have been affected tremendously. Lee's plan to create a baby Singapore in the city of Suzhou, China, where life is to be modelled on that in the Lion City, has run into serious problems—problems that Singaporeans have been whispering about but heard little of from the state controlled media. That is, until Lee Kuan Yew, unable to contain his displeasure at the 'municipal shenanigans' of the Suzhou authorities, decided to censure his Chinese counterparts. He was angry at local Suzhou entrepreneurs who had built the neighbouring Suzhou New District, a 'rival economic zone' with his Suzhou Industrial Park (SIP). The 'shenanigans' of the Chinese authorities had apparently led to the New District being 'chock-a-block with factories' while the SIP 'is notable for its vast tracts of wasteland'. The irony, however, is that the New District was set up a whole three years before the SIP. Lee publicly threatened to 'bow out' of the project, which is estimated to have cost the island republic a cool US$20 billion. Bow out? Who accounts for the lost dollars?

Singaporeans are seldom told of such debacles in Lee's 'information age'. They are not informed of the investments—which are taken care of by the Government of Singapore Investment Corporation (GIC)—in the first place. Handling the staggering billions (80 at last count) is the GIC's board of directors, which Lee chairs but of which the country's Prime Minister, Goh Chok Tong, is not even a member.

There was also little public accountability when a computer company, Micropolis—owned and managed by the Government-run Singapore Technologies headed by Lee's daughter-in-law—failed, costing the taxpayer more than US$400 million. The Government simply told everyone what they already knew: that the loss resulted 'in a diminution of the government's assets'.

At the onset of the monetary crisis when the Indonesian economy started to hyperventilate, Singapore wasted little time in sending its Prime Minister to Jakarta to prescribe a US$10 billion loan in an attempt to prevent the crisis from slipping into an unrecoverable coma. Parliament in Singapore knew nothing about the deal, and Singaporeans came to learn of it not from their Prime Minister but from Suharto, who happened to make some off-the-cuff remarks during a visit to a town in East Java.

The news shocked and confused political and economic analysts in the region. The International Monetary Funds (IMF) had always insisted that any financial aid must be tied to economic reform. Apparently, Singapore had not insisted on any conditions from Suharto who later confirmed this view when he said that 'the situation is not that we are asking for money from the IMF, then we are tied to this or that condition' implying that money not linked with the IMF, as in the US$10 billion from Goh, was an unconditional pledge. This notion was reinforced when a Singaporean Government official said that the money 'would help to *supplement* the IMF effort' (emphasis added), followed by another Singaporean source who reported that the cash, or at least the first $5 billion, came 'with no conditions imposed.' Goh himself had said earlier that the help from Singapore would supplement the IMF's assistance. The Prime Minister later backtracked and noted that the funds would be tied to conditions set by the IMF.

When Goh subsequently heard that Suharto had 'instructed' his central bank to use the money from the Singapore loan to rescue ailing Indonesian banks, some of which were owned by Suharto's relatives, the Singaporean buttonholed the Indonesian during the Asia Pacific Economic Conference in Vancouver in November 1997 and got the assurance that the Indonesian Government would not do such a thing.

The perplexing episode raises two questions: One, what transpired between Goh and Suharto when the loan was first offered and why was there the contradiction between the two leaders? Information on how and under what conditions the deal was made remains sketchy. Two, did Goh not know Suharto's penchant to siphon off foreign capital for personal gain? Through his years as President, Suharto had acquired an international reputation for his corrupt ways. When asked by the IMF why special funds reserved for reafforestation in Indonesia were not being used to fight the country's forest fires, the former President replied that the money had been set aside for his son's national car project. The Singapore Government's judgement of Suharto raises grave concerns. Goh Chok Tong had told Suharto during the last days of the despot's political career: 'Your vigour and stamina in the face of intense pressure speak volumes for your resolve to overcome these problems.' He added that the dictator's election to a seventh term was a 'reaffirmation of the people's trust' in him and that the people 'had benefited from his leadership.' Two months later, the people dumped their benefactor and called for him to return the billions of dollars he had taken from the country.

Whatever the answers, the secretive manner in which the deal between the two governments was made is disturbing.

According to an American journalist, however, Singapore was showing leadership in a time of turmoil in Indonesia and that critics tended to 'dismiss the island city-state as little more than a cauldron of caning, not caring.' United States Senator Diane Feinstein, mesmerised by all this caring for Indonesia, said, 'Singapore has been remarkable. It is probably showing more leadership per capita than any of us.'

This was not lost on the PAP, which has often accused the United States of interfering in Singapore's domestic affairs whenever the Americans offer criticism. But compliments are different for they are not interference, and thus welcomed. Goh claimed that, 'It is no longer possible nor right for us to close our eyes or fold our arms and ignore the problems of our neighbours.' It was not hard to see that his feet were stuck firmly in the Indonesian economic quicksand. As Singapore's trade with Indonesia continue to get that sinking feeling, could all the caring mask a startled, if subtle, signal to the United States and Europe to throw a lifeline? The record of transparency and accountability by both governments is appalling. The Singapore Government does not publish statistics about its trade with Indonesia—estimated at about US$20 billion a year—as the 'information is deemed too sensitive'.

According to Lee Kuan Yew, Asia's economic collapse has come about because of a lack of systems, especially 'the rule of law'. Wasn't this the same man who said that it was not his practice to produce 'evidence that will stand up to the strict rules of evidence of a court of law' when he arrested and imprisoned all his opponents? The rule of law can only come about when government institutions are not manipulated willy-nilly by the ruling elite. Lee showed further confusion when he elucidated that on the one hand, 'East Asia needs to strengthen its institutions of government', but on the other, 'authoritarian arrangements are essential to economic success'.

If transparency and accountability are going to make any difference in the way that matters are conducted in Asia, the mass media must have a role in disseminating the information.

Regimes in Asia still find it distressing to have the international media freely report about events in their countries; this is a shame because the lack of information has aggravated, if not precipitated, the economic skid. When foreign currency debts are not disclosed, mismanagement of resources goes uncommented, and corruption is left to spawn without public scrutiny, serious economic problems will turn into disastrous ones.

Transparency and authoritarianism are, however, sworn enemies. As their economies become more and more sophisticated, governments become less and less tolerant about the information that becomes public. In Bangkok, police raided the offices of two brokerage firms, ABN-Amro Hoare Govett and Capital Nomura, when they published some rather unflattering news about business prospects in Thailand. Malaysia banned discussions by academics on the problems caused by the haze from forest fires that had shrouded much of the country. A bomb threat was issued to Bloomberg's office in Seoul following a critical analysis the news agency made of South Korea's troubled economy. Indonesia closed down a journal and jailed its editor for publishing caricatures of President Suharto.

Nowhere is the control of the media more insidious than in Singapore, however. With the local press and the single television station already well trained, the Government turned on the more errant foreign media by curtailing its circulation: *Time* magazine from 18,000 to 2,000 copies per issue, *Asian Wall Street Journal* 5,100 to 400, *Asiaweek* 10,000 to 500, *Far Eastern Economic Review* 9,000 to 500, and *The Economist* restricted to 7,500 copies per week. Alternatively they are sued till they abjectly beg for clemency, as in the case of the *International Herald Tribune*, which ended up paying Lee Kuan Yew, his son Lee Hsien Loong and Goh Chok Tong hundreds of thousands of dollars in costs and damages.

'The truth of the matter is that we're trying to increase our circulation in Singapore,' a foreign journalist told me after an interview. 'There's a lot of self-censorship going on whenever we report about the situation here. I know it stinks but we have to take care of business as well.' In 1997, I wrote an article for an international newspaper about the Singapore Government's business involvement with Burma's druglords.

The editor first replied that the piece would be published. A few days later, the newspaper reversed its decision because, as it said in rather vague terms, some people might read too much into it.

The tendency of Asian authoritarians to shoot the messenger is epitomised in a case concerning Christopher Lingle, an American academic. In the *The Rise and Decline of the Asian Century*, Lingle wrote:

> Stock markets in East Asia have exhibited a considerable amount of volatility that should generate serious questions about the integrity and their long-term viability...and there is an incomplete evaluation of the risk factors inherent in the region. It may be true that high rates of return are often available under situations where there are great risks. Unfortunately, the popular perception of sustainable, robust economic growth in East Asia has resulted in a distorted picture of the risk/return profile.

What makes the observation remarkable is the author's anticipation of Asia's economic troubles. The book was published in early 1997, before the meltdown began. Its original publisher, a Western company with an office in Singapore, had decided not to proceed with the publication. Lingle then asked me to look for printers in Singapore. Unfortunately, there were none who were willing to do the job. This came as no surprise to me as he was, in the eyes of the Singapore Government, a fugitive. He was teaching at the National University of Singapore in 1994 when he wrote an article published by the *International Herald Tribune* (IHT) which contained a sentence commenting on the judiciary of some of the countries in Asia. The Singapore Government took offence at the statement even though no country or persons were named, and charged Lingle and the IHT for criminal contempt. Both parties were convicted.

I met Lingle for the first time about a week after the piece appeared in the newspaper. He did not realise at that time that his article was going to bring him so much attention. Days after our encounter I received news that Lingle was in trouble with the authorities and that detectives had questioned him at length and seized his files from his office and home. (I discovered later that the authorities suspected that I was involved in the writing of the article.) When he learned that Lee Kuan Yew had also 'demanded a full retraction and an apology' failing which he would 'initiate civil proceedings' against him, Lingle hurriedly caught a flight out of the country.

If the media is cowed, how can abuses of power and corruption be kept in check? Governments and their institutions are able to monitor businesses and banks to ensure that regulations are complied with, but who monitors the monitors? In some Asian societies, autocrats have been so entrenched in their positions that no amount of elections can dislodge them from power. Systems have been manipulated to ensure victory, or money is bartered for votes, or both.

Suharto subjected himself to his own will once every five years in the Peoples Consultative Assembly, a system designed to give him a lifetime warranty.

In cash-rich Taiwan, Kuomintang candidates dispatch their assistants to hand out small sums of money for wink-and-nod support. 'This is for you and your husband,' the neighbourhood committee leader grinned as he pushed $200 into my Taiwanese friend's hand. 'I have a daughter as well and she is eligible to vote this year,' my friend told him. 'Oh, is that so?' the grin widened as he pushed another $100 note forward. 'Take the money and vote for the opposition,' she told me later. 'That's the only way to stop them from buying votes.' The idea seemed to work because, as the number of opposition parliamentarians increases, vote buying by the Kuomintang officials has seen a steady decline.

Candidates in Thailand are a little more wily. Trudging out to the poorest of rural areas, they hand out cherished commodities like shoes and sandals. The trick, of course, is to give them only half a pair, and to hand them the other only if the candidate is elected.

In the Philippines, where the sheer number of candidates can stump even the most discerning, campaign workers pay voters to smuggle out blank ballot slips so that they can be marked and handed to the next voter, who in turn sells his unmarked paper, thus carrying on a most ingenious racket.

In Singapore, the ruling PAP entices voters with new train lines, libraries, playgrounds and refurbishment of their apartments, all funded by the public largesse. There is, of course, nothing wrong with such a scheme—that is, if it ends there. The caveat is that delivery of the goods will be delayed, or even withheld, in constituencies where the ruling party's candidates are not successful. For good measure, the PAP announces that it will be monitoring the percentage of votes it receives from each small cluster of blocks of apartments. This is, as the PAP calls it, a 'national upgrading' policy. There's a more common and better known term for it—corruption.

Messrs Science and Democracy

Proponents of 'Asian' values will claim that democracy in the region has a short history. Perhaps. They forget, however, that it has a long past.

This is an important point. All this talk about Asian values, by those who applaud it and others who assail it, still doesn't answer the question of whether the ideals embodied in the concept of democracy have any basis within Asia's historical context.

Kim Dae-jung insists: 'There are no ideas more fundamental to democracy than the teachings of Confucianism, Buddhism, and the Tonghak. Clearly, Asia has democratic philosophies as profound as those of the West.' Tonghak is the native religion in Korea. Its essence is predicated on the belief that 'man is Heaven' and 'to serve man is to serve Heaven.' It was this notion that motivated peasants to revolt against their feudal rulers in 1894. Even during the fifteenth and sixteenth centuries, Kim relates, 'Thinkers such as Cho Kwangju and Yi Yulgok advocated freedom of expression as a basic value in governing a country and argued that the rise and fall of a dynasty depended on whether speech was free or suppressed.'

In China, history has consisted of long lulls of nepotistic rule of a few hundred years, followed by a gradual corruption and decline of power, giving way in turn to an intense burst of calamity instigated by mutinous armies and popular insurrections, only to result in another despot taking over and the advent of yet another dynasty. The uprising against an emperor is often justified, in a sleight of logic, by the argument that the incumbent lost the 'mandate of Heaven', which, presumably, will be passed on to whoever has the mightier army and, therefore, the right to rule.

Meng Zi or Mencius, a faithful student of Confucius, was adamant that his master-teacher, though he had advocated strict obedience by the people, had taught that a ruler's mandate from Heaven was really a public endorsement of his reign because 'the king has received a mandate to rule the people with justice on behalf of Heaven. Now, if the king goes against the will of Heaven and rules the people in a tyrannical manner, the people will have the right not to recognise him as a king any more and to overthrow him and usher in a new king.' Even the 'will of Heaven', according to Mencius, was the 'will of the people'. He went on to advocate a system of 'people based politics' as early as 300 BC, which sounded suspiciously like the basis for the democratic process. Although it was not institutionalised in the East as it was in the West, the idea of a people's government may not have been as alien to Asia as some would like to believe.

China's modern history is also replete with catastrophic struggles. When the Manchus invaded the Middle Kingdom in the seventeenth century to establish the Qing dynasty, they showed little fondness for progress, preferring a lifestyle of imperial navel gazing with all its trappings and traditions of courtly profligacy. That continued until the reign of Emperor Guang Xu, who was struck by the way knowledge had been put to use by those Western 'foreign devils' to expand their empires. And so in 1898, in a rare burst of dynastic energy and vision, the young emperor issued edict after edict to revive China's love for learning and to instil in the people the importance of applying knowledge to life. It was an idea that the Chinese language didn't even have a term for—science.

The Empress Dowager, interested only in maintaining the status quo and thus her power over the Kingdom, engineered the emperor's downfall. He was replaced by his nephew, Pu Yi, China's last emperor.

But this could not stop the Chinese people, led by a contumacious Hawaii-trained medical doctor, from mounting a campaign against corrupt monarchical rule. In 1911 Sun Yat-sen succeeded in ending China's 4,000 years of imperial rule. He proclaimed the Republic of China and presided over a period of modernisation. Having been pinned painfully under successive incompetent and vacuous mandates of Heaven which seemed unable to ward off bullies from Europe and

Japan who had sliced up their country and passed out the pieces like it was some kind of delicacy, the liberated nationalists were in no mood for autocracy. In addition to science, the Chinese wanted democracy.

The two subjects were elevated to the honorific positions of 'Mr Science' and 'Mr Democracy'. Education for the masses—as opposed to the practice of restricting scholarship to privileged mandarins which had until then been based on the study of the ancient Chinese classics understood only by the aristocratic class—would be the means to study and practise the two.

But it was more than serendipity that Messrs Science and Democracy came to be seen as twin engineers for China's growth. Following the emancipation from centuries of tyranny, transparency and order were desired as mainstays of modern society. Since science—embedded in the principles of empiricism, verification and self-correction—rejects opacity and arbitrariness, it seemed the most appropriate approach for conducting intellectual pursuits. Empirical evidence necessitates that data is produced for everyone to examine, unreliability and even deceit is quickly exposed by the process of verification and testing, and changes to theories are facilitated through a methodical, self-correcting course. For the scientific process to take place, open debate is a prerequisite and this occurs through scientific journals and conferences.

Intelligent debate often begins with intrepid dissent, and science has had its share of rebellious swots. Nicolaus Copernicus was castigated by the powerful medieval church for blasphemy when he made the crazy claim that the earth was round instead of flat; Galileo Galilei, tried before the Inquisition, was sentenced to life imprisonment for advocating the profane notion of planetary motion (his Law of Inertia was to later inspire Isaac Newton to develop his First Law of Motion); and Giordano Bruno was jailed for eight years and finally burned at the stake for heresy when he stated that 'innumerable suns exist'.

Without freedom of expression, science degenerates into a dangerous tinkering with nature. In the nineteenth century, Franz Joseph Gall and Johann Spurzheim, two German anatomists, believed that human behavioural traits could be determined according to the contour of one's head, through a technique they called phrenology. The way that Gall and Spurzheim obtained their data and arrived at their conclusions were highly questionable. And yet, the popularity of phrenology took America and Europe by storm, and was even taught in medical schools until the turn of the century. Science, of course, had something else to say and, through its own laws of freedom, consigned phrenology to its rightful place in neurological history—the garbage can. Because the laws of science—and therefore nature—rule supreme, progress and direction of scientific endeavour has been most evident and least contentious as a way to settle disputes.

Similarly, democracy requires that, firstly, a majority come to a consensus on a particular leader through an empirically determined vote, as opposed to being subjected to rule by an authoritarian claiming supernatural mandates. Secondly, political chicanery by those who aspire to lead would be exposed and debunked under the scrutiny of public forums and debates. Thirdly, dithering and withering leaders can be replaced in an orderly fashion through constitutional elections, minimising upheaval to society.

Albert Einstein, a self-confessed liberal who barely escaped Nazi oppression, saw the connection between his world of mathematical formulas and the one that he lived in, and enjoined that 'every citizen should be equally responsible for defending the constitutional liberties of his country,' especially the intelligentsia, because authoritarian governments 'are particularly anxious to intimidate and silence the intellectual.'

Open debate, as in science, is crucial to the process of societal development which offers the best possible method of discovering the truth, elusive as it often is. Even as autocrats argue that a good form of government may be far from the democratic one, the process of free inquiry and debate that democratic ideals embrace allows truth to be approximated, better than any other political practice. Some may bristle at the thought of likening democracy—a political process not readily reducible to laws and formulas—to science. It is not unreasonable to argue that the two are different as chalk and cheese. Yet, there are similarities:

Science	Democracy
Theories are formulated and debated.	Policies are formulated and debated.
Theories are accepted only after they pass empirical tests.	Policies are implemented only after they examined by the various segments of society.
Theories are discarded if they are not supported by data.	Policies are abandoned if they are harmful to society (the government that implements the policies is sometimes voted out of power).
Information is readily available through journals, books, seminars, and conferences to all scientists.	Information is readily available through the mass media, political parties, public forums and rallies to all citizens.
The openness of science makes the discipline reliable.	The openness of democracy gives the society long-term stability.

Few dispute the efficacy of science, and scientific values are universally held in high regard without any dismemberment of the subject into 'Asian' or 'Western' versions. With democratic principles mirroring scientific ones, a dichotomy of Asian democracy versus Western-style democracy makes just as little sense.

The principles of science and democracy came to grief even before they could be established in the Chinese society. No sooner had Sun Yat-sen gathered his supporters to form a government than a warlord, Yuan Shi-kai, demanded that he be the ruler of the new republic, and set about achieving his ambition in a most brutal manner. Sun yielded the presidency, for not doing so would have torn the country apart again. Yuan yanked China back into despotic rule but died in 1916. Meanwhile Sun had formed the Huangpu Military Academy to counter Yuan's government in Beijing. On 4 May 1919, students, activists and academics sent the government reeling in the massive May Fourth Movement, rekindling the republican spirit and establishing Sun Yat-sen as President of the southern government in Nanjing. Unluckily for China, he died in 1925, and Chiang Kai-shek succeeded him as leader.

Somewhere out in the heady morass of political turbulence, a young librarian from Beijing University joined the Chinese Communist Party and advocated a revolution of the Chinese peasantry. His name was Mao Zedong.

In 1989, after 40 turbulent years of communist rule, the Chinese people rallied for democracy in Tiananmen Square. One has to reach back into the past to catch a glimpse of the future and, by all accounts, there will be another battle against the emperors in Beijing.

The universality of human rights and wrongs

Two white jeeps pulled up in the driveway and a bunch of masked men jumped out. They started shooting at a another group of men who were resting on a lawn outside the Capital building, taking a break from quarrelling over the counting of votes in the 1986 presidential elections.

Evelio Javier, a former governor and one of Corazon Aquino's campaign managers, took off towards a nearby building, darting this way and that to evade the bullets. One found its mark in his shoulder and sent him crashing into a pond. As onlookers nervously yelled in support, the politician struggled to his feet and tottered across the street. He tried to open the first door he came to but found it locked. His enemies were closing in and more shots were fired. Javier ducked into an alley and hid behind the door of a toilet. The gunmen followed the trail of blood and closed in on their prey. They cornered him in the alley and finished off the dying man with a burst of gunfire.

Later, ten more bodies were found in Quirino province, all understood to be Aquino's supporters. At least 156 people were killed in the presidential race in 1986. Despite the fraud, intimidation and killings, Marcos claimed victory and Reagan gained infamy by announcing that there was only an 'appearance of fraud' in the elections and, worse, that it had occurred 'on both sides'.

When Filipinos subsequently started demonstrating against Marcos's machinations, a White House official scoffed that the opposition should not protest 'just because [they] did not like the elections'.

But Reagan's dismissive attitude surprised few in the Philippines especially after Vice-President George Bush, at the height of the dictator's repressive rule, said that America loved Marcos's 'adherence to democratic principles'.

Despite Washington's amour for the absurd, the people of the Philippines went on to topple their tyrant in a revolution that spilled little blood.

Compare this to another coup 20 years earlier, this time in Indonesia. Suharto came into power by eliminating half a million Indonesian lives—five times the number of people killed in the Vietnam War and 500 times the number of deaths in the Tiananmen Square massacre—and later added to the tally thousands more in East Timor. Throughout Suharto's rule of more than three decades, democratic pretence was never the dictator's practice. And yet the West continued to pour economic aid into Jakarta.

During the Vietnam War, United States troops dropped bomb after bomb on the Vietnamese, creating instant clearings in the jungles. Villages were torched and their inhabitants herded into concentration camps. Defoliants and napalm, with hideous efficiency, killed Charlies and children alike in their thousands—all in the name of liberty. Nearly two million tons of bombs and 150,000 deaths later, the Vietnamese people began to wonder whose liberty they were dying for anyway.

In South Korea, Taiwan and Thailand, murderous military regimes killed their freedom fighters by day and slept soundly at night knowing that Uncle Sam watched protectively over them.

Of course, the United States was primarily concerned about the spread of communism. A chastity belt of anti-communist nations, democratic or otherwise, had to be stitched together in Asia to prevent the communist rape of the region. Asian peoples had to be protected from cruel, despotic, anti-democratic regimes of communists—even if it meant subjecting them to cruel, despotic, anti-democratic regimes of anti-communists.

The war against the communists dragged in Cambodia and Laos which were just as callously bombed. When it ended in 1973, Indochina was all red. The United States flew out its men from Saigon to escape the advancing Vietcong, and the United States Secretary of State, Henry Kissinger, went to Stockholm, incredibly, to collect his Nobel Peace Prize.

So who or what is the United States Government really trying to protect? According to George Kennan, an official in the State Department after World War II, the 'real task in the coming period is to devise a pattern of relationships which will permit us to maintain this position of disparity'—the disparity that the United States, with only 6.3% of the world's population, controls 50% of its wealth. These 'immediate national objectives,' Kennan urged, could be achieved when the United States ceased to talk about 'unreal objectives such as human rights, the raising of living standards, and democratisation.'

This goal can be easily achieved by an annual defence budget of more than 300 billion dollars, over a million armed forces personnel stationed in more than 100 countries, an alliance network with over 50 countries, and an arsenal capable of blowing this planet to smithereens. It has fought many wars, with and without its allies, and lost few. It has shipped arms and cash to its friends, and arrested the leaders of its enemies.

Then the Berlin Wall crashed and killed the Soviet Union, removing its most formidable challenger for world power. In supreme command of earthly affairs, its armies now invade other countries in suits instead of boots, carrying with them the flag of corporate America. Again, pragmatists like Henry Kissinger are in the fore, leading the investment charge into China through his consulting firm, Kissinger & Associates, which handles clients like American Express, H. J. Heinz, ITT and Lockheed. Following the Tiananmen uprising, Kissinger defended the dictators in Beijing: 'No government in the world would have tolerated having the main square of its capital occupied for eight weeks by tens of thousands of demonstrators.' But then, he forgets, no people in the world would have tolerated having its capital occupied for half a century by a couple of dictators who have killed millions of people.

The United States is not alone. The British colonised Hong Kong, Burma and Malaya, the Netherlands Indonesia, and the French Cambodia, Laos and Vietnam. Western powers, for much of the nineteenth and twentieth centuries, ruled Asia.

Then there is East Timor. The island of Timor was divided into two, one half occupied by the Dutch and the other by the Portuguese colonial governments. When Indonesia got rid of the Dutch in 1949, West Timor automatically reverted to Indonesian control. The East Timorese started fighting for independence from the Portuguese. In December 1975, however, Suharto sent his troops in to take over the territory and ended up slaughtering between one-fifth and one-third of the population of 600,000. Suharto warned everyone to stay clear of the issue and, for their own reasons, everyone did.

Particularly interesting was Australia. It seemed that the Australian embassy in Jakarta knew of the impending invasion and furtively advised its Government to be understanding because, as John Pilger wrote, 'Australia would consequently be able to exploit East Timor's huge oil and gas resources.' Pilger went on to point out: 'The terrible irony for the people of illegally occupied East Timor was that 60,000 of them had died defending Australia against the Japanese in 1942 when the Australian air force dropped leaflets that promised: "We will never forget you."' Australia remains the only country to recognise Suharto's annexation of East Timor.

And yet the West knows that its amoral pragmatic approach has limits because, if nothing else, its leaders and people will not stand for an international community devoid of moral fibre. In the United States, President Carter made human rights the 'soul' of his foreign policy and resolved to clip the feathers of repressive right-wing regimes the world over. Critics point out (and not incorrectly) that Carter's foreign policy was wrecked with controversy, the most glaring being the embassy hostage crisis in Iran which caused him to lose the 1980 presidential elections to Ronald Reagan by a landslide. (Reagan, interestingly, was alleged to have exploited the situation by striking 'a private deal with Khomeini' and promising to pay ransom to the Iranians if they would 'hold the hostages until after the election'.) Criticisms of Carter's 'naivete and inconsistency' in his fight for international human rights became increasingly louder. His support for the Shah of Iran and his muffled objections to the atrocities committed by the Park and Chun regimes in Korea came in for particularly heavy disapprobation among human rights groups.

Still, Carter maintained, he wanted foreign leaders to know that a 'significant element' in the United States's relationship with other countries would be governments 'providing basic freedoms to their peoples.' At that time it was difficult to see how the principle would translate into tangible results, as the former President acknowledged in his memoirs published in 1982:

> It will always be impossible to measure how much was accomplished by our nation's policy when the units of measurement are not inches or pounds or dollars. The lifting of the human spirit, the revival of hope, the absence of fear, the release from prison, the end of torture, the reunion of a family, the newfound sense of human dignity—these are difficult to quantify, but I am certain that many people were able to experience them because the United States of America let it be known that we stood for freedom and justice for all people.

What Carter pushed for only came to bear fruit in Asia years after he left office. It was through his efforts that Shih, Kim and Aquino were able to tear down dictatorships in their own countries and restore the democratic process. 'Carter's concerns about human rights helped tremendously,' Shih Ming-teh told me. 'Otherwise, I would have been imprisoned for many more years.' Kim Dae Jung wrote in his memoirs that 'President Jimmy Carter pressured the military junta and stopped [my] execution. But when Reagan beat Carter for the presidency, the Korean colonels were ecstatic and proclaimed, "Now, we can kill Kim Dae Jung."' When he was in Boston, Ninoy Aquino enjoyed strong support from the White House until Reagan walked in and returned the smile to Marcos's face.

In his memoirs, Carter defended his approach to foreign policy:

> There is no doubt that a few of these [dictators] could have been spared both embarrassment and the danger of being overthrown if they had strengthened themselves by eliminating the abuses. For those who did not survive, it may be that our emphasis on human rights was not wrong, but too late. Had America argued for these principles sooner, such foreign leaders might not have allowed themselves to become too isolated to correct the abuses without violence.

The experience of Ferdinand Marcos, Chun Doo Hwan and Suharto seems to have vindicated Carter's prescience.

As a result of his continued humanitarian work after his White House years, Carter today remains one of the most respected ex-presidents among Americans and has been repeatedly called upon to act as an international peace-broker.

The forceful emphasis on human rights in America's foreign policy had earlier been outlined by President Harry Truman, who announced 'that it must be the policy of the United States to support free peoples' after the ravages of World War II into which it had been reluctantly dragged. But when disinclined push came to puissant shove, America's power had saved Europe and Russia from Hitler, driven Mussolini from Africa, and forced Hirohito to withdraw from China and Southeast Asia. But even as it crushed its enemies during the War, it helped rebuild them so that today, Germany and Japan can rival it again—as economic powers.

The American people themselves are no pushovers when it comes to questions of human rights. Noam Chomsky, the country's leading linguist and activist, continues to remind his fellow citizens that 'the struggle for freedom is never over. The people of the Third World need our sympathetic understanding and, much more than that, they need our help.' Chomsky rattles the gates of Washington, calling on Americans to make 'life uncomfortable' for their own Government by 'not [being] passive and quiescent'.

So is America Seraph or Satan? Neither. It is just doing what comes naturally: being heartless, greedy, ignorant, compassionate, magnanimous and insightful. In short, being human as humans would be in any other country.

But with its capacity to influence world affairs, the United States is also like no other country, and how it acts must perforce be widely discussed, especially if its power is amassed in the hands of the few in Washington. Whether those in power believe in the hardheaded realist approach, where the means and ends are coldly calculated to advance national interests, or in the moral justification of policies, where human rights and democracy form the core of American foreign policy, world opinion, solicited or not, must matter.

Few these days believe that the United States' interests in Asia are served by right-wing autocratic regimes which claim that domestic affairs are better handled by anti-democratic principles so that stability can blissfully wed economic growth. For a moment, with the once mighty Kuomintang in full control of Taiwan's politics and economics, the late Park Chung Hee driving South Korea's economy skywards and his opponents deathwards, and Singapore as the shining example of the give-me-liberty-or-give-me-wealth syndrome, it seemed that pragmatism was the way to go. It mattered little that democratic ideals weren't being pursued in Asia as long as the countries supplied labour and material for United States businesses.

Asian autocrats told the world that there was such a thing as 'Korean style democracy', Indonesia's 'guided democracy', Singapore's 'Asian democracy' and Burma's 'disciplined democracy'. Authoritarianism, by any other name, reeks as odious. Malaysia's Prime Minister, Mahathir Mohamad, admonished that too much democracy leads to 'homosexuality, moral decay, racial intolerance, economic decline, single parent families and a lax work ethic.' Marcos warned of the 'paralysing system of checks and balances.' Lee Kuan Yew threatened to change the one-man-one-vote system and told the West 'not to foist their system indiscriminately on societies in which it will not work' (little wonder that Kissinger considers Lee to be a 'true friend of the United States'). Korea's Chun Doo Hwan predated Singapore's Lee: 'If a Western version of democracy should be transplanted in an oriental society, it will not take root.' Burma's Ohn Gyaw lectured that 'the Eastern concept of human rights is not the same as the Western concept', and Shintaro Ishihara, in a rare show of Japanese leadership, proclaimed: 'The Asia century is at hand.'

It was an intriguing theory to say the least. The region registering dizzying economic growth rates of almost 10% in the late 1980s, twice the world average. Western businessmen descended upon Asia screaming for the region's governments to take their money and make it grow. Carter's insistence that democracy and human rights take precedence in United States Asian policy seemed outrageous, out-argued and out of date.

Fast forward to 1998, and the picture takes a dramatic discolouration. With whole nations going bankrupt, how has authoritarianism ensured stability and progress? Through the years of heady economic expansion, which sceptics warned was unsustainable growth, Asia's authoritarians pretended that they actually knew what they were doing and their banks pretended that they actually had money. One such sceptic was economist Paul Krugman, who said: 'When Asian economies delivered nothing but good news, it was easy to hold such beliefs. It was easy to assume that so-called planners knew what they were doing. It is easy for government policy makers to look competent in a prosperous economy. But they may not have a clue!'

It seemed like a good, perhaps the only, idea 30 years ago to let a certain Indonesian general oust his communist leaning President. As the world looked the other way, Suharto grew less tolerant and his wallet more corpulent. Because there seemed to be this miraculous generation of wealth for the corporate world, human rights and democracy became nothing more than a mindless incantation that no one cared about. What is happening today in Indonesia is the result of unsustainable economic growth that was based on plunder and deceit.

What about Burma? 'If Burma is stable, think of what we could be doing for the region,' Aung San Suu Kyi told me during my visit to Rangoon. 'Since we're not in a position to help, it means that we are only contributing to the general depression of the area.'

Singapore, 'one of the big trees that have not been blown down' according to Lee Kuan Yew, is teetering on the brink of a recession. Singaporeans don't seem to care that their ability to remain economically viable is entirely dependent on a secretive Government that has lost billions of dollars of the country's reserves. The lack of accountability has led to a situation where the city-state's future is inextricably bound to that of Indonesia. Singaporeans, in the words of a former deputy prime minister, don't know if they are on 'thin ice or solid rock'.

In South Korea, Kim Dae Jung seems to be a stabiliser in the aftermath of the waning won. How the country emerges from the meltdown will depend on how Kim leads the Korean people and, from all accounts, he seems to have moved decisively to prevent the situation from deteriorating into turmoil on the scale of Indonesia.

Ironically, it is the *chaebol*, which once despised the liberal democrat (and perhaps still do) for his championing of workers' rights, which have run aground and, however grudgingly, are now locking to Kim to straighten out the economy. This is more painful than what the conglomerates may have expected. President Kim is now pursuing the 'mass participatory economic principle' that prisoner Kim espoused, which includes the eradication of the corrupt business-politics-banking nexus. Ever since South Korea started receiving foreign investments after the end of the Korean War, bankers and politicians have colluded to give low-rate credit to the *chaebol* which, in return, ensured that their accomplices were financially well looked after. The unwholesome relationship resulted in South Korean financial institutions being saddled with huge amounts of non-performing loans, causing several banks to close when the Asian crisis visited the country.

As an oppositionist, Kim had repeatedly criticised successive presidents for appointing retired military officials to key positions in government and quasi-government organisations in order to secure the cooperation of the army. This led to a system encumbered by patronage, so much so that when the financial crisis came, South Korea was unable to prevent itself from falling deeper into a recession than it otherwise would have.

Kim has also moved to streamline the *chaebol* and forced these massive corporations to scale back and concentrate on core business activities, enhance management transparency and increase the accountability of their owner-managers. The initiative was also aimed at giving credit-starved small and medium sized businesses a chance to compete.

Ironically, Kim Dae Jung's biggest problem as President is with the labour unions that he fought for during his years as a dissident. With massive layoffs occurring everywhere, he is faced with strikes and labour actions almost on a daily basis. Still, the President is committed to ensuring that the rights of labour movements are protected.

Chuan Leekpai, the most democratically-minded and abstemious leader that Thailand has had for a while, has been pushed back into the prime ministership by popular demand to steer the country out of its economic mess. Democratic Taiwan is holding its own, at least at the time of writing this book, even as its Asian neighbours succumb to the economic weight all around.

To draw the conclusion that democracy will restore wealth to Asia, however, is just as ingenuous as saying that authoritarianism was responsible for the heady growth in the first place. No intelligent democrat has ever claimed that democracy is the miracle cure for economic illness. But honest-to-goodness development cannot occur without democracy, any more than doughnuts can be made without dough. The idea that development should first lay the foundation for a population to understand and subsequently practise democracy is to political science what phrenology is to neuroscience.

Social scientists tell us that without human rights, 'economic growth may occur but economic development will not.' Or simply, the rich get to buy jets instead of just Jaguars, and the poor continue to live in slums. And 'even if economic rights do tend to shift resources from the richer to the poorer, this does not necessarily lead to a greater propensity to consumption, that what consumption does take place will be more conducive to production and that in any case capital accumulation by elites in developing countries tends to be concentrated offshore.' In everyday English, what Suharto did for the poor masses did not necessarily make them richer, only better equipped to make more money for the companies owned by his family and cronies, who then stashed their profits in European banks. With Indonesia now lacking in food and essential commodities—scenes reminiscent of the 1960s when Sukarno was President—economic development clearly hasn't progressed very much. Similarly, development in Burma is almost imperceptible.

America has many enemies in the world. Democrats in Asia are not among them. But if the United States continues to treat Asia as a source for raw materials and a market for its products without concerning itself with the democratic development of the region, it will unavoidably alienate Asian peoples. The 'keep away' signs that Asian authoritarians put up for meddling democrats from the West belie the fact that Western governments are already deeply involved in the politics of such countries when aid money is used, directly or otherwise, to suppress internal democratic movements. When authoritarians stop the West from interfering in their domestic politics with one hand, how many of them are not asking for aid, either in cash or through trade, with the other? An exasperated Kim Dae Jung exclaimed while he was in exile, 'If only the United States would stop helping the dictators, the people could do the rest.'

When the needs of governments and peoples become polarised, progress cannot continue for long. Political chickens, if the lesson hasn't been already learned, have this habit of coming home to roost. And when development does take place, democracy doesn't necessarily follow, as shown in the case of Singapore, where the Government remains unapologetic about its authoritarian ways. Worse, after more than 30 years of development, the ruling elite now argues that the progress that has been made will 'perish' or 'be finished' with the advent of democracy. It's back to the future.

If there is a genuine belief (and all signatories to the United Nation Human Rights Declaration in 1949 would claim there is) that dissidents should not be tortured and killed for opposing their governments, then the West must also realise that Asian peoples will not live quietly under subjugation, first by the colonialists and now by their own governments. And if Western governments do not wish for a world insuperably dichotomised into antagonistic regions, then they must also accept that Asian peoples, just like Westerners, long for freedom and security. Anti-American sentiment has repeatedly lashed through Asia because the United States Government is often perceived as exploiting the region and subjecting people to conditions that it would not even think of imposing on its own citizens.

With the end of the Cold War and an increasingly intricate global interdependency, it makes little sense for any country to talk about national interests instead of international interests. The Golden Rule of 'doing unto others what you would have others do unto you' may not be as sentimentally nonsensical as hardnosed politicians think. We conclude erroneously, writes Anwar Ibrahim, that 'by pursuing selfish interests we somehow contribute to the safety and progress of all. Ethics and morality are scoffed at as intrusions of the unrealistic into the cold-blooded affairs of the state.'

On the other hand, if human rights form the bedrock of United States policy on Asia, and indeed anywhere in the world, people will reciprocate the goodwill in the long term. American idealism and hardheadedness, whichever way one looks at them, cannot remain as two sides of a coin, but must instead melt into a single, inseparable currency through which politics can be elevated to a nobler plane where all humanity is cared for. For its own sake, humanity must rid itself of the East versus West mentality.

I borrowed *The Voice of Asia* from the library and noticed that beside the paragraph where Mahathir Mohamad had written, 'It is even fair to say that tolerance is a typically Asian quality. Indeed, it is the core of the Eastern way of thinking, so unlike the Western predisposition to impose, by force if necessary, one's own point of view on others,' some wit had scribbled an incredulous '*What?*' West bad, East good. That is the general thesis of the book, which, of course, raises the ire of those under Mahathir's fire.

On the other side of the world, Max Weber, the German philosopher, insisted that Chinese civilisation got nowhere because of its dependence on Confucian thought. This same Confucian civilisation had already shaped cast iron to make axes, spades, chisels and hoes in the first century. The technique of making steel, employed by present-day companies such as Siemens-Martin, first took place during the Han dynasty. Paper which enables Bill Gates to disseminate his Microsoft instruction manuals, was invented almost 2,000 years ago by a castrated Cai Lun. Chinese astronomers documented sunspots, noted Halley's comet and charted the celestial heavens centuries before Galileo was born. Machines that could extract brine 2,000 feet below the ground were in operation around the time of Christ's birth. The first dissection of a cadaver to measure and weigh the entrails occurred hundreds of years before sixteenth century French philosopher Rene Descartes attempted to explain human movement.

From paper to porcelain, silk to stirrups, compass to coins to canals, winnowing machines to wheelbarrows, fireworks to flotillas, Chinese minds were at the cutting edge of what is now ancient technology. As Francis Bacon was to note, the three Chinese inventions—printing, gunpowder and the compass—'have changed the whole face and state of things throughout the world.' It is not doubted that modern technology from the West is indebted to Chinese contributions to science. By the time Westerners learned from Asia to enter into the Renaissance and Reformation periods in the fourteenth century, the East had already undergone development for two millennia.

In return, the West has given to the world modern science and democracy, which have made life much more orderly and comfortable. As the West learned from the East, now must the East reciprocate the honourable endeavour.

What has made the West so successful is not only its ability to dominate the world through capitalism but also (and primarily) by its understanding of the power of the scientific method. Having understood the great moment of the Chinese inventions, Bacon presciently declared that 'knowledge itself is power'.

Asian countries have been lured by the bright lights of capitalism and consumerism in the West without adequately understanding the pains that were needed to bring about the success—the pains of educating its masses, not just to read and score wonders in mathematics contests, but in the powerful process of discovery and learning. The Singapore Government, for example, continues to talk about the upgrading of workers' skills but, conspicuously, not their minds. Asian governments scrambled to attract computer making companies, set up trading systems that moved dollars by the billions (though few of them understood the workings and mechanisms of the markets) and hocked their land insatiably. Ironically, it is the West, and in particular Australia, which has the most established research institutions in the academic field of Asian studies.

Inquiry is going to be the staple of success in the future. What the authoritarians want is riches from the West without the rocking of their power base. To a certain extent, wealth can be generated in this manner because technology is easy to use and even easier to produce. The mass production of commodities, however, goes only as far as the mass infusion of capital. Economies without a culture of learning and innovation go bust; worse, they find it hard to regenerate themselves when investors don't hang around.

Politics is dirty and politicians are all the same.

Such cynicism by the masses will transform percept into precept if ethics continues to be teased away from politics. As capitalism sweeps the world, the tendency is, for those living under autocratic regimes, to recoil from engaging their ruling elites and bow their heads before the altar of the GNP. The political stability from such situations is transient and fragile. When economies stumble, as they have in Asia, the dislocation between the rulers and the ruled will result in painful upheavals, as they have in Asia.

The pursuit of material wealth must not be carried out at the expense of human rights. At the moment, however, autocrats are burning the Asian candle with capitalism from one end and authoritarianism from the other, leaving the people with the charred remains of the worst of two worlds.

Politics is only as good or as bad as the people who practice it. And politicians will all be the same only if those who wish differently remain pusillanimous in mind and parsimonious in energy.

Let those who seek the democratic process come forward and speak out loudly, not merely whisper it. Let the industrialised world engage the developing world on the basis of what is right and wrong, not merely capitalise on it. Let politics reconcile with ethics, not merely patronise it.

In Asia, the 1990s will be remembered for economic turmoil. There is little doubt that the crisis will pass. As the restructuring of the region's devastated fiscal system takes place, much talk has been centred on getting the 'fundamentals' right, fundamentals such as keeping up high savings rates, regulating financial systems and opening up markets. If the havoc of high stakes economic poker has taught Asia anything, it is that the most important of all fundamentals—to nurture people before profits, environment before investment, democracy before deals—have not been given enough prominence. If there must be a set of Asian values, let it not be for the kinds in stockmarkets. Instead, let it be for the ideals of wisdom and harmony. If priorities remain right-side up, then riches—both in spirit and in kind—will follow.

As sure as Asia will recover from its present turmoil, Asian authoritarians will continue to subject their political opponents to jail and torture. It cannot, therefore, be said that the struggle of the Aung San Suu Kyis, Ninoy Aquinos, Chia Thye Pohs, Kim Dae Jungs, Shih Ming-tehs and Pramoedya Ananta Toers will end soon. But when it does end, there is not a shred of doubt in my mind as to who will emerge victorious, for the human spirit can only be suppressed, never crushed.

Reference notes

Prologue

1 'Friday,' said Robin Crusoe—Rosen and Widgery 1991, 208.

Taiwan

7 'Nori! They're here to arrest you!'—Lee 1993, 294-300.

9 Shih Ming-teh was born—*An Introduction of Shih Ming-teh of Taiwan* 1995, 1.

9 The Portuguese had named Taiwan—Lee 1993, 6-12.

9 His name 'teh'—Lee 1993, 6-12.

9 When he was four—Lee 1993, 6-12.

10 Led by General Chen Yi—Jacobs July 1993, 116; Lee 1993, 17-19. A detailed account of the Republican movement in Taiwan is given in Shu 1996, *Taiwan History After World War II*.

11 When he was six years old— *An Introduction of Shih Ming-teh of Taiwan* 1995, 3.

11 With martial law, political parties— *An Introduction of Shih Ming-teh of Taiwan* 1995, 3.

12 'When we were in school'—Hsiao Li-rong December 1997, personal communication.

12 'make a glorious return to the mainland'—*Newsweek* 1 November 1982, 10.

13 The 2-2-8 Incident had lit the flame—Lee 1993, 21-45.

13 In his high school days— *An Introduction of Shih Ming-teh of Taiwan* 1995, 4.

14 In 1962 at the age of 21— *An Introduction of Shih Ming-teh of Taiwan* 1995, 5; Lee 1993, 49-92.

18 To many people—Lee 1993, 49.

19 Taiyuan prison is a concrete—Lee 1993, 93-110.

20 His mother passed away in 1968— *An Introduction of Shih Ming-teh of Taiwan* 1995, 6.

21 'This is the only real family life'— *An Introduction of Shih Ming-teh of Taiwan* 1995, 7.

21 On 8 February 1970— *An Introduction of Shih Ming-teh of Taiwan* 1995, 7-8; Lee 1993, 110-119.

23 Taiwan's economy was expanding—*Newsweek* 1 November 1982, 13.

24 'We do not have political prisoners here'—*Newsweek* 1 November 1982, 14.

24 Following his release— *An Introduction of Shih Ming-teh of Taiwan* 1995, 8-9.

25 It was now even more difficult—Lee 1993, 121-138.
27 Nixon's visit to China in February 1972—Jacobs July 1993, 118.
27 Japan, with the tacit acquiescence—Jacobs July 1993, 118.
27 In April 1975, Chiang Kai-shek—*An Introduction of Shih Ming-teh of Taiwan* 1995, 9.
28 In the meantime, Vice-President Yen Chia-kan—Jacobs July 1993 , 121.
28 stepped aside for Chiang Ching-kuo—*Asiaweek* 20 January 1978, 22.
28 Hsu wanted to go places—*Newsweek* 5 December 1977, 9.
28 'I won't be campaigning'—*Newsweek* 5 December 1977, 9.
28 On polling day— *An Introduction of Shih Ming-teh of Taiwan* 1995, 12.
28 This triggered an angry protest—Jacobs 1981, 27.
29 On 16 June 1977— *An Introduction of Shih Ming-teh of Taiwan* 1995, 10.
29 Before he left—Lee 1993, 151-171.
30 'You say you suffered'— *An Introduction of Shih Ming-teh of Taiwan* 1995, 10.
30 'I won back my confidence'— *An Introduction of Shih Ming-teh of Taiwan* 1995, 11.
30 Following the win—Lee 1993, 173-175
30 The booklets also caught— *An Introduction of Shih Ming-teh of Taiwan* 1995, 14-18.
32 At two in the morning—*Newsweek* 1 January 1979, 6.
33 'the entire free world'—*Time* 25 December 1978, 8.
33 Meanwhile, Shih had come—Lee 1993, 211.
33 'We used to conduct'—Yao Chia-wen November 1995, personal communication.
34 By the late 1970s, the *dangwai*—Jacobs 1981, 38.
34 On 10 December 1979—*Asiaweek* 4 April 1980, 14.
34 'If I have to sit in jail'—Lee 1993, 288.
35 'Where to, mister?'—Lee 1993, 301-339.
38 The Reverend Kao Jun-ming—*Asiaweek* 11 July 1980, 28.
38 'Christian love and sympathy'—*Asiaweek* 30 May 1980, 19.
38 Lin Yi-hsiung's wife—A detailed account of the Lin murders is given in *Ten Years of Life and Death* 1991.
39 Seventeen years after the murders—Lin Yi-hsiung December 1997, personal communication.
39 He was elected Chairman—*The Straits Times* 9 June 1998.
40 'It was a very dark period in Taiwan'—Bruce Jacobs March 1998, personal communication.
41 Foremost on their minds—*Asiaweek* 11 April 1980, 12.

41 'not to act recklessly outside'—*Asiaweek* 11 April 1980, 12.
41 'At that point'—*Asiaweek* 4 April 1980, 14.
41 Annette Lu Shiu-lien—*Asiaweek* 4 April 1980, 14.
42 Yao Chia-wen repeated—*Asiaweek* 4 April 1980, 14.
42 'give me the death sentence'—*Asiaweek* 11 April 1980, 12.
42 Less than three years—Lee 1993, 357-368.
43 Chiang Ching-kuo called for elections—*Asiaweek* 12 December 1980, 20.
43 It began with the visit—*Asiaweek* 31 July 1981, 14.
43 'could have committed suicide'—*Asiaweek* 31 July 1981, 14.
44 He revealed that Chen—*Asiaweek* 31 July 1981, 14.
44 On 15 October 1984—Lee 1993, 374-382.
46 Hsu put together a committed—*An Introduction of Shih Ming-teh of Taiwan* 1995, 25.
46 In September 1986—*An Introduction of Shih Ming-teh of Taiwan* 1995, 25.
47 Former journalist Cheng Nan-rong—A detailed account Cheng's fight with the Kuomintang Government is given in *For the Love of Taiwan* 1992.
48 On 20 May 1990—Lee 1993, 1-2.
49 'The most difficult part'—Shih Ming-teh December 1997, personal communication.
50 In every era—Shih 1990, 170.
51 I have not come here—Shih 1992, 183-188.

Burma

56 While Ne Win was an incorrigible gambler—Lintner 1990, 22.
56 There he formed the bluntly named—Lintner 1990, 24.
56 The British Prime Minister—Lintner 1990, 24.
56 General elections were held—Lintner 1990, 25.
57 But, like many youthful leaders—Lintner 1990, 26.
57 The widow reluctantly—Lintner 1990, 108-109.
57 On 26 August 1988—Lintner 1990, 115.
58 'During my visits to Rangoon'—Clements 1997, 98-99.
58 'I'm just the sort of person'—Clements 1997, 98-99.
58 'I only ask one thing'—Clements 1997, 151.
59 'fine porcelain, a beauty'—Clements 1997, xvi.
59 'The present crisis'—Lintner 1990, 115.
60 That day was Saturday—Lintner 1990, 1-9.
64 The ethnic minorities—A detailed account of Burma's ethnic insurgency is given in Smith 1991; and Lintner 1994.
64 The mansion is protected by soldiers—Sesser 1993, 188.
64 A licentious man with a libido—Sesser 1993, 188.

65 Astrology and numerology—Lintner 1990, 62.
65 While travelling from the airport—Smith 1991, 431.
66 By the mid-1980s Burma—Smith 1991, 24.
66 Overnight, the old notes—Smith 1991, 25-26.
66 They finally pontificated—Sesser 1993, 205.
67 On 23 July 1988—Sesser 1993, 208.
68 Sein Lwin, nicknamed the 'Butcher'—Lintner 1990, 88.
68 In 1974 Thant—Lintner 1990, 52.
69 The students knew—Lintner 1990, 87-105.
71 As suddenly as it had erupted—Lintner 1990, 107.
72 Aung Gyi was as puzzling—Sesser 1993, 225.
73 With no scheme too contemptible—Lintner 1990, 121.
74 'Get off the road!' the captain ordered—Clements 1997, 25.
74 'The point is that demonstrations'—Sesser 1993, 231.
74 On another occasion—Clements 1997, 215.
75 He ordered soldiers—Lintner 1990, 120.
75 Earthen containers that provided—Lintner 1990, 121.
76 Arsonists went on a burning spree—Lintner 1990, 122.
76 The question was answered—Lintner 1990, 131.
76 Next day, machine guns—Lintner 1990, 133.
77 [The furnace] was supposed—Webb 1993, 7.
77 Myint (not his real name).
79 To make room for—Sesser 1993, 234.
79 Former Prime Minister Nu—Lintner 1990, 125.
79 The NLD won 392 of the 485 seats—Clements 1997, xv.
80 'only the SLORC has the right'—Lintner 1994, 309.
80 The most likely explanation—Sesser 1993, 235.
80 it was the monks' turn—Lintner 1994, 311.
81 The SLORC seized the opportunity—Ibid.
81 Those who escaped made—Lintner 1994, 319.
81 Naw Mya Thaung—Webb 1993, 20.
82 Private Maung Po Pain— Webb 1993, 20.
82 In order to maintain—Lintner 1990, 140.
83 'never even applied for such a permit'— Lintner 1990, 140.
83 The first country to come—Selth 1995, 4.
83 'domestic phone, fax and e-mail lines'—*Bangkok Post* 17 October 1997, internet communication.
84 'thought to be training'—A detailed account of Singapore's involvement in arms transactions and military relations with the Burmese army is given in Selth September/October 1997, 5; *Jane's Intelligence Review* March 1998, 32-34.
84 'My first visit to Rangoon'—Lintner 1990, 140.
84 'non-interference in the internal affairs'—Maung 1992, 189.
84 Petroleum companies—Lintner 1990, 178.

84 Sein Lwin's son and relatives'—Maung 1992, 236.
85 'has direct business interests'— Maung 1992, 236.
85 'So it is no surprise'—*The New York Times* 20 October 1991.
86 'You know, I've never'—Clements 1997, 10.
87 'I liked most of them as human'—Clements 1997, 104.
87 In Buddhism, as you know—Clements 1997, 127.
87 I remind people that *karma*—Clements 1997, 124.
87 'People must ask questions'—Clements 1997, 40.
87 'Complacency is very dangerous'—Clements 1997, 124.
88 But what impressed me most—Clements 1997, 167.
88 On the morning of her arrest in 1989—Clements 1997, 100.
88 As a mother—Clements 1997, 102.
89 During the years of her house arrest—Clements 1997, 104.
89 Hunger strike—Clements 1997, 180.
89 Aung San Suu Kyi takes pains—Pantoja-Hidalgo 1991, 119.
90 I read somewhere—Clements 1997, 131-132.
90 On 10 July 1995—Clements 1997, 184.
91 Before the massacre in 1988—Lintner 1990, 147.
91 The Kuomintang soldiers—The relationship between the Kuomintang troops and the ethnic states vis-a-vis the production of drugs is detailed in Lintner 1994, 239-271.
92 By agreeing to stop the fighting—Accounts of drug trafficking and money laundering by Burma's druglords are given in *Asiaweek* 23 January 1997, internet communication; *The Nation* 20 October 1997, 11-16; *Covert Action Quarterly* Spring 1998, 45-51.
93 'It's ridiculous'—Sein Lwin 1995, personal communication.
93 'over half [of the investments in Burma]'—*The Nation* 20 October 1997, 13-14.
93 'without whose support and encouragement'—*Covert Action Quarterly* Spring 1998, 48.
93 'a majority of the shareholders'—*The Nation* 24 November 1997, internet communication.
94 Months later on 24 July 1998—Unpublished news release 31 August 1998, internet communication.

Indonesia

101 Lieutenant-General Achmad Yani—May 1978, 95-96.
102 Five other military generals—May 1978, 98-100.
103 Untung was later tried—May 1978, 139.
104 The influence of a mixture—May 1978, 9-12.
105 He was enrolled in a private school—Pramoedya 1995, 1-2.
105 In 1942, before he could complete—Pramoedya, 'Silent Song of a Mute'.

106 'The Japanese Are Your Elder Brothers'—*The New Yorker* 1996, 3.
106 Pramoedya sought the shelter—James 1996, 3.
106 With the paltry salary he earned—Pramoedya, 'Silent Song of a Mute'.
106 Pramoedya seized the opportunity—*The New Yorker* 1996, 4.
107 Prison had failed to arrest—Pramoedya, 'Silent Song of a Mute'.
107 Pramoedya witnessed the full glory—Pramoedya, 'Silent Song of a Mute'.
109 part-god, part-man—Bloodworth 1992, 156.
109 The PKI grew in strength—May 1978, 113.
109 Sukarno's bitter experience—May 1978, 78.
109 It was at this time that Sukarno—May 1978, 82-83.
110 Suspecting that the British—May 1978, 87.
110 The British embassy in Jakarta—May 1978, 93.
110 'They must be smashed immediately'—May 1978, 120.
111 Many observers at that time—A more detailed analysis of the possible reasons and players in the putsch is given in May, 91-128; Kingsbury 1998.
112 Following the 30 September putsch—The political struggle between Sukarno and Suharto is described in May 1978, 129-159.
114 One of the targeted—Pramoedya November 1991, 6.
114 Lekra seemed an appropriate vehicle—Pramoedya 1995, 5.
114 In 1960, he wrote *Hoakiau di Indonesia*—Pramoedya 1995, 2.
114 '[Sukarno] was capable of creating'—Pramoedya 1995, 4.
115 Between 1983 and 1984—Heryanto 1993, p. 37.
115 'Why flee?'—*Indonesia Reports* August 1986, 3.
119 'Now don't think I have'—*Indonesia Reports* August 1986, 5.
119 That night, the room—*Inside Indonesia* October 1990, 2.
119 The number of detainees—*Indonesia Reports* August 1986, 3-7.
121 *Adri XV*, a 300,000 tonne ship—Pramoedya, 'Silent Song of a Mute'.
124 Experienced farmers and young men—May 1978, 37.
124 The penal complex housed—Pramoedya, 'Silent Song of a Mute'.
138 Critics were often made to pay—May 1978, 215.
138 'How much [rice] went'—May 1978, 405.
139 'Let me first say that I am happy'—Pramoedya, 'Silent song of a Mute'.
146 'a dam breaking'—James 1996, 2.
146 'Hugo and Dostoyevski are the writers'—James 1996, 8.

147 His name has been on the lips—*The New Straits Times* 21 August 1996, 1.
147 In 1995 he won—*Indonesia* 1996, 6.
139 'led the oppression'—*International Press Service* 10 August 1995, 1.
147 'It was indeed fierce'—*Indonesia Reports* August 1986, 2; Interview 1997, 1.
147 The murmuring found its way—Heryanto 1993, 93.
148 Talk about the impending release—Pramoedya, 'Silent song of a Mute'.
151 His political demise—*Asiaweek* 24 July 1998, 30-41.
152 'man was not born'—Radio Netherland Interview, *Weekend Focus* 1995, 1.
152 'I don't think that'—Pramoedya October 1997, personal communication.

Philippines

155 It was Saturday—Salonga 1998, unpublished manuscript; Crisostomo 1987, 66.
156 'I still have more than'—Salonga February 1998, personal communication.
157 'an unmitigated crime'—Daza, Abad, Florencio and Angeles 1996, 54.
157 Aquino replied that—Daza, Abad, Florencio and Angeles 1996, 57-58.
157 For good measure—Crisostomo 1987, 67.
158 The television appearance—*Far Eastern Economic Review* 4 September 1971, 18.
158 Goons, guns and gold—Burton 1989, 65-66.
158 'Ninoy could not only talk'—Anonymous source November 1997, personal communication.
159 'Ninoy could talk'—Tess Oreta November 1997, personal communication.
159 As a 17-year-old journalist—Soliven 1984, 8.
159 He was put in charge—Crisostomo 1987, 46.
159 he later died in a plane crash—Daza, Abad, Florencio and Angeles 1996, 36.
159 Aquino senior died—Benigno 1993, 11.
160 became the youngest mayor—Soliven 1984, 9.
160 Tarlac was shorn of all funds—Soliven 1984, 9.
160 The Liberal Party was founded—Daza, Abad, Florencio and Angeles 1996, 3.
160 In 1963, President Macapagal—Burton 1989, 63.
161 And what better way—Burton 1989, 65.

161 Aquino realised that Marcos—Soliven 1984, 10.
161 He took to the streets— Soliven 1984, 10.
162 When the campaign began—Benigno 1993, 14.
162 One of them concerned—Burton 1989, 70.
163 'a 50 million peso cultural centre'—Burton 1989, 71.
163 Discontent with the administration—Crisostomo 1987, 60.
163 'We should allow'— Daza, Abad, Florencio and Angeles 1996, 46.
164 Marcos suspended habeas corpus—Crisostomo 1987, 66.
164 'was trying to create an atmosphere'—Burton 1989, 82.
164 At about the same time—Burton 1989, 82.
164 'Mr Marcos, if I die'—Soliven 1984, 11.
165 Then one night—Burton 1989, 84.
165 'imperilled by the danger'—Crisostomo 1987, 71.
165 It happened on 23 September 1972—Burton 1989, 87.
166 When he was still a law student—Burton 1989, 37-39.
167 Marcos was drafted to defend Bataan—Burton 1989, 42.
167 The months following—*Newsweek* 3 November 1975, 6.
167 Economic confidence returned—Burton 1989, 89.
167 This so impressed—*Newsweek* 3 November 1975, 6.
167 One afternoon—Ninoy 1983, 3-5.
169 The families of Aquino and Diokno—Burton 1989, 91-93.
170 Sirs, I know you—Ninoy 1983, 20-21.
171 in protest against a procedure—Ninoy 1983, 36.
171 I know I have caused—Ninoy 1983, 45.
171 As the days passed—Benigno 1993, 24.
172 His family and closest friends—Burton 1989, 97.
172 Sentence: death by firing squad—Soliven 1984, 12.
172 Marcos even allowed Aquino—Burton 1989, 102-104.
173 'Ingrates! Let them vote'—*Newsweek* 24 April 1978, 6.
173 Suddenly, blessing came—Benigno 1993, 27.
174 'It helped me these last seven years'—*Newsweek* 19 May 1980, 8.
174 'A week ago I was in my cell'—*Newsweek* 19 May 1980, 8.
174 Aquino then went to Boston—Crisostomo 1987, 79-83.
175 Back in Manila, a storm was brewing—*Newsweek* 18 August 1980, 6.
175 The more militant groups—Burton 1989, 108.
176 'He was profoundly'—Tess Oreta November 1997, personal communication.
176 'I believe that unfortunately history'—*Newsweek* 15 August 1983, 50.
176 He ventured to Saudi Arabia—Burton 1989, 110.
176 'a pact with the devil was no pact at all'—Benigno 1993, 31.

177 I have decided to pursue—Ninoy 1983, 60.
177 'I've met with men and women'—*Newsweek* 18 August 1980, 7.
177 Barely a month later—*Newsweek* 3 November 1980, 24.
177 'Mad Bomber'—Soliven 1984, 13.
177 Under Carter—Burton 1989, 16.
178 'Carter refused'—Raul Manglapus November 1997, personal communication.
178 'democratic principles'—Burton 1989, 111.
179 'violence would develop'—Ninoy 1983, 56.
179 'Since you were the one'—Burton 1989, 11.
180 On 13 August 1983—Crisostomo 1987, 95.
180 The flight took him—Burton 1989, 113.
181 As before, Cory read —Crisostomo 1987, 96.
182 I put on a big smile—Burton 1989, 28.
183 It was 11.15 a.m.—Burton 1989, 29.
184 His gaze had turned—Burton 1989, 31.
185 As the plane started its descent—A detailed account of Aquino's assassination is given in Burton 1989, 32-35; Hill and Hill 1983, 25-52.
186 Back in Boston—Crisostomo 1984, 99.
188 The room was packed—A detailed account of the investigation of Aquino's assassination is given in *Reports of the Fact-Finding Board* 1984.
192 A horde of media personnel—Burton 1989, 263.
193 True to his word—Burton 1989, 305.
193 In Manila, when they—Tess Oreta November 1997, personal communication.
194 Cory took the lonely flight—Burton 1989, 138.
194 During the days of Aquino's—Burton 1989, 133.
194 '49 million cowards'—Benigno 1993, 20.
194 As Aquino's body lay—Benigno 1993, 3-8.
194 'The mass has ended'—Burton 1989, 143.

South Korea

197 Kim was born in 1925—Kim 1996, 9.
197 His father was a kindly man—Kim 1996, 3.
197 The history of Korea's—*Korea in Focus* 1998, 2.
198 Two colonels—Cumings 1997, 187.
198 In June 1950—A detailed account of the Korean War is given in Stueck 1995.
199 Rhee had spent—Cumings 1997, 195.
199 After the war—Cumings 1997, 195.
199 When the election—Cumings 1997, 212.

200 Democratically installed—Cumings 1997, 340-346.
200 The Government was left—Cumings, 347.
200 'which may have included'—Cumings 1997, 350.
200 Immediately after the coup—Cumings 1997, 350.
201 Kim had become—Kim 1996, 175.
201 In order to avoid conscription—Kim 1996, 5.
201 In 1954 he ran unsuccessfully—Kim 1996, 176.
202 'Be brave and fight!'—Kim 1996, 129.
202 In 1962 Kim married Lee Hee Ho—Kim 1996, 129.
203 in selected industries—Cumings 1997, 316.
203 'could work a crowd'—Cumings 1997, 316.
203 'generalissimo system'—*Newsweek* 10 May 1971, 18.
203 and not a little vote buying—Cumings 1998, 361.
205 'The opposition has charged'—*The People vs. Park Chung Hee* 1976, 82.
205 On 8 August 1973— Kim 1996, 136; *Newsweek* 20 August 1973, 10; *Newsweek* 27 August 1973, 11; Kim 1994, 30; *Korea Scope* March 1983, 34-35.
206 'if [the United States]'—*Time* 2 March 1998, 20-21.
206 'Don't move for three minutes'—*Newsweek* 27 August 1973, 11.
207 the first secretary—Cumings 1997, 362.
207 The agency was a product—Cumings 1997, 363.
207 At its most fearsome—*Newsweek* 8 October 1973, 13.
207 'campaigning prior'—*The People vs Park Chung Hee* 1976, 79.
207 'making a false charge'—*The People vs Park Chung Hee* 1976, 79.
207 'generalissimo regime'—*The People vs Park Chung Hee* 1976, 79.
208 the GNP bounded to $7.2 billion—*Time* 10 May 1971, 29.
208 'every straw-thatched home in Korea'— *Time* 10 May 1971, 29.
208 He cited the raging conflict—Cumings 1997, 359.
209 Decree no. 9 of 1974—Cumings 1997, 358.
209 The *Dong-A Ilbo*—Ogle 1977, 99-102; *The People vs Park Chung Hee* 1976, 86.
210 whom Park accused—Ogle 1977, 94-98.
210 'This time we'll scare'—Ogle 1977, 99.
210 'Korean-style democracy'—Cumings 1997, 359.
210 Prisoners were electrically shocked—*Report of an Amnesty International Mission to The Republic of Korea (27 March–9 April 1975)* 1977, 28.
211 A concert pianist—Cumings 1997, 366.
211 In 1978 about 70 textile workers—Ogle 1990, 85-87.
211 The 'largest single gift'—Ogle 1977, 87.

211 But by the late 1970s—*Newsweek* 12 Nov 1979, 17; *Newsweek* 16 February 1981, 11.
212 Park Chung Hee was delivering—*Newsweek* 26 August 1974, 11.
212 The gunman was 22-year-old—*The People vs. Park Chung Hee* 1976, 54.
213 The ballistic records—*The People vs. Park Chung Hee* 1976, 55.
213 'jetted back to Seoul'—*The People vs. Park Chung Hee* 1976, 58.
213 The less salacious rumours—*The People vs. Park Chung Hee* 1976, 56.
213 'were paid by the Seoul government'—*The People vs. Park Chung Hee* 1976, 11.
214 On 1 March 1976—*Newsweek* 26 May 1980, 10.
214 'Long Live Democracy!'—*Newsweek* 14 March 1977, 19.
214 'nation-ruining plot'—*Newsweek* 17 May 1976, 17.
214 'Democracy in Korea is crucified!'—*Newsweek* 17 May 1976, p. 17.
214 During the trial itself—*Korea Scope* March 1983, 36.
215 'I want an opposition party'—*Newsweek* 2 August 1976, 13.
216 Your Blood—*Korea Communiqué*, 20 October 1979, 26.
217 I want to identify with the oppressed—Kim Chi Ha 1978, 18-19.
217 On 26 October 1979—*Newsweek* 5 November 1979, 10; *Newsweek* 19 November 1979, 22.
217 'How can we conduct our policies'—Cumings 1997, 374.
218 He called for Kim Chae Gyu's trial—*Korea Communiqué* 15 July 1980, 47.
218 'be given the post of commander-in-chief'—*Newsweek* 10 December 1979, 21.
218 A month later Chun Doo Hwan—*Newsweek* 24 December 1979, 6; Cumings 1997, 375.
218 Following his grab of political leadership—*Newsweek* 25 August 1980, 7.
218 'It is time to Koreanize democracy'—*Newsweek* 25 August 1980, 6.
218 More than 170 newspapers—*Newsweek* 25 August 1980, 17.
219 Limping, with a cane in one hand—*Newsweek* 8 January 1979, 7.
219 On 14 May 1980—Kim 1996, 44.
219 'to leave politics'—*Newsweek* 26 May 1980, 11.
220 'If you had not scrapped'—Kim 1996, 46.
220 In Kwangju, the struggle—*Korea Communiqué* 15 July 1980, 5-34.
221 'If you try to hide'—*Korea Communiqué* 15 July 1980, 21.

221 'Please, please leave this area'—*Korea Communiqué* 15 July 1980, 21.
221 'Students and citizens'—*Korea Communiqué* 15 July 1980, 22.
222 'This police station'—*Korea Communiqué* 15 July 1980, 29.
222 156 page indictment—*Republic of Korea: Violations of human rights* 1981, 14.
222 A two hour documentary—*Newsweek* 8 September 1980, 11.
222 Local newspapers—*Korea Herald* 5 July 1980.
223 Meanwhile, in an underground cell—*Newsweek* 22 Sept 1980, 8.
223 For more than two—*South Korea: Violations of Human Rights* 1986, 71-74.
224 In prison, his interrogators—Kim 1994, 219.
224 There were vague references—Kim 1996, 34.
224 'I am a Christian'—*Asiaweek* 26 Sept 1980, 10.
224 Kim, 'an agitator-politician'—*Newsweek* 22 Sept 1980, 8.
224 When I stood at the bar—Kim 1996, 121.
225 'Even if I die'—*Asiaweek* 26 Sept 1980, 10.
225 'As my death seemed to draw nearer'—*Korea Scope* March 1983, 36.
225 'even if I were killed by Chun Doo Hwan'—*Korea Scope* March 1983, 36.
225 Kim's life now depended on clemency—*Newsweek* 25 August 1980, 8.
225 We talked about what was being done—Carter 1982, 578.
226 Richard von Weizsacker—Kim 1996, 122.
226 The German foreign minister—*Newsweek* 29 Sept 1980, 6.
226 Only weeks earlier—*Newsweek* 8 Sept 1980, 11.
226 Chun quickly got down to doing—Cumings 1997, 379.
226 'Kim Dae Jung was a dead man'—*Time*, 2 March 1998, 21.
226 He finally relented—*Korea Communiqué* 1 March 1981, 31.
227 Chun promptly declared—*Newsweek* 16 Feb 1981, 11.
227 'shrewdly used Kim's death sentence'—The Nation 1998, 17.
227 Within 48 hours of Reagan's— *Korea Scope* March 1983, 44-45; *Far Eastern Economic Review* 7 February 1985, 39.
227 The local press made sure—Kim 1996, 122.
227 Kim was incarcerated in Chongju Prison—Kim 1996, 107.
227 His hair was shaven—Kim 1996, 122.
227 A little window—Kim 1996, 108.
228 A few weeks after his—*Move*, date unknown, 83.
228 His arthritis plagued him—*Aiusa Matchbox* 1983, 3.
228 Totally cut off from civilisation— *Aiusa Matchbox* 1983, 3.
228 Kim started to carry on— *Aiusa Matchbox* 1983, 2.
228 'My faith in God'— *Aiusa Matchbox* 1983, 2.

229 'spiritual fulfilment and elevation'—Kim 1996, 109.
229 His second right—Kim 1996, 110.
229 The third pleasure—Kim 1996, 110.
229 On the wooden floor—Kim 1996, 111.
230 Kim used his hour of exercise—Kim 1996, 111-112.
230 'filled with dozens and dozens of clocks'—Kim 1996, 113.
230 'That this flower has bloomed'—Kim 1996, 113.
231 Kim was still under heavy guard—*Washington Post* 24 December 1982.
231 Hours later, the Chun regime—*The New York Times* 25 December 1982.
231 'The main object of my'—*Washington Post* 26 December 1982.
231 Not only did Reagan ignore—*Newsweek* 16 February 1981, 10.
231 'Even if I couldn't come out'—*Washington Post* 26 December 1982.
232 'In reality, America has helped'—*The New York Times* 26 December 1982.
232 'we must have peace with'—*The New York Times* 26 December 1982.
232 'my wife believes in the same ideals'—Seiden, journal unknown.
232 He had asked his—*Far Eastern Economic Review* 7 February 1985, 37.
233 'return will be trouble-free'—*Far Eastern Economic Review* 25 October 1984, 38.
233 Kim Dae Jung returned in—Cumings 1997, 381.
234 The hawkish generals—*Far Eastern Economic Review* 25 October 1984, 38.
234 If the military saw Kim as poison—Cumings 1998, 20.
234 'I will have earth cover my eyes'—Cumings 1997, 328.
234 'ten families control 60 per cent'—Cumings 1997, 330.
235 University students have always—*Newsweek* 2 June 1980, 9.
235 'best organised and most articulate'—*Newsweek* 2 June 1980, 9.
235 Through the 1980s—Cumings 1997, 387.
235 Having amassed a kingly fortune— Cumings 1997, 387.
235 As protests grew—Cumings 1997, 388.
236 To make sure that he—Cumings 1997, 390.
236 With his new found freedom—Lee 1990, 58.
236 In the 1987 presidential elections—Lee 1990, 85.
236 he was attacked by stones—Lee 1990, 75.
236 His critics—Lee 1990, 58.
237 Midway through his term—Kim 1996, 32.
237 Not long after he stepped—Cumings 1997, 391.

238 In December 1992—Kim 1996, 7.
238 'I narrowly escaped death'—Kim 1996, 7.
238 'I hope he runs again'—Anonymous source 1995, personal communication.
238 'A man should finish clean'—Kim 1996, 9.
239 'Sorry I walk so slow'—Kim Dae Jung 1995, personal communication.
239 'I will consult you on all issues'—*The Korea Times*, 26 February 1998.
239 visited Park Chung Hee's grave—Kim 1996, 123.
239 'Someone who stands for liberty'—*Time* 2 March 1998, 22.

Singapore

242 'As long as Nelson Mandela'—Anonymous source 1996, personal communication.
242 'a democratic society'—Singapore's National Pledge.
242 There, he was kept—Pollack and Telkämper October 1992, 1.
242 'not even a chess club'—Pollack and Telkämper October 1992, 2.
243 One day he decided to visit—Pollack and Telkämper October 1992, 2.
244 'allegations were deliberate'—Chia Thye Poh 14 July 1990, interview with the Special Broadcasting Service, Australia.
244 I joined the Barisan Sosialis—*Silencing All Critics* 1990, 12.
245 They tried very hard—Sesser 1993, 33-34.
246 'will succumb to psychological'—Pollack and Telkämper October 1992, 3.
246 'This is not about a personal battle'—Chia Thye Poh October 1997, personal communication.
248 The elections were won handsomely—Josey 1982, 1.
248 The Chief Minister led—Bloodworth 1986, 137-139.
249 was replaced by Lim Yew Hock—George 1974, 41.
249 'Don't trifle with this man'—David Marshall 1995, personal communication.
249 'At the height of the struggle'—Anonymous source February 1998, personal communication.
250 'In his heyday'—Anonymous source June 1996, personal communication.
250 'best bloody Englishman'—Sesser 1993, 16.
250 'were a communist'—Josey 1982, 78.
250 'I cannot in all honesty'—Josey 1982, 41.
251 'if I have to choose'—Josey 1982, 42.
251 Lim Chin Siong had qualities—George 1974, 47.

251 Lim Chin Siong proved—George 1974, 42.
251 'Repeated government intervention'—George 1974, 43.
252 Lee Kuan Yew knew—Bloodworth 1986, 184-185.
252 In one of their discussions—George 1974, 49.
252 'Lee used information'—George 1974, 43.
253 But either we believe—*Silencing All Critics* 1990, 11.
253 He even pledged that—Bloodworth 1986, 192.
253 'I'm told it is'—George 1974, 111.
253 'What he [Marshall] is seeking'—George 1974, 145.
254 'If the Government'—Josey 1982, 77.
254 'I wish to point out'—Josey 1982, 37.
254 'At a time when you want'—George 1974, 114.
255 he was offered a job—Bloodworth 1986, 194.
255 Lim had promised—Josey 1982, 94.
255 'reckless adventure'—Josey 1982, 165.
255 'took instruction from'— Josey 1982, 165.
255 Lim, piqued by the treatment—George 1974, 62.
255 'three ways of saying'—Bloodworth 1986, 260.
255 'lost the referendum'—Josey 1982, 166.
255 'There can never be two'—George 1974, 82.
256 'For me it is a moment of anguish'—Bloodworth 1986, 288.
256 'I don't know why'—George 1974, 88.
256 'Lord Selkirk was then'—Anonymous source November 1997, personal communication.
257 'came from [the PAP] Government'—Josey 1982, 162.
257 'We were riding a tiger'—Bloodworth 1986, cover.
258 While imprisoned, he came close—Bloodworth 1986,
258 'finally come to the conclusion'—George 1974, 118.
258 'This is not the Lim Chin Siong'—Anonymous source July 1995, personal communication.
258 Its victory was not—George 1974, 67.
259 'As a minister'—*Asiaweek* 1984, cited in *The New Democrat*.
259 'The British may be'—Josey 1982, 177-178.
260 'That time, 1963 to 1966'—Chia Thye Poh 14 July 1990, interview with the Special Broadcasting Service, Australia.
260 'When they first brought me'—Anonymous source March 1996, personal communication.
264 Through the years, the PAP—*Silencing All Critics* 1990, 45.
265 The Singapore Government's policies—Chia Thye Poh 14 July 1990, interview with the Special Broadcasting Service, Australia.
266 'continue until all the prisoners'—George 1974, 119.
266 'the absurd allegations'—Seow 1994, xx.
266 'I am obliged to eat'—Seow 1994, xx.

266 Within a week of the humiliating—*Japan-Asia Quarterly Review* August-September 1976, 30-33.
267 'This whole day'—*Report of an Amnesty International Mission to Singapore* 1980, 38-39.
268 Chua Hock Hua was thrashed—*Report of an Amnesty International Mission to Singapore* 1980, 36.
268 'a lacerated liver caused by beatings'—*Report of an Amnesty International Mission to Singapore.*
268 'no newspaper in the Republic'—*Report of an Amnesty International Mission to Singapore* 1980, 41.
269 Prisoners had their jaws broken—A detailed account of the treatment of political prisoners in Singapore is given in *Report of an Amnesty International Mission to Singapore* 1980.
269 'The Government does not'—Seow 1994, xxii.
269 'We don't ill treat people'—*Far Eastern Economic Review* 28 April 1988, 16.
269 'We don't do these things'—*Asiaweek* 13 September 1987, 19.
269 'In Singapore, we believe'—*The Straits Times* 20 August 1997, 24.
269 'live comfortably in prison'—George 1974, 191.
269 'abjure violence'—Josey 1982, 15.
269 'There is one thing—Josey 1982, 36.
270 'it should be made clear'—*The Straits Times* 28 January 1998.
270 'We are a different society'—*Asiaweek* 17 June 1988, 13.
270 'We are a different society'—*The Straits Times* 20 August 1997, 24.
270 In Lee's vision of a different society—George 1974, 134.
271 'communist united front tactics'—*Silencing All Critics* 1990, 69.
271 In 1974, when he was a student—*Japan-Asia Quarterly Review* April-June 1975, 60-62.
272 The *Straits Times*—O'Grady 1990, 38.
272 'to incite disaffection'—*Silencing All Critics* 1990, 16.
272 'manipulate and instigate'—*Silencing All Critics* 1990, 19.
272 The office of the CCA—O'Grady 1990, 9-12.
273 In the midst of the accusations—Tang Fong Har 1997, internet communication.
273 'for the [ISD's] effectiveness'—*Far Eastern Economic Review* 28 April 1988, 16.
274 'any officer who assaults'—*The Age* 8 February 1978, 8.
274 'But [Chia] has never accepted'—Lee Kuan Yew's speeach in Australia. Date unknown.
274 '[The officers] told me'—Chia Thye Poh 14 July 1990, interview with the Special Broadcasting Service, Australia.

274 In its present form—*Silencing All Critics* 1990, 9.
274 nine of the 22 detainees—*Silencing All Critics* 1990, 69.
275 When Seow arrived—Seow 1994, 106.
275 'So you think you can take on'—Seow 1994, 128.
276 'I am a firm supporter'—Josey 1982, 104.
276 On 29 June 1988—*Far Eastern Economic Review* 14 July 1988, 37.
276 'so that Singaporeans'—*Far Eastern Economic Review* 14 July 1988, 38.
277 In an open letter to 'Kuan Yew'—Seow 1994, 273-282.
277 When Francis Seow visited—*Far Eastern Economic Review* 26 January 1989, 12.
277 A similar matter was reported—*Sydney Morning Herald* 21 October 1997.
279 In 1984, Jeyaretnam and his co-accused—*Silencing All Critics* 1990, 55-59.
280 'loitering inside the polling station'—Letter by Attorney-General Chan Sek Keong 21 July 1997.
281 'HPL rapped for delay'—*The Straits Times* 23 April 1996.
283 'Drop me off at home'—Tang Liang Hong 1997, personal communication.
285 'Chinese communist style'—Sesser 1993, 48.
285 'Do I look like a policeman?'—Lee Kuan Yew 1997, interview with the Australian Broadcasting Corporation.
285 'It is in the nature'—*Asiaweek* 6 May 1988, 18.

Conclusion

288 On 22 February Defence Secretary—Burton 1989, 354-410.
289 As the masses cheered the victory—*Time* 3 March 1986, 4.
290 'We are finally free'—*Time* 10 March 1986, 6.
290 'The global tide'—Fidel Ramos 3 December 1997, speech given at his conferment ceremony of the Aristides Calvani Award.
290 'if a government'—Kaur 1986, 60.
291 Civil disobedience is really—Kaur 1986, 79.
291 'it's a crime for anyone'—Dalton 1993, 176.
291 'According to Gandhi'—Ninoy 1983, 65.
292 'a saint and a superior strategist'—Kim Dae Jung 1986, 209.
293 'encourage anyone to sacrifice'—*For the Love of Taiwan* 1992, 95.
294 'I have carefully weighed'—Benigno 1993, 37.
294 'not everyone is brave enough'—Aung San Suu Kyi February 1998, personal communication.
294 'Every book that is banned'—*Asiaweek* 24 April 1998, internet communication.

295 'I always tell him'—Maimunah Thamrin November 1997, personal communication.
295 Kim Dae Jung's two sons—Kim 1996, 36.
295 'long overdue homework'—Kim 1996, 52.
296 'Anyone who carries'—Shih Ming-teh December 1997, personal communication.
296 'Twenty-three years'—Chia Thye Poh 14 July 1990, interview with the Special Broadcasting Service, Australia.
296 'Our tragedy is that'—George 1974, 191.
296 'We, the government'—Clements 1997, 130.
296 'has been one of the'—*Newsweek* 24 April 1978, 7.
297 'Power removes the humiliation'—Minchin 1990.
297 'If they think that it is'—Clements 1997, 129-130
297 involves deliberate coercion—Stohl and Lopez 1986, 5.
298 'Between being loved'—*South China Morning Post* 6 October 1997, internet communication.
299 the bigger the crisis—Barnet and Raskin, cited in George 1974, 203.
300 the most effective use—Mitchell, Stohl, Carleton and Lopez 1986, 12.
301 'If we are able to weather'— Fidel Ramos 3 December 1997, speech given at his conferment ceremony of the Aristides Calvani Award.
302 Tommy Koh, its ambassador at large—*The Straits Times* 8 January 1998, internet communication.
303 Lee Kuan Yew and Goh Chok Tong—*The Straits Times* 12 January 1998, internet communication; *The Straits Times* 22 January 1998, internet communication.
303 'they think of it as'—*The Straits Times* 11 May 1998, internet communication.
303 When it was pointed out—*Time* 16 March 1998, internet communication.
304 There are, nevertheless—Engholm 1991, 128.
305 Complex behaviour is represented—A. R. Luria attempted to describe the neuropsychological functions of the human brain in *The Working Brain* 1973.
305 'We, whether Americans'—*Time* 15 June 1998, 35.
306 'You don't understand this'—*The Asian Age* 13 April 1998, internet communication.
306 His people seemed—*Washington Post Foreign Service* 26 May 1998, A01.
306 When she pleaded—*The Straits Times* 11 December 1997, internet communication.
306 'as though they'—*The Straits Times* 12 December 1997, internet communication.

307 'While the other countries'—*The Nation* 20 October 1997, 13.
307 'seem to have turned'—*Jane's Intelligence Review* March 1998, 33.
307 'including the satellite'—*Jane's Intelligence Review* March 1998, 33.
308 'During the time'—Huang Yen-hua December 1997, personal communication.
309 'The Kuomintang used'—Anonymous source November 1995, personal communication.
309 'Those who think that'—Shih Ming-teh December 1997, personal communication.
309 'The saddest thing'—Lin Yi-hsiung December 1997, personal communication.
309 'Lee's [Kuan Yew] view'—Kim 1994, 239.
310 'I think all the talk'—Aung San Suu Kyi February 1998, personal communication.
310 If we in Asia— Cited in Chee 1995, 98 (*The Straits Times* 13 March 1995).
310 'As long as Asians are oppressed'—Syed Hussin Ali April 1998, personal communication.
310 dubious national car project—*Sydney Morning Herald* 11 December 1997, internet communication.
311 By 1999, an estimated—*Hong Kong Standard* 1 September 1998, internet communication.
311 'After 30 years'—*Far Eastern Economic Review* 12 May 1998, 114.
314 And, as if to wake—*The Economist* 28 February 1998, 29.
314 'Perhaps it is time'—*The Straits Times* 14 June 1998, internet communication.
315 it was revealed that—Djin Siauw 1998, 3.
315 Similar demonstrations—Djin Siauw 1998, 6.
315 Evidence that the killings—Djin Siauw 1998, 3.
315 The Food and Horticultural Minister —Djin Siauw 1998, 7.
315 'a natural reluctance'—*The Straits Times* 28 October 1997, internet communication.
315 'not receptive of'—*The Straits Times* 14 September 1997, internet communication.
315 'to waste time talking'—*Asia Times* 24 June 1997, internet communication.
316 'the question mark'—*The Straits Times* 23 January 1998, internet communication.
316 'change the nature'—*The Straits Times* 21 March 1998, internet communication.
316 'to strengthen [their] institutions'—*The Straits Times* 21 February 1998, internet communication.

316 'Nobody has the right'—*Asiaweek* 17 June 1988, 13.
316 'stupidity and weakness'—*Los Angeles Times* 22 February 1998, Internet communication.
316 'been part of the information age'—*Hong Kong Standard* 17 June 1998, internet communication.
316 'municipal shenanigans'—*The Economist* 3 January 1998, internet communication.
317 'in a diminution'—*The Straits Times* 15 January 1998, internet communication.
317 At the onset of the monetary—*Sydney Morning Herald* 30 October 1997, internet communication; *The Straits Time* 29 October 1997, internet communication; and CNN 30 October 1997, internet communication.
318 When Goh subsequently heard—*The Economist* 29 November 1997, 29.
318 'Your vigour and stamina'—*The Straits Times* 12 March 1998, internet communication.
319 'dismiss the island'—*The Straits Times* 7 March 1998, internet communication.
319 'Singapore has been'—*The Straits Times* 7 March 1998, internet communication.
319 'It is no longer possible'— *The Straits Times* 7 March 1998, internet communication.
319 'information is deemed too sensitive'—Reuters 4 June 1998, internet communication.
319 especially 'the rule of law'—*Time* 16 March 1998, internet communication.
319 'authoritarian arrangements'—*The Straits Times* 15 April 1998, internet communication.
320 As their economies—*Far Eastern Economic Review* 20 November 1997, internet communication.
320 Nowhere is the control—A detailed account of the control of the mass media in Singapore is given in Seow 1998.
320 'The truth of the matter'—Anonymous source June 1996, personal communication.
321 Stock markets in East Asia—Lingle 1997, 3.
322 'This is for you'—Anonymous source December 1997, personal communication.
322 Candidates in Thailand—Anonymous source February 1996, personal communication.
322 In the Philippines—Anonymous source January 1998, personal communication.
322 'There are no ideas'—Kim 1994, 243.
323 'the king has received'—Kim 1996, 63.

324 China's modern history—*History of China*, internet communication.
325 In the nineteenth century—Levinthal 1990, 5.
327 No sooner had Sun Yat-sen—*History of China*, internet communication.
328 Two white jeeps pulled up—Burton 1989, 358-360.
328 'on both sides'—Burton 1989, 361.
329 'just because [they] did not'—Burton 1989, 360.
329 150,000 deaths later—Bloodworth 1987, 219.
330 'real task in the coming period'—Chomsky 1992, 9.
330 with only 6.3%—Chomsky 1992, 9.
330 'immediate national objectives'—Chomsky 1992, 10.
330 'unreal objectives such'— Chomsky 1992, 10.
330 This goal can be easily—Ambrose and Brinkley 1997, 1.
330 Again, pragmatists like—*Extra!* 1989, internet communication.
330 'No government in the world'—*Extra!* 1989, internet communication.
331 The East Timorese started—*The Age* 27 May 1998, internet communication.
331 'Australia would consequently'—*The Age* 27 May 1998, internet communication.
331 'soul' of his foreign policy—Ambrose and Brinkley 1997, 281.
331 Reagan, interestingly—Ambrose and Brinkley 1997, 301.
331 Criticisms of Carter's—Carter 1982, 145.
332 It will always be impossible—Carter 1982, 150.
332 'Carter's concerns about'—Shih Ming-teh December 1997, personal communication.
332 'President Jimmy Carter pressured'—Kim 1996, 34.
333 There is no doubt—Carter 1982, 151.
333 'that it must be the policy'—Ambrose and Brinkley 1997, 75.
333 'the struggle for freedom'—Chomsky 1992, 100.
333 'life uncomfortable'—Chomsky 1992, 98.
334 'homosexuality, moral decay'—*Sydney Morning Herald* 4 September 1998, internet communication.
334 'paralysing system'—*Newsweek* 2 April 1984, 13.
334 'not to foist their system'—Kim 1994, 238.
334 'true friend of the United States'—Kissinger 1982, 124.
334 'If a Western version'—*Newsweek* 1 September 1980, 7.
334 'the Eastern concept'—Clements 1997, 130.
334 'The Asia century is at hand'—Mahathir and Ishihara 1995, 21.
335 'When Asian economies'—*Asian Affairs* Spring 1988, internet communication.

335 'If Burma is stable'—Aung San Suu Kyi February 1998, personal communication.
335 'one of the big trees'—*The Straits Times* 3 November 1997, internet communication.
336 'thin ice or solid rock'—*Asiaweek* 1984, cited in *The New Democrat*.
336 In South Korea—*The Korea Times* 16 July 1998, 1-2.
337 'economic growth may occur'—Kingsbury and Barton 1994, 50.
337 'even if economic rights'— Kingsbury and Barton 1994, 50.
338 'If only the United States'—Seiden, journal unknown.
339 'by pursuing selfish interests'—*International Herald Tribune* May 1998, internet communication.
339 'It is even fair to say'—Mahathir and Ishihara 1995, 74.
339 cast iron to make—Cotterell 1988, 64.
339 The technique of making steel—Cotterell 1988, 124.
339 Chinese astronomers—Bloodworth 1982, 5.
340 From paper to porcelain—A detailed account of Chinese historical inventions is given in Cotterell 1988.
340 'have changed the whole'—Cotterell 1988, 173.

Bibliography

Aiusa Matchbox February 1983, In prison: Flowers, a spiderweb and prayer—An interview with Kim Dae Jung.

AKSI National Secretariat 18 August 18 1995, Hasta Mitra statement on Pramoedya protests.

Ambrose, Stephen E & Brinkley, Douglas G 1997, *Rise To Globalism: American Foreign Policy Since 1938*. Penguin Books.

An Introduction to Shih Ming-teh of Taiwan 1995, Taipei: Democratic Progressive Party.

Anwar Ibrahim 19 June 1997, *Speech at the AMIC Annual Conference in Kuala Lumpur*.

Asia Times 24 June 1997, Singapore makes bold bet on the future of democracy.

Asiaweek 24 July 1998, Ten days that shook Indonesia.

—— 24 April 1998, Fighting words: Neither prison nor the passing of years has weakened Pramoedya Ananta Toer's passion for justice in Indonesia.

——23 January 1997, Business is blooming.

——2 June 1989, Singapore: The release of Chia Thye Poh.

——17 June 1988, 'We are different.'

——6 May 1988, Singapore: Now, going head to head.

——13 September 1987, Singapore: Battle against leftism.

——7 June 1987, Singapore: A "Marxist conspiracy".

——15 February 1987, The Philippines: 'People Power, Part II.'

——31 July 1981, Taiwan: A strange death.

——6 February 1981, Korea: Clemency for Kim Dae Jung.

——12 December 1980, Taiwan: Election time.

——26 September 1980, Dissidents: Death verdict in Seoul.

——11 July 1980, Taiwan: Kaohsiung finale.

——30 May 1980, Taiwan: Sedition.

——16 May 1980, Taiwan: Kaohsiung's ripples.

——11 April 1980, The twin: A sudden chill.

——4 April 1980, Trials: The 'Kaohsiung 8' fight back.

——20 January 1978, Taiwan: An offer he can's refuse.

Aung San Suu Kyi 1991, *Freedom from Fear and other writings (ed by Michael Aris)*. London: Viking. London.

Aye Saung 1989, *Burman in the Back Row: An Autobiography*. Bangkok: White Lotus.

Bangkok Post 17 October 1997, *Singapore Helps Burma's Spies*.

Benigno, Teodoro 1993, *Ninoy Aquino: Portrait of A Hero*. Benigno S Aquino, Jr. Foundation.

Bloodworth, Dennis 1987, *An Eye for the Dragon*, Singapore: Times Books International.
——1986, *The Tiger and the Trojan Horse.* Singapore: Times Books International.
——1982, *The Messiah and The Mandarins: The Paradox of Mao's China.* London: Weidenfeld & Nicolson.
Burma: Extrajudicial Execution and Torture of Members of Ethnic Minorities 1988, Amnesty International Publications.
Burton, Sandra 1989, *Impossible Dream: The Marcoses, the Aquinos, and the Unfinished Revolution.* New York: Warner Books.
Carter, Jimmy 1982, *Keeping Faith: Memoirs of A President*. Bantam Books.
Chee, Soon Juan 1995, *Singapore, My Home Too.* Singapore: CSJ Publications.
Chomsky, Noam 1993, *What Uncle Sam Really Wants*. Odonian Press.
Clements, Alan 1997, *The Voice of Hope*. London: Penguin Books.
——1994, *Burma's Revolution of the Spirit*. Aperture.
——1992, *Burma: The New Killing Fields*. Odonian Press.
CNN 30 October 1997, Singapore aid for Indonesia likely to have strings.
Cotterell, Arthur 1988, *China: A cultural history*. Penguin Books.
Covert Action Quarterly Spring 1998, *The Burma-Singapore Axis: Globalizing the Heroin Trade*.
Crisostomo, Isabelo T 1987, *Cory: Profile of A President.* Selangor: Pelanduk Publications (M) Sdn Bhd.
Cumings, Bruce 1997, *Korea's Place in the Sun: A Modern History*. W. W. Norton & Co.
Dalton, Dennis 1993, *Mahatma Gandhi: Nonviolent Power in Action*. New York: Columbia University Press.
Daza, Raul A, Abad, Florencio B and Angeles, J. I. 1996, The Steadfast Keepers: Keeping Alive the Vision of Liberal Democracy in the Philippines. Philippines: National Institute for Policy Studies.
Djin Siauw August 1998, *Racism in Indonesia*. Committee Against Racism in Indonesia.
Engholm, Christopher 1991, *When Business East Meets Business West: The Guide to Practices and Protocol in The Pacific Rim*. John Wiley & Sons Inc.
Extra! 10 November 1989, Henry Kissinger: The walking, talking conflict of interest.
Far Eastern Economic Review 20 August 1998, Singapore's psyche.
——12 May 1998, To the Barricades: As economic hardship mounts, student protests are gaining support from other segments of society—And starting to look like a nationwide movement.

——20 November 1997, The Better to see you: Investors want more transparent markets and companies.

——26 January 1989, Singapore: Dissident under watch in New York, Eyes on the job.

——14 July 1988, Singapore: Delving the mud, Lee escalates campaign against colleague-turned-critic Nair.

——28 April 1988, Singapore: Behind bars, again.

——18 June 1987, Singapore: Airing a confession, Alleged ringleader buttresses government's case.

——11 June 1987, Marxists in the church: The Archbishop says he is swayed by the evidence.

——1 January 1987, South Korea: Dissent and detention, Kim Dae Jung remains the top symbol of the opposition.

——7 February 1985, A hushed homecoming: The US watches to see how the returning Kim Dae Jung is treated.

——25 October 1984, South Korea: The Aquino factor.

——4 September 1971, Philippines: The fall out.

For the Love of Taiwan: The memorial collections for the third anniversary of Cheng Nan-rong's death (Chinese) 1992, Taipei: Cheng Nan-rong Foundation.

George, T J S 1974, *Lee Kuan Yew's Singapore.* Andre Deutsch.

Heryanto, Ariel 1993, *Discourse and State-Terrorism: A Case Study of Political Trials in New Order Indonesia, 1989-1990.* Melbourne: Monash University.

Hill, Gerald N & Hill, Kathleen T 1984, *The True Story and Analysis of the Aquino Assassination.* Hilltop Publishing Co.

Hong Kong Standard 1 September 1998, Food fight: Indonesians battle to get a cheap bag of rice being distributed in Jakarta, where basic food prices have soared over the past year.

——17 June 1998, Asean leaders' comments aggravating crisis: Lee.

Index on Censorship, UK August 1989, A first-hand account of arrest, interrogation, mistreatment and detention by Tang Fong Har.

Indonesia 16 September 1996, Java Jive.

——October 1983, *Perburuan 1950 & Keluarga Gerilya 1950* (translated by Benedict Anderson).

Indonesia Report-Culture & Society Supplement, No. 17 August 1986, An Open Letter by Pramoedya Ananta Toer.

Inside Indonesia October 1990, My life as a prisoner: Interview with Pramoedya Ananta Toer, the internationally renowned Indonesian novelist and critic.

Inter Press Service 10 August 1995, Indonesia: Cold war-like storm over jailed writer's award.

Jacobs, J Bruce 1993, Democratisation in Taiwan, *Asian Studies Review*, Vol 17, No 1, July.

——1981, Political opposition and Taiwan's political future, *The Australian Journal of Chinese Affairs*, No 1.

Jane's Intelligence Review February-March 1998, Burma receives advances from its silent suitors in Singapore.

Jane's Intelligence Review 1 March 1998, Burma the country that won't kick the habit.

Japan-Asia Quarterly Review Vol 7, No 2, April-June 1975, Tokyo: AMPO.

Josey, Alex 1982, *David Marshall's Political Interlude*. Eastern University Press Sdn. Bhd.

Kampas 13 June 1996, Maemunah's complaints: Pramoedya's wife brings complaint to National Commission for Human rights (translated by Alex Bardsley).

Kaur, Harpinder 1986, *Gandhi's Concept of Civil Disobedience: A Study with Special Reference to Thoreau's Influence on Gandhi*. New Delhi: Intellectual Book Corner.

Kim, Chi-ha 1978, *The Gold-Crowned Jesus and Other Writings (edited by Kim Chong-sun & Shelly Killen)*. New York: Orbis Books.

Kim, Dae-jung 1996, *A New Beginning: Kim Dae Jung Reviews His Career (translated by Young J. L. & Yong M. K.)*. The Centre for Multiethnic and Transnational Studies, University of Southern California.

——1994, *Korea and Asia: A Collection of Essays, Speeches and Discussions*. The Kim Dae Jung Peace Foundation Press.

——1987, *Prison Writings (translated by Choi Sung-il & David R. McCann)*. University of California Press.

Kingsbury, Damien 1998, *The Politics of Indonesia*. Melbourne: Oxford University Press.

Kingsbury, Damien & Barton, Greg (eds) 1994, *Difference And Tolerance: Human Rights Issues in Southeast Asia*. Melbourne: Deakin University Press.

Kissinger, Henry 1982, *Years of Upheaval*. Little, Brown & Co.

Korea Communique 1976-1983, Tokyo: Japan Emergency Christian Conference on Korean Problems.

Korea in Focus February 1998, Seoul: Korean Overseas Culture and Information Service.

Korea Scope (Special Issue on : Kim Dae Jung in America.) Vol 3, No 1, 1983, The International Christian Network for Democracy in Korea.

Asian Affairs Vol 1, No 3, Spring 1998, Interview of Paul Krugman about financial crisis.

Lee, Ang 1993, *Biography of Shih Ming-teh, Part I (Chinese)*. Taipei: New Taiwan Foundation.

Lee, Manwoo 1990, *The Odyssey of Korean Democracy: Korean Politics 1987-1990*. New York: Praeger.

Letter by Singapore Attorney General Chan Sek Keong to Minister for Law Prof S Jayakumar 21 July 1997, Presence of unauthorised person inside polling stations.

Levinthal, Charles F 1990, *Introduction to Physiological Psychology (3rd ed)*. Prentice-Hall, Inc.

Lin, Yi-hsiung 1991, *Ten Years of Life and Death (Chinese)*. Taipei: Chilin Foundation.

Lingle, Christopher 1997, *The Rise and Decline of the Asian Century: False starts on the path to the global millennium*. Barcelona: Sirocco.

Lintner, Bertil 1994, *Burma in Revolt*. Westview Press, Inc.

——1990, *Outrage: Burma's Struggle for Democracy*. White Lotus.

Luria, A. R. 1978, *The Working Brain: An introduction to Neuropsychology*. Penguin Books Ltd.

Mahathir, Mohamad & Ishihara 1995, *The Voice of Asia: Two Leaders Discuss the Coming Century (translated by Frank Baldwin)*. Kodansha International.

Maung, Mya 1992, *Totalitarianism in Burma: Prospects for Economic Development*. Paragon House.

May, Brian 1978, *The Indonesia Tragedy*. Boston: Routledge & K. Paul.

Minchin, James 1990, *No Man Is An Island: A Portrait of Singapore's Lee Kuan Yew*. Allen & Unwin Australia Pty Ltd.

Myanmar: Amnesty International Briefing 1990, Amnesty International Publications.

New Straits Times 21 August 1996, Pramoedya and independence.

Newsweek 2 April 1984, Philippines: Stumbling toward elections.

——12 September 1983, Manila's time of mourning: Filipinos throng to Aquino's funeral, and many blame the regime for his death.

——5 September 1983, A welcome-home murder: The Aquino assassination is a disaster for democracyÍ and possibly for Marcos.

——15 August 1983, 'We must build a new leadership.' Interview: Benigno Aquino.

——1 November 1982, Taiwan's time of troubles.

——20 September 1982, 'We have a society of peace and order.' Interview: Ferdinand Marcos.

——23 February 1981, Manila's house divided.

——16 February 1981, Closing ranks with Seoul.

——3 November 1980, Terror in the Philippines.

——6 October 1980, The Philippines: Urban bomb wave rattles Marcos.

——29 September 1980, A death sentence in Seoul.

——22 September 1980, Going for the death sentence.

——8 September 1980, South Korea: A strongman takes command in Seoul.

——1 September 1980, South Korea's time of trial.

——25 August 1980, Chon 'Koreanizes' democracy.

——18 August 1980, A 'gathering storm' in Manila.
——9 June 1980, Korea's day of the generals.
——2 June 1980, A bloody rebellion in Korea.
——26 May 1980, 'There's no way to topple Marcos.'
——26 May 1980, A new crackdown in Korea.
——19 May 1980, A puzzling release in Manila.
——21 January 1980, Taiwan: Battering the opposition.
——10 December 1979, Storm warnings in Seoul.
——12 November 1979, South Korea after Park.
——5 November 1979, A shoot-out in Seoul.
——8 January 1979, Free at last.
——1 January 1979, Anger on Taiwan.
——24 April 1978, Crackdown on dissent.
——5 December 1977, Taiwan: The Chungli Incident.
——14 March 1977, South Korea: Prayer meeting.
——22 November 1976, 'Someday we will be free.'
——2 August 1976, The Philippines: The winds of change?
——17 May 1976, Korea: Song of protest.
——22 March 1976, Crackdown in the Cathedral.
——3 November 1975, Marcos's brave new world.
——19 May 1975, The Philippines: The making of a martyr.
——30 September 1974, A personal vision.
——26 August 1974, Enter the assassin.
——8 October 1973, South Korea's sordid spooks.
——10 September 1973, The Philippines: Man's fate.
——27 August 1973, South Korea: The Seoul survivor.
——20 August 1973, Espionage: The Kim kidnap case.
——10 May 1971, South Korea: Choosing the familiar.

Ninoy, Letters—Prison and Exile 1983. La Ignaciana Apostolic Centre.

O'grady, Ron 1990, *Banished*. Hong Kong: The Christian Conference of Asia.

Ogle, George E 1977, *Liberty To The Captives: The Struggle against Oppression in South Korea*. Atlanta: John Knox Press.

Pantoja-Hidalgo, Christina 1991, *Five Years in a Forgotten Land*. University of the Philippines Press.

Pollack, Anita & Telkämper, Wilfréd October 1992, *Singapore: MEPs Visit Chia Thye Poh*. European Parliament Report.

Pramoedya, Ananta Toer 1995, *Nyanyi Sunyi Seorang Bisu (Bahasa Indonesian), A Silent Song of The Mute*. Jarkata: Lentera.

——24 August 1995, *Literature, censorship and the State: To what extent is a novel dangerous? (translated by Alex Bardsley)*.

——November 1991, *My apologies, in the name of experience (translated by Alex Bardsley)*.

Radio Netherlands Interview 22 July 1995, Weekend Focus: Interview with Pramoedya Ananta Toer (translated by Alex Bardsley).

Report of An Amnesty International Mission to Singapore 1980, Amnesty International Publications.

Reports of The Fact-Finding Board on The Assassination of Senator Benigno S. Aquino Jr 1984. Manila: Mr & Mrs Publishing Co.

Republic of Korea Violations of Human Rights: An Amnesty International Report 1981, Amnesty International Publications.

Reuters 4 June 1998, Singapore's economy quakes as Asian cracks widen.

Rosen, Michael and Widgery, David 1991. *The Chatto Book of Dissent*. London: Chatto & Windus.

Seiden, Matt. Date and journal unknown.

Selth, Andrew June 1997, *Burma's Intelligence Apparatus*. Canberra: Strategic and Defence Studies Centre, Australia National University.

——1995, *Burma's Arms Procurement Programme*. Canberra: Strategic and Defence Studies Centre, Australia National University.

Seow, Francis T 1997, *The Media Enthralled: Singapore Revisited*. Westview Book.

——1994, *To Catch A Tartar: A Dissident in Lee Kuan Yew's Prison*. Yale Southeast Asia Studies.

Sesser, Stan 1993, *The Lands of Charm and Cruelty*. Alfred A. Knopf, Inc.

Shih, Ming-teh 1992, *Spring in the Prison Cell (Chinese)*. Taipei: Chien Wei Publications.

——1990, *Spring in the Prison Cell (Chinese)*. Taipei: Dun Li Publications.

Shu, Jie-ling 1996, *Taiwan History After WWII, Volume I-IV (Chinese)*. Taipei: Wen Ying Tang Publications.

Silencing All Critics: Human Rights Violations in Singapore 1990, An Asia Watch Report.

Singapore Continuing Detentions under the Internal Security Act: Further Evidence of Torture and Ill-treatment of Detainees 1988, Amnesty International Publications.

Smith, Martin J. 1991, *Burma: Insurgency and the Politics of Ethnicity*. London: Zed Books.

Soliven, Maximo V. 1984, Benigno 'Ninoy' Aquino in the eye of memory, in *Reports of The Fact-Finding Board on The Assassination of Senator Benigno S. Aquino Jr 1984*. Manila: Mr & Mrs Publishing Co.

South China Morning Post 6 October 1997, Leaders must inspire fear: Lee Kuan Yew.

South Korea Violations of Human Rights 1986, Amnesty International Publications.

Special Broadcasting Services (Australia) 14 July 1990, 'Dateline' Interview of Singapore's Chia Thye Poh.

Stohl, Michael & Lopez, George A (eds) 1986, *Government Violence and Repression: An Agenda for Research*. Greenwood Press.
Stueck, William 1995, *The Korean War: An International History*, Princeton University Press.
Suara Independen No. 3/I August 1995, *Saya sudah tutup buku dengan kekuasaan (Bahasa Indonesian), I have closed the book on power*, by Pramoedya Ananta Toer (translated by Alex Bardsley).
Sydney Morning Herald 4 April 1998, Naked truth: It's Asian values or bust.
——11 December 1997, Region in Crisis: World Bank blasts 'Asia model'.
——21 October 1997, FBI investigates burglary with claimed links to Singapore.
——20 October 1997, The Singapore sling.
Tempo Interaktif 1996, *Apa dan Siapa: Pramudya, 1985-1986* (translated by Alex Bardsley).
The Age 27 May 1998, How Australia toadied to a dictator.
——20 January 1994, Pramoedya tests limits of Suharto's new openness.
——8 February 1978, Lee sets sights on trade changes & Singapore and political prisoners.
The Asian Age 13 April 1998, Are Asian values a justification for repression?
The Economist 28 February 1998, Asean's Failure: The limits of politeness.
——3 January 1998, The trouble with Singapore's clone.
——29 November 1997, Meanwhile, back where the wagons are circling...
The Korea Herald 5 July 1980, Kim Dae-jung masterminds Kwangju riot.
The Korea Times 16 July 1998, Korea—A lab for 'DJ-nomics': Business community wants 'Sunshine policy'.
——26 February 1998, 'Let us open a new era': Overcoming national crisis and talking a new leap forward.
The Nation 30 March 1998, Korea's other miracle: In a triumph of democratization, the country's best-known dissident takes office.
——20 October 1997, Singapore's blood money: Hanging drug couriers but investing with their suppliers.
——24 November 1997, Reply to Singapore's blood money.
The New Democrat Issue No. 4 1996, Singapore Democratic Party Publications.
The New York Times 1 November 1996, Indonesia writer vents his fury in a garbage dump.
——20 October 1991, The power of the Peace Prize may be lost on Myanmar.

——25 December 1982, U. S. Welcomes Seoul's move to release 1,200 prisoners.

The New Yorker 27 May 1996, The Indonesiad.

The People vs Park Chung Hee: Voice of the Korean Resistance May 1974-March 1976.

The Straits Times 27 June 1998, Thais retract call for Asean intervention.

——14 June 1998, Call to review Asean's non-interference policy.

——9 June 1998, Hard-liner elected DPP chief.

——11 May 1998, Asian sates 'not all of same shade.'

——15 April 1998, Cultural side of the Asian crisis.

——24 March 1998, Show Asian nations that you care, Europe.

——21 March 1998, Chaebols have to reform, plug into global system, says SM.

——12 March 1998, Warmest congrats from PM Goh.

——7 March 1998, Currency crisis will reveal the true leaders.

——22 February 1998, Singapore relies on efficiency to survive regional woes.

——21 February 1998, East Asian governments have to take painful reforms, says SM Lee.

——28 January 1998, Feedback: Not in Singapore...

——23 January 1998, Suharto 'will see nation through crisis'.

——23 January 1998, Forest funds redirected to national car.

——22 January 1998, Currency crisis: How and when will East Asia recover? (Lee Kuan Yew's speech at the Thai National Defence College in Bangkok.)

——22 January 1998, SM Lee urges US and Japan to help Asia out of crisis.

——15 January 1998, Unexpected downturn led to Micropolis' liquidation.

——12 January 1998, PM renews call to Japan, US, Europe for help.

——8 January 1998, Perspective: What seemed impossible then is now a reality.

——7 January 1998, Asia didn't heed warning signs, by Keith B. Richburg and Steven Mufson (*Washington Post)*.

——12 December 1997, Was apathy a factor in East Coast tragedy?

——11 December 1997, Not good to die on Singapore streets.

——3 November 1997, Singapore tree stands tall in typhoon.

——29 October 1997, Singapore offered US$10 billion to help out, says Suharto.

——28 October 1997, Comments by SM Lee 'inappropriate'.

——14 September 1997, SM's comment on Japan draws response.

——20 August 1997, Leaders in a Confucian society "must be Junzi".

——23 April 1996, HPL rapped for delay in disclosing condo sale at discount.

Time 16 March 1998, In defence of "Asian values": Singapore's Lee Kuan Yew reflects on China and the Asian crisis.
——2 March 1998, Destiny's choice: Jailed, beaten, marked for death. To Kim Dae Jung, it was all preparation for this moment.
——10 March 1986, Now the hard part: A new President faces Communist rebels and a failing economy.
——3 March 1986, Rebelling against Marcos: With tacit US backing two top military leaders accuse him of fraud.
——24 February 1986, Going into the streets: As Marcos wins a tainted election victory, Aquino vows to go on fighting.
——25 December 1978, Taiwan: Shock and fury.
——10 May 1971, South Korea: Landslide for Stone Face.
Torture in the eighties: An amnesty international report 1984, Amnesty International Publications
Washington Post 26 May 1998, Hong Kong residents back democracy slate: Voices creates Opposition Bloc on Chinese soil.
——26 December 1982, S. Korea urges US to alter rights policy.
——24 December 1982, S. Korean frees Kim Dae Jung; Dissident flies to Washington.
Webb, Paul 1993, *Escape from Burma*. Centre for Southeast Asia Studies, Northern Territory University.
Wei Jingshen 1998, *Speech at Columbia University*. Date unknown.

Index